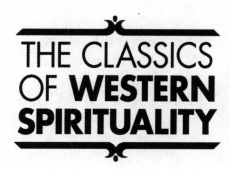

THE CLASSICS
OF **WESTERN**
SPIRITUALITY

THE CLASSICS OF WESTERN SPIRITUALITY
A Library of the Great Spiritual Masters

President and Publisher
Mark-David Janus, CSP

EDITORIAL BOARD

SØREN KIERKEGAARD

Discourses and Writings on Spirituality

Introduced and translated by
Christopher B. Barnett

Paulist Press
New York / Mahwah, NJ

Caseside image: Portrait of Søren Kierkegaard at his desk by Luplau Janssen, 1902, The Museum of Natural History, Frederiksborg Castle, Denmark.

Caseside design by Sharyn Banks
Book design by Lynn Else

Library of Congress Cataloging-in-Publication Data

Names: Kierkegaard, Søren, 1813-1855, author. | Barnett, Christopher B. (Christopher Baldwin), 1976– editor, translator.
Title: Søren Kierkegaard : discourses and writings on spirituality / introduced and translated by Christopher B. Barnett.
Description: Mahwah, New Jersey : Paulist Press, [2018] | Series: The classics of Western spirituality | In English, translated from the original Danish. | Includes bibliographical references and index.
Identifiers: LCCN 2018023980 (print) | LCCN 2018049982 (ebook) | ISBN 9781587687396 (ebook) | ISBN 9780809106486 (hardcover : alk. paper)
Subjects: LCSH: Theology.
Classification: LCC BX4827.K5 (ebook) | LCC BX4827.K5 A25 2018 (print) | DDC 248—dc23
LC record available at https://lccn.loc.gov/2018023980

ISBN 978-0-8091-0648-6 (hardcover)
ISBN 978-1-58768-739-6 (e-book)

Published by Paulist Press
997 Macarthur Boulevard
Mahwah, New Jersey 07430

www.paulistpress.com

Printed and bound in the United States of America

This book is dedicated to my teachers
Videnskab kan man maaskee banke ind i et Menneske,
men det Ethiske maa man banke ud af dem.
—Kierkegaard (1847)

CONTENTS

ABOUT THE CONTRIBUTOR

Christopher B. Barnett specializes in modern theology, Christian spirituality, the philosophy of technology, and the relation between theology and the arts (especially cinema and literature). He received his doctor of philosophy in theology from the University of Oxford and taught at Berry College in Mount Berry, Georgia, prior to coming to Villanova University, where he is currently Associate Professor in the Department of Theology and Religious Studies. He also has served as Guest Researcher at the Unitätsarchiv in Herrnhut, Germany, and at Søren Kierkegaard Forskningscenteret in Copenhagen.

In addition to several articles and book chapters, Dr. Barnett has authored three books, *Kierkegaard, Pietism and Holiness* (Ashgate, 2011), *From Despair to Faith: The Spirituality of Søren Kierkegaard* (Fortress, 2014), and *Kierkegaard and the Question Concerning Technology* (Bloomsbury Academic, 2019), and is working on *Historical Dictionary of Kierkegaard's Philosophy* (Rowman and Littlefield, 2021). He has also coedited two volumes, *Theology and the Films of Terrence Malick* (Routledge, 2016) and *Scorsese as Theologian* (Brill, 2019). Raised in Birmingham, Alabama, he now lives in the Philadelphia area.

TRANSLATOR'S NOTE

These translations follow the standard Danish edition of Kierkegaard's writings, *Søren Kierkegaards Skrifter*. A complete reference for each selection will be provided in a footnote at the beginning of its given chapter.[1] Otherwise, I have kept footnotes to a minimum, so as to avoid distracting the reader with concerns that would apply primarily to specialists.

Translating Kierkegaard is, to borrow the phrase, no walk in the park. There is the fundamental challenge of aligning nineteenth-century Danish with twenty-first-century English—a substantial problem in and of itself, made even more difficult by Kierkegaard's complex (if often alluring) use of punctuation, syntax, grammatical mood, and the like. Among these traits, Kierkegaard's use of punctuation is particularly taxing for the translator. Kierkegaard was intrigued by how punctuation could influence meaning, so much so that he considered himself a master at pairing rhetoric and punctuation. As he bluntly puts it in an 1847 journal entry, "[With punctuation] I defer to absolutely no one, and I very much doubt that there is any Danish author who can equal me in this respect."[2] At the same time, however, it must be said that Kierkegaard's protracted sentences and his idiosyncratic use of colons and dashes (among other signs) can be disruptive for readers, especially for those who are accustomed to twenty-first-century English. As a translator, then, I have been tasked not only with making Kierkegaard's language as readable as possible for contemporary Anglophone audiences, but also with preserving his distinctive style. It is a delicate balance, to be sure, and I readily confess that some interpretive decisions have been easier than others. Still, since this translation is intended for the general reader first and foremost, I have given preference to linguistic clarity over textual eccentricities and scholarly niceties.

Next, there are accompanying yet significant issues pertaining to Kierkegaard's sociocultural location and perspective. For example, Kierkegaard's views on gender roles tend to echo the presuppositions of his own day, though occasionally he does push against patriarchal assumptions in subtle yet decisive ways. Something similar might be said about Kierkegaard's use of exclusive language. In keeping with the conventions of nineteenth-century Western literature, he frequently uses the third-person singular masculine pronoun (*han*, or "he," as well as *ham*, or "him") when speaking about people in general. With regard to such issues, I typically have left Kierkegaard's language intact, lest I intrude upon his text and, perhaps even more importantly, further complicate his already complicated sentence structure. On the other hand, I have tended to render Kierkegaard's use of the Danish noun *Menneske* (and its derivatives) as "human being" or as "person," rather than as "man." This is, indeed, quite appropriate in Danish, even if its generality at times jars with Kierkegaard's masculine pronoun use. But this tension was present even in Kierkegaard's day, and, as discussed in the general introduction, it by no means discouraged Kierkegaard's contemporary female audience. In any case, one may safely assume that Kierkegaard's use of *han* or *ham* is intended to encourage the reader to think in terms of individual applicability, rather than to limit the content to the male gender alone.

A final complexity has to do with Kierkegaard's use of the Bible. In many cases, he refers to biblical texts in offhand ways, while at other points he directly quotes Scripture but does not provide a citation. I have chosen not to identify these sorts of biblical references, since they are plentiful and would burden the text with notes. On the other hand, I have followed Kierkegaard himself whenever he parenthetically cites a biblical passage. Even more difficult has been deciding on how to translate Kierkegaard's quotations from the Bible. Should one simply render Kierkegaard's Danish into English? This approach would have the benefit of closely adhering to Kierkegaard's text itself, though, inasmuch as Kierkegaard's Bible was *already* a translation of the original biblical languages, it would also have the dubious distinction of being a translation of a translation. Should one use an existing English translation of the Bible whenever Kierkegaard quotes Scripture? This has the advantage of cultural familiarity and linguistic reliability, though, of course, it occasions yet another question about *which* translation to utilize—a question that remains hotly debated even (or perhaps especially) today.

Ultimately, after much vacillation, I have come to accept that there is no clear-cut solution to this conundrum. What I have elected to do, then, is no doubt imperfect, though I trust that Kierkegaard's thinking will eclipse the peccadilloes of the translator. First, since the standard Danish Bible of Kierkegaard's era combined an 1819 translation of the New Testament with an adaptation of the Old Testament from the eighteenth century, it bears a noticeable stylistic relation to the King James (or Authorized) Version of the Bible, originally published in 1611. Hence, in order to preserve these textual echoes, I have basically used the King James Version whenever Kierkegaard quotes the Bible.[3] Moreover, according to "The Bible in American Life," a 2014 study released by The Center for the Study of Religion and American Culture at Indiana University–Purdue University Indianapolis (IUPUI),[4] the King James Version remains by far the most popular translation of the Bible in America—a point also confirmed by translation-related searches on Google since 2005.[5] Of course, whether or not this is a good thing remains an open question, and my use of the King James Version is not meant to indicate an opinion in one direction or another. At the same time, however, I do want Kierkegaard's employment of Scripture to bear cultural resonance, and it seems that the King James Version will best facilitate that aim, even though I have eliminated some of its more archaic features (e.g., its "thees" and "doths") in order to avoid too much discordance with my translation of Kierkegaard's writings themselves.

I conclude with a word of appreciation. I have been chipping away at this project for years now, and, along the way, I have received help from a number of people, whether in the form of linguistic insight, methodological advice, proofreading, or just old-fashioned sympathy. Given such wide-ranging support, it would be impossible to list everyone involved. Still, I would be remiss if I failed to mention the following persons: Stacy Barnett, Andrew Burgess, John

Cacchione, Nancy de Flon, Josh Furnal, Jake Given, Marty Laird, Vincent McCarthy, George Pattison, and Brian Söderquist. Of course, to mention such excellent colleagues and friends should not imply that they bear responsibility for any mistakes in the text, which, alas, are attributable solely to me.

Notes

1. See the section entitled "Abbreviations and Forms of Reference" for more details.

2. *SKS* 20, NB:146.

3. More specifically, I have used the Oxford World's Classics edition: *The Bible: Authorized King James Version with Apocrypha* (Oxford: Oxford University Press, 1997).

4. See Philip Goff, Arthur E. Farnsley II, and Peter J. Thuesen, "The Bible in American Life Today," in *The Bible in American Life*, ed. Philip Goff, Arthur E. Farnsley II, and Peter J. Thuesen (Oxford: Oxford University Press, 2017), 10.

5. Sarah Eekhoff Zylstra, "The Most Popular and Fastest Growing Bible Translation Isn't What You Think It Is," *Christianity Today*, March 13, 2014, http://www.christianitytoday.com/news/2014/march/most-popular-and -fastest-growing-bible-translation-niv-kjv.html.

ABBREVIATIONS AND FORMS OF REFERENCE

In a sense, this volume can be thought of as two projects in one. First, there is the introductory material, which proceeds along the lines of a typical Anglophone contribution to Kierkegaard scholarship. Next, there are the translations of Kierkegaard's writings themselves.

With regard to the former—that is to say, both the "General Introduction" and the brief section introductions—quotations from Kierkegaard's published work generally have been taken from the current standard English translations of his work *Kierkegaard's Writings*, issued by Princeton University Press under the direction of Howard and Edna Hong. On occasion, however, I have elected to provide my own translations of Kierkegaard's writings, and, when appropriate, I have made a note of that decision. Accordingly, the standard Danish edition of Kierkegaard's works, *Søren Kierkegaards Skrifter* [*SKS*] is also indicated.[1] Many quotations from Kierkegaard's *Nachlaß* have been taken from *Søren Kierkegaard's Journals and Papers* [*JP*], the seven-volume set arranged by the Hongs, and, as with the published writings, I have linked these references to *SKS* as well.[2] However, in other instances, I have translated journal passages myself, noting their location in *SKS* or, even more rarely, in the older *Papirer*.[3] Below, a register of abbreviations has been included, and complete documentary information can be accessed in the works cited section.

With regard to the translations per se, I have elected only to cite their location in *SKS*. This information can be found at the beginning of each chapter and is indicated by the first note in the chapter. Rather than use abbreviations, I have tried to keep this data as simple and as unobtrusive as possible, featuring the *SKS* series volume and corresponding page numbers, along with a handful of other factual details. Any other notes that appear in these chapters—and there will be only a few—will not require special abbreviations or forms of reference.

ABBREVIATIONS

DANISH[4]

| SKS | *Søren Kierkegaards Skrifter* (1997–2013) |
| Pap. | *Søren Kierkegaards Papirer* (1909–48) |

ENGLISH[5]

BA	*The Book on Adler* (1995)
CA	*The Concept of Anxiety* (1980)
CD	*Christian Discourses/The Crisis and a Crisis in the Life of an Actress* (1997)
CI	*The Concept of Irony* (1989)
COR	*The Corsair Affair* (1982)
CUP1	*Concluding Unscientific Postscript to "Philosophical Fragments,"* vol. 1 (1992)
EO1	*Either/Or,* vol. 1 (1987)
EO2	*Either/Or,* vol. 2 (1987)
EUD	*Eighteen Upbuilding Discourses* (1990)
FSE/JFY	*For Self-Examination/Judge for Yourself!* (1990)
FT	*Fear and Trembling* (1983)
JP	*Søren Kierkegaard's Journals and Papers,* vols. 1–7 (1967–78)
KJN	*Kierkegaard's Journals and Notebooks* (2007–)

LD	*Letters and Documents* (1978)
M	*"The Moment" and Late Writings* (1998)
PC	*Practice in Christianity* (1991)
PF/JC	*Philosophical Fragments/Johannes Climacus* (1985)
PV	*The Point of View* (1998)
SLW	*Stages on Life's Way* (1988)
SUD	*The Sickness unto Death* (1980)
TA	*Two Ages* (1978)
TD	*Three Discourses on Imagined Occasions* (1993)
UDVS	*Upbuilding Discourses in Various Spirits* (1993)
WA	*Without Authority* (1997)
WL	*Works of Love* (1995)

Notes

1. Full citations list the text in question, the volume number (when apt), and the page number(s): e.g., *SKS* 7, 41 / *CUP* 1, 34.

2. Volume number, journal designation, and journal entry number are provided for *SKS*, while volume number and entry number are supplied from the Hong edition: e.g., *SKS* 17, AA:13 / *JP* 3, 3245.

3. E.g., *SKS* 20, NB4:5 or *Pap.* V B 227.

4. See the works cited section (p. 331) for complete details.

5. With the exception of *Søren Kierkegaard's Journals and Papers*, all abbreviations in this list correspond to editions of *Kierkegaard's Writings*, edited by Howard and Edna Hong. Again, see works cited for more information.

GENERAL INTRODUCTION

PROLOGUE

The great Austrian philosopher Ludwig Wittgenstein (1889–1951) once remarked to a friend, "Kierkegaard was by far the most profound thinker of the last century. Kierkegaard was a saint."[1] Just what Wittgenstein meant by this statement is unclear. After all, there is not a direct correlation between intellectual accomplishment and holiness. We do not say a thinker is excellent on account of holiness, nor do we understand holiness as a guarantee of intellectual excellence. When the two do seem to coincide—as in the case of a Thomas Aquinas or an Edith Stein—we may very well appreciate the concurrence. And yet, Thomas's *Summa Theologica* remains widely read today not due to the saint's religious virtue but, rather, to his philosophical and theological insight.

How, then, should Wittgenstein's claim about Kierkegaard be taken? Perhaps the juxtaposition of "thinker" and "saint" is instructive enough, for, as this volume will demonstrate, Kierkegaard was a thinker deeply concerned with the problem of being a saint—that is to say, with the problem of holiness.

What is holiness? Is holiness possible for human beings? If so, what are its characteristics? What implications does it have for one's social life? Both in his published and unpublished writings, these are questions to which Kierkegaard directly and indirectly returned. Moreover, he dedicated a significant portion of his authorship to fostering holiness, though, as will be seen, he preferred the term *upbuilding*. Thus it appears that Wittgenstein actually gets to the heart of the matter: Kierkegaard's holiness, however it be construed, cannot be

1

separated from his willingness to think about and think through holiness.

The purpose of this volume is to acquaint readers with this fundamental aspect of Kierkegaard's thought. Included here are some of Kierkegaard's most important spiritual writings, ranging from his early "upbuilding discourses," which gently encourage the reader to consider a life lived in and for God, to his late broadsides against the Danish state church, which shock in their condemnation of bourgeois Christianity. In between are a variety of pieces that see Kierkegaard develop his spiritual insights and methods. His discourses on the lilies of the field and the birds of the air are lyrical parables that treat the natural world as an image of the human being's spiritual condition. His analysis of the human self in *The Sickness unto Death* uses philosophical language in order to make a spiritual point—namely, that happiness stems from the self's willingness to find "rest" in God. In every case, Kierkegaard establishes himself as one of the key figures in modern Christian spirituality.

A SHORT BIOGRAPHY OF KIERKEGAARD

For all its complexity, Kierkegaard's life loosely resembles the structure of a three-act play: (1) an early period in which his habits and interests were formed; (2) a middle stage during which his literary career began to thrive, even as he was slowly pressed into conflict with certain elements of Danish society; and (3) a dramatic final phase culminating in his so-called attack upon Christendom and his untimely death at forty-two years of age.

Kierkegaard's Upbringing

Though born into a well-heeled family in Copenhagen, Kierkegaard should not be confused with a typical member of the *haute bourgeoisie*. In fact, one could argue that Kierkegaard's authorship is an outgrowth of his inability to fit into polite Danish society. The primary source of this tension was Kierkegaard's father, Michael Pedersen Kierkegaard (1756–1838), a man whose combination of brooding melancholy and religious piety has become legendary in Kierkegaard studies.

The son of a peasant whose surname was adopted from the small churchyard (*kirkegaard*) he managed, M. P. Kierkegaard grew up in the West Jutland parish of Sædding, an area of limited economic opportunity, known for its bucolic way of life and traditional values. Even as the Enlightenment compelled the Danish state church to exchange older catechetical and liturgical materials for works more compatible with modern rationalism, Jutlanders remained committed to the Christianity of previous generations. A nearby village served as a base for Pietist evangelization and, with it, the proclamation of what the great Pietist forefather Johann Arndt (1555–1621) called "true Christianity." For Arndt and his followers, the Christian life was not a matter of social propriety but of repentance for sin, faith in salvation, and constant growth in holiness.[2]

Driven by economic necessity, M. P. Kierkegaard would leave his home as a youth, but he sustained an "unbroken connection with the religious awakening movement of the faraway West Jutland village of [his] childhood."[3] This was evident in the way he ordered his family's religious affairs. Despite his rise as a successful businessman in Copenhagen, M. P. Kierkegaard almost exclusively associated with Pietist-minded clergy and organizations. The Kierkegaard family became involved in Copenhagen's Moravian *Brødresocietet* (Society of Brothers) and regularly attended its services, which combined homiletic stress on what was referred to as "upbuilding"[4] (*opbyggelse*) with liturgical attention to the crucified Christ—themes that, notably, would come to dominate Søren Kierkegaard's own writings. Likewise, the *Brødresocietet* nurtured the long-standing Moravian practice of spiritual reading. Books such as Thomas à Kempis's *The Imitation of Christ* and Arndt's *True Christianity*, both drawing from the complex legacy of Catholic mystics such as Meister Eckhart (ca. 1260–1327) and Johannes Tauler (1300–1360), were staples in Moravian households. Kierkegaard himself kept volumes by Tauler, Thomas à Kempis, and Arndt, and he read and admired spiritual writers as diverse as Henry Suso, Angelus Silesius, Jakob Böhme, and Gerhard Tersteegen.

This lifelong interest in Pietist literature adds another layer of complexity to Kierkegaard's relationship with his father, whose religious piety was equaled only by a "melancholy mingled with a strong dose of guilt."[5] The precise origin of this guilt is difficult to pin down, but, whatever the case, "it appears that Søren believed quite literally that his father's sins had been transmitted to him as well."[6] Precisely how or why Kierkegaard arrived at this conclusion has puzzled scholars for decades. Certainly the fact that *five* of Søren's siblings died before his father was received as evidence that a "guilt must remain on the entire family."[7] Yet, in the end, the lone certainty is that the Kierkegaard family sought to wrench theological meaning from personal sorrow.

Something similar could be said of the other major event in Kierkegaard's background, namely, his broken engagement to Regine Olsen in 1841. On the surface, their match seemed almost ideal. Both families were affluent. Both were pious: Regine's family, too, attended the *Brødresocietet*'s meetings when she was a child. And yet, Regine and Søren did not respond to their backgrounds in the same way. Kierkegaard could not shake an ambivalence about wealth, even as he relied on it to support his literary career. Moreover, he struggled to reconcile Christian asceticism with conjugal life. Regine, on the other hand, had a jaunty, "cheerful personality."[8] She did not see a conflict between earthly happiness and religious devotion.[9] It is hardly surprising, then, that she fought to preserve the engagement.[10]

But it was not to be, for reasons that "may not have been completely clear even to [Kierkegaard] himself."[11] What is evident is that Kierkegaard "came to believe that he had some personal impediment or flaw that made it impossible for him to marry."[12] This obstacle may have involved his father's murky past[13] or an altruistic desire to shield Regine from his own "melancholy and sadness."[14] It almost certainly had to do with Kierkegaard's sense of religious vocation, which, in his mind, placed him outside of "normal" cultural expectations. Ironically, Regine's resistance on the latter point persuaded him to play the rake. He even told her that the breakup was simply an occasion to have a fling[15]—hardly a mature decision, but one he hoped would demonstrate that the relationship was untenable. Ultimately, Regine relented.

The end of the affair was indelibly painful. Regine would go on to marry Frederik Schlegel, a finance minister who, in 1855, assumed the governorship of the Danish West Indies. Schlegel was a "stable, harmonious"[16] person, and, by all accounts, his marriage to Regine was a contented one. Still, Regine remained captivated by her first love,[17] just as Kierkegaard never stopped loving Regine. References to her populate his authorship, and there is "evidence that Kierkegaard's writings...are partly intended as ways of communicating with Regine."[18] Indeed, Kierkegaard's break with Regine catapulted him into a new phase in life. He was a writer now, and it would not be long until he made his mark in Danish letters.

Kierkegaard's Literary Career

Kierkegaard's literary output in the years following the breakup rivals that of anyone in Western intellectual history, though, in a sense, it started accidentally. Still distraught, Kierkegaard journeyed to Berlin in October 1841, citing a desire to hear the lectures of one of the day's leading philosophers, Friedrich Schelling. Kierkegaard was hardly the only burgeoning thinker to attend,[19] but Schelling failed to retain the Dane's attention: "Schelling talks the most insufferable nonsense,"[20] as he bluntly put it. So Kierkegaard elected to immerse himself in his own writing. By the time he returned to Copenhagen in 1842, he had "serviceable drafts"[21] of his own literary-cum-philosophical opus, *Either/Or*. The finished product, which numbers well over seven hundred pages, would be published in 1843.

Thus began a remarkable stretch of creative activity. From 1843 to 1846, Kierkegaard issued an assortment of works. On the one hand were his pseudonymous writings, whose prolix, lyrical élan belied philosophical and theological ruminations on all manner of topics—the origin of melancholy, the beauty of monogamous love, the challenge of faith, the anxiety of freedom, and the relation between faith and reason. A number of these works, including *Fear and Trembling* (1843) and *Philosophical Fragments* (1844), have since been reckoned among the most significant in Western thought. On the other hand were Kierkegaard's many upbuilding discourses, which bore his own name and were published more or less concurrently with his pseudonymous works. These discourses will be discussed in greater detail later. For now, suffice it to say that Kierkegaard considered them "directly religious"[22] and thus a decisive counterbalance to the searching, even skeptical tone of their pseudonymous relatives. That, indeed, was why he deemed them "upbuilding" (*opbyggelige*), a term he encountered among Copenhagen's Moravians. They are intended to fill the reader who, "like [an] empty jar,"[23] is receptive to spiritual wisdom.

Yet, despite his productivity, the life of an author did not sit easily with Kierkegaard. He periodically floated other pursuits—teaching, traveling, and, perhaps most seriously, pastoring. This vocational tension came to a head in 1846. In February of that year, he published *Concluding Unscientific Postscript to Philosophical Fragments*, which would prove to be another pseudonymous masterwork. Unlike its predecessors, however, the *Postscript* ends with a brief appendix, "A First and Last Explanation." In it, Kierkegaard discloses that *he* stands behind the series of pseudonymous writings that began with *Either/Or*. This admission afforded Kierkegaard the opportunity to stipulate "what to make of his 'authorship,'"[24] particularly by underscoring that the author himself is not to be identified with the pseudonyms, who are more like characters in a play than facsimiles of his own personality. It also reflected his desire to take leave of his literary pursuits and to become a parish priest. As he writes in a February 1846 journal entry, "My idea is now to qualify myself for the priesthood[.] For several months I have prayed to God to help me along, for it has long been clear to me that I ought not continue as an author, which is something I want to be entirely or not at all."[25]

Kierkegaard's interest in becoming a pastor was not new. He entered the Royal Pastoral Seminary in 1840 and delivered his final qualifying sermon for the priesthood in February 1844. He had delayed ordination on account of his authorial career—a career that suddenly seemed less appealing. "If only I could make myself become a priest....Out [in a rural parish], in quiet activity, granting myself a bit of literary productivity in my free moments, I would breathe more easily."[26] To understand this change, not to mention Kierkegaard's post-1846 writings, attention has to be paid to what scholars call "the *Corsair* affair."

The *Corsair* (*Corsaren*) was a satirical periodical well known for its scandalous attacks on the leaders of Danish culture. In December 1845, one of its anonymous contributors, a literary critic and poet named Peder Ludvig Møller, published an acerbic critique of Kierkegaard's pseudonymous text *Stages on Life's Way*, even questioning the mental stability and moral probity of its "author." Many in Copenhagen's intellectual circles understood that Møller was attacking Kierkegaard. Of course, Kierkegaard did too. Soon he responded with a polemical article of his own, poking fun at Møller's literary and personal foibles and tempting *The Corsair* to ridicule him in its pages. The magazine took the bait. In January 1846, it launched a sustained literary assault on Kierkegaard, repeatedly lampooning his external appearance and depicting him as naive, self-centered, and even insane.

These incidents carried profound consequences. In fomenting the scandal, Kierkegaard called attention to *The Corsair*'s malevolence and, incidentally or not, wrecked Møller's chances of becoming a professor at the University of Copenhagen. But it was a Pyrrhic victory. Now an object of open ridicule, "it became literally impossible for [Kierkegaard] to walk around Copenhagen without crowds of curious and sometimes jeering onlookers."[27] In this way, his life came to resemble an archetype all too familiar today—that of the disgraced celebrity, hounded by the press and mocked in society. He did not expect this outcome. He was publicly isolated and, despite his literary achievements, made into a laughingstock.

The *Corsair* affair forced Kierkegaard to reconsider his vocational intentions. His plans to enter the ministry were put on hold, and, in March 1846, he published *A Literary Review*—a brief but significant work that signaled a change in his activity and in his outlook. Ostensibly a work of literary criticism, occasioned by Thomasine Gyllembourg's 1845 novel *Two Ages* [*To Tidsaldre*], *A Literary Review* provided Kierkegaard with an opportunity to assess Western society at the midpoint of the nineteenth century. What he found was grim indeed. Kierkegaard argues that, despite its intellectual and technological progress, "the present age" was morally and religiously bankrupt. Enervated by the press, which facilitates envy, gossip, and skepticism, social life has turned away from the noble if sometimes violent aims of the past and been set on a course of decay. Cocktail parties and dilettantes have usurped the place of sacred ceremonies and heroes. This deterioration cannot be easily reformed, since, unlike previous eras, the press now stands between individuals and meaningful action, showcasing the flaws of would-be leaders and undermining the bonds that once held society together. In conclusion, Kierkegaard suggests that religious life may offer an egress from the present age's iniquity, but only if it is patterned on the example of Christ—rigorous in self-dispossession, unafraid of persecution, patient in adversity, and obedient to God in all things.

Emerging from this newfound point of view was, in many respects, a new body of literature, sometimes referred to as Kierkegaard's "second authorship." These post-1846 writings display a marked emphasis on Christian discipleship, paying an increased amount of attention to the theme of *imitatio Christi*. This tendency begins with *Upbuilding Discourses in Various Spirits* (1847) and turns up in several signed works, including *Works of Love* (1847), *Christian Discourses* (1848), *The Lily in the Field and the Bird of the Air* (1849), and *For Self-Examination* (1851). Kierkegaard also continued to develop a pseudonymous authorship, albeit with some differences. For example, two of his most celebrated later works, *The Sickness unto Death* (1849) and *Practice in Christianity* (1850), are attributed to Anti-Climacus—a name that harks back to Johannes Climacus, the pseudonymous author of *Philosophical Fragments* and *Concluding Unscientific Postscript*. Yet, whereas Johannes Climacus epitomizes an ironic, quizzical approach to Christianity, Anti-Climacus stands as a Christian of penetrating insight. The prefix *Anti-* ("opposite" or "before") already discloses this point, as it signals both a contrast to and a precedence over his predecessor. For that reason, some commentators have noted a "change from the old lower-level pseudonyms to the new higher-level religious ones."[28]

In any case, after the publication of *For Self-Examination*, Kierkegaard's activity as an author ground to a halt, at least *publicly*. For over three years, he confined himself to private matters, committing "to his journals many reflections about himself, his 'task' and project, and his past, and about his relationship to Regine."²⁹ He increasingly registered disdain for modern society in general and for the Danish state church in particular. As he saw it, an authorship that had unfolded as an endeavor to awaken and to upbuild³⁰ Danish Christianity had proven unsuccessful.³¹ He would have to ponder what went wrong and what else, if anything, could be done. He also hoped that members of the clergy, headed by Jacob Peter Mynster, bishop of Zealand, would come forward and admit that institutional Christianity had failed to uphold traditional Christian ideals, particularly those involving the imitation of Christ. Only such an admission, he concluded, would truly recover the church in Denmark. And so he waited and waited. These were the "'silent years' before the storm."³²

The Final Act:
Kierkegaard's "Attack upon Christendom"

To get a sense of how controversial Kierkegaard's last years were, one might well start with his funeral. It was held on November 18, 1855—a week after his passing. The service concluded at Assistens Cemetery, the burial place of many of Copenhagen's notables. The cemetery "soon became a sea of people; groups large and small surged over the graves and their little gated plots of flowers."³³ After ceremonial rites, a "tall, pale man clad in black, stepped forward from the crowd"³⁴ and doffed his hat. The man's name was Henrik Sigvard Lund—a son of Kierkegaard's deceased sister, Nicoline Christine. Observing his uncle commemorated by the very institution he had died condemning, Lund could not help but register both irony and horror. He read from Kierkegaard's short essay "We Are All Christians" and then addressed the gathering:

> Isn't [Kierkegaard] correct? Is not what we are all witnessing today—namely, that this poor man, despite all his energetic protests in thought, word, and deed, in life and death, is being buried by "the Official Church" as a beloved member—isn't this in accordance with his words? It would never have happened in a Jewish society, not even among

9

the Turks and Mohammedans: that a member of their society, who had left it so decisively, would, after his death and without any prior recantation of his views, nevertheless be viewed as a member of that society. That was something reserved for "official Christianity" to commit. Can this be "God's true Church," then?[35]

Applause briefly rang out, but Lund's words did not so much produce fury as silence. A few people began to leave. Others waited expectantly, wondering "what would happen *next*."[36]

This scene was, in a sense, a fitting summary of Kierkegaard's authorship. His doctoral dissertation on irony focused, among other things, on Socrates's "divine mission"[37] to undermine the establishment of ancient Athens. In similar fashion, Kierkegaard's copious pseudonymous writings were intended to needle the reader, forcing him or her to "consider what is put forward and make the decision to choose or not to choose the…ethical-religious path."[38] The *Corsair* affair only intensified these tendencies. Moreover, it convinced him of the poverty of the present age, which, despite its celebration of "progress" and nominal acceptance of Christian doctrine, lacked the moral and spiritual resources to seek justice and truth. Thus the stage was set for Kierkegaard's attack upon Christendom.

By "Christendom" (*Christenheden*) Kierkegaard understood something quite different from "Christianity" (*Christendommen*). He equated Christianity with the teachings of the New Testament, particularly as embodied in the lives of Jesus Christ and the apostles. Furthermore, he insisted that genuine Christianity involves striving to realize their example, even if such a standard exceeds one's own capability. That is why true Christianity also entails the need for "forgiveness for sin through faith in Christ."[39] The Christian may fall short of holiness, but, if he or she is honest about such failures, God will both forgive and provide the grace needed to resume and, hopefully, to fulfill the task of sanctity.

In contrast, "Christendom" describes the attempt to translate Christianity into the sociopolitical sphere. It encompasses a peculiar conception of the church—namely, as an institution dedicated to indoctrinating persons into a given society or, simply put, as a wing of the state. For Kierkegaard, the trouble with this ecclesiology is manifold. Christendom "tones down the radical character of God's demands on a person's life. Christ's life was a decisive challenge to the established order of his day, and he paid the price for this challenge with his life. On Kierkegaard's view, the Christian who becomes a follower of Christ can expect to suffer opposition and persecution from the established order as well."[40] Thus Kierkegaard rejected the assumption that Western society had become Christian. For him, the "Church in this life must always be a Church militant, struggling to define itself over against the world."[41]

Kierkegaard had adumbrated such views for years—a tendency that became unmistakable with the publication of *Practice in Christianity* and *For Self-Examination*. Still, he had avoided a direct and public confrontation with the Danish church, partly because J. P. Mynster was his father's pastor and partly because he continued to hope for change. Mynster's death in 1854 would force him to reassess the situation.

Mynster was eulogized by Hans Lassen Martensen, an upwardly mobile churchman and theologian. With an eye on the deceased's bishopric, Martensen highlighted the triumphs of Mynster's twenty-year episcopacy, even declaring him a true imitator of Christ, a "link in [the] holy chain of witnesses to the truth," which stretches "across the ages, from the days of the Apostles up to our own times."[42] This statement "was [either] too much for Kierkegaard, or it was just what he was waiting for, the moment for decisive action."[43] Kierkegaard dashed off a critical rejoinder, in which he maintained that, however great Mynster's earthly accomplishments, the bishop should in no way be confused with a "witness of truth." The latter is characterized by a total commitment to the life and teachings of Jesus Christ, while Mynster ought to be seen as a career-minded ecclesiastic, who tendered a diluted version of Christianity in exchange for political stability and personal gain.

Bearing the title "Was Bishop Mynster a 'Truth-Witness,' One of 'the Authentic Truth-Witnesses'—Is *This the Truth?*," the piece appeared in December 1854. The reaction was "one of stunned incomprehension."[44] Mynster's association with the Kierkegaard family was well known, and despite Kierkegaard's protests to the contrary, his article was widely regarded as an unwarranted betrayal of the deceased. "Only those who had read Kierkegaard's works and understood them, or were privy to the journals, could have appreciated the reasons for the collision."[45] Yet, at that time, the journals were unpublished, and Kierkegaard remained an elusive figure for many. Misunderstandings abounded. Conservatives, among whom he was once numbered, were scandalized by the antiestablishment undercurrent of his polemics. Liberals, of whom he had been critical, supported him in private and eventually in public.[46] Martensen, for his part, published a brief reply and then refused to comment again. The vast majority of the "clergy simply let the incident pass them by."[47]

But Kierkegaard was determined to press the issue. At first he simply wanted to provoke further reaction from Martensen. When a response failed to materialize, Kierkegaard released a series of articles and, in time, his own periodical, *The Moment* (*Øieblikket*). This was an ironic decision, given Kierkegaard's criticism of the press in *A Literary Review*. Nevertheless, *The Moment* stands as a "classic of satirical literature,"[48] in which Kierkegaard not only chastises the Danish church but, indeed, seeks to embarrass it. As he writes in the fifth edition of *The Moment*,

> Beware of the pastors! It belongs to being a Christian…to have suffered for the doctrine. And believe me, as sure as my name is Søren Kierkegaard, you will get no official pastor to say that—which is natural, since to do so would be suicide for him. At the same moment it is said that to have suffered for the doctrine is required even for being any ordinary Christian, at the same moment the whole machinery…is exposed. That is why you will get no official pastor to say it. On the contrary, you can be completely sure that he with all his might will…prevent you from thinking those thoughts so that you can be kept in the condition he considers to be Christian: a good sheep for shearing, a harmless mediocrity, to whom eternity is closed.[49]

It is not only the clergy who get a drubbing. In one piece, dubbed "The Sort of Person Who Is Called a Christian," Kierkegaard lampoons the status of the Danish laity. Its opening vignette describes a "young man," blessed with "more than ordinary capacities," who marries, has a child, and only then feels "compelled to have religion."[50] Thus he has the child baptized—a decision that makes a mockery of the sacrament by which Christians pledge "to live as sacrificed ones in this world of lies and evil."[51] A second picture portrays a hardened tradesman, who reasons that a moral person cannot succeed in the business world.[52] And yet, this same tradesman maintains his ties to Christianity, since his association with the church allows him to cultivate the appearance of integrity:

> Two or four times a year this man dresses up in his best clothes and goes to Communion. There a pastor makes his appearance, a pastor who (like those figures that jump out of a snuffbox when the spring is touched) jumps as soon as he sees "a blue banknote." And then the holy ceremony is celebrated, from which the tradesman, or rather both of the tradesmen...return home to their ordinary way of life.[53]

Kierkegaard drives home the point with ferocity: "And one dares to offer this to God in the name of the Sacrament of the Altar, the Communion of Christ's body and blood!"[54]

In spite of its vitriol, Kierkegaard's attack was not so much trying to *destroy* the Danish church as trying to *keep* it from destroying itself. "I am only a corrective," he once wrote, "I have nothing new to bring."[55] Its negativity gestures toward something positive—namely, the kind of faith celebrated in the lives of the great martyrs and saints, whose pursuit of justice, truth, and love did not cower before convention or prejudice, precisely because it shared in the overflowing, unlimited generosity of God himself.

Not long before the tenth issue of *The Moment* was to go to press, Kierkegaard became ill. On October 2, 1855, he collapsed in the street, and, just over a month later, he was dead. The cause of his deterioration was unclear. Kierkegaard himself associated his sickness with his attack upon the Danish church, "the cause [to] which he has devoted all his intellectual strength to resolving...and for which alone he believes that he has been intended."[56] Indeed, it appears that Kierkegaard understood his death as essential to the continuation of his "religious battle."[57] Otherwise his polemic would trudge on indefinitely and, in the long run, "peter out."[58] In death, however, "it will maintain its strength."[59]

And yet, there is a sense in which *The Moment* does not represent Kierkegaard's last word. In 1846, as he approached his thirty-third year of life, Kierkegaard drew up details for the reparation of the family burial site at Assistens Cemetery—a place that can be visited to this day. After mentioning a few details, he adds, "And then there will be enough space for a little verse which may be done in small type."[60] The "little verse" was from one of Kierkegaard's most cherished poets, the Pietist hymn writer Hans Adolph Brorson (1694–1764). Kierkegaard refers to Brorson's songs throughout his authorship, citing, for example, Brorson's hymn, "I Go in Danger, Where I Go," in both *Stages on Life's Way* and *Concluding Unscientific Postscript*, and using "Draw Me, Jesus," as inspiration for the third section of *Practice of Christianity*.[61] For his gravestone, Kierkegaard would choose the tenth stanza of Brorson's "Hallelujah! I Have Found My Jesus":

> In yet a little time,
> I will have won,
> Then will the whole struggle
> Be over and done,
> Then I can rest [*hvile*]
> In halls of roses,
> And continually,
> And continually
> Talk with my Jesus.[62]

In selecting this verse for his tombstone, Kierkegaard did more than acknowledge his debt to Brorson. He also made Brorson's words his own—indeed, his last communication with the world. As Johannes Climacus explains in the *Postscript*—a work that dates from the same year that Kierkegaard sketched out the plans for his burial site—the words on one's headstone signify what "the dead person calls out"[63] from the grave. Thus Kierkegaard, dead now for more than 150 years, continues to "call out" what he saw as the essence of Christian existence—that, while always a struggle, it nevertheless tends toward and culminates in the joy and "rest"[64] of a relationship with Christ. As will be seen, his spiritual discourses and writings bear out this declaration.

KIERKEGAARD'S PLACE IN THE HISTORY OF CHRISTIAN SPIRITUALITY

Spirituality has been defined as the pursuit of "life integration" by way of a process of "self-transcendence toward the ultimate value one perceives."[65] Thus particular doctrines underlie every spirituality—for they articulate the "ultimate value" in question—but spirituality itself is not a mere set of doctrines or rules. Rather, it involves the existential application of such principles, whether they concern "the Transcendent, the flourishing of humanity, or some other value."[66]

With this in mind, "Christian spirituality" refers to that spirituality whose "horizon of ultimate value is the triune God revealed in Jesus Christ and communicated through his Holy Spirit, and the project of self-transcendence is the living of the paschal mystery within the context of the church community."[67] The person concerned with Christian spirituality, then, will have certain presuppositions about who God is. Her task, however, will not be to elucidate and to expand on those presuppositions—as it is in theology—but to relate them to who she is and to what she wants in life. On this understanding, Christianity is always already more than a cognitive assent or an interior "feeling." It is a *mode de vie*, which involves political, sexual, social, and spiritual matrices.

As a thinker, Kierkegaard has often been labeled as an "existentialist" or, more forcefully, as the "father of existentialism." As Robert Solomon explains, "It is generally acknowledged that if existentialism is a 'movement' at all, Kierkegaard is its prime mover."[68]

Existentialism can be defined as a way of philosophizing that stresses the importance of the human subject, not only as a thinker, but also as a concrete, acting individual confronted by a variety of problems—for example, the experience of freedom in a world that often seems hostile, even absurd. But this is, doubtless, an extensive definition, and, as Simon Blackburn notes, "existentialism" is not so much a unified philosophy as a "loose title for various philosophies that emphasize certain common themes."[69] Thus existentialist themes crop up in writers of various stripes, from the ontological ruminations of Martin Heidegger to the probing of meaninglessness by Jean-Paul Sartre. In other cases, what seems to be "existentialism" may not be that at all. Thomas Merton once observed that the differences between existentialism and mysticism are not always clear-cut, for both focus "on the ineluctable fact of death, on man's need for authenticity, and on a kind of spiritual liberation."[70] Similarly, James Collins argues that existentialism cannot be reduced to a modern phenomenon, given that it has "striking parallels" in thinkers such as Augustine of Hippo and Blaise Pascal.[71] With this in mind, it is worth adding that Collins does not view Kierkegaard as an existentialist per se but instead as one who, along with Friedrich Nietzsche and Edmund Husserl, strongly "contributed to the current of thought from which existentialism stems."[72]

Identifying Kierkegaard with "existentialism," then, is hardly a straightforward matter. It may be that the very themes that Kierkegaard bequeathed to existentialism are better understood in light of Christian spirituality, since a number of Kierkegaard's most cherished ideas and motifs follow the "contours of Christian spirituality."[73] Lawrence S. Cunningham and Keith J. Egan maintain that "any authentic Christian spirituality"[74] must possess each of these general features: (1) an emphasis on Christianity as a *way of life,* rather than "an abstract philosophy or a code of beliefs"; (2) a thematization of the Christian way of life as discipleship, understood, in particular, as the following of Jesus Christ; (3) a recognition that discipleship is not purely an individual matter, but also entails interpersonal involvement; (4) a stress on the reception of the Eucharist; (5) a sensitivity to the role of the Holy Spirit in the life of discipleship; and (6) an openness to the world, rather than a longing for a "shield from the exigent realities around us."[75] Kierkegaard's authorship displays each of these qualities. The upbuilding writings, in particular, might be taken as manifestly spiritual. And yet, even Kierkegaard's more philosophical works, many of which are seen as existentialism's *loci classici*, either highlight or, at least, hint at the contours of Christian spirituality. Hence, rather than portion out a "philosophical" and a "religious" Kierkegaard, it is better to view his authorship as a *whole*, which, at any juncture, is capable of moving from irony to upbuilding.[76]

Whatever the case, the persistence of spiritual themes in Kierkegaard's authorship raises the question, Where do they come from? In other words, if thinkers such as Kant and Hegel form the background of Kierkegaard's philosophical output, who are the key sources behind Kierkegaard's spiritual writings? Answering this question will not only better situate Kierkegaard in the history of Christian spirituality, but, eventually, will also bring his own contribution to Christian spirituality into sharper relief.

The Pietist Influence on Kierkegaard

Among the myriad influences on Kierkegaard, it may have been the Pietists who mattered most to him. He remained a lifelong devotee of Pietist literature, reading figures such as Johann Arndt and Gerhard Tersteegen for edification and frequently alluding to them with great reverence in his writings, whether published or unpublished. As he put it in an 1850 journal entry,

> Yes, indeed, pietism [*Pietisme*] (properly understood...in the sense of witnessing for the truth and suffering for it, together with the understanding that suffering in this world belongs to being a Christian, and that a shrewd and secular conformity with this world is unchristian)—yes, indeed, pietism is the one and only consequence of Christianity.[77]

What, exactly, did he learn from the Pietists? A number of answers might be ventured here. First, it is clear that, in Pietism, he saw an emphasis on Christianity as a way of life, namely, a way of life centered on the example of Jesus Christ. The theme of *imitatio Christi*, common among Pietists, garnered decisive impetus in Johann Arndt's groundbreaking work *True Christianity*. For Arndt, Christ stands as the "example, mirror, and rule for [one's] life."[78] What this means, in particular, is that the Christian's life is to express the virtues incarnated by Christ—humility and love, to be sure, but also all types of suffering, from poverty to persecution. This stress gives Arndtian piety an "ethical focal point"[79] that would come to be characteristic of Pietism and, later, of Kierkegaard's thinking, especially in post-1846 works such as *Works of Love* and *Practice in Christianity*.

Second, Kierkegaard was attracted to the Pietist emphasis on sanctification, that is, on the process by which one becomes holy. In order to appreciate this emphasis, it must be remembered that, after Martin Luther, sanctification was a point of controversy in Protestant circles. While it would be false to accuse Luther of lacking an interest in holiness, it is nevertheless true that he disdained the notion that holiness is an outcome of a "heavenward journey,"[80] achieved gradually, if also painfully, by the Christian pilgrim. As Carter Lindberg puts it, "For Luther salvation is not the process or goal of life, but rather the presupposition of life, [thus] his theology became a transvaluation of all values."[81] For that reason, Luther could not endorse the imitation of Christ, at least not understood as a deliberate "imitation of the suffering *Christus exemplum*."[82] For him, any such human attempt to approach God is nothing but temptation, since the "desire to be as God (*homo deificatus*) is the root of all sin."[83]

The Pietists, however, tended to take a different position. While accepting Luther's stress on faith as the *terminus a quo* of holiness, they added that the process of sanctification *presupposes* evangelical faith, and so the one who grows in holiness does so on the basis of faith and not on that of human works.[84] Thus the Pietists were able to combine the Lutheran principle of *sola fide* with an emphasis on constant progress in holiness. Moreover, they were bold enough to thematize this process in categories borrowed from Catholic mysticism—most notably, the notion of "detachment" (*Gelassenheit*). For Arndt, who, indeed, was strongly indebted to Catholic spiritual authors such as Johannes Tauler and Thomas à Kempis, "detachment" is synonymous with resignation from earthly goods. This sort of restraint is necessary not because such goods are intrinsically evil, but so that "nothing other is to live, shine, act, will, love, think, speak, or rejoice in man except God himself."[85] In this way, "Tauler's emphasis on *Gelassenheit*," which was otherwise more speculative and metaphysical, "worked easily into Arndt's order of salvation."[86]

Kierkegaard, too, was adamant that Luther's *sola fide* be understood as a starting point for ethical striving, and he was highly critical of those who would suggest otherwise, including Luther himself. Moreover, he credits spiritual authors such as Tauler[87] and Arndt[88] for upholding the connection between faith, suffering, and progress in the spiritual life. As will be seen, he was to replicate this tendency in his own authorship.

A third way in which Pietism shaped Kierkegaard was its promotion of what might be termed "countercultural" Christianity—an inclination that was characteristic of the Moravian Brethren, with whom, as has been noted, Kierkegaard was personally familiar. In conducting missions in harsh environments,[89] and in separating into semimonastic communities such as Christiansfeld in southern Jutland, Denmark's Moravians represented a Christianity that refused to assimilate willy-nilly into the burgeoning secular world. This radical commitment made a significant impression on Kierkegaard. On the one hand, he admired the Moravians' dedication to social equality,[90] and in one 1848 journal entry, he even suggested that they are the only true Christians left in Denmark.[91] On the other hand, he saw their tendency to cluster in like-minded communities—in which "all people [are] alike...dressed alike, praying at specified times, marrying by drawing lots, going to bed by the clock"[92]—as an evasion of the demand to suffer in the world as Christ did. As he notes, "There is much that is beautiful in their lives, but their quietness is still not Christianity, not in the deepest sense."[93]

Yet, even here, Kierkegaard betrays the influence of Pietism, for he uses the Pietist emphasis on *imitatio Christi* as a means of critiquing a certain aspect of the movement. Indeed, it could be argued that his evaluation of the Moravians is representative of a larger debate within Pietism vis-à-vis the proper locus of the religious life. Namely, are Christians to pursue holiness within a secular and perhaps even hostile society, or are they to separate from such a society so as to practice their faith more freely?[94] For Kierkegaard, these are not easy questions: a dialectic of confrontation and retreat can be found in his own writings. Still, in the end, he is certain that Jesus Christ must remain the standard by which Christians are measured. Thus he concludes that the countercultural Christianity of the Moravians is not *really* countercultural if it fails to confront the established order as Jesus did—namely, head-on.

Kierkegaard's Anticipation of Modern Christian Spirituality

In pondering Kierkegaard's role in the history of Christian spirituality, it is important not just to look behind but also to look forward. He did not just receive a number of insights from figures such as Tauler and Arndt, but he anticipated some of the key themes of late nineteenth- and twentieth-century Christian spirituality. Thus it is worthwhile to consider where Kierkegaard's spiritual writings overlap with those of subsequent authors.

Still, this task is more than a little difficult. First, and most obviously, Kierkegaard has been received primarily as a philosopher of existence or of religion, rather than as an *Erbauungsautor*. Thus his relation to Christian spirituality has garnered a relatively small degree of attention, whether in the secondary literature or, even more significantly, among spiritual writers themselves.

Yet, the absence of direct influence hardly means that Kierkegaard is irrelevant to the development of Christian spirituality. Just as he dealt with issues that would become familiar in twentieth-century philosophy, so are there thematic correspondences between his writings of those of later spiritual authors. The goal here is to highlight a couple of these common points of emphasis and, in turn, to demonstrate that Kierkegaard stands as a pertinent—and seemingly prescient—figure in modern Christian spirituality.

The first such thematic correspondence is what Kierkegaard terms *unrecognizability*—a motif that plays a pivotal role in his 1846 work, *A Literary Review*. As mentioned earlier, Kierkegaard is damning of modernity's preoccupation with objective information, which, he argues, has been legitimized by philosophy and then popularized by the press. The upshot is a coolness toward ethical-religious ideals. People are so busy gobbling up facts, figures, gossip, and news that self-knowledge and the contemplation of the meaning and purpose of human life are forgotten. Even worse, this cycle is almost impossible to break, since anyone who tries to bring reform will be subjected to the same apathy, resentment, and scorn that drives the media in the first place. Kierkegaard terms this process "leveling," likening it to a "deathly stillness in which nothing can rise up but everything sinks down into it, impotent."[95] It is a form of violence, but in a negative sense: it robs individuals and, with them, society of zeal for the good. Hence, far from bringing *liberté, egalité*, and *fraternité*, "the present age" ensnares individuals in a crude desire for aesthetic stimulation and, in turn, weakens the principled creativity needed for social flourishing. Even if a certain "numerical equality"[96] follows, it is but a shadow of true egalitarianism, "the idea of religiousness,"[97] which is based on the unconditional love of the neighbor.[98]

But where can this true equality be found? Is it a purely eschatological notion? Kierkegaard is loath to give an answer. While acknowledging that the Moravian Brethren provide an intimation of genuine unity, he refuses to endorse what he saw as their preference for separatism. Remote religious societies that define themselves over against the larger society are not the answer, nor is the hierarchical ecclesial establishment. Consequently, there is no *given* religious community into which one can enter. Rather, one must cultivate it in the midst of worldly opposition: "Only when the single individual in himself has won ethical firmness despite the whole world, not until then can there be talk about uniting in truth."[99]

With this in mind, Kierkegaard turns to "the unrecognizables"—a religious community that will neither disclose nor proclaim itself as such, since the individuals who constitute it "have divinely understood the diabolical principle of the leveling process."[100] Kierkegaard likens the unrecognizables to "plainclothes policeman" or to "secret agents."[101] They work for the good within common society, yet must guard their true identities, lest their mission be exposed and undermined. Herein lies an immense burden. The unrecognizables must serve in quiet, even in the face of rampant criminality, so that their larger aims can be met. Thus their unrecognizability is not a flight from the world but, rather, a solidarity so deep that it is willing to suffer evil for the sake of good. And Kierkegaard does think that good will come in this way—indeed, perhaps *only* in this way:

> The unrecognizables recognize the servants of leveling but dare not use power or authority against them, for then there would be a regression, because it would be instantly obvious to a third party that the unrecognizable one was an authority, and then the third party would be hindered from attaining the highest....He does not dare to defeat leveling outright—he would be dismissed for that, since it would be acting with authority—but in suffering he will defeat it and thereby experience in turn the law of his existence, which is not to rule, to guide, to lead, but in suffering to serve, to help indirectly.[102]

This orientation, as Kierkegaard sees it, is ultimately an expression of the love of Christ. For just as Christ let go of the reins of history, refusing to seek worldly power, so have the unrecognizables learned that loving others is not about "ruling" them but about "constraining oneself on their behalf."[103]

A few decades later, a similar emphasis on unrecognizability would be taken up by one of the great mystics of modern times, Charles de Foucauld (1858–1916). Born into an aristocratic family in Strasbourg, Charles grew up with the advantages of nobility but lacked "any wider purpose or ambition."[104] Yet, a turning point arrived when Charles was sent to North Africa as part of a French regiment. He became fascinated with the region and undertook a geographical expedition to Morocco. This experience led Charles to reconsider not only his lifestyle, but also his relation to God. He joined a Trappist monastery in Syria but found its order too comforting, its poverty too respectable. As he saw it, the Trappists had not renounced *everything* in the manner of Christ; they retained an evident measure of dignity. Receiving a dispensation, he left the monastery and began another period of vocational discernment, eventually settling in Algeria.

His primary goal there was to "live among the poor in a spirit of service and solidarity."[105] In other words, he wanted to interact with Algeria's Muslim population, not as one who wanted to control or to convert them, but as a lowly "Christian presence in their midst."[106] He expounded on this approach to Christian mission—with more than a little resemblance to Kierkegaard—in his various writings. He wrote in 1897,

> I must...embrace humility, poverty, detachment, abjection, solitude, suffering. I must make little of human greatness and the respect and approval of men, but I must respect the poor as much as the rich. For myself I must always seek the lowest of the low places, and arrange my life so that I may be the last and the most despised among men.[107]

Like Kierkegaard, then, Charles insists that the Christian life must be patterned after the example of the abased Christ. What's more, he describes this as a "hidden life," wherein Christian devotion is misunderstood and, indeed, unrecognized: "You are...unknown, inordinately poor, lowly in your smock and sandals....Some take you for a laborer of the lowest kind; others think you are an outcast....Most—nearly all, in fact—take you for a fool."[108]

But what, exactly, is the purpose of such piety? Just as Kierkegaard saw the unrecognizables as serving the good apart from sociopolitical power, so does Charles appeal to those who "lead hidden lives, possessing [Christ] without having been given a mission to preach."[109] These hidden ones, Charles explains, carry "the Gospel... not by word of mouth but by the persuasive force of example, not by speaking, but by living."[110] In this way, they "work for the sanctification of the world," even "in the midst of those who do not know [Christ]."[111] While differences between Charles and Kierkegaard might be found, it is nevertheless remarkable that both writers, when confronted with the barriers that sociopolitical power presents to evangelization, maintained that the Christian life must return to the example of the Son of God, whose incarnation not only promised salvation, but dared unrecognizability.

A second thematic correspondence between Kierkegaard and later spiritual authors is the *absolute otherness of God*. Kierkegaard's fervent and repeated insistence that God lies beyond all human conceptions and conventions harks back to older ways of understanding the relation between divine reality and human understanding—ways that, notably, were prevalent among Christian mystics. As developed in pseudonymous works such as *Concluding Unscientific Postscript* and *The Sickness unto Death*, as well as his signed upbuilding writings, Kierkegaard assumes that religiousness is not limited to organized churches or groups but is present within the human as such. Inasmuch as all human beings ask questions of existential consequence, they are capable of a "dialectical inward deepening"[112] that leads to a confrontation with ultimate reality—or, at least, with the possibility of such a reality. This view means that, for Kierkegaard, religion is not something imposed on human beings from the outside; rather, it emerges out of the concern and curiosity endemic to human life and thought.

Still, as Johannes Climacus insists in the *Postscript*, the immanence of religiousness ought not be confused with the *comprehensibility* of the eternal. In fact, the more one progresses down the road of immanent religiousness (what Climacus dubs "Religiousness A"), the more one realizes that human existence cannot be brought into correspondence with the eternal. Every human step toward God bears the recognition that this gap can only be bridged by God himself, though, by the same token, to come to this recognition is to open oneself up to divine activity. Hence, for Climacus, the spiritual life is not only perfected by God's absolute otherness (as in traditional Christian accounts of salvation), but also and ever spurred on by it, so much so that one cannot be a Christian if the inward-directed, contemplative passion of immanent religiousness is missing.[113]

Thus a Kierkegaardian approach to spirituality hinges on correctly understanding who God is and who human beings are in relation to God. As Sylvia Walsh puts it, "[A] true conception of God is [for Kierkegaard] required in order to have a true conception of life and oneself, but one cannot have a true conception of

God without also having a corresponding true conception of life and oneself."[114] Here the unconditional distinction between divine and human, Creator and creature, is fundamental—a distinction that may seem like a given for much of Christian history but, in truth, has been challenged on a number of fronts, particularly in modernity. For example, the great German theologian Friedrich Schleiermacher (1768–1834) formulated a so-called theology of experience, whose Romantic tendencies situated human feeling at the starting point of Christian theology. Consequently, Schleiermacher risked the immanentization of God and, in turn, the blurring of the divine and the human—a point that Kierkegaard recognized and, indeed, warned against.[115] Moreover, Hans Lassen Martensen—the same Martensen whom Kierkegaard so vehemently opposed in his polemics against the Danish state church—advocated for a "modern philosophical approach to God [which has] its starting-point in human self-consciousness."[116] For Kierkegaard, a key problem with this Hegelian-tinged theology lies in its assumption that a phenomenological analysis of consciousness can illuminate precisely how human beings stand vis-à-vis God, whereas Christian faith is a personal commitment to the God who reveals himself *to* humanity. God is not an object of philosophical scrutiny but a subject in whom "we live and move and have our being" (Acts 17:28). That the Hegelian theologians miss this point is the reason why Kierkegaard says they lead to "the philosophical volatilization of Christian doctrines."[117]

Kierkegaard's response to speculative theology would prove to be "the nineteenth century's sharpest statement of the difference between the divine and the human,"[118] and, in turn, it would come to exercise major influence on subsequent thinkers. Karl Barth, to cite the most famous example, once wrote, "If I have a system, it is limited to a recognition of what Kierkegaard called the 'infinite qualitative distinction' between time and eternity, and to my regarding this as possessing negative as well as positive significance: 'God is in heaven, and thou art on earth.'"[119] At the same time, however, Barth *contrasts* Kierkegaard's "dialectical audacity" with the human desire for holiness, since, in his view, spiritual discipline "presents piety as a human achievement, [and] evokes worship which knows not how to be silent before God."[120] In short, for Barth, the religious impulse in human

beings is not liberating but enslaving: "Religion is that human necessity in which the power exercised over men by sin is clearly demonstrated."[121]

Thus Barth effectively inverts Kierkegaard's conception of religiousness, which does not depict God's absolute transcendence as an
unconditional *Nein* to human religiousness but, rather, as that which
draws one along the path of the human to the divine.[122] In this
approach, Kierkegaard not only recalls the spirituality of earlier
Christian mystics but also anticipates that of one of the twentieth
century's most important thinkers, Simone Weil. Weil was a Marxist
philosopher and activist who grew interested in religious ideas and,
in time, began to have what might be termed mystical experiences:

> In a moment of intense physical suffering, when I was
> forcing myself to feel love, but without desiring to give a
> name to that love, I felt, without being in any way prepared
> for it (for I had never read the mystical writers) a presence
> more personal, more certain, more real than that of a
> human being, though inaccessible to the senses and the
> imagination.[123]

This juxtaposition of God's inaccessibility and presence would come
to characterize Weil's thought. On the one hand, she insists that God
"is infinitely beyond our reach," so much so that, in a sense, God "is
absent."[124] On the other hand, this divine distance makes possible
divine intimacy: "We can only turn our eyes toward him. We do not
have to search for him....It is for him to search for us."[125] Indeed, Weil
recounts a number of encounters with "Christ himself."[126] At one
point, she recalls, "I felt in the midst of my suffering the presence of
a love, like that which one can read in the smile on a beloved face."[127]
Elsewhere she tells of a mysterious visitor with whom she shared
bread and wine—a visitor whose love she cannot fathom and of
whom she "cannot help thinking, with fear and trembling, that perhaps, in spite of all, he loves me."[128]

Such ideas were developed further in *Gravity and Grace*—a collection of Weil's notebook entries. There she writes that "God can
only be present in creation under the form of absence."[129] This is not

a hollow paradox; rather, it is a metaphysical point. For Weil, as for Kierkegaard, God is utterly distinct from the universe and, therefore, by no means related to what William Blake once called "Nobodaddy"— the proverbial great man in the sky, frequently assumed to be the object of religious worship. On the contrary, God is beyond conceptualization, beyond predication. For that reason, Weil goes so far as to say that God does not exist, since "existence," as applied to creatures, connotes a number of conditions (birth, composition, death) that necessarily fall short of divine reality. To confront God, then, is to enter into a kind of intellectual and spiritual void. But this void, once accepted, is the prerequisite for religious growth. Here Weil comes much closer to Kierkegaard than Barth does. As she sees it, the infinite qualitative difference between God and creatures *occasions* the religious life, even as it serves as a check against religious hubris. Indeed, for that reason, Weil does not so much call persons to seek God as to *receive* God.

Once more, such an approach bears a notable resemblance to Kierkegaard, whose pseudonymous work *The Sickness unto Death* describes faith as a transparent *rest* in God.[130] This phrase means that the ideal relation to God is not attained through autonomous striving but through spiritual openness and repose.[131] It has been frequently noted that Kierkegaard's contributions to modern philosophy include his stress on the limitations of the human condition and on the hazards of putatively comprehensive systems of human thinking. What has been suggested above is that this stress resonates with later spirituality too. Kierkegaard may not have directly influenced Weil, but his thinking tilled the soil, as it were, for the development and the reception of her ideas.

The Prominence of "Upbuilding" in Kierkegaard's Spirituality

There is little doubt that Kierkegaard's legacy rests primarily with his pseudonymous writings, especially those published between 1843 and 1846. It was in and through these texts, from *Either/Or* to *Fear and Trembling* to *Concluding Unscientific Postscript*, that Kierkegaard emerged as one of the modern world's most important and controversial thinkers. In this, however, lies a striking irony. For these pseudonymous *magna opera* are not so much independent, self-contained pieces as parts of a larger authorial task—a task that marshaled a range of literary devices and philosophical-theological insights for its achievement. Later in his career, Kierkegaard described this task as follows: "The truth about me as an author is that I am and was a religious author, that the whole of my authorial activity is related to Christianity, to the problem: how to become a Christian."[132] In other words, Kierkegaard retroactively understood his authorship as an exercise in *upbuilding*, in facilitating the spiritual development of persons, particularly in relation to Christianity.

Admittedly, Kierkegaard is not always read in this way. Some commentators disregard his Christian interests, preferring to treat him as a philosopher instead. Others attend to his entire corpus, including his directly religious writings, yet with an eye to their philosophical import.[133] Still others question Kierkegaard's stated authorial mission, which, in the wake of postmodernity and its suspicions about (or even hostility toward) a unitary presence behind a given text,[134] looks misleading at best and incoherent at worst.[135] Nevertheless, Kierkegaard's own understanding of his literary career endures and, at the very least, stands as an intriguing line of interpretation—one that is more supple than it may appear prima facie. After all, as George Pattison has suggested, the choice between perfect authorial clarity and deconstructive self-invention is a false one. Instead, it makes sense to see Kierkegaard's authorship as "an ongoing quest to gain clarity and understanding about the meaning of his own words and works, a quest that involved him in experimenting with a variety of self-representations and points of view, and testing these out in relation to…issues that recur throughout the authorship."[136] The pseudonyms, then, are not *opposed* to clarity; they belong to the means by which Kierkegaard *obtained* clarity.

Thus Kierkegaard's elucidation of the nature and purpose of his writings may be simplified, but it is hardly incoherent. As he took stock of his literary career, he perceived that he always was a "religious author," even as the process by which he arrived at this realization was not linear. Yet, adds Pattison, this is not "only…an experience familiar to many authors, but…one that lies at the heart of philosophy itself, namely the never-ending attempt to reach clarity about what it is we really are saying."[137] Doubtless this conclusion will go a bridge too far for an ardent poststructuralist, though it may simply be the case that a thoroughgoing postmodern reading of Kierkegaard is not sustainable. As C. Stephen Evans writes,

> The radical postmodern Kierkegaard is a Kierkegaard who is an object of aesthetic appreciation. Such an approach to Kierkegaard allows a person to enjoy the style and literary techniques of Kierkegaard without fear of being challenged by Kierkegaard as one human person speaking to another about issues of ultimate importance.[138]

Kierkegaard's authorship may be play, but it is not *just* play. The goal of upbuilding, however concealed at times, is ever present.

And yet, one may very well ask, Why *conceal* anything at all? Why did Kierkegaard not just come out and say what he wanted to say? There is a philosophical and a historical answer to these questions. The former has to do with Kierkegaard's peculiar philosophy of pedagogy, which, during the period of 1847–48, he hoped to turn into a series of lectures. The lectures themselves never materialized, but Kierkegaard left a number of drafts, notes, and sketches among his journals and papers. They are collected under the title *The Dialectic of Ethical and Ethical-Religious Communication*.

Kierkegaard opens by criticizing the modern notion that ethics should be taught *scientifically*, that is, in objective fashion. There is undue focus on *knowing* what is right, when, in truth, ethics is best communicated by *practicing* what is right. For living well is an art rather than a science. People implicitly know the difference between right and wrong; the problem is that they often fail to actualize this knowledge. The modern world, then, has it backward. It craves information when what it really needs is exemplarity; it is so busy telling that it neglects to show.

With this in mind, Kierkegaard shifts his attention to indirect communication—the best way, in his opinion, to teach the ethical. This belief is grounded in his conviction that, insofar as the attainment of ethical perfection lies outside human capability, one can never arrogate the title of "master-teacher."[139] On the contrary, God alone is to be thought of as master, and, for that reason, the best a teacher of ethics can do is to facilitate the individual's God-relationship. Put differently, in relation to ethics, *direct* communication is impossible on two counts: it is ineffectual for the teacher to simply impart a catalog of ethical rules, and it is intolerable for the teacher to stand before the student as master. The teacher's role, then, is to lead in such a way that she disappears, to put herself out of a job, as it were. Kierkegaard likens this approach to that of Socrates, whose maieutic method sought to bring "to birth the ethical possibilities latent in the pupil."[140]

It is well known that Kierkegaard's pseudonymous writings represent the use of this approach. The various pseudonyms signify Kierkegaard's attempt to communicate with the reader via the portrayal of certain *Weltanschauungen* and thus are not to be identified with Kierkegaard himself. He makes this point explicit in "A First and Last Explanation," a short appendix to the *Postscript*: "What has been written...is mine, but only insofar as I...have placed the life-view of the creat*ing*, poetically actual individuality in his mouth."[141] He compares his role to that of a "secretary" and adds that he, too, has sought to learn from the pseudonyms, whose ideas are "dialectically reduplicated" in his own person.[142] This point underlines that the pseudonymous writings by no means lie outside the scope of Kierkegaard's larger task of upbuilding. Rather, they are a crucial part of building up the reader, since, in their variegated moods and perspectives, they facilitate ethical-religious reflection and prompt the reader to deepen her own self-knowledge and relation to the eternal.

Yet, if the pseudonymous treatises belong to the upbuilding, what is the purpose of Kierkegaard's nonpseudonymous ("signed") and presumably *direct* writings? Before addressing this question, it is worth pointing out that, for Kierkegaard, religious communication is not identical with ethical communication. One may very well have an a priori understanding of right and wrong, but knowledge of, say, Jesus Christ is not intrinsic to human nature. Therefore some objective knowledge of Christianity is required, and, consequently, there is warrant for direct communication among Christians—a point that explains why Kierkegaard was not hesitant to call his signed discourses "directly religious."[143] He intended these writings to supplement or, in a sense, complete their pseudonymous counterparts. Whereas the latter seek to cast the reader into ethical-religious reflection, the former aim to communicate religious truth. As Kierkegaard expounds, "In relation to pure receptivity, like the empty jar that is to be filled, *direct* communication is appropriate, but when illusion is involved, consequently something that must first be removed, direct communication is inappropriate."[144]

At the same time, however, it would be wrong to label Kierkegaard's signed works as "dogmatic." In fact, Kierkegaard is at pains to distinguish his signed discourses—which, unlike the pseudonymous treatises, are frequently specified as *opbyggelse* (upbuilding)—from doctrinal teaching or official instruction. This qualification partly has to do with Kierkegaard's lack of ecclesiastical authority, which he tends to underline in the forewords to the discourses. It also, however, involves the *kind* of direct communication necessitated by his authorial context. Writing in Denmark, which was and is a formally Christian nation, Kierkegaard presupposed that his reader already had adequate knowledge of church doctrine and the like. The trouble lay with the application of that knowledge, with getting persons to appropriate the teachings they already know. Thus religious instruction circles back to the problem of ethics. How can the communicator facilitate the actualization of the ethical possibility latent in the knowledge of Christian truth?

With this mind, it is clear that Kierkegaard's signed discourses are not *that* different from the pseudonymous ones. Their focus on ethical actuality and their disclaimers of ecclesial authority, not to mention "Kierkegaard's insistence that ethical communication of this kind is necessarily indirect, would...seem to mark them out as indirect communication after all."[145] Indeed, the very rhetoric of the discourses supports this point. At first glance, they appear to be transcripts of formal addresses or perhaps even sermons; yet, as noted, Kierkegaard explicitly precludes the latter possibility. Besides, the incorporation of other elements—for example, direct references to the reader ("my listener"), the usage of the first-person plural personal pronoun ("we"), and the recurrent (bordering on incessant) utilization of interrogative sentences—give the discourses a decidedly conversational feel. It is as if Kierkegaard is not only speaking to, but also *with*, his audience. In this way, his language instantiates his communicative theory, deflecting attention away from the author's authority and toward the individual's understanding both of herself and of God. Ultimately, then, the signed discourses are both direct *and* indirect. They bear Kierkegaard's name and often accentuate the Christian presuppositions underlying his thought, even as they attempt to avoid the objectivism that, according to Kierkegaard, plagues so much religious instruction.

And yet, amid Kierkegaard's shifting strategies and voices, there is a constant goal—to upbuild his readers. But upbuild to what? Or for what? What does Kierkegaard envision as the outcome of *opbyggelse*? It should be clear that Kierkegaard's oeuvre is not designed for pat answers. Its complexity demands the reader's effort, juxtaposing the extensive *points de vue* of the pseudonymous works with the intensive dialectic of the signed discourses. Indeed, the indirect and direct writings were not issued in linear fashion, as if one might simply march from one side of the authorship to another, but were, quite literally, issued together. Kierkegaard inaugurated this approach in 1843, when, after publishing the pseudonymous *Either/Or* in February, he issued the signed *Two Upbuilding Discourses* in May. Later that year, he repeated this practice: the pseudonymous works *Fear and Trembling* and *Repetition* were published on the same day (October 16) as the signed *Three Upbuilding Discourses*. This pattern would come to characterize Kierkegaard's literary career. As he put it, "The religious is present from the very beginning. Conversely, the esthetic is still present even in the last moment. After the publication of only religious works for two years, a little esthetic article follows....The duplexity is both first and last."[146]

Thus the upbuilding and its attendant religious concerns are present at every stage of Kierkegaard's oeuvre. But insofar as those concerns are existential in nature (that is, they do not involve dogmatic instruction), they have to do with developing and strengthening the individual's spiritual life. This goal especially relates to a pair of excellences that, in the larger Christian tradition, are often described as "theological virtues"—namely, faith and love.

Kierkegaard connects the latter to *opbyggelse* in explicit fashion. Drawing on the words of Paul—who famously told the church in Corinth that "love builds up" (1 Cor 8:1)—Kierkegaard asserts that the upbuilding "is exclusively characteristic of love."[147] Here he does not mean that all forms or manifestations of love are upbuilding. An erotic relationship can become twisted by greed and selfishness; a friendship can become warped by elitism and pride. Nor does Kierkegaard mean that love upbuilds at the *exclusion* of other activities. Indeed, he quotes Paul to the contrary: "[Love] does not insist on its own way" (1 Cor 13:5).[148] For Kierkegaard, this means that love has a noncompetitive relationship with the world. It does not have to get out of the way in order for another activity to take place. Rather, it is capable of "being able to give itself in everything, be present in everything."[149] In this sense, love is identical to upbuilding: "Everything can be upbuilding in the same sense as love can be everywhere present."[150] Kierkegaard illustrates this point with an example:

> We would not think that the sight of a person sleeping could be upbuilding. Yet if you see a baby sleeping on its mother's breast—and you see the mother's love, see that she has, so to speak, waited for and now makes use of the moment while the baby is sleeping really to rejoice in it because she hardly dares let the baby notice how inexpressibly she loves it—then this is an upbuilding sight.... Just to see the baby sleeping is a friendly, benevolent, soothing sight, but it is not upbuilding. If you still want to call it upbuilding, it is because you see love present, it is because you see God's love encompass the baby.[151]

Here Kierkegaard does not bother to account for the shift from "the mother's love" to "God's love." Elsewhere, however, he is clear that human love is but a sharing in the love of God, the "Eternal Love," who is the "source of all love in heaven and on earth," "so that the one who loves is what he is only by being in you."[152]

Hence, for Kierkegaard, there is an intrinsic bond between upbuilding, love, and God that makes up a type of trinity. Wherever love is present, so is the upbuilding. Yet, since God is love, it is also true that the presence of the upbuilding signifies the presence of God. Again, Kierkegaard's task as an upbuilding author is to manifest these connections, not in dogmatic fashion,[153] but in such a way that they come to develop the reader's spiritual life.

One might object that other facets of life are upbuilding—for instance, political competence, artistic skill, and scholarly erudition. But these talents, *sensu stricto*, do not concern themselves with love, and so Kierkegaard maintains that their upbuilding "is still not upbuilding in the deepest sense."[154] "This is because, spiritually, love is the *ground*, and to build up means to erect from *the ground up*."[155]

Yet, in so elevating love, Kierkegaard might be seen as diminishing the centrality of faith. His words call to mind the viewpoint of the Apostle Paul, whose famed encomium on love states that, in relation to other Christian virtues, "the greatest of these is love" (1 Cor 13:13). How, then, does Kierkegaard conceive of the relation between faith and love and, in turn, faith's role in his larger authorial project of upbuilding?

Kierkegaard wrestled with this question for some time. Already in 1834 a pair of journal entries question the link between faith and volitional activity.[156] Then, in 1836, Kierkegaard hits on an understanding that will come to characterize his analysis of the problem. Comparing faith to a "vital fluid" and to "the atmosphere we breathe," he concludes that it is "the prerequisite for everything."[157] He later reworks this notion, explaining that faith is the "a priori" that "hovers over all the a posteriori of works."[158] Intriguingly, Kierkegaard likens this position to that of Paul[159]—a point borne out by scholarship on the apostle's epistles. According to J. Paul Sampley, Paul understands faith as "the right relation to God," which, in turn, "makes love possible."[160] In other words, "love presupposes faith."[161] But this perspective does not place faith *over* love. Faith is a "human commitment" that "may end," whereas love, "grounded as it is in God and a signal and eternal characteristic of God's commitment toward all creatures, is the one disposition that believers share most fully with God."[162] Thus love flows from faith and, indeed, is its perfection. But without faith it could not begin. To return to Kierkegaard's language, faith is the prerequisite for everything.

Kierkegaard develops this line of reasoning at the outset of *Works of Love*. He opens with a prayer that lauds the "God of love."[163] Here the term he uses for "love" is *Kjerlighed*, which can be compared to the Latin term *caritas*, signifying nonerotic benevolence or kindness.[164] Thus God is *Kjerlighed*. Kierkegaard presents this point in trinitarian fashion, describing God as "the source of all love in heaven and on earth,"[165] "the Savior and Redeemer," "who revealed what love is," and the "Spirit of love," who reminds "the believer to love as he is loved and his neighbor as himself."[166] In emphasizing love's divine origin, Kierkegaard is also stressing its mystery. As M. Jamie Ferreira puts it, "Love is hidden because its source is God, who is hidden, who is invisible, a 'secret source.'"[167] The same is true for *Kjerlighed* in human life, which, stemming from God, "dwells in hiding or is hidden in the innermost being."[168] In turn, *Kjerlighed* does not proceed from a calculus of cost-benefit. It is not like a coin, which is presented in exchange for something else. Rather, it is given, even without recognition, for the sake of the beloved.

Yet, precisely because this sort of love confounds ordinary ways of doing things, precisely because its saturation of the created order renders it incomprehensible, one must have *faith* in it. *Works of Love* emphasizes this point. The tendency of "conceited sagacity," Kierkegaard writes, is to "believe nothing that we cannot see with our physical eyes."[169] But this way of thinking carries a decisive implication: "we first and foremost ought to give up believing in love,"[170] which cannot be empirically demonstrated. Such logic, says Kierkegaard, ought to give one pause for thought. It is true that no one in life wants to be "deceived by believing what is untrue."[171] And yet, this impulse can be taken too far. One can become obsessed with wanting to make oneself "absolutely secure against being deceived,"[172] policing out anything that lacks experimental proof. But this is itself a deception—indeed, a more intractable and damaging deception. For such a person, proud of his or her intelligence, is "deceived by not believing what is true."[173]

The challenge, then, is to have faith in love. It is to believe that love is present, not only in human life, but also in eternity. In fact, these two loves go hand in hand:

35

SØREN KIERKEGAARD

[Love] is in an unfathomable connectedness with all existence. Just as the quiet lake originates deep down in hidden springs no eye has seen, so also does a person's love
[*Kjerlighed*] originate even more deeply in God's love
[*Kjerlighed*]. If there were no gushing spring at the bottom, if God were not love, then there would be neither the
little lake nor a human being's love.[174]

Thus love cannot be seen, much less comprehended. "When you
think that you see [love's essence], you are deceived by a reflected
image."[175] That is why faith is necessary. It does not seek to infiltrate
the mystery of love but, rather, to presuppose it, to rest in its presence.[176] In this way, faith is like a channel, which allows one to "tune
in" to the reality of love. Faith does not create love but enables the
human being to grow in it—a point that brings this discussion back
to Paul. For Kierkegaard, as for Paul, love and its works are the perfection of faith. Yet, it is also true that love is an aspect of faith, since,
without faith, love could not be known in the world.

It would seem critical, then, that Kierkegaard's writings seek to
upbuild the reader's faith. But herein lies a problem, already laid out
in Kierkegaard's pseudonymous treatise *Philosophical Fragments*. In
that work, Johannes Climacus argues that faith cannot be taught,
since its condition is not intrinsic to human nature. After all, if it
were, then Socrates has done the most that can be done for a human
being, and Christian teaching about the incarnation of the Son of
God is superfluous. In contrast, Christianity teaches that the condition for faith is supplied by God himself. As Climacus explains,

When does [a person] receive [the condition for faith]? In
the moment. This condition, what does it condition? His
understanding of the eternal. But a condition such as this
surely must be an eternal condition. —In the moment,
therefore, he receives the eternal condition, and he knows
this from his having received it in the moment, for otherwise he merely calls to mind that he had it from eternity.
He receives the condition in the moment and receives it
from that teacher himself.[177]

36

Climacus, then, endorses the longstanding Christian position that faith is not a product of human effort but a divine gift: "The god gave the follower the condition to see…and opened for him the eyes of faith."[178] And yet, this top-down model of faith risks nullifying human participation altogether. It seems that one is either zapped by the deity or destined to go without faith—a conclusion that would render any attempt to "build up" another's faith pointless.

In *Concluding Unscientific Postscript*, however, Climacus expands on his position. While he continues to insist that faith in the revelation of the incarnate Son of God "depends on the active assistance of God, giving the ability to recognize the truth as such, and not on the inherent powers of human reason,"[179] he argues that this assistance does not come at the expense of human effort—a claim that emerges as one of the focal points of the *Postscript*. At the heart of Climacus's argument is the idea that, even though Christian faith is not a faculty latent in the human self, *all* human beings do possess a capacity for religion. He is not talking about, say, the practice of prayer or of ceremonial ritual but, rather, about a dedicated exploration of existential questions. Here, again, he cites as an example "the Socrates of Socratic ignorance (objective uncertainty), of Socratic irony (indirect communication), and of Socratic uncertainty 'if there is an immortality' (objective uncertainty again)."[180] Put differently, this sort of religiousness arises whenever one probes the meaning of life, particularly with regard to the possibility of an eternal origin and purpose. It is, in short, a religiousness of passionate (or impassioned) inward deepening.

Such a broad conception of human religiousness necessitates a broad name, and so, as alluded to above, Climacus calls it "Religiousness A." The "A" indicates its relation to Christianity (or "Religiousness B"), which Climacus treats as transcendent, emerging solely through divine initiative. Hence, on Climacus's analysis, not all religious persons are Christian, but all Christians are religious in the sense of Religiousness A. Climacus goes so far as to insist that one cannot be Christian without having passed through the crucible of Religiousness A. This should not give the impression that Religiousness A is a simple affair, as if it were a baby step prior to the sprint of Christianity. Climacus divides Religiousness A into a trio of stages, wherein the person slowly but surely comes to face the para-doxes of human existence—that one desires eternal life yet is unable to procure it; that every movement toward the divine only illumines its distance; that the greatest of all human tasks (the pursuit of eter-nity) terminates in the failure of human effort.

It is clear that this "Socratic form of the religious life"[181] is, for Kierkegaard, critical for the development of Christian faith. And it is on that level that most of his signed, upbuilding discourses work. They are not written as apologies for Christian revelation, nor do they attempt to explicate systematically the various tenets of Christian faith. And though they *do* draw on motifs and persons from the Christian tradition, they do so with an eye to understanding and to stirring immanent religious passion and its interleaving desires for eternal justice and happiness. In short, these discourses try to foster the reader's spiritual life, precisely because "the development of gen-uine 'inwardness' in a person is a process that also involves the devel-opment of a knowledge of God and a relation to God."[182] They facilitate Religiousness A but, in doing so, open up a space for the reception of Religiousness B, that is, for the faith that comes from God alone.

Thus Kierkegaard's project is, in the end, very much about the building up of love and faith, not in opposition to an otherwise recal-citrant human nature, but *through* the faculties most characteristic of the human—intellect, memory, and will. That this process encom-passes both the pseudonymous and signed works suggests that there is, after all, a unifying purpose to Kierkegaard's oeuvre. Kierkegaard has a Socratic side, and Kierkegaard has a Christian side. Yet, "the point of similarity between irony and radical [Christian] discipleship is to be located precisely in the category of the upbuilding."[183]

If, for Kierkegaard, the goal of human life lies in faith's happy rest in God, which positions one to love God and neighbor in *imita-tio Christi*, it is also true that not everyone gets there the same way. Some respond to philosophical interrogation, others to the tradi-tional doctrines of Christianity, and still more, perhaps, to some combination of the two. Kierkegaard's authorial task was to address just such a variety of persons—a task that was as ambitious as it was distinctive. In an authorship famed for polyphony, it is not an exaggeration to say that "the upbuilding" is its *cantus firmus*.

CONCLUSION

In closing, it seems appropriate (if also ironic) to register Kierkegaard's disdain for the kind of material presented here. He writes in an 1848 journal entry,

> What I have to say may not be taught; by being taught it turns into something entirely different. What I need is a man who does not gesticulate with his arms up in a pulpit or with his fingers upon a podium, but a person who gesticulates with his entire personal existence [*Existents*], with the willingness in every danger to will to express in action precisely what he teaches....Precisely this is the profound untruth in all modern teaching, that there is no notion at all of how thought is influenced by the fact that the one presenting it does not dare to express it in action, that in this very way the flower of the thought or the heart of the thought vanishes and the power of the thought disappears.[184]

Scholars often ascribe such complaints to Kierkegaard's opposition to the Hegelian system and its concomitant model of philosophy as objective science—an interpretation that is not without merit. And yet, to prioritize this reading is to suggest that Kierkegaard is best defined by what he is *against* rather than what he is *for*. It is to treat him as a detractor rather than as an advocate.

Gradually, however, the notion that Kierkegaard is a mere voice of existentialist angst and protest is fading. Since the 1980s, increasing attention has been paid to Kierkegaard's category of *opbyggelse*,[185] and there has been a resurgence of interest in Kierkegaard's mystical-cum-Pietist sources and their influence on his thinking.[186] To say the least, then, Kierkegaard's connection to and treatment of Christian spirituality is a live issue in the scholarly world, and the upshot is a fuller understanding of the Dane's work.

I hope this book will contribute to this ongoing development, demonstrating that Kierkegaard wants to provoke existential transformation and to foster Christian holiness. Moreover, in devising and effecting such a project, Kierkegaard finds himself not at the margins of Western thought but, rather, as part of an intellectual tradition that stretches back to antiquity, finds its full flowering in the Christian era, and remains prominent to this day. This is the tradition of spiritual writing, and it boasts some of the most important thinkers in Western history, from Plato and Augustine to Meister Eckhart and Teresa of Ávila. To the extent that this volume encourages one to situate Kierkegaard among their kind, it will have met its aim.

Notes

1. Maurice O'Connor Drury, "Conversations with Wittgenstein," in *Recollections of Wittgenstein*, ed. Rush Rhees (Oxford: Oxford University Press, 1984), 87–88.

2. I have treated these issues extensively elsewhere. See, first and foremost, Christopher B. Barnett, *Kierkegaard, Pietism and Holiness* (Farnham: Ashgate, 2011).

3. Jørgen Bukdahl, *Søren Kierkegaard and the Common Man*, trans. Bruce H. Kirmmse (Grand Rapids: Eerdmans, 2001), 35.

4. Kaj Baagø, *Vækkelse og Kirkeliv in København og Omegn* (Copenhagen: Gads Forlag, 1960), 23.

5. C. Stephen Evans, *Kierkegaard: An Introduction* (Cambridge: Cambridge University Press, 2009), 4.

6. Evans, *Kierkegaard*, 5.

7. *SKS* 27, 292, *Pap.* 305:3, my translation. Also see Joakim Garff, *Søren Kierkegaard: A Biography* (Princeton, NJ: Princeton University Press, 2005), 346–47.

8. Garff, *Kierkegaard*, 176. Also see Joakim Garff, *Kierkegaard's Muse: The Mystery of Regine Olsen*, trans. Alastair Hannay (Princeton, NJ: Princeton University Press, 2017).

9. See, e.g., Bruce Kirmmse, ed., *Encounters with Kierkegaard* (Princeton, NJ: Princeton University Press, 1996), 35.

10. Alastair Hannay, *Kierkegaard: A Biography* (Cambridge: Cambridge University Press, 2001), 158.

11. Evans, *Kierkegaard*, 5.

12. Evans, *Kierkegaard*, 5.

13. Evans, *Kierkegaard*, 5.

14. Hannay, *Kierkegaard*, 154.

15. Hannay, *Kierkegaard*, 158.

16. Garff, *Kierkegaard*, 485.

17. Kirmmse, *Encounters with Kierkegaard*, 53–54.

18. Evans, *Kierkegaard*, 5.

19. Hannay, *Kierkegaard*, 160. Jacob Burckhardt, Friedrich Engels, and (according to some reports) Karl Marx likewise attended Schelling's lectures.

20. *SKS* 28, Brev 4 / *LD*, 141.

21. Hannay, *Kierkegaard*, 164.

22. *SKS* 13, 14 / *PV*, 496.

23. *SKS* 13, 14 / *PV*, 497.

24. Hannay, *Kierkegaard*, 315.

25. *SKS* 18, 278, JJ 415 / *KJN* 2, 257.

26. *SKS* 20, 19, NB:7 / *KJN* 4, 16–17.

27. Evans, *Kierkegaard*, 7.

28. Julia Watkin, *Historical Dictionary of Kierkegaard's Philosophy* (Lanham, UK: Scarecrow Press, 2001), 404.

29. Hannay, *Kierkegaard*, 401.

30. See, e.g., *SKS* 22, 298, NB13:37 / *JP* 6, 6511.

31. See, e.g., *SKS* 22, 141, NB11:233.

32. Hannay, *Kierkegaard*, 401.

33. Garff, *Kierkegaard*, 798.

34. Garff, *Kierkegaard*, 798.

35. Quoted in Garff, *Kierkegaard*, 798.

36. Garff, *Kierkegaard*, 798.

37. *SKS* 1, 221 / *CI*, 173.

38. Watkin, *Kierkegaard's Philosophy*, 129.

39. Evans, *Kierkegaard*, 9.

40. Evans, *Kierkegaard*, 9.

41. Evans, *Kierkegaard*, 9.

42. Quoted in Garff, *Kierkegaard*, 729.

43. Hannay, *Kierkegaard*, 402.

44. Hannay, *Kierkegaard*, 405.

45. Hannay, *Kierkegaard*, 405.
46. Hannay, *Kierkegaard*, 407.
47. Hannay, *Kierkegaard*, 407.
48. Hannay, *Kierkegaard*, 410.
49. *SKS* 13, 248 / *M*, 197.
50. *SKS* 13, 286 / *M*, 229.
51. *SKS* 13, 287 / *M*, 230.
52. *SKS* 13, 288 / *M*, 230.
53. *SKS* 13, 288 / *M*, 231.
54. *SKS* 13, 288 / *M*, 231.
55. *SKS* 24, 197, NB22:172.
56. *LD*, 28.
57. *LD*, 28.
58. *LD*, 28.
59. *LD*, 28.
60. *SKS* 28, Brev 39 / *LD*, 26–27.
61. For more on Brorson and on Kierkegaard's interest in him, see my "Hans Adolph Brorson: Danish Pietism's Greatest Hymn Writer and His Relation to Kierkegaard," in *Kierkegaard and the Renaissance and Modern Traditions—Theology*, ed. Jon Stewart (Farnham, UK: Ashgate, 2009), 63–80.
62. Hans Adolph Brorson, *Udvalgte salmer og digter*, ed. Steffen Arndal (Borgen: Det Danske Sprog- og Litteraturselskab, 1994), 99–101. Also see *SKS* 28, Brev 39 / *LD*, 26–27.
63. *SKS* 7, 214 / *CUP1*, 235.
64. As will be explained, the notion of "rest" (*Hvile/Ro*) is an important one in Kierkegaard's spirituality. Indeed, it is by no means insignificant that his tombstone inscription features "rest" (*hvile*), in addition to the more celebrated—even stereotypical—Kierkegaardian motifs such as "struggle."
65. Sandra M. Schneiders, "Christian Spirituality: Definition, Methods and Types," in *The New Westminster Dictionary of Christian Spirituality*, ed. Philip Sheldrake (Louisville, KY: Westminster John Knox Press, 2005), 1.
66. Schneiders, "Christian Spirituality, 1.
67. Schneiders, "Christian Spirituality, 1.
68. Robert Solomon, "Introduction," in *Existentialism*, ed. Robert C. Solomon (Oxford: Oxford University Press, 2005), 1.
69. Simon Blackburn, *Oxford Dictionary of Philosophy* (Oxford: Oxford University Press, 1996), 129.

70. Thomas Merton, *Contemplative Prayer* (London: Darton, Longman & Todd, 1969), 24.

71. James Collins, *The Existentialists: A Critical Study* (Chicago: Regnery, 1952), 2.

72. Collins, *The Existentialists*, 3.

73. Lawrence S. Cunningham and Keith J. Egan, *Christian Spirituality: Themes from the Tradition* (Mahwah, NJ: Paulist Press, 1996), 9.

74. Cunningham and Egan, *Christian Spirituality*, 14.

75. Cunningham and Egan, *Christian Spirituality*, 9–14.

76. See Michael Strawser, *Both/And: Reading Kierkegaard from Irony to Edification* (New York: Fordham University Press, 1999). Strawser would add, however, that the reverse is also possible. George Pattison, while agreeing with Strawser's attempt to read Kierkegaard in holistic fashion, nevertheless breaks from "Strawser's apparent acceptance of a complete equivocation between irony and upbuilding." See George Pattison, *Kierkegaard's Upbuilding Discourses: Philosophy, Literature and Theology* (London: Routledge, 2002), 139.

77. NB20:175, NB20:175a / *JP* 3, 3318.

78. Johann Arndt, *True Christianity*, ed. and trans. Peter C. Erb (New York: Paulist Press, 1979), 39.

79. Christian Braw, *Bücher im Staube: Die Theologie Johann Arndts in ihrem Verhältnis zur Mystik* (Leiden: E.J. Brill, 1985), 43–44.

80. Carter Lindberg, "Luther's Struggle with Social-Ethical Issues," in *The Cambridge Companion to Martin Luther*, ed. Donald K. McKim (Cambridge: Cambridge University Press, 2003), 165.

81. Lindberg, "Luther's Struggle with Social-Ethical Issues," 166.

82. Dietmar Lage, *Martin Luther's Christology and Ethics* (Lewiston, NY: Edwin Mellen Press, 1990), 60.

83. Lage, *Martin Luther's Christology and Ethics*, 81.

84. See, e.g., Braw, *Bücher im Staube*, 80.

85. Arndt, *True Christianity*, 30.

86. Peter C. Erb, "Introduction," in *True Christianity*, trans. Peter C. Erb (New York: Paulist Press, 1979), 13.

87. See, e.g., *SKS* 20, NB2:10 / *JP* 4, 4598.

88. See, e.g., *SKS* 18, JJ:451 / *JP* 5, 5920.

89. On this point, see, above all, Andrew Burgess, "Kierkegaard, Moravian Missions, and Martyrdom," in *International Kierkegaard Commentary: Without Authority*, ed. Robert L. Perkins (Macon, GA: Mercer University Press, 2007), 177–201.

90. *SKS* 8, 64 / *TA*, 65–66.

91. *SKS* 21, NB7:101 / *JP* 3, 2751.

92. *Pap.* IX B 22.

93. *SKS* 21, NB7:101 / *JP* 3, 2751.

94. These questions remain vital today, as evidenced by the controversy surrounding the so-called Benedict Option. See, e.g., Rod Dreher, *The Benedict Option: A Strategy for Christians in a Post-Christian Nation* (New York: Sentinel, 2017).

95. *SKS* 8, 81 / *TA*, 84.

96. *SKS* 8, 102 / *TA*, 108.

97. *SKS* 8, 85 / *TA*, 88.

98. See, e.g., *SKS* 9, 87 / *WL*, 81.

99. *SKS* 8, 101 / *TA*, 106, my translation.

100. *SKS* 8, 101 / *TA*, 107.

101. *SKS* 8, 102 / *TA*, 107.

102. *SKS* 8, 103–4 / *TA*, 109.

103. *SKS* 8, 104 / *TA*, 109, my translation.

104. Robert Ellsberg, "Introduction: Little Brother of Jesus," in *Charles de Foucauld: Essential Writings* (Maryknoll, NY: Orbis Books, 1999), 15.

105. Ellsberg, "Introduction: Little Brother of Jesus," 20.

106. Ellsberg, "Introduction: Little Brother of Jesus," 21.

107. Charles de Foucauld, *Charles de Foucauld: Essential Writings* (Maryknoll, NY: Orbis Books, 1999), 65.

108. *Charles de Foucauld: Essential Writings*, 42.

109. *Charles de Foucauld: Essential Writings*, 44.

110. *Charles de Foucauld: Essential Writings*, 44.

111. *Charles de Foucauld: Essential Writings*, 44.

112. *SKS* 7, 505 / *CUP1*, 556.

113. *SKS* 7, 352 / *CUP1*, 386.

114. Sylvia Walsh, "Kierkegaard's Theology," in *The Oxford Handbook of Kierkegaard*, ed. John Lippitt and George Pattison (Oxford: Oxford University Press, 2013), 295.

115. *SKS* 27, *Pap.* 13:11.

116. George Pattison, *Kierkegaard and the Theology of the Nineteenth Century: The Paradox and the "Point of Contact"* (Cambridge: Cambridge University Press, 2012), 49.

117. *SKS* 19, Not8:52 / *JP* 3, 3285.

118. Pattison, *Kierkegaard and the Theology of the Nineteenth Century*, 27.

119. Karl Barth, *The Epistle to the Romans*, trans. Edwyn Hoskyns (London: Oxford University Press, 1933), 10.

120. Barth, *The Epistle to the Romans*, 252–53.

121. Barth, *The Epistle to the Romans*, 253.

122. For more on this topic, see my *From Despair to Faith: The Spirituality of Søren Kierkegaard* (Minneapolis: Fortress Press, 2014), esp. chap. 2, "Kierkegaard on God, Self, and the Spiritual Journey."

123. Quoted in Leslie A. Fiedler, "Introduction," in Simone Weil, *Waiting for God*, trans. Emma Craufurd (New York: Harper Perennial Modern Classics, 2009), xxiii.

124. Weil, *Waiting for God*, 143.

125. Weil, *Waiting for God*, 143.

126. Weil, *Waiting for God*, 27.

127. Weil, *Waiting for God*, 27.

128. Simone Weil, *The Notebooks of Simone Weil*, vol. 2, trans. Arthur Wills (London: Routledge, 1976), 638–39.

129. Simone Weil, *Gravity and Grace*, trans. Emma Crawford and Mario von der Ruhr (London: Routledge Classics, 2002), 109.

130. *SKS* 11, 242 / *SUD*, 131.

131. Again, see my *From Despair to Faith: The Spirituality of Søren Kierkegaard* for more on this topic. Also see Paul Cruysberghs, "Transparency to Oneself and to God," in *At være sig selv nærværende: Festskrift til Niels Jørgen Cappelørn*, ed. Joakim Garff, Ettore Rocca, and Pia Søltoft (Copenhagen: Kristeligt Dagblads Forlag, 2010), 138–39.

132. *SKS* 16, 11 / *PV*, 23, my translation.

133. Here one might cite the example of Martin Heidegger, who, far from dismissing Kierkegaard's upbuilding writings as merely devotional, argued that they bear significant *philosophical* import. As Heidegger once wrote, "There is more to be learned philosophically from Kierkegaard's 'edifying' writings than from his theoretical ones—with the exception of his treatise on the concept of anxiety" (Martin Heidegger, *Being and Time*, trans. John Macquarrie and Edward Robinson [San Francisco: Harper Collins, 1962], 494).

134. See, e.g., Roland Barthes, "The Death of the Author," in *Image-Music-Text*, trans. Stephen Heath (New York: Hill and Wang, 1977), 142–48. As Barthes writes, "[A] text is not a line of words releasing a single 'theological' meaning (the message of the 'Author-God') but a multi-dimensional space in which a variety of writings, none of them original, blend and clash" (146).

135. One well-known proponent of this perspective was the late Roger Poole, who argued that Kierkegaard's "irony and his many-voiced-ness, his *heteroglossia*, distance him from any position that could be asserted to be finally 'his' position" (Roger Poole, "The Unknown Kierkegaard: Twentieth-Century Receptions," in *The Cambridge Companion to Kierkegaard*, ed. Alastair Hannay and Gordon D. Marino [Cambridge: Cambridge University Press, 1998], 48).

136. Pattison, *Kierkegaard's Upbuilding Discourses*, 14.

137. Pattison, *Kierkegaard's Upbuilding Discourses*, 14.

138. Evans, *Kierkegaard*, 13. It should be noted, however, that some postmodern readings of Kierkegaard do, in fact, stress the socioethical thrust of his authorship. See, e.g., Mark Dooley, *The Politics of Exodus: Søren Kierkegaard's Ethics of Responsibility* (New York: Fordham University Press, 2001).

139. *SKS* 27, 396, *Pap.* 365:12 / *JP* 1, 649.

140. Pattison, *Kierkegaard's Upbuilding Discourses*, 18.

141. *SKS* 7, 569 / *CUP1*, 625.

142. *SKS* 7, 571 / *CUP1*, 627.

143. *SKS* 13, 14 / *PV*, 8.

144. *SKS* 13, 14 / *PV*, 8.

145. Pattison, *Kierkegaard's Upbuilding Discourses*, 21.

146. *SKS* 16, 16–17 / *PV*, 30.

147. *SKS* 9, 215 / *WL*, 212.

148. *SKS* 9, 215 / *WL*, 212.

149. *SKS* 9, 215 / *WL*, 212.

150. *SKS* 9, 216 / *WL*, 213.

151. *SKS* 9, 217 / *WL*, 214.

152. *SKS* 9, 12 / *WL*, 4.

153. As Paul Müller puts it, "Kierkegaard proves himself a...*theologian,*— for the sake of upbuilding" ("Begrebet 'det Opbyggelige' hos Søren Kierkegaard," *Fønix* 7 [1983]: 15).

154. *SKS* 9, 219 / *WL*, 216.

155. *SKS* 9, 219 / *WL*, 216.

156. *SKS*, 27, 97, *Pap.* 58 / *JP* 2, 1094; *SKS*, 27, 99, *Pap.* 62 / *JP* 2, 1095.

157. *SKS* 27, 112, *Pap.* 92 / *JP* 2, 1096.

158. *SKS* 17, 247, DD:79 / *JP* 2, 1097.

159. See, e.g., Rom 8:35–39.

160. J. Paul Sampley, "The First Letter to the Corinthians," *The New Interpreter's Bible*, vol. 10, ed. Leander E. Keck et al. (Nashville: Abingdon Press, 2002), 955.

161. Sampley, "The First Letter to the Corinthians," 955.

162. Sampley, "The First Letter to the Corinthians," 955.

163. *SKS* 9, 12 / *WL*, 3.

164. For that reason, *Kjerlighed* is often contrasted with its Danish counterpart, *Elskov*, which indicates erotic or sensual love. That does not mean, however, that the two are mutually exclusive. For Kierkegaard in particular, *Kjerlighed* might be seen as the completion of *Elskov*, since, without *Kjerlighed*, *Elskov* cannot be sustained in nonviolent fashion. As he explains, Christianity "has made erotic love a matter of conscience," since it refuses to reduce love to "drives and inclination" (*SKS* 9, 142 / *WL*, 140). Put simply, Christianity also treats the erotic lover as "the neighbor," whom one is supposed to love as oneself. In this way, the Christian stress on *Kjerlighed*, which reflects a participation in the nature of God, protects "what was begun on the basis of the erotic" (Watkin, *Kierkegaard's Philosophy*, 155).

165. *SKS* 9, 12 / *WL*, 3.

166. *SKS* 9, 12 / *WL*, 3–4.

167. M. Jamie Ferreira, *Love's Grateful Striving: A Commentary on Kierkegaard's Works of Love* (Oxford: Oxford University Press, 2001), 22.

168. *SKS* 9, 17 / *WL*, 9.

169. *SKS* 9, 13 / *WL*, 5.

170. *SKS* 9, 13 / *WL*, 5.

171. *SKS* 9, 13 / *WL*, 5.

172. *SKS* 9, 13 / *WL*, 5.

173. *SKS* 9, 13 / *WL*, 5.

174. *SKS* 9, 17–18 / *WL*, 9–10.

175. *SKS* 9, 18 / *WL*, 10.

176. Kierkegaard develops this insight poignantly later in *Works of Love*, namely, in the discourse "Love Hides a Multitude of Sins."

177. *SKS* 4, 265–66 / *PF*, 64.

178. *SKS* 4, 266 / *PF*, 65.

179. Merold Westphal, *Kierkegaard's Concept of Faith* (Grand Rapids, MI: Eerdmans, 2014), 131.

180. Westphal, *Kierkegaard's Concept of Faith*, 208.

181. Westphal, *Kierkegaard's Concept of Faith*, 111.

182. Westphal, *Kierkegaard's Concept of Faith*, 123.

183. Westphal, *Kierkegaard's Concept of Faith*, 123.

184. *SKS* 20, 321, NB4:72 / *JP* 1, 646.

185. See, e.g., Paul Müller, "Begrebet 'det Opbyggelige' hos Søren Kierkegaard," *Fønix* 7 (1983): 1–16; Anders Kingo, *Den Opbyggelige Tale: En Systematisk-Teologisk Studie over Søren Kierkegaards Opbyggelige Forfatterskab* (Copenhagen: Gad, 1987); and Anders Kingo, *Analogiens Teologi: En Dogmatisk Studie over Dialektikken i Søren Kierkegaards Opbyggelige og Pseudonyme Forfatterskab* (Copenhagen: Gad, 1995). Also see George Pattison, *The Philosophy of Kierkegaard* (Chesham, UK: Acumen, 2005) and especially his *Kierkegaard's Upbuilding Discourses*, cited earlier.

186. See, e.g., Andrew Burgess, "Kierkegaard, Brorson, and Moravian Music," in *International Kierkegaard Commentary: Practice in Christianity*, ed. Robert L. Perkins (Macon, GA: Mercer University Press, 2004), 211–43; Andrew Burgess, "Kierkegaard, Moravian Missions, and Martyrdom," in Perkins, *International Kierkegaard Commentary: Without Authority*, 177–201; Peter Šajda, "Kierkegaard's Encounter with Rhineland-Flemish Mystics: A Case Study," in *Kierkegaard Studies Yearbook 2009: Kierkegaard's Concept of Irony*, ed. Niels Jørgen Cappelørn, Hermann Deuser, and K. Brian Söderquist (Berlin: de Gruyter, 2009), 559–84; Simon Podmore, *Kierkegaard and the Self Before God: Anatomy of the Abyss* (Bloomington: Indiana University Press, 2011); Simon D. Podmore, *Struggling with God: Kierkegaard and the Temptation of Spiritual Trial* (Cambridge: James Clarke, 2013); and Peter Kline, *Passion for Nothing: Kierkegaard's Apophatic Theology* (Minneapolis: Fortress Press, 2017).

Part One

God

～

INTRODUCTION
TO PART ONE

The first sequence in this work has to do with God—a voluminous topic if there ever was one. Indeed, Kierkegaard employs the word *God* (*Gud*) almost nine thousand times in his authorship, and he uses the more prosaic terms "the God" (*Guden*) and "the god" (*guden*) hundreds of additional times. Furthermore, these figures say nothing about supplementary allusions or references to God in his oeuvre, whether indirect (as in mentions of divine providence) or particular (as in mentions of trinitarian theology). It stands to reason, then, that a comprehensive overview of Kierkegaard's conception of God is simply not possible in this context. Thus the aim of this section is more modest—namely, to introduce the reader to a few writings that indicate the Dane's most consistent and enduring insights regarding who God is and how human beings ought to relate to God.

The great Swiss theologian Karl Barth once wrote, "If I have a system, it is limited to a recognition of what Kierkegaard called the 'infinite qualitative distinction' between time and eternity."[1] Barth goes on to explain this distinction by way of a passage from the Bible: "God is in heaven, and thou art on earth."[2] For Barth, as for Kierkegaard, this point has been all too easily misunderstood in the modern, secular West, where God is often treated either as the other-worldly object of a purely private faith or as the immanent benefactor of a given community's sociopolitical program. In fact, Kierkegaard

---

1. Karl Barth, *The Epistle to the Romans*, trans. Edwyn C. Hoskins (London: Oxford University Press, 1933), 10.
2. Quoted in Barth, *The Epistle to the Romans*. Also see Eccl 5:2.

might be seen as one of the first, and certainly one of the most outstanding, modern Christian thinkers to criticize this ostensible
dichotomy—thus his influence on Barth and on a host of other
twentieth-century Christian authors, from Dietrich Bonhoeffer to
Thomas Merton. And yet, while such an impact suggests that
Kierkegaard was an innovator, he actually saw himself as a kind of
traditionalist, whose mission was to remind persons of the
intellectual-cum-spiritual challenges always already present in what
he liked to call "New Testament Christianity" (*nye Testamentes
Christendom*).[3]

Kierkegaard's understanding of God—what Barth refers to as
the "infinite qualitative distinction"—does indeed follow this pattern. In an 1849 journal entry, he writes that the "major premise" of
Christianity is that there "is an infinite, radical, qualitative difference
between God and man."[4] What he has in mind here is parallel to the
statement of the Fourth Lateran Council (1215), which, in repudiat-
ing univocal language about God and humanity, famously proclaimed, "For between Creator and creature no similitude can be
expressed without implying a greater dissimilitude."[5] God's otherness
is so absolute that human beings, in and of themselves, are incapable
of delineating the divine nature. Hence, as Thomas Aquinas later put
it, "We have no means for considering how God is, but rather how He
is not."[6] Traditionally, however, this realization has not foreclosed on
theological reflection but, rather, encouraged thinkers to explore the
implications of God's indefinable nature—an exploration that has
centered on several *negative* attributes, including God's eternity,
immutability, infinity, and simplicity.[7]

---

3. See, e.g., *SKS* 25, NB29:24 / *JP* 3, 2902.
4. *SKS* 21, NB9:59 / *JP* 2, 1383.
5. Jacques Dupuis, ed., *The Christian Faith in the Doctrinal Documents of the
Catholic Church* (New York: Alba House, 2001), 153.
6. St. Thomas Aquinas, *Summa Theologica*, vol. 1 (Notre Dame: Ave Maria
Press, 1948), 14. Alternatively, this quotation might be cited as follows: *ST* I, pr.
Q. 3.
7. Aquinas, *Summa Theologica*, 1:11–143 or *ST* I, Q. 2–Q. 26.

In works such as Thomas's *Summa Theologica*, these characteristics stand primarily as objects for philosophical consideration. But Kierkegaard tends to take a different approach. That is to say, he *presupposes* the classical tradition's insistence on the negative attributes of God—indeed, one will search Kierkegaard's authorship in vain for systematic demonstrations of why God should be viewed as impassible rather than passible, immutable rather than mutable—and instead concentrates on what these attributes mean for human existence and for its relation to the infinite and qualitative otherness of God. As he explains in another 1849 journal passage,

> First the infinite conception of God's infinite sublimity, and then, then the next, the childlike openness to become involved with him earnestly and in truth. But Christendom has made God so sublime that in the long run we really have spirited him away or smuggled him out of life....
>
> In the conversation of the apostles one continually gets the impression that they had been personally in the company of Christ, had lived with him as with a human being. Therefore their speech is very human, although they never do forget the infinite qualitative difference.[8]

For Kierkegaard, in other words, it is not enough simply to acknowledge the infinite qualitative difference; one must relate oneself to it and find *upbuilding* in it.

Each of the writings in this section works toward that end. The first is taken from one of Kierkegaard's earliest and most famous books—*Either/Or*. Published in 1843, it might be considered a philosophical novel, in which Kierkegaard, writing under a variety of pseudonyms, juxtaposes an aesthetic worldview on the one hand and an ethical one on the other. And yet, as this sprawling opus comes to a close, Kierkegaard appends a final pseudonymous text—this one supposedly penned by a pastor from Denmark's rural Jutland peninsula. The overarching title of the pastor's section is simply "Ultimatum," and it does indeed have the character of a "final proposition." For in

---

8. *SKS* 21, NB9:64 / *JP* 2, 1385.

a way that refines (if not contradicts) the preceding reflections on the ethical, the pastor's "sermon" (*Prædiken*), prosaically named "The Upbuilding That Lies in the Thought That Compared to God We Are Always in the Wrong," highlights both the moral humility and the gracious comfort that comes from contemplating the absolute difference between God and human beings.

The second piece in this section was first published in *Two Upbuilding Discourses*—a slight and then overlooked volume that appeared in May 1843, just a few months after the popular *Either/Or*. Moreover, also unlike *Either/Or*, *Two Upbuilding Discourses* was issued under Kierkegaard's own name, thereby beginning a trend that would come to mark the Dane's authorship, namely, the near simultaneous publication of both pseudonymous and "signed" works. Kierkegaard himself later described this approach as a "duplexity" in which his own writings "offered with the right hand" what the pseudonymous ones "held out with the left hand."[9] This difference is often taken to refer to the mode of transmission, since the pseudonyms represent maieutic, or indirect, communication, whereas the signed works epitomize direct communication. Of course, such distinctions are rarely so neat, and, indeed, there is a great deal of similarity between the Jutland pastor's "sermon" and the discourse included here. Entitled "Every Good and Every Perfect Gift Is from Above," words taken from one of Kierkegaard's most cherished biblical pericopes (Jas 1:17–22) and on which he would continue to base further writings, this discourse is not only a meditation on God as the eternal and immutable giver of gifts, but also a dialectical rumination on the various ways persons struggle to accept and to profit from these gifts.

Part 1's third and final selection came out in September 1855, just a short time before Kierkegaard's death in November of the same year. Kierkegaard had been working on this discourse since 1851, however, and he bases it on the familiar passage of James 1:17–21. Thus this exposition, aptly named "The Unchangeableness of God," might be seen as the consummation of Kierkegaard's authorship, since it recapitulates, right at the very end, Kierkegaard's longstand-

---

9. *SKS* 11, 9 / *WA*, 3.

ing interest in the "infinite qualitative distinction." Indeed, Kierkegaard is at pains here to remind the reader that, even though the notion of divine immutability heightens the difference between God and creation, this difference is not alienating but is the very source of human hope. For, as unchangeable love, God is eternally available to persons in need.

Chapter One

THE UPBUILDING THAT LIES IN THE THOUGHT THAT COMPARED TO GOD WE ARE ALWAYS IN THE WRONG[1]

PRAYER

Father in heaven! Teach us to pray rightly so that our hearts may open themselves to you in prayer and supplication and to keep no secret desire that we know is not pleasing to you, nor any private fear that you will deny us something that is truly for our own good, in order that the toiling thoughts, the restless mind, the apprehensive heart may find rest in and through that alone in which and through which it is to be found—by always gladly thanking you, since we gladly admit that compared to you we are always in the wrong. Amen.

In the nineteenth chapter of The Gospel of St. Luke, from the forty-first verse to the end, the Holy Gospel is written as follows:

> And when he had come near, he beheld the city, and wept over it, saying, If you had known, even you, at least in this your day, the things which belong unto your peace! but now they are hid from your eyes. For the days shall come

---

1. From Niels Jørgen Cappelørn et al., eds., *Søren Kierkegaards Skrifter*, vol. 3 (Copenhagen: Gads Forlag, 1997), 320–32.

upon you, that your enemies shall cast a trench about you, and compass you round, and keep you in on every side, and shall lay you even with the ground, and your children within you; and they shall not leave in you one stone upon another; because you knew not the time of your visitation. And he went into the temple, and began to cast out them that sold therein, and them that bought; saying unto them, It is written, My house is the house of prayer: but you have made it a den of thieves. And he taught daily in the temple. But the chief priests and the scribes and the chief of the people sought to destroy him, and could not find what they might do: for all the people were very attentive to hear him.

What the Spirit had revealed to the prophets in visions and dreams, what these had proclaimed in a portentous voice to one generation after another—the chosen people's repudiation, proud Jerusalem's terrible destruction—was drawing ever closer. Christ goes up to Jerusalem. He is no prophet who proclaims the future. His speech does not cause anxious unrest, because he sees before his eyes what is still hidden there. He does not prophesy. There is no more time for that—he weeps over Jerusalem. And yet the city still stood in its glory, and the temple still towered as always, higher than any other building in the world, and Christ himself says: "If you knew today what was best for you." But he also adds: "Yet, it is hidden before your eyes." In God's eternal counsel, its downfall is decided, and salvation is hidden before the eyes of its inhabitants.

Was, then, the generation that lived at that time more reprehensible than the one before it, to which it owed its life? Was the entire people vicious? Was there no righteous person in Jerusalem, no one who could stop the deity's wrath? Was there no devout person among all those before whose eyes salvation was hidden? And if there was such a person, was there no gateway opened for him in the time of fear and distress, when the enemies besieged it all around and applied force on every side? Did no angel come down and save him before all gateways were closed? Was no sign done for his sake?

Still, its downfall was fixed. In its fear, the besieged city vainly searched for a way out. The enemy's army squeezed it in its mighty embrace, and no one slipped away, and heaven was locked, and no angel was sent out but the angel of death, who swung its sword over the city. What the people had committed this generation had to pay for. What this generation had committed each individual member of generation had to pay for.

Shall, then, the righteous suffer with the unrighteous? Is this God's zeal—that he inflicts the father's guilt on the children to the third and fourth generation, that he does not punish the fathers but the children? What should we answer? Should we say that now almost two millennia have passed since those days, a horror such that the world never before and will probably never again have to see? We thank God that we live in peace and safety, that the scream of angst from those days only sounds faint to us. We will hope and believe that our days and our children's days may go forward calmly, unaffected by the storms of existence! We do not feel capable to think about such things, but we will thank God that we are not tested in them.

Can anything more cowardly and more comfortless be imagined than this sort of talk? Has the unexplainable been explained when one has said: "It has only happened once in the world"? Or is this not the unexplainable—that it has happened? Or does not this—that it has happened—have the power to make everything else unexplainable, even the explainable? If it happened once in the world that the human being's conditions were essentially different from what they otherwise always are, then what certainty is there that it cannot happen again? What certainty is there that this was not true and that which ordinarily happens false? Or is it a demonstration of the truth when something happens more frequently? And does what those times witnessed not actually recur more often? Is it not what we all in so many ways have experienced, that what happens in great things is experienced in lesser things as well? "Do you suppose," Christ says, "that those Galileans whose blood Pilate had mingled with their sacrifices were sinners above all the Galileans, because they suffered such things? Or those eighteen, upon whom the tower in Siloam fell, and killed them, do you think that they were sinners above all men that dwelled in Jerusalem?" Accordingly, some of these Galileans were not worse sinners than other people. Those eighteen were not guiltier than other people living in Jerusalem—and yet the innocent shared the fate of the guilty. It was an accident, perhaps you will say, not a punishment. But Jerusalem's downfall was a punishment, and it hit the guilty and the innocent equally hard. That is why you will not worry yourself with fretting about such things, for you can grasp that someone can have troubles and sufferings, that these fall both on good and evil just like the rain, but that it is supposed to be a punishment....And yet, Scripture presents it in this way.

Is, then, the fate of the righteous the same as the unrighteous? Does the fear of God have no promise for this life, such as it is? Is, then, every uplifting thought that at one time made you so rich in courage and confidence, is it a fancy, an illusion, which the child believes in, the youth hopes for, but in which someone a bit older finds no blessing, but only mockery and scandal? But this thought outrages you. It cannot and shall not get power to captivate you; it must not be able to make your soul listless. You will love righteousness. You will practice righteousness early and late. Even if it has no reward, you will practice it nonetheless. You feel that a demand lies in it, which still must be fulfilled some day. You will not sink into lethargy, and then at some point realize that righteousness did have promises, but that you had locked yourself away from them by not performing righteousness. You will not struggle with human beings; you will struggle with God and hold fast to him. He won't be able to break away from you without blessing you!

Yet, Scripture says: "You shall not contend with God." Are you not doing that? Indeed, is this not hopeless talk once again? Is, then, holy Scripture only given to people in order to humiliate and to devastate them? By no means! When it is said that you shall not contend with God, then it means that you must not want to be in the right against God. You are to contend with him only like this: you learn that you are in the wrong. Yes, that is what you yourself ought to want. When you are forbidden to contend with God, your perfection is thereby signified, and in no way is it said that you are a trifling being who has no significance for him. The sparrow falls to the ground; in a sense it has a right relation to God. The lily fades; it has a right relation to God. Only human beings fall into what is unrighteous; to them alone is reserved what was denied to everything else—to be in the wrong compared to God.

If I were to put it differently, I would remind you about a wisdom that you certainly have heard often—a wisdom that knows easily enough how to explain everything without doing an injustice either to God or to human beings. It says that a human being is a fragile creature; it would be unreasonable of God to ask for the impossible from him. One does what one can, and if at some time one is rather negligent, God will never forget that we are weak and imperfect beings. Shall I mostly admire the exalted conceptions of the deity's nature that this shrewdness peddles, or that deep insight into the human heart, that searching consciousness which scours one's heart and then comes to the comfortable and convenient realization: "One does what one can"? Was it such an easy matter for you, my listener, to determine how much it is you can do? Were you never in a dangerous situation, where, almost in despair, you exerted your powers and yet certainly wished to do more, and perhaps another person looked at you with a doubtful and pleading glance, whether or not it was possible that you could do more? Or were you never anxious about yourself, so anxious that, to you, there was no sin so dark, no self-centeredness so hateful, that it could not creep into you and like an alien power gain control over you? Did you not feel this anxiety? If you did not feel it, then do not open your mouth to answer, for you cannot speak to what is being asked. But if you did feel it, my listener, then I ask you: did you find rest in those words: "One does what one can"?

Or were you never anxious about others? Did you not see them faltering in life, those you used to look up to with confidence and trust? And did you not hear a soft voice whispering to you: "When even these people cannot attain great things, what is life but evil pain and what is faith but a trap, which pulls us out into the infinite, where we really cannot live—far better, then, to forget, to give up every demand." Did you not hear this voice? If you did not hear it, do not open your mouth to answer. You cannot speak to what is being asked about. But if you did hear it, my listener, I ask you: did you find comfort in the saying, "One does what one can"? Was this not precisely the basis of your unrest—that you yourself did not know how much one can do, that at one time it seemed so infinitely great, in the next moment so very little? For that reason, was not your angst so painful, because you could not pierce through your consciousness, because the more sincerely you would, the more deeply you wished to act, the more terrible was the dichotomy you found yourself in: that you might not have done what you could, or that you actually might have done what you could but no one came to help you?

Hence, every more sincere doubt, every deeper worry is not calmed by the maxim "One does what one can." If a person is in the right at times, in the wrong at times, in the right to a certain degree, in the wrong to a certain degree, who is the one who determines that but the person himself? And yet, can he not once more be in the right to a certain degree and in the wrong to a certain degree in this determination? Or is he another person when he assesses his action rather than when he acts? Shall, then, doubt rule, constantly to discover new difficulties, and shall worry go alongside of and impress past experiences on the troubled soul? Or ought we to prefer constantly to be in the right in the sense that creatures without reason are? Thus we have only the choice between being nothing before God or to begin again each moment in eternal agony, yet without being able to begin. For if we are to be able to determine with certainty whether we are in the right in the present moment, then this question must be determined with certainty about the previous moment, and so on further and further back.

Once more, doubt is set in motion, once more worry is awakened. So let us strive to soothe it by contemplating:

The *upbuilding* that lies in the thought that compared to God we are *always* in the wrong.

To be in the wrong—can a feeling more painful than this be conceived? And do we not see that people would rather suffer everything than confess that they are in the wrong? We certainly do not approve of such obstinacy, neither in ourselves nor in others; we think that to confess that we are in the wrong is the wiser and better course of action when we actually are that; we then say that the pain that follows from confession would be like a bitter medicine, which would restore to health. But we do not conceal that it is painful to be in the wrong, painful to confess we are in the wrong. We suffer the pain because we know that it is to our good; we trust that one day we will succeed in making a more powerful resistance, that we perhaps will progress to the point of being in the wrong only very seldom. This reflection is so natural, so obvious to everyone. There lies, then, something upbuilding in being in the wrong, provided that, as we confess being in the wrong, we build ourselves up by the possibility that it will be the case more and more infrequently. And yet, it was not by this consideration that we would calm doubt; it was by contemplating what is upbuilding in the fact that we are always in the wrong. If, then, this first reflection—which gave the hope that, with time, one no longer would be in the wrong—was upbuilding, how can the opposite point of view also be upbuilding, the one that would teach us that we are always in the wrong, including both the past and the future.

Your life brings you into various relations with other people. Some of them love justice and righteousness; others seem not to want to practice them; they do wrong to you. Your soul is not hardened to the suffering they cause you, but you search and examine your heart. You make certain that you are in the right, and you rest quietly and strongly in this conviction. "No matter how much they hurt me," you say, "they will not be able to take away from me this peace—that I know I'm in the right and that I suffer wrong." There is a satisfaction, a joy in this thought, which probably everyone of us has tasted. And when you continue to suffer injustice, you are upbuilt by the thought that you are in the right. This way of thinking is so natural, so understandable, so often proven in life. Nevertheless, we do not want to calm doubt and heal worry with it, but by contemplating the upbuilding that lies in the thought that we are always in the wrong. Can, then, the opposite thought have the same effect?

Your life brings you into a variety of relations to other people. To some you are drawn with a deeper love than to others. Now, if such a person who was the object of your love were to do wrong to you, it would pain you. You would carefully examine everything, but then you would say: "I know myself that I am in the right; is this thought supposed to calm me?" Oh, if you loved him, it would not calm you. You would inquire into everything. You would not be able to see anything but that he was in the wrong, and yet this certainty would disturb you. You would wish that you might be in the wrong; you would try to find something that would speak in his defense, and, if you could not find it, you would only find rest in the thought that you were in the wrong. Or if you were directed to bear responsibility for such a person's welfare, you would do everything in your power, and when the other person nevertheless paid no attention to it and only caused you worry, is it not true that you would try to account for it? Would you say: "I know I am in the right toward him"?—Oh, no! If you loved him, this thought would only make you anxious. You would grab after every probability, and, if you found none, you would tear up the account in order to forget it, and you would strive to build yourself up by the thought that you were in the wrong.

So, then, it is painful to be in the wrong, and even more painful the more often one is in the wrong; it is upbuilding to be in the wrong, and even more upbuilding the more often one is in the wrong! Indeed, it is a contradiction. In what manner can this be explained but this—that you in the one case are obliged to acknowledge what you in the second case wish to acknowledge? Yet, is not the acknowledgment the same? Does the fact that one wishes or does not wish have any influence on it? In what manner can this be explained but this—that you in the one case loved, but not in the second case? In other words, that you in the one case were in an infinite relationship with a person, in the second case in a finite relationship? Thus to wish to be in the wrong is an expression for an infinite relationship, but to want to be in the right or to find it painful to be in the wrong is an expression for a finite relationship! For that reason, it is upbuilding always to be in the wrong, for only the infinite upbuilds. The finite does not!

Now, if it were a person you loved, even if your love piously managed to deceive your thinking and yourself, you were nevertheless in a constant contradiction, because you knew you were in the right but wished and wished to believe you were in the wrong. On the other hand, if it were God you loved, is talk about such a contradiction possible? Could you be aware of anything other than what you wished to believe? Should he, who is in heaven, not be greater than you, who lives on the earth? Should his riches not be more surpassing than your measure, his wisdom not deeper than your ingenuity, his holiness greater than your righteousness? You must acknowledge this as a matter of course, no? But if you must acknowledge it, then there is no contradiction between your knowledge and your wish. And yet, if you must acknowledge it as a matter of course, then there is indeed nothing upbuilding in the thought that you are always in the wrong. After all, it was said that the reason why it is painful to be in the wrong on one occasion and upbuilding to be in the wrong on another was because, in the first case, one is compelled to acknowledge what one wished to acknowledge in the second case. So, then, in your relation to God you were freed from contradiction, but you had lost the upbuilding. Still, that was precisely what we wanted to think over: the upbuilding in the fact that we are always in the wrong in relation to God.

Might it actually be like this? Why did you wish to be in the wrong in relation to a person? Because you loved. Why did you find it upbuilding? Because you loved. The more you loved, the less time you spent thinking about whether or not you were in the right. Your love had only one wish—that you must constantly be in the wrong. Likewise in your relation to God. You loved God, and therefore your soul could only find rest and joy in the fact that you always must be in the wrong. You did not come to this recognition from the difficulty of thought. You were not compelled, for when you are in love you are in freedom. When the thought assured you that this is right, that it could not be otherwise than you always must be in the wrong or God always must be in the right, then this followed behind. And you did not become certain that you are in the wrong from the acknowledgment that God is in the right; rather, you came to the recognition that God is always in the right from love's only and highest wish—that you always must be in the wrong. But this is love's wish and therefore freedom's concern, and by no means are you compelled to acknowledge that you are always in the wrong. You did not become certain that you were always in the wrong by deliberation, but the certainty lay in the fact that you were upbuilt by it.

It is, then, an upbuilding thought that compared to God we are always in the wrong. If that were not the case, if this certainty did not have its source from the whole of your being—that is, from the love within you—then your reflection would have taken a different form. You would have acknowledged that God is always in the right; you would have been compelled to acknowledge this as a consequence of being compelled to acknowledge that you were always in the wrong. The latter was already difficult, because it is true that you can be compelled to acknowledge that God is always in the right. But to make the application to yourself, to take up this acknowledgment in your whole being—you cannot be compelled to do that. You acknowledged, then, that God is always in the right and that you, in turn, are always in the wrong. However, this acknowledgment did not upbuild you. There is nothing upbuilding in acknowledging that God is always in the right, and thus there is nothing upbuilding in any thought that follows from it as a matter of course. When you acknowledge that God is always in the right, you stand aloof from God, and the same holds true when you consequently acknowledge that you are always in the wrong. On the other hand, when you—not by virtue of any prior acknowledgment—demand and are made certain that you are always in the wrong, then you are hidden in God. This is your worship, your devotion, your fear of God.

You loved a person; you wished always to be in the wrong compared to him—ah, but he grew faithless to you, and no matter how reluctant you were, no matter how much it hurt you, you still were in the right toward him and wrong in that you loved him so greatly. And yet your soul demanded to love in that way. Only in that could you find rest and peace and blessing. Then your soul turned away from the finite to the infinite; it found its object, which made your soul happy. "I will love God," you said, "he gives everything to the person who loves. He fulfills my highest, my sole wish—that I must always be in the wrong compared to him. No worrisome doubt will ever tear me away from him. Never shall the thought terrify me that I could prove right compared to him. For compared to God I am always in the wrong."

Or is it not so? Was this not your sole wish, your highest, and did not a terrifying anguish grip you when, in an instant, the thought would emerge in your soul—that you could be in the right; that your plans, rather than God's Providence, were wisdom; that your games, rather than God's thoughts, were righteousness; that your feelings, rather than God's heart, were love? And was it not your salvation that you could never love as you were loved? So, then, this—that compared to God you are always in the wrong—is not a truth you must acknowledge, not a comfort that relieves your pain, not a payment for something better, but it is a joy in which you triumph over yourself and the world, your delight, your hymn of thanksgiving, your adoration, a demonstration that your love is happy, as only the love with which one loves God is.

In this way, the thought that compared to God we are always in the wrong is upbuilding. It is upbuilding that we are in the wrong, upbuilding that we are always so. It shows its upbuilding power in dual fashion, in part by stopping doubt and by calming the worries of doubt, in part by encouraging action.

My listener, do you still remember a wisdom that was denoted earlier? It looked so faithful and reliable. It explained everything so easily. It was willing to rescue every person all through life, unaffected by the storms of doubt. "One does what one can," it shouted to the perplexed. And, to be sure, it is undeniable that, when one does just that, one is helped. It had nothing else to say; it disappeared like a dream, or it became a monotonous repetition in the ear of the person doubting. When, then, he would use it, it turned out that he could not use it; it turned out that it caught him in a snare of difficulties. He could not find the time to think about what he could do, because, at the same time, he had to do what he could do. Or if he got time to think it over, then the examination gave him a more or a less, an approximation, but never something comprehensive. Likewise, how should a person be able to measure his relation to God by a more or a less, or by a determination of an approximation? He learned that this wisdom was a treasonous friend, who, under the appearance of helping him, entangled him in doubt, worried him into a continuous cycle of confusion. What before had been obscure but not worrying to him did not become clearer now, though his mind was anxious with doubt and worried. Only in an infinite relation to God could doubt be calmed; only in an infinitely free relation to God could his worry be turned to joy. He is in an infinite relation to God when he acknowledges that God is always in the right; he is in an infinite relation to God when he acknowledges that he is always in the wrong.

In this way, then, doubt is brought to a standstill. For the movement of doubt lay precisely in this—that in the one moment he was to be in the right, in the next moment in the wrong, to a certain degree to be in the right, to a certain degree in the wrong, and this was to mark his relation to God. But such a relation to God is no relation, and this was the fuel of doubt. In his relation to another person, it was certainly possible that he could be partly in the wrong, partly in the right, to a certain degree in the wrong, to a certain degree in the right. For he himself as well as every human being is a finite entity, and their relation is a finite relation, which consists in a more or a less. So long as doubt, then, would render the finite relation infinite, and so long as wisdom would fill up the infinite relation with finitude, just so long would he remain in doubt. Every time, then, doubt wants to worry him with the particular, wants to teach him that he suffers too much or is tested beyond his powers, he loses the finite in the infinite—that he is always in the wrong. Every time the disquiet of doubt wants to make him sad, he lifts himself up over the finite into the infinite. For this—that he is always in the wrong—is the wing on which he rises over finitude. It is the longing with which he seeks God. It is the love in which he finds God.

Compared to God we are always in the wrong. But is this thought not anesthetizing? However upbuilding it may be, is it not dangerous for a human being? Does it not lull him into a sleep in which he dreams about a relation to God that is no actual relation? Does it not consume the will's power and resolution's strength? By no means! Was, then, the person who, in relation to another person, wished always to be in the wrong—was he listless and stagnant? Did he not do everything in his power to be in the right and yet wished only to be in the wrong? And then should not the thought that compared to God we are always in the wrong be inspiring, for what does it express but that God's love is always greater than our love? Does not this thought make him glad to act, because when he doubts he has no energy to act? Does it not ignite the spirit, for when he calculates in finite terms the spirit's fire is put out? If, then, your only wish was denied to you, my listener, you are still happy. You do not say: "God is always in the right," because there is no joy in that. You say: "Compared to God I am always in the wrong." If you yourself were the one who had to deny yourself your highest wish, you are still happy. You do not say: "God is always in the right," because there is no cheer in that. You say: "Compared to God I am always in the wrong." If your wish was what, in a certain sense, other people and yourself must call your duty, if you not only have to deny your wish but betray your duty in some way, if you not only lost your joy but even your honor, you are glad nevertheless. "Compared to God," you say, "I am always in the wrong." If you knocked but it was not opened, if you searched but did not find, if you worked but got nothing, if you planted and watered but saw no blessing, if heaven was closed and the witness failed to come, you are still glad in your work. If the punishment that the father's guilt had called down came over you, you are still glad. For compared to God we are always in the wrong.

Compared to God we are always in the wrong—this thought, then, brings doubt to a standstill and calms its worries. It enlivens and fills one with enthusiasm for action.

Your thought has now followed the course of the exposition, perhaps quickly hurrying ahead when it led you on well-known paths, perhaps slowly, reluctantly when the way was strange to you. Still, though, you must confess that the situation is as it was worked out, and your thinking had nothing to say against it. Before we part, my listener, one more question: would you wish, could you wish, that it might be different? Could you wish that you are supposed to be in the right? Could you wish that this beautiful law, which, for thousands of years, has borne the generation through life and each member of the generation—this beautiful law, more glorious than that which bears the stars on their course over the vault of heaven—could you wish that this law be shattered, something more terrible than if the law of nature lost its power and everything was broken up into frightful chaos? Could you wish that? I have no words of anger to terrify you with. Your wish must not emerge from anxiety over the presumption in the thought of wanting to be in the right compared to God. I ask you only: would you wish that it be otherwise?

Perhaps my tone does not have enough power and fervor; my voice cannot penetrate into your innermost thinking. O, but ask yourself—ask yourself with the solemn uncertainty with which you would turn to a person who you knew was able to determine your life's happiness with a single word—ask yourself even more earnestly than that. For, in truth, it is a matter of salvation. Do not stop the flight of your soul. Do not distress the best in you. Do not dull your spirit with half wishes and half thoughts. Ask yourself, and keep on asking, until you find the answer. For one may have known a thing many times, acknowledged it. One may have willed a thing many times, attempted it. And yet, only the deep inner movement, only the heart's indescribable emotion—only that convinces you that what you have recognized belongs to you, that no power can take it from you. For only the truth that upbuilds is truth for you.

Chapter Two

EVERY GOOD AND EVERY PERFECT GIFT IS FROM ABOVE[1]

PRAYER

From your hand, O God, we desire to receive everything! You stretch it out, your mighty hand, and catch the wise in their foolishness. You open it, your gentle hand, and fill everything that lives with blessing. And even if it seems that your arm has become shorter, increase our faith and our trust, so that we still hold fast to you. And if at times it seems that you draw your hand away from us, oh, we know well that it is only because you close it—that you only close it in order to open it again and fill everything that lives with blessing. Amen.

It is written in the Epistle of St. James the Apostle, chapter 1, verses 17–22:

> Every good gift and every perfect gift is from above, and comes down from the Father of lights, with whom is no variableness, neither shadow of turning. Of his own will, he gave birth to us with the word of truth, that we should be a kind of firstfruits of his creatures. Wherefore, my beloved brethren, let every person be swift to hear, slow to speak, slow to wrath: for the wrath of man does not work the righteousness of God. Wherefore lay apart all

---

1. From Niels Jørgen Cappelørn et al., eds., *Søren Kierkegaards Skrifter*, vol. 5 (Copenhagen: Gads Forlag, 2009), 41–56.

filthiness and superfluity of naughtiness, and receive with meekness the engrafted word, which is able to save your souls.

"Every good gift and every perfect gift is from above, and comes down from the Father of lights, with whom is no variableness, neither shadow of turning." These words are so beautiful, so inviting, so moving, that it assuredly would not be the fault of the words if they did not find a way into the listener's ears, if they did not find any resonance in his heart. They are by one of the Lord's apostles, and insofar as we ourselves have not deeply perceived their meaning, we still dare to trust that they are not casual and idle chatter, not a meticulous expression of a flimsy thought, but that they are faithful and unfailing, tried and tested as the life of the apostle who wrote them. They are not said occasionally, but with special emphasis, not in passing, but accompanied by an urgent admonition: "Do not err, my beloved brethren" (v. 16). We dare to trust, then, that they not only have power to lift up the soul but also strength to carry it—these words that bore an apostle through a turbulent life. They are not said without connection to other words. That the apostle says, "Do not err, my beloved brethren," is to warn against the terrible delusion that God would tempt a person, to warn against the allurement of the heart that would tempt God. Thus we dare to be convinced that the words are also powerful to unmask allurement, powerful to stop the errant thought.

"Every good gift and every perfect gift is from above, and comes down from the Father of lights, with whom is no variableness, neither shadow of turning." Again and again these words have been repeated in the world, and yet many live as if they had never heard them, and it would perhaps have had a disturbing effect on them if they had done so. Carefree, they go on their way. A friendly lot in life makes everything so easy for them, every wish fulfilled, every task making progress. Without knowing how, they are in the midst of the movement of life, a link in the chain that binds a past to a future. Unconcerned about how it happens, they are borne on the wave of the present. Resting in the law of nature that lets a human life develop in the world, as if it spreads a carpet of flowers over the earth, they go on

living, cheerful and contented in life's variation. At no moment do they wish to break away from this, to honestly give each his due: thankfulness to the one to whom they attribute good gifts, helpfulness to the one they think has need of it and in the way they think it useful to him. They certainly know that there are good and perfect gifts. They also know where they come from, because the earth gives its growth and the sky gives rain early and late, and family and friends intend the best for them, and their wise and sensible plans make progress, which is natural, since they are wise and sensible. For them, life has no mystery, and yet their life is a mystery, a dream, and the apostle's earnest admonition, "Do not err," does not bring them to a standstill. They have no time to pay attention to it or to the words, and what does the wave care about whence it comes or whither it goes? Or if certain ones among them, in consideration of something higher, paid attention to the apostle's words, they would soon be done with them. They would let their thought be occupied with them for a moment, and then they would say, "Now we have understood them; do bring us new thoughts that we have not understood." Nor would they be wrong, for the apostle's words are not difficult. And yet, they showed that, after having understood them, they wished to abandon them; in this way, they had not understood them.

"Every good gift and every perfect gift is from above, and comes down from the Father of lights, with whom is no variableness, neither shadow of turning." These words are very soothing and alleviating, and yet how many were they who rightly knew how to soak up the rich nourishment of comfort from them, rightly knew how to appropriate it! The worried ones, those whom life did not allow to grow old and who die as children, whom it did not suckle with the milk of success but weaned early; the mourning ones, whose thought sought to pierce through the changing to the lasting—they felt the apostle's words and respected them. The more they were able to sink their souls into them, to forget everything on account of them, the more they felt themselves strengthened and full of confidence. Yet it soon turned out that this strength was a disappointment. However much confidence they gained, they still did not gain power to pierce through life. Sometimes the worried mind and the confused thought

turned to that rich comfort; sometimes they sensed the contradiction again. At last, perhaps, it seemed to them that these words were almost dangerous to their peace. They awakened a confidence in them that was continually disappointed; they gave them wings that surely could lift them up to God but did not help them in their walk through life. They did not deny the inexhaustible comfort in the words, but they almost feared it even though they praised it. If a person owned a glorious piece of jewelry, and there was never a time when he would deny that it was glorious, then certainly he would get it out now and then, enjoy it, but soon he would say, "I cannot adorn myself with this for everyday use, and I wait in vain for the festive occasion that would properly suit it." Undoubtedly, then, he would set the piece of jewelry aside and, with sadness, contemplate that he owned such a piece of jewelry and that life did not grant him with the occasion to take it out with rightful joy.

So they sat there in quiet sorrow. They did not harden themselves against the comfort in those words. They were humble enough to admit that life is a dark saying, and just as they, in their thoughts, were swift to hear if an explanatory word might ring out, so were they also slow to speak, slow to anger. They did not have the audacity to cast away the words, if only the opportune hour would come. If this came, then they would be saved. That was their opinion, and you, my listener, said it was bound to happen. Or is there only one spirit who witnesses in heaven, yet no spirit who witnesses on earth! Do only heaven and the spirit that flies away from the earth know that God is good! Does life on earth know nothing of it! Is there no harmony between what happens in heaven and what happens on earth! Is there joy in heaven, only sorrow on earth, or really only the news that there is joy in heaven! Does God in heaven produce the good gifts and save them for us in heaven, so that one day we can receive them in the next world! Perhaps this is the way you talked in your heart's curiosity. You did not demand that, for your sake, signs and wondrous works should take place. You did not childishly demand that every one of your wishes should be fulfilled. You only asked for a witness, whether early or late, because your worried soul hid a wish. If this were granted, then all would be well, then your thanks and your praise would be eternal, then the festive occasion would have come, then you would, with your whole heart, give testimony to the saying that all good and all perfect gifts come from above.

But see, that was denied you, and your soul became restless, tossed about by the passion of the wish. It did not become defiant and wild; you did not impatiently cast off humility's harness; you had not forgotten that you are on earth and God is in heaven. With humble prayers, with burning desire, you sought to tempt God, as it were: this wish is so important to me; my joy, my peace, my future—all hang on this. For me it is so very important; for God it is so easy, since he is, after all, almighty. But it was not granted. In vain you sought tranquility; you left no stone unturned in your fruitless restlessness. You ascended suspicion's staggering pinnacle in order to be on the look-out for an emerging possibility. If you believed you saw one, then right away you were ready with prayers, so that, with their help, you could fashion the actual from the apparent. But it was a mirage. You climbed down again; you gave yourself over to sorrow's numbing dullness—that the time is bound to pass, as surely as it came. And it became morning, and it became night, but the day you longed for did not come. And yet you certainly did everything. You prayed early and late, more and more deeply, more and more temptingly. Alas, and still it did not happen.

Then you gave up on it. You wanted to make your soul be patient; you wanted to wait in quiet longing, if only you could gain certainty that eternity would bring you your wish, bring you that which was your eyes' wish and your heart's demand. Alas, this certainty was denied you as well. But then when the busy thoughts had worked themselves weary, when the fruitless wishes had worn out your soul, then perhaps your being grew more quiet, then perhaps had your mind, secretly and unnoticeably, developed in itself the meekness that receives the word that was implanted within you and that was able to render your soul blessed, the word that all good and all perfect gifts come from above. Doubtless, then, you confessed in all humility that God assuredly did not deceive you when he received your worldly wishes and miserable covetousness, swapped them for you and instead gave you divine comfort and holy thoughts; that he did not treat you unfairly when he denied you a wish, but in compensation created this faith in your heart; when instead of a wish, which, even if it conquered everything, was at most able to give you the whole world, he blessed you with a faith by which you won God and overcame the whole world. Then you acknowledged with humble joy that God was still the almighty Creator of heaven and earth, who not only created the world from nothing but did something even more wonderful: he created the incorruptible nature of a quiet spirit from your impatient and inconstant heart. Ashamed, you then confessed that it was good, so very good for you that God does not let himself be tempted; then you understood the apostle's admonition and why it is connected with the delusion that would tempt God. Then you realized how wrong your behavior was. You wanted God's ideas about what was right for you to be your ideas, but, in addition, you wished that he would be the almighty Creator of heaven and earth so that he could properly fulfill your wish. And yet, if he were to share your ideas, he would cease to be the almighty Father. You wanted to distort, as it were, God's eternal nature in your childish impatience, and you were dazzled enough to enchant yourself, as if you would be helped if God in heaven did not know better than you what was helpful for you, as if some day you would not discover to your horror that you had wished what no human being would be able to bear if it happened.

Let us for a moment speak inadequately and in a human way. If there was a person in whom you had rightful confidence because you believed he wanted what was good for you, but you had one idea of what was beneficial for you and he another, is it not true that you would try to persuade him? You would perhaps entreat and implore him to fulfill your wish. But when he continued to refuse your wish, then you would cease to beg him. You would say: "If my petitions were to move him to do what he did not consider to be right, then something even more horrible would happen—that I would have been weak enough to make him just as weak. Then I would have only lost him and my trust in him, even if I would have called his weakness love in the moment of intoxication."

Or perhaps this was not the case with you; perhaps you grew too old to entertain childish ideas about God, too mature to possibly think about him. Maybe you would move him by your defiance. That life was a dark saying you readily admitted, but you were not, following the apostle's admonition, quick to hear if a clarifying word might ring out. Contrary to his admonition, you were swift to anger. Is life a dark saying? Then let it be. You should not care about the explanation—and your heart shall be hardened. Your appearance was perhaps calm, perhaps friendly, your conversation even kind. But deep down in the secret workshop of your thoughts you said—no, you did not say it, but there you heard a voice that said: "God does tempt a person." And the cold of despair made your spirit shiver, and its death brooded over your heart. When at times life stirred again in your inner being, savage voices raged there, voices that did not belong to you but nevertheless rang out from your inner being. For why was your complaint so unyielding? Why was your scream so penetrating? Why was even your prayer so aggressive? Or was it not because you believed that your sufferings were so great, your sorrows so devastating, and that consequently your complaint so just, your voice so mighty, that it had to ring throughout the heavens and summon God from his secretive depths, where, as it seemed to you, he sat, calm and indifferent without paying attention to the world and its destinies? But heaven shuts itself off from such presumptuous talk, and it is written that God is not tempted by anyone. Your speech was powerless, as powerless as your thought, as powerless as your arm, and heaven did not hear your prayer. But when you then humbled yourself under God's tremendous hand and, spiritually broken, sighed: "My God, my God, great is my sin, greater than can be forgiven"— then heaven opened again, then God, as a prophet writes, looked down from his window at you and said: "Yet a little while; yet a little while and I shall renew the face of the earth"—and see, your face was renewed, and God's merciful grace had nurtured in your barren mind the meekness that receives the words. Then you humbly confessed before God that God tempts no one, but that everyone is tempted when he is lured and drawn by his own greedy desires, just as you were tempted by proud and haughty and defiant thoughts. Then you were horrified that your confused notion—that God tempts a person—is supposed to make life clearer. For then life to you would become a dark saying, then you would indeed listen to this explanation, which, as you would have to admit, simply made everything unclear. Then you, humbled and shamed, confessed that it was good that God does not allow himself to be tempted, that he is the almighty God who can crush every presumptuous thought, that in your despair you had not found an explanation of life's dark saying, which no person is able to maintain.

"*Every good gift and every perfect gift is from above, and comes down from the Father of lights, with whom is no variableness, neither shadow of turning.*" These words are so comprehensible, so simple, and yet how many were they who rightly understood them, who rightly understood that they were a magnificent coin, which is more glorious than all the world's treasure, but also pocket change, which is usable in life's everyday circumstances.

"Every good and every perfect gift is from God." The apostle uses two phrases. "Every good gift," he says and, in turn, signifies the inner nature of the gift—that it is healthy and blessed fruit, which does not hide any unwholesome or harmful additive. "Every perfect gift," the apostle says and, in turn, signifies the closer relation into which the good gifts, with God's assistance, enter with the individual who receives them, so that in and of themselves goods do not become trouble and perdition to him. Two other phrases correspond to these. "The gift is from above and comes down from the Father of lights." "It is from above," the apostle says and thereby turns the believer's thoughts up toward heaven, where, indeed, every good thing—the blessing that satisfies the mouth and the one that satisfies the heart—has its home; up toward heaven, from where the good spirits proceed for the salvation of human beings; up toward heaven, from where good intentions return as heavenly gifts. "From the Father of lights," says the apostle and, in turn, means that God penetrates everything with his eternal clarity, that he understands people's thoughts from afar and knows their ways clearly that his eternal love hurries ahead and prepares everything and thus makes "the good gift" into a "perfect gift." For God in heaven is not like a person who, if he had a good gift to give, nevertheless gave it away in darkness and in uncertainty— glad, no doubt, because it was a good gift and he a glad giver, but also sad because he did not know whether or not it would really be of benefit to the other.

78

"Every good and every perfect gift," says the apostle. "*Every*"—
what does this mean? Does the apostle mean thereby that heaven's
extensive fortification is a great storeroom and, nevertheless, that
heaven only holds good gifts? Does he mean that God takes from this
rich supply and now and then dispatches, according to time and
occasion, sometimes to the one, sometimes to the other, to one more,
to the other less, to the odd one nothing at all, but what he sends is
good and perfect? Let us heed the ensuing words: "with whom is no
variableness, neither shadow of turning." If that is what the apostle
had wanted to convey, then, instead of these words, he probably
would have added: "from the God of love, the God of mercy and
comfort, the giver of good gifts" or however he would have expressed
it otherwise, better and more pithily than we are able to do it. He
almost certainly would have admonished the believers to gratitude
according to time and occasion, inasmuch as the good gifts were
allotted to them. He does not do this. What he warns against is the
delusion that God would tempt a person, the delusion that God
would let himself be tempted. What he emphasizes is that God is the
constant who remains the same, whereas everything else changes. He
admonishes us to love God in such a way that our nature might
become like his, that we might attain God in constancy and rescue
our soul in patience. He says nothing in these words about the nature
of the specific gifts, but he talks about God's eternal relation to the
believer. When joy enlightens life and everything is bright and clear,
he warns against this enlightenment and counsels us to attribute it to
the Father of lights, with whom is no variableness, neither shadow of
turning. When sorrow casts its shadow over our lives, when dejec-
tion makes our vision woozy, when the cloud of worry takes him
away from our eyes, then the apostle's admonition—that with God
there is no shadow of turning—rings out. What the apostle warns
against is disturbing God's blessed nature through the restlessness of
temptation, as if his heart had become either cold or weak. What he
impresses is that, as God's almighty hand made everything good, so
he, the Father of lights, ever constant, at every moment makes everything good, everything into a good and perfect gift for everyone who
has enough heart to be humble, enough heart to be trustful.

But doubt is cunning and scheming, not at all noisy and defiant, as it certainly is described at times. It is inconspicuous and subtle, not brazen and presumptuous, and the more inconspicuous it is, the more dangerous it is. It does not deny that these words are beautiful, that they are comforting; if it did this, the heart would rebel against it. It merely says that the words are difficult, almost inscrutable. It wants to help the worried mind to understand the apostolic saying that all good and all perfect gifts are from God. "What does this want to express? What else but that everything that comes from God is a good and a perfect gift, and that everything that is a good and a perfect gift is from God." This explanation is, indeed, simple and natural, and yet doubt has subtly concealed itself in it. Therefore it goes on: "In order that a person might be able to find peace in these words in his lifetime, he must be able to decide either what it is that comes from God or what can be justly and truly called a good and a perfect gift. But how is this possible? Is every human life, then, a continual chain of miracles? Or is it possible for a human being's understanding to forge its way through the unmanageable number of derived causes and effects, to penetrate any intervening thing, and in that way to find God? Or is it possible for a human being's understanding to decide with certainty what is a good and a perfect gift for him? Is it not wrecked on this again and again? How often has humankind, how often has every single person, lived through the painful experience that it is a folly—one that does not go unpunished—to want to dare what has been denied to humanity?" Then doubt was finished with its explanation of the words and, moreover, finished with the words. It had transformed the apostolic, authoritative saying into blustery talk that went from mouth to mouth without pith and meaning. It was modest enough not to demand that the words should be erased and handed over to eternal forgetfulness. It wrested them from the heart and left them to the lips.

Was it like this, my listener? Are these words perhaps not the work of an apostle of the Lord? Are they perhaps the work of that spiritual host below heaven? Was it a curse that rested upon them—that they were to be homeless in the world and find no place in a person's heart? Was it their destiny to perplex people? Is it not possible to stop that alarming movement in which thinking exhausts itself and yet never goes further? Was it perhaps nevertheless the case that God does tempt a person, even if in no other way than by proclaiming a word that only confuses his thinking?

The Apostle Paul says, "For every creature of God *is* good, and nothing to be refused, if it be received with thanksgiving." It is, if anything, to warn against an earthly shrewdness that would enslave believers in the service of ceremony that the apostle says these words. At the same time, what does the apostle do? He raises the believer's mind above earthly and finite worries, above worldly shrewdness and doubt, by means of a devout contemplation—that we always ought to thank God. For, after all, the thankfulness that the apostle talks about cannot be a thankfulness that is to be shown from one person to another, and those false teachers also thought that the faithful, by violating the ceremony, sinned against God. Should not the same apply to every person's relation to God—that every gift is a good and a perfect gift when it is received with thankfulness?

Is it not true, my listener, that you interpreted those apostolic words in this way and that you were not confused about what was a good and a perfect gift or about what came from God. For, you said, every gift is good when it is received with thankfulness from the hand of God, and from God comes every good and every perfect gift. You did not anxiously question what it is that comes from God; you happily and openly said: "This thing, for which I thank God." You did not trouble your mind with thinking over what was a good and a perfect gift, because you confidently said: "I know what it is that I thank God for, and therefore I thank him for it." You interpreted the apostolic words as your heart expanded. You did not demand to learn much from life. You only wanted to learn one thing—always to thank God and, in turn, to learn to simply understand that all things serve for good those who love God.

Are, then, the apostolic words that every good and every perfect gift is from above and comes down from the Father of lights—is it a dark and difficult saying? And if you think that you cannot understand it, do you then dare to maintain that you have wanted to understand it? When you doubted about what came from God or about what was a good and a perfect gift, did you risk the attempt? And when the easy play of joy beckoned you, did you thank God for it? And when you were so strong that it was as if you needed no help, did you then thank God? And when your appointed portion was little, did you thank God? And when your appointed portion was sufferings, did you thank God? And when your wish was denied, did you thank God? And when you yourself had to deny your wish, did you thank God? And when people did you wrong and hurt you, did you thank God? We are not saying that the wrong of such persons thereby stopped being wrong. What would be the purpose of such corrupt and wicked talk? Whether it was wrong you will determine yourself. But have you attributed the wrong and insult to God and by your thanksgiving received it from his hand as a good and a perfect gift? Have you done that? Well, then you have worthily interpreted the apostolic words to the honor of God and to your own salvation. For it is beautiful that a person prays, and many a promise is said to the one who prays without ceasing, but it is more blessed always to give thanks. Then you have worthily interpreted those apostolic words more gloriously than if all the angels spoke in flaming tongues.

But who had such courage, such faith? Who loved God in this way? Who was the joyous and steadfast warrior who stood such a long time at life's post that he never slumbered? And if you did that, my listener, have you not concealed it from yourself? Have you then said to yourself: "I well understand the apostolic words, but I also understand that I am too cowardly or too proud or too sluggish to want to understand them properly"? Have you admonished yourself? Have you taken into consideration that, even if this seems to be a hard saying, the timorous person also has a deceitful heart and is not an upright lover? Have you taken into consideration that there is a judgment also upon the despondent, but the humble heart does not come to judgment? Have you taken into consideration that the melancholy person, too, does not love God with his whole heart, but the person who is happy in God has overcome the world? Have you at least watched over yourself? Have you observed the apostolic words in sacred fashion? Have you treasured them in a pure and beautiful heart and for no price, for no shrewdness of cunning bribery, wanted to ransom yourself from the deep pain of having to confess again and again that you never loved as you were loved? That you were faithless when God was faithful; that you were lukewarm when he was aflame; that he sent good gifts, which you perverted to your own injury; that he asked about you but you would not answer; that he called to you but you would not listen; that he spoke to you as a friend but you ignored it; that he spoke to you earnestly but you misunderstood it; that he fulfilled your wish and, as thanks, you produced new wishes; that he fulfilled your wish but you had not wished for the right thing and were quick to anger? Have you really felt how sad it is that you, in order to describe your relation to God, need so many words? With this in mind, have you at least been honest with yourself and with your God in your relation to him? Have you not postponed the reckoning, not rather preferred to be ashamed of yourself in your solitude? Have you been ready to endure the reckoning's pain? Have you borne in mind that he loved you first? Have you yourself been quick to judge that he should not continue to love you, while you, in turn, were slow to love? If you have done this, then you will probably win the courage to give thanks from time to time, even when what happens is strange in your eyes—the courage to understand that every good and every perfect gift is from above, the courage to explain it in love, the faith to receive this courage. For it, too, is a good and a perfect gift.

"Every good gift and every perfect gift is from above, and comes down from the Father of lights, with whom is no variableness, neither shadow of turning." These words are so restorative, so healing, and yet how often did the penitent soul allow himself to be healed by them, how often did he understand their discriminating earnestness but also their merciful grace.

Or, my listener, was there perhaps in your own life no occasion to find these words difficult? Were you always contented with yourself, so contented that you perhaps thanked God that you were not like other persons? Did you, perhaps, become so wise that you grasped the profound meaning in the meaningless talk that it was wonderful not to be like other persons?…What was it, then, that made them difficult? If a person is himself a good and a perfect gift, if, indeed, he is only receiving and has received everything from God's hand! How could he, then, receive anything but good and perfect gifts?

Yet, when you stooped under the lot of the ordinary human being, then you confessed that you were neither good nor perfect—that you do not only relate to others as receiver but, in everything, what you received underwent a transformation. Can the like, then, be understood by anything other than the like? Can the good remain good in anything other than the good? Can healthy food preserve its nourishment in the sick soul? A person is not in purely receptive relationships. He himself is communicating, and it became difficult for you to understand how the unwholesomeness that came from you could be anything other than trouble for others. You well understood that it was only in giving thanks to God that everything became a good and a perfect gift for you. You maintained that other persons also must appropriate everything in the same way. But, then, was even the love that gave birth to gratitude—was even it pure? Did it not transform what was received?

Hence, can a person do more than love? Have thought and language any higher expression for loving than to give thanks always? Not at all. It has an inferior, a humbler expression, for even the one who always wants to give thanks nevertheless loves according to his own perfection, and a person can only love God in truth when he loves him according to his own imperfection. Which love is this? Repentance's love is more beautiful than any other love, since you love God in it! It is more faithful and more heartfelt than any other love, because in repentance it is God who loves you. In repentance you receive everything from God, even the thanksgiving that you bring him, so that even this is what the child's gift is in parents' eyes—a jest, a receiving of something one has given oneself. Was it not like this, my listener? You would always thank God, but even this was very imperfect. Then you understood that God is the one who does everything in you and who vouchsafes to you the childlike joy over the fact that he considers your thanksgiving as a gift from you. He bestows this joy upon you when you have not been afraid of the pain of repentance and the deep sorrow in which a person comes to rejoice in God like a child, when you have not been afraid to understand that this is love—not that we love God, but that God loves us.

And you, my listener, you who in a simpler and humbler way understood the profound meaning of the thought that you were not like other persons, was it so easy for you not to understand the apostolic words? You fully grasped that every good and every perfect gift comes from God. Alas! Could you not grasp that it could become anything other than a wound to you? Dew and rain are, indeed, a good gift from above, but if the poisonous herb understood itself and could talk, it would perhaps say: "Oh, stop! Go back to heaven again, so that I may perish of drought. Do not refresh my root, so that I do not thrive and increase and become even more dangerous!" And you neither understood yourself nor the apostolic words. For if it were so, then it would not be true that every perfect gift comes from God, then God would not be greater than a person's distressed heart. And how, then, could every good and perfect gift come from him?

Perhaps there was something in your life that you wished undone. If this were possible, then, you would take every perfect gift from God's hand with joyful thanksgiving. Just by thinking about it, your joy was so great that it was as if it would tempt God to undo what had been done. But God is tempted by no one. Perhaps you strove to forget it, so that your thanksgiving ought not to be weak and like a snuffed-out candle. Alas, and if you could forget it, then how would it be possible for you to understand the apostolic words? If it were possible for you to forget it, then not every good and perfect gift would come from God, after all. You would close yourself off from the blessing, not by what you had done, but by your poor and self-absorbed and capricious understanding of the words, just like the one whose wish was denied would close himself off from the blessing by wanting to think that the wish that was denied was also not a good and a perfect gift, even though it seemed much harder to you than to him to dare to understand it.

Perhaps you understood the apostolic words in a different way—that punishment from God is a good and a perfect gift too. Your inner wrath wanted to come to help the divine wrath, as it were, so that the punishment would consume you. And yet, the punishment that you suffered was different than you had imagined it. Perhaps it reached more persons than you, but, nevertheless, you were the guilty one. Perhaps its grip went beyond you, but, nevertheless, you were the only one who should have been its object. Even if you, in secret, admitted that divine providence knows how to hit a person, knows how to make itself understandable to him, even if no one else understood it, the apostolic words became obscure to you. It was as if the punishment itself became a new temptation. What was punishment and what was incident became ambiguous to you. If it were only incident, then your soul demanded punishment; if it were nothing but punishment, then you could not take it on. You would forsake everything, every wish, every desire. You would give up the notion that, in your soul's extreme exertion, you had done your best—the assurance that it was good, that it was other than folly and sin. You would suffer every punishment, but you could not bear the *more* that was linked to it. Was it also a good and a perfect gift? Then your soul was darkened. Could you not understand the words? But what did you do then? Did you cast the words aside? Oh no! You held them fast in all your distress. And when all the devils stood ready and willing to save your soul from the madness of despair, explaining that God is not love, is it not true that you then clung tightly to the words, even if you did not understand them? For you still faintly hoped in them, and to relinquish them was more horrible than anything else.

Did you do this, my listener? Then, even if the external person was harmed, the inner person was renewed nonetheless. Then you understood that every good and every perfect gift is from above when it is received with thanksgiving. You understood that repentance is a thanksgiving, not only for punishment, but also for what is given out, and that the penitent who only wants to suffer punishment will still not, in the deepest sense, love according to his imperfection. Just as the Lord himself says, "This very day," so does the Lord's apostle say: "This very day, every good and every perfect gift is from above and comes down from the Father of lights, with whom is no variableness, neither shadow of turning, this very day, and this in spite of the fact that he is the same today as he was yesterday."

"Every good gift and every perfect gift is from above, and comes down from the Father of lights, with whom is no variableness, neither shadow of turning." These words are so beautiful, so appealing, so moving; they are so consoling, so comforting, so simple and comprehensible, so healing and curing. Thus we pray to you, O God, that you would make the ears of those who have not venerated them up to now

willing to receive them; that, in accordance with the words' knowl-edge, you would heal the misunderstanding heart so that it under-stands the words; that you would bow the erring thought under the words' saving obedience; that you would give the penitent soul the boldness to dare to understand the words; and that you would make those who have understood them more and more blessed by them, so that they understand them again and again. Amen.

Chapter Three

THE UNCHANGEABLENESS OF GOD[1]

PRAYER

You unchangeable one, whom nothing changes! You who are unchangeable in love, who, just for our benefit, do not let yourself change—would that we also might will our own well-being. By your unchangeableness let us be brought up in unconditional obedience to find rest and to rest in your unchangeableness! You are not like a human being. If he were to preserve only some unchangeableness, he must not have too much that can move him and not let himself be moved too much. You, on the other hand, are moved by everything—and in infinite love. Even the sparrow's need, which we persons call unimportant and pass by unmoved, moves you. A human sigh, which we so often scarcely pay attention to, moves you, Infinite Love. But nothing changes you, you Unchangeable One! O you who in infinite love let yourself be moved, let this our prayer also move you, so that you may bless it. In this way, the prayer changes the one who prays in accordance with your unchanging will, you unchanging one!

James 1:17–21

> Every good gift and every perfect gift is from above, and comes down from the Father of lights, with whom is no variableness, neither shadow of turning. Of his own will, he gave birth to us with the word of truth, that we should

---

1. From Niels Jørgen Cappelørn et al., eds., *Søren Kierkegaards Skrifter*, vol. 13 (Copenhagen: Gads Forlag, 2009), 327–39.

be a kind of firstfruits of his creatures. Wherefore, my beloved brethren, let every person be swift to hear, slow to speak, slow to wrath: for the wrath of man does not work the righteousness of God. Wherefore lay apart all filthiness and superfluity of naughtiness, and receive with meekness the engrafted word, which is able to save your souls.

My listener, you have heard the text read. Now, how natural to think of the opposite: the temporal, the changeableness of earthly things, and the changeableness of human beings! How depressing, how tiring, that everything is corruptibility, that human beings are changeableness—you, my listener, and I! How sad that the change is so often for the worse! What poor human comfort, and yet a comfort that there is still one change among the changeable: it has an end!

However, if we want to talk like this, especially in this gloomy mood—therefore not like when there is earnest talk about corruptibility, about "human inconstancy"—then we not only would not stick to the text. No, we would forsake it—indeed, we would change it. For in the text the opposite is talked about: God's unchangeableness. The text is sheer delight and joy. As from the peak of the mountain, where silence dwells, so is the apostle's language lifted up over all the changeableness of earthly life. He talks about God's unchangeableness, not about something else. About a "Father of lights," who dwells up there, where no changeableness reaches, not even the shadow of it. About "good and perfect gifts," which come down from above, from this Father, who, as Father "of lights" or as the light's Father, infinitely knows how to make sure that what comes from him truly is considered good and perfect as well, and as "Father" wants nothing else, thinks of nothing other, than to send good and perfect gifts without change. And therefore, my beloved brethren, let each person be "swift to hear," that is, not to listen to loose and fast talk but in accordance with what is above, for nothing but good news is ever heard from *there*. "Slow to speak," for the chatter we persons take part in, especially in relation to the here and now, can only most often serve to make the good and perfect gifts less good and less perfect. "Slow to wrath," that we do not become angry when the gifts do not seem good and perfect to us and, by our own guilt, effect the corruption of the good and perfect things that were provided for our well-being—that is what a person's anger can do, and "the wrath of man does not work the righteousness of God." "Wherefore lay apart all filthiness and superfluity of naughtiness"—just as one cleans and decorates one's house and sits dressed up, festively awaiting the visit, so we are to receive the good and perfect gifts in this way. "And receive with meekness the engrafted word, which is able to save your souls." With meekness! In truth, if it were not the apostle who was speaking, and if we did not immediately comply with the command "to be slow to speak, slow to wrath," we might well say that it was an odd way of talking. Are we, then, so foolish that we need to be admonished to meekness in relation to the one who only wants our well-being?

Indeed, it is almost mocking us to use the word "meekness" in this way. See, if one wanted to hurt me unjustly, and another standing by said admonishingly, "Submit to it with meekness," this is straight talk. But think of the friendliest being, love itself, who has picked out a gift intended for me, and the gift is good and perfect, yes, like love itself. He comes and wants to bestow this gift upon me—then another is standing by, and he says to me admonishingly: now let me see you submit to it with meekness. And yet, this is how it is with human beings. A pagan, and a mere human being, that simple wise man from antiquity,[2] complains about having often experienced that, when he would deprive a person of one or another folly in order to impart better knowledge to him—therefore in order to do good for him—the other person could then become so angry that he would like to bite him, as the simple one jokingly says in earnest.

Alas, and what has God not had to experience in these 6,000 years, what does he not experience every day from morning till night with every last one of these millions of people. We sometimes become most angry when he wants to do the most good for us. Indeed, if we human beings truly knew our own good and, in the deepest sense,

---

2. Whenever Kierkegaard refers to "that simple wise man from antiquity" (*den eenfoldige Vise i Oldtiden*), he is referring to the classical Athenian philosopher, Socrates. (Tr.)

truly willed our own good, no admonition to meekness would be needed in this situation. But we human beings (who has not experienced this personally!) are still like children in relation to God. And therefore the admonition about meekness is needed in relation to receiving what is good and perfect—so convinced is the apostle that only good and perfect gifts come down from him, the eternally unchangeable one.

Such different points of view! The merely human one (what, indeed, paganism shows) talks less about God and has a prevailing tendency to only want to talk sadly about the changeableness of human things; the apostle simply and solely wants to talk about God's unchangeableness. This is the way it is with the apostle. For him, the thought of God's unchangeableness is simply and solely sheer consolation, peace, joy, blessedness. And, to be sure, this is also eternally true. But let us not forget: the fact that it is like this for the apostle lies in the fact that the apostle is the apostle—that he already long since abandoned himself to God's unchangeableness in unconditioned obedience, that he did not stand at the beginning but at the end of the way instead, the narrow but also the good way that he, forsaking everything, had chosen and, unchanged, followed without looking back, hastening toward eternity with stronger and stronger movement. In contrast, we who are still only beginners under instruction, with us God's unchangeableness must also have another side to be seen, and, if we forget this, we easily run the risk of taking the apostle's sublimity in vain.

Hence, if possible both in terror and in reassurance, we will talk *about you, you unchangeable one,* or *about your unchangeableness.*

God is unchangeable. Almighty, he created this visible world—and made himself invisible. He donned the visible world like a piece of clothing; he changes it like one switches a piece of clothing—himself unchanged. So it is in the sensory world. In the world's course of events, he is present everywhere in every moment. In a truer sense than the most vigilant human justice is said to be in all places, he is—never seen by any mortal—omnipresent, present everywhere, by the least and by the greatest, by what only figuratively can be called an event and by what is the extraordinary event, when a sparrow dies and when the savior of the human race is born. In his almighty hand, he holds all actuality as possibility at every moment, has everything in preparedness at every moment, changes everything in an instant—the opinions of human beings, judgments, human sovereignty and mediocrity. He changes everything—himself unchanged. When everything is apparent unchangingness (for it is only apparent that the external is unchanged for a certain time; it is always being changed), he remains just as unchanged amid the upheaval of everything; no variableness touches him, not even the shadow of turning. He is, in unchanged brightness, the Father of lights, eternally unchanged. In unchanged brightness—yes, it is just for that reason that he is unchanged, because he is sheer brightness, a brightness that has no darkness in it and that no darkness can come near. It is not so with persons like us. We are not brightness in this fashion, and just for that reason we are changeable: sometimes a thing becomes clearer in us, and sometimes a thing is darkened, and we are changed. Now it alternates around us, and the shadow of turning slides changingly over us. Now a changing light falls over us from the outside world, while, in all of this, we ourselves are changed within ourselves again. But God is unchangeable.

This thought is *terrifying, sheer fear and trembling*. In general, this is perhaps less emphasized. One complains about the variability of humanity, of everything temporal, but God is unchangeable. "That is the consolation, sheer consolation," even carelessness says, "Yes, God is certainly unchangeable."

But first and foremost, are you, too, in agreement with God? Are you considering this with proper earnestness? Are you sincerely striving to understand—and that a person is to strive after this is God's eternally unchanging will for you, as for every person—are you sincerely striving to understand what God's will for you can be? Or do you live in such a way that this has not occurred to you? So, how terrible that he is the eternally unchangeable one! For one day, sooner or later, you still have to collide with this unchangeable will, which, because it willed your well-being, willed that you would consider this matter—this unchanging will that must therefore crush you, if you collide with it in any other way.

Next, you who are still in agreement with God, are you also in good agreement with him? Is your will—is it, and unconditionally, his will? Are your wishes, each wish of yours, his command? Are your thoughts, the first and the last, his thoughts? If not, how terrible that God is unchangeable, eternally, eternally unchangeable! How terrible just to be in disagreement with a person! Yet perhaps you are the stronger and say about the other: "Yes, well, he is sure to change." But, now, what if he is the stronger? Perhaps you still think that you could hold out longer. But, now, what if it is a whole era? Yet perhaps you say: "70 years is surely no eternity." But the eternally unchangeable one—what if you were in a disagreement with him? Indeed, it is an eternity. How terrible!

Imagine a wanderer. He has come to a stop at the foot of an immense, an insurmountable mountain. It is this he...no, he shall not cross, but it is this he wants to cross, for his wishes, his longings, his demands, his soul—which has an easier kind of passage—is already over on the other side, and what is missing is just that he follow after. Imagine he became 70 years old, but the mountain stands unchanged, insurmountable. Let him remain a period of 70 years more, but the mountain stands unchanged before him in the path, unchanged, insurmountable. So, during all this, he is perhaps changed. He dies to his longings, his wishes, his demands. He scarcely knows himself anymore. Now, in this way, a later generation meets him sitting, changed, at the foot of the mountain, which stands unchanged, insurmountable. Let it be 1,000 years since. He, the changed one, is long since dead. Only a legend is told about him; it is the only thing that remains—yes, and then the mountain, which stands unchanged, insurmountable. And now the eternally unchanged one, for whom 1,000 years is like a day. Alas, and even this has said too much. They are for him like an instant; yes, strictly speaking, they are for him like they were not for him. If you, even in the slightest, want to go another way than he wants you to: terrible!

True enough, if your will, if my will, if the will of these thousands and thousands is not exactly in complete agreement with God's will, things obviously go on the best they can out there in the bustle of the so-called real world. After all, God really acts as if nothing has happened. If anything, it is likely that if there were a righteous person—if there were such a one!—who considered this world, a world that lies in evil as Scripture says, he would have to become disheartened over the fact that God acts as if nothing has happened. But do you therefore believe that God has changed? Or is the fact that he acts as if nothing has happened less terrible when it is nevertheless certain that he is eternally unchangeable? It does not seem like that to me. Consider this, however, and then tell which is the most terrible. Either this: the infinitely strong one who, tired of letting himself be mocked, rises up in his power and crushes the recalcitrant—it is terrible, and it is even represented in this way, when it is told that God does not let himself be mocked, and there is reference to the times when his punitive judgment devastatingly overran the generation. But is that actually the most terrible? Is this not even more terrible: the infinitely strong one, who—eternally unchangeable!—sits entirely still and watches without a change of expression, almost like he did not exist. But at the same time, as the righteous person is certainly bound to lament, untruth prospers, has power. Violence and injustice prevail and yet in such a way that even a better person can be tempted to consider having to use something of the same measures, if there is to be hope of doing anything for the good. Thus it is as if he is derided—he, the infinitely strong one, the eternally unchangeable one, who really neither lets himself be mocked nor changed. Is this not the most terrible?

For why do you think that he is so quiet? Because he is conscious that he is eternally unchangeable. One who was not eternally sure of oneself—sure that he is the unchangeable—he himself could not keep calm in this way; he would spring up in his power. But only the eternally unchangeable one can sit so still. He takes his time; that he can do as well. He has eternity, and he is eternally unchangeable. He takes his time; that he does on purpose. Then comes eternity's reckoning, where nothing is forgotten, not a single abusive word that was said, and eternally he is unchangeable. However, it can also be merciful that he thus gives time—time for repentance and improvement. But how terrible if this time is not used in this way, for then the iniquity and the irresponsibility in us would instead wish that he was immediately at hand with punishment, rather than that he give time like this, act like nothing, and yet be eternally unchangeable.

Ask one who educates children (and, after all, we are all more or less children in relation to God!), ask one who has had to do with erring persons (and, after all, each one of us has been in error at least once, for a longer or shorter time, at greater or lesser intervals), and you will hear that he will verify that it is a great help to irresponsibility—or, rather, in order to prevent irresponsibility (and who dares claim to be entirely free of irresponsibility!)—that the hardship of punishment come the very instant after the violation, if possible. Thus the memory of the irresponsible one is habituated to remember the punishment simultaneously with the guilt.

Yes, if it were the case that straying and punishment stood in relation to one another like this—that one pressed on a spring and at the very instant one seized the forbidden pleasure or went astray punishment immediately followed, just as with a double-barreled gun—I believe that irresponsibility would be on guard. But the longer the time between guilt and punishment (which, understood in truth, expresses the measure of the case's seriousness), the more tempting for irresponsibility, as if the whole thing could perhaps be forgotten or justice itself could perhaps change and at that time acquire entirely different concepts or as if it would, in the end, at least be so long since it happened that it would be impossible to depict the matter unchanged. Then irresponsibility changes and not for the better; then irresponsibility becomes secure. And when such irresponsibility has become secure, then it ventures more, and so it goes year after year—the punishment fails to come, and forgetfulness sets in, and again punishment fails to come, but new sins do not fail to come, and the old sins have now become more vicious. And then it is over; then death closes—and to all this (it was only irresponsibility!) there was an eternally unchangeable witness. Was that also irresponsibility? An eternally unchangeable one, and it is with him that you will have to make an accounting. In the moment when temporality's hand—the minute hand—indicated 70 years, and the person died, in that time eternity's hand had scarcely moved a trifle. To that degree is everything present for eternity and for him, the unchangeable one!

And therefore, no matter who you are, remember what I say to myself—that nothing is significant for God and nothing insignificant, that in one sense the significant is insignificant for him, in another sense even the least insignificance is something infinitely significant. If your will, then, is not in keeping with his, consider that you will never slip away from him. Thank him if he—by mildness or by strictness—teaches you to bring your will into agreement with his. How terrible if he acts as if nothing has happened, how terrible if it could come so far with a person that he boasts that God either does not exist or that he has changed or even simply that he is too great to notice what we call trivialities. For he both exists, and he is eternally unchangeable, and his infinite greatness is precisely that he sees even the least thing, remembers even the least thing—yes, and if you do not will as he wills, he remembers it unchanged for an eternity!

For that reason, there is sheer fear and trembling for us irresponsible and inconstant persons in this thought about God's unchangeableness. Oh, consider it well! Whether or not he acts as if nothing has happened, he is eternally unchangeable. Consider it well: he is eternally unchangeable if, as it is said, you have something outstanding with him. He is unchangeable. Perhaps you have promised him something, have committed yourself by a sacred vow...but in the course of time you have changed. Now you seldom think about God (as an older person, have you perhaps got more important things to think about?) or perhaps you think differently about God— that he does not care about the trivialities of your life, that such faith is childishness. In any case, you have forgotten in this way what you promised him, then after that forgotten that you promised anything, and then finally forgotten, forgotten—yes, forgotten that he forgets nothing, he the eternally unchangeable one. You have forgotten that it is just the upside-down childishness of age to think that something is insignificant for God and that God forgets anything—he the eternally unchangeable one!

In the relationship between one person and another, so often there is complaint about changefulness. The one complains about the other—that he has changed. But, at times, even in the relationship between one person and another, the one's unchangingness can be like a plague. Perhaps one has talked to another person about himself. Perhaps it was somewhat childish, forgivable talk that he conveyed. But perhaps the matter was also more serious: it tempted the poor, vain heart to talk in high tones about its enthusiasm, its emotional stability, its will in this world. The other then listened calmly. He did not even smile or prevent him from talking. He let him talk. He listened. He was silent. He only promised what was demanded—not to forget the matter. Then time passed, and the first person had long since forgotten all this; however, the other had not forgotten it. Indeed, let us consider something much stranger. He had let himself be moved by the thoughts that the first person had talked about and, alas, almost surrendered in a moody moment. He had, with honest efforts, shaped his life in relation to these thoughts. He who only too clearly demonstrated that he remembered to the last what was said in that moment—what a plague to the unchangingness of his memory!

And now the eternally unchangeable one—and this human heart! Oh, this human heart, what do you not hide in your mysterious enclosure, unbeknownst to others (that would not be so bad) but sometimes almost unbeknownst to the person himself! Indeed, it is almost, as soon as a person has become only some years older, it is almost like a burial plot, this human heart! There they lie buried, buried in oblivion—promises, intentions, resolutions, entire plans and fragments of plans and God knows what. Yes, we human beings talk in this way, for we human beings seldom think about what we are saying. We say: God knows what is there. And we say that half carelessly, half tired of life—and then it is so frightfully true that God knows what. He knows, down to the least thing, what you have forgotten. He knows what has changed for your memory; he knows it unchanged. He does not even remember it as if it were really something past; no, he knows it as if it were today, and he knows if, in relation to some of these wishes, intentions, resolutions, something was said to him, so to speak—and he is eternally unchanged and eternally unchangeable. Oh, another person's memory can be a burden to a person—now, it is still never entirely reliable, and in any case it surely cannot be eternal. After all, I will become free from this other person and his memory. But an omniscient one, and an eternally unchangeable memory from which you do not then escape, least of all in eternity—frightful! No, everything is for him—eternally unchangeable—eternally present, present in eternal equality. No changing shadow changes him, neither of morning nor of evening, neither of youth nor of old age, neither of forgetfulness nor of excuse.

No, for him, there is no shadow. We are, as it is said, shadows; he is eternal brightness in his eternal unchangeableness. We are shadows that hurry away—my soul, do look out, for whether you want to or do not want to, you are hurrying to eternity, to him, and he is eternal brightness! Therefore he does not only hold a reckoning, but he is the reckoning. It is said that we persons are to make a reckoning, as if there were perhaps a long time to it, and so perhaps an overwhelming mass of details in order to get the reckoning brought about. O my soul, it is made every moment, for his unchangeable brightness is the reckoning, completely ready down to the last thing and preserved by him, the eternally unchangeable one, who has forgotten nothing of what I have forgotten. Neither does he remember something other than what was really real, as I do.

Thus there is sheer fear and trembling in this thought about God's unchangeableness. It is almost as if it were far, far beyond a human being's powers to have to do with such an unchangeableness. Yes, it is as if this thought must steer a person into anxiety and unrest to the point of despair.

But then it is also the case *that there is reassurance and blessedness in this thought.* It is really so that when you, tired of all this human, all this temporal and earthly changeableness and vicissitude, tired of your own inconstancy, could wish for a place where you could rest your weary head, your weary thoughts, your weary mind, in order to rest and to have a good rest—oh, in God's unchangeableness there is rest! Therefore, when you let his unchangeableness serve you—as he wants it to—for your good, for your eternal good, when you let yourself be brought up so that your self-will (and it has come more from your own changeableness than from without) dies away, the sooner the better—it does not help you; you are either with the good or with the bad. Consider the vanity in wanting to be at odds with an eternal unchangeableness. Be like the child when it profoundly senses that, over against itself, it has a will where it only helps one to obey. When you let yourself be brought up by his unchangeableness so that you forsake inconstancy and changeableness and caprice and willfulness, then you rest ever more confidently and more and more blessedly in this unchangeableness of God.

The Unchangeableness of God

That the thought about God's unchangeableness is blessed—yes, who doubts that? But just take care that you grow in this way so that, blessedly, you can rest in this unchangeableness! O, such a person speaks like one who has a happy home: "My home has been made eternally secure; I rest in God's unchangeableness." No one can disturb this rest but you yourself. If you could become entirely obedient in unchanged obedience, then—with the same necessity as a heavy body sinks into the earth, or with the same necessity as that which is light rises toward the sky—you would freely rest in God in every moment.

And, so, let everything else change, as it does. If you find your activity on a great stage, you will experience the changeableness of everything on a great scale. Yet, on a lesser stage, on the least one, you will really experience the same thing, perhaps just as painfully. You will experience how persons change, how you yourself change. At times it will even seem as if God changes, which is part of the upbringing. About this, about the changeableness of everything, an older person will be better able to talk than I, while what I could say, perhaps, could seem new to the very young. Still, we will not develop this further but let life's manifoldness unfold for each person as it is determined for him, so that he can come to experience what all others have experienced before him. At times the change will be such that you are reminded of the saying: "Change is pleasing"—yes, indescribably! There will also come times when you yourself invent a saying that language has suppressed, and you say: "Change is not pleasing—how could I even say change is pleasing?" When that happens, you will be particularly led (what in the first case you certainly will not forget either) to seek him, the unchangeable one.

My listener! This hour, and the discourse, are now soon past. If you yourself do not want it otherwise, this hour, and the discourse, soon will be forgotten too. And if you yourself do not want it otherwise, soon the thought about God's unchangeableness will be forgotten in changeableness too. Still, in this, he is surely not to blame, he the unchangeable one! But if you do not make yourself guilty of forgetting it, you will be supported by this thought for your lifetime, for an eternity.

Imagine a solitary person in the desert. Nearly burnt by the sun's heat, languishing, he finds a spring. O delicious coolness! "God be praised," he says, "now I am provided for"—and, after all, he found only a spring. How must the person who found God talk! And yet, he must also say, "God be praised. I found God! God be praised, now am I provided for. Your faithful coolness, O beloved spring, is not conquered by change. In winter's cold, if it were to reach here, you do not become colder but retain precisely the same coolness. The water of a spring does not freeze! In summer's midday fire, you retain precisely your unchanged coolness. The water of a spring is not lukewarm!" And there is nothing untrue in what he says (he who, in my opinion, did not choose some thankless subject for a eulogy, a spring, what everyone better understands the better one knows the meaning of desert and solitude); there is no untrue exaggeration in his eulogy. In the meantime, his life took an entirely different turn than he had thought. He once strayed away, then was tugged out into the wide world. Many years later he turned back. His first thought was the spring. It was not there; it was dried up. He stood silent for a moment in sorrow. Then he pulled himself together and said: "No, I still do not take back one word of what I said in your praise; it was all true. And if I praised your delicious coolness while you were there, O beloved spring, then let me also praise it now that you have vanished, so that it may be true that there is unchangingness in a human being's breast. Nor can I say that you deceived me. No, had I found you, I am convinced your coolness would be unchanged—and more you had not promised."

But you, O God, you unchangeable one, you are always to be found unchanged and let yourself always be found unchanged. Neither in life nor death does anyone travel so far away that you are not to be found, that you are not there. Indeed, you are everywhere. No springs on earth are like this; springs are only in particular places. And besides—what overwhelming security!—you do not remain in place like a spring. You travel with a person. Ah, and no one goes so far astray that he cannot make it back to you, you who are not only like a spring that lets itself be found—what a poor description of your nature!—you who are like a spring that even seeks the thirsty, the lost—something no one has ever heard about any spring. Thus you are always unchanged and to be found everywhere. And whenever a person comes to you, at whatever age, at whatever time of day, in whatever condition: if he comes sincerely, he always finds (like the spring's unchanged coolness) your love equally warm, you unchangeable one! Amen.

Part Two

Creation

⁓

INTRODUCTION
TO PART TWO

The second part of this volume is dedicated to the theme of creation and, more specifically, to writings in which Kierkegaard focuses on the spiritual significance of creation. In theological terms, "creation" can denote, on the one hand, the process by which God brings about and sustains all existing things. Here the emphasis traditionally falls on questions about whether or not God needs anything in order to create or about God's reasons for creating. On the other hand, "creation" also can refer to that which has been created by God—in other words, "creatures" that are not God and, indeed, are dependent upon God in order to exist. Here the emphasis traditionally falls upon the degree to which created things are able to interact with God and, in turn, fulfill their divinely ordained purposes. As a whole, then, theological reflection on creation engages matters that are both deeply theoretical and immediately practicable, relying on philosophical and, perhaps above all, biblical claims about God in order to understand and to guide creaturely life, especially the life of human beings.

This twofold emphasis is certainly not foreign to Kierkegaard's authorship, though he tends to approach creation in the second sense. In other words, much like his reflections on the nature of God, he is generally willing to *assume* the veracity of traditional Christian teaching about God's creative activity, so that, instead, he can focus and expound on what this teaching means for the ways in which human beings are to relate to God and to one another. Even his denser philosophical treatises regarding creation—above all, *The Concept of Anxiety* (1844), which explores how human freedom fosters an ambivalent anxiety (*Angest*) within the individual, thereby imparting a precondition for either ethical or sinful action—make clear that they are not attempting to encroach upon

Christian "dogmatics."[1] Indeed, Kierkegaard's pseudonym, Vigilius Haufniensis, notes that his task is "the psychological treatment of the concept of 'anxiety,'" which concerns "persistent observation" rather than the dogmatic stress on resisting and overcoming sin.[2]

As a pseudonymous work of philosophical psychology, *The Concept of Anxiety* stands in contrast, both in form and in tone, to the four pieces included here. And yet, its fundamental interest in theological anthropology indicates the crimson thread running through part 2. The first selection, "To Need God Is the Human Being's Highest Perfection," is the opening chapter of *Four Upbuilding Discourses*, published in August 1844 during a striking period of productivity, even by Kierkegaard's lofty standards. Roughly two months earlier, Kierkegaard had issued a trio of pseudonymous works— *Philosophical Fragments*, *The Concept of Anxiety*, and *Prefaces*. These were accompanied by two signed collections, *Three Upbuilding Discourses*, published in early June 1844, and the aforementioned *Four Upbuilding Discourses*. All told, then, Kierkegaard put out *five* books during the summer of 1844, two of which are now widely counted among his finest and most influential efforts, *Philosophical Fragments* and *The Concept of Anxiety*.

It is understandable, then, that a discourse such as "To Need God" might be overlooked amid such literary abundance; however, it stands as an important addendum to *The Concept of Anxiety* and as a clear precursor to *The Sickness unto Death* (1849). Kierkegaard's fundamental task in the discourse is to explore the inner dynamics of the human being, particularly in terms of the self's quest for fulfillment. There is, he posits, an interplay of selves within the human being—a "first self" that seeks gratification in and through earthly goods, and a "deeper self" that recognizes the impermanence of phenomenal things and thus seeks to orient the person to that which is eternal. The tension between these two ways of relating to reality effectively cripples the person, especially if the deeper self assumes that it has overwhelmed the first self, thereby giving the deeper self a sense of mastery that belies its intrinsic fragility. No, says Kierkegaard, the

---

1. *SKS* 317–31 / *CA*, 9–24.
2. *SKS* 4, 321 / *CA*, 14.

solution to the self's quandary is not strength but weakness, not a self-confident autonomy but a humble reliance on God—a point that at once hints at the Dane's indebtedness to mystics such as Johannes Tauler[3] and establishes one of the key themes of his oeuvre.

Indeed, part 2's second selection arrives at a similar conclusion, though it is distinguished by *how* it gets there. Entitled *What We Learn from the Lilies in the Field and from the Birds of the Air*, this short treatise makes up the second section of *Upbuilding Discourses in Various Spirits*, which Kierkegaard published in March 1847. The word *Spirits* here is taken from the Danish noun *Ånd*, which indeed can refer to the immaterial aspect of a human being, but also connotes a way of thinking or a mindset. Thus each treatise in *Upbuilding Discourses in Various Spirits* exemplifies a certain way of contemplating the world, and *What We Learn* in particular demonstrates an attitude of humble *disponibilité* toward creation. The prayer that opens the discourse establishes this outlook from the start:

> Father in heaven! From you come only good and perfect gifts. It must also be beneficial to follow the guidance and teaching of whomever you appoint as a teacher to human beings, as a guide to the worried. So, then, grant that the worried may truly learn from the divinely appointed teachers: the lilies in the field and the birds of the air! Amen.[4]

Here, again, Kierkegaard's indebtedness to classical Christian doctrine is manifest: God is the unchangeably benevolent Creator who creates all things good and whose gifts are offered to human beings for their own well-being. And yet, Kierkegaard especially wants to focus on creation's own capacity to *teach* human beings, and *What*

---

3. For more on the links between "To Need God" and mystical theology, see Christopher B. Barnett, "The Mystical Influence on Kierkegaard's Theological Anthropology," *Acta Kierkegaardiana* 6 (2013): 105–22. Also see Christopher B. Barnett, *From Despair to Faith: The Spirituality of Søren Kierkegaard* (Minneapolis: Fortress Press, 2014), 33–38.
4. *SKS* 8, 258 / *UDVS*, 57, my translation.

We Learn—the longest selection in the present volume—develops this point over three substantial sections. Drawing on a pericope from Jesus's Sermon on the Mount (Matt 6:24–34), and employing some of the richest and most poetic writing in his entire corpus, Kierkegaard argues that created things such as lilies and birds can show human beings that it is good to be a part of creation, that the glory of human life is to share in God's life, and that what dignifies human beings is that they are granted the freedom to receive this glory.

If Kierkegaard, by way of the lilies and the birds, calls persons to come to participate in the divine life, one still might ask, What, exactly, is the nature of this divine life, and what would it mean for human beings to involve themselves with it? Kierkegaard addresses these questions in the third piece included in this section, namely, "Love Upbuilds." Also stemming from 1847, "Love Upbuilds" opens the second sequence of *Works of Love*, which arguably is Kierkegaard's most popular collection of signed writings, though it is hardly unique in its focus on the question of "love." As M. Jamie Ferreira puts it,

> The bulk of Kierkegaard's authorship provokes us to ask ourselves "Am I loving rightly and well?" precisely because he complicates the story of love. The figure of the lover winds its way throughout his authorship, clothed in aesthetic, ethical, and religious categories.[5]

Unsurprisingly, "Love Upbuilds," like the rest of *Works of Love*, tends to focus on the religious aspect of love. Indeed, the volume itself starts with a prayer, one that invokes the Holy Trinity, the "God of love," the one who is "Eternal Love,"[6] from whom love originates and through whom it is redeemed and strengthened. It is this "love"—

---

5. M. Jamie Ferreira, "Love," in *The Oxford Handbook of Kierkegaard*, ed. John Lippitt and George Pattison (Oxford: Oxford University Press, 2013), 328. Also see Ferreira's important study on *Works of Love*: M. Jamie Ferreira, *Love's Grateful Striving: A Commentary on Kierkegaard's* Works of Love (Oxford: Oxford University Press, 2001).

6. *SKS* 9, 12 / *WL*, 4.

Kierkegaard uses the term *Kjerlighed*, which, like the Latin *caritas*, refers to a self-giving benevolence toward the other—that Kierkegaard principally identifies with the Christian life. Indeed, "Love Upbuilds" expands on this very point, maintaining that what distinguishes *Kjerlighed* is not a given action or a certain turn of phrase but an inner commitment to edifying other persons, not through force or through manipulation but, rather, through always trusting that love is present in them.

In contrast to its predecessors, the fourth and final piece in this section is neither mellifluous nor obviously spiritual. It warrants inclusion here, however, because it expounds, albeit in a thick philosophical idiom, the core of Kierkegaard's theological anthropology. The piece in question is the first section of *The Sickness unto Death*—one of two texts attributed to the pseudonym Anti-Climacus, who aims to delineate "the summit of Christianity in ethical rigor."[7] Indeed, according to Kierkegaard, what distinguishes Anti-Climacus among Kierkegaard's pseudonyms is his acute "exposition of ideality," so much so that he risks confusing "himself with ideality."[8] Despite this danger, however, Kierkegaard insists that Anti-Climacus's "account of ideality can be absolutely true, and I bow to it."[9]

But what, exactly, does Kierkegaard mean by "ideality" (*Idealiteten*)? Derived from the Latin *idealis* ("existing as an archetype"), the word itself refers to the quality of being or of expressing a standard of perfection, an *ideal*. Anti-Climacus emphasizes distinct but complementary ideals in his two books, *The Sickness unto Death* and *Practice in Christianity* (1850). For example, in the latter text (selections from which are included in this volume), Anti-Climacus tends to focus on how Christ's life of humility and suffering is archetypal for the ordinary Christian believer, even for one who lives in Christendom. *The Sickness unto Death*, however, takes a more methodical and thereby less hortatory approach, attending to the nature of the human self and its concomitant need to overcome despair and sin and to arrive at perfection—a state that, for

---

7. *SKS* 22, NB12:7, my translation.
8. *SKS* 22, NB11:209 / *JP* 6, 6433.
9. *SKS* 22, NB11:209 / *JP* 6, 6433.

Anti-Climacus, is synonymous with the harmonization of the self's dialectical elements, which can only occur when the self properly relates to itself and to God.[10]

The portion from *The Sickness unto Death* included here, entitled "The Sickness unto Death Is Despair," sets forth precisely this argument. Again, it is a challenging read, though one worth the effort. As one commentator has put it, *The Sickness unto Death* not only represents "the unifying focus of all of Kierkegaard's writings," but it endures as Kierkegaard's "most mature work, his masterpiece."[11]

---

10. For a more in-depth discussion of *The Sickness unto Death* and its centrality to Kierkegaard's spiritual thought, see Barnett, *The Spirituality of Søren Kierkegaard*, 25–61.

11. Arnold B. Come, *Kierkegaard as Humanist: Discovering My Self* (Montreal: McGill-Queen's University Press, 1995), xxi.

Chapter Four

TO NEED GOD IS THE HUMAN BEING'S HIGHEST PERFECTION[1]

"A person needs only a little in order to live, and he needs this little only a little while"—this is a magnanimous saying, which is worth being received and understood as it wants to be understood. For it is too earnest to want to be admired as a beautiful expression or as a stylish phrase. At times it is certainly thrown around in this way. One shouts it to the needy person, perhaps in order to comfort him in passing, perhaps only in order to say something as well. One says it to oneself even on a lucky day, for the human heart is very deceitful and therefore only gladly takes magnanimity in vain and is proud of only needing a little—while using much. One says it to oneself on a day of need and, in admiration, hurries ahead to meet oneself at the goal—when one completed something glorious. In doing so, however, one is as little served as the saying is.

"One needs it only a little while." Yet, just as it sometimes happens that when the days lengthen, winter also strengthens, so is it always the case that the winter of privation and hardship makes the days long even if time and life are short. How much, then, is the little that a person needs? Actually, one cannot at all answer this question in general. And even the one who has experienced it—if not needing little, then nevertheless of having to manage with little—even he will not be able to define in general what that little is. In particular, just as time often brings the grieving one new comfort, the brokenhearted

1. From Niels Jørgen Cappelørn et al., eds., *Søren Kierkegaards Skrifter*, vol. 5 (Copenhagen: Gads Forlag, 1998), 291–316.

one new satisfaction, the one who lost much new compensation, so is it gentle with the suffering one, even when it continues to take. It seldom takes everything at once but does so little by little, and, in this way, it little by little gets him used to going without, until he himself sees with wonder that he needs even less than what he once considered the least—indeed, needs so little that he would think about having to need so little with dismay (even if he would not express himself with perfect clarity, for truly the dismay does not lie only in needing little) and would almost be provoked by the contradictory notion of having to need it in order to be able to continue needing it, even if he would not entirely understand himself, since the perfection really would not consist in coming to need more.

But how much, then, is the little that a human being needs? Let life answer, and let the discourse do what life's distress and hardship sometimes do—strip a human being in order to see how little it is that he needs. And now you, my listener, join in or wish to join in as you must in relation to your particular circumstances. For the discourse will not arouse dismay if, on the contrary, it is considering how to find comfort, and it does not intend to deceive you, as when the ice and snow of despair forms the deceptive mountain torrent, according to which the caravan changes its route, goes into the desert, and perishes (Job 6:15–18). It cannot arouse your dismay, if you yourself have experienced it and found comfort. And, if you have not experienced it, then the discourse about this will only dismay you if your strength lies in the thought that such a thing happens but rarely. But who, then, is the most miserable: the one who has experienced it, or the cowardly and soft fool who does not notice that his comfort is a fraud—that his comfort is only of little benefit when misfortune hits, that this is the rare occasion?

So, then, take it away from him: wealth and power and might, and the treasonous servility of false friends, and the submissiveness of desires to the caprice of pleasure, and the triumphs of vanity over pleading admiration, and the flattering attention of the crowd, and all of his appearance's envied glory—he has lost this and is content with less. Just as the world cannot recognize him because of this immense change, so can he hardly recognize himself—so changed is he that he, who needed so much, now needs so much less. In truth, it is far easier and far more joyful to understand how this change can make him unrecognizable to himself than how that other change can make him unrecognizable to other persons. For is it not foolishness that it is the clothes that make a man unrecognizable, so that one cannot recognize him when he is naked? And is it not sad that it is the clothes that one admires, not the man! But a more godly way of looking easily sees that he is about to be clothed and is being arrayed in festive garb, for the earthly wedding outfit and the heavenly one are exceedingly different.

Nevertheless, a few possessions with contentment is already a great gain indeed. So, then, take that away from him—not the contentment but the last thing that he owned. He does not suffer distress; he does not go to bed hungry. But where is he to get what is necessary? That he does not know, not at night when he falls asleep from worry, not in the morning when he awakens to it. But he still gets it—the little he needs in order to live. So, then, he is poor, and the saying that is so hard to hear he must hear said about himself. He feels it doubly hard, because he himself did not choose this condition, like the one who cast away his possessions in order to test himself and who perhaps submits himself to voluntary poverty more easily, albeit not always better if he merely renounced vanity with the help of a still greater vanity.

"Only needs a little," as the saying goes. But to know that a person only needs a little without nevertheless knowing at any moment with certainty that one can get the little that one needs—the person who bears this only needs a little. He does not even need—what still amounts to something—to know this little with certainty. A person, then, does not need more, if it is true that he only needs a little...in order to live. For he will find a grave, won't he? And in the grave every human being needs just a little. Whether the dead man owns the grave in which he lies, perhaps for a hundred years (alas, what a peculiar contradiction!), or he has had to trespass among others, even in death has had to fight his way in order to get a little place— they own equally much and need equally little, and need it only for a little while. But the previous "little while" that the saying speaks about can perhaps become long. For even if the way to the grave was not long—if you perhaps not infrequently saw him wearily make his way out there, in order to conquer with his eyes the little land that he intended to capture as a dead man—could not the way, therefore, become very long in another sense? If, then, he grew despondent at times, if he did not always understand that a human being only needs a little, did you have nothing else to say to him than to repeat that saying? Or did you probably say to him what came quite naturally, so naturally that, in your heart, perhaps even you yourself did not have confidence in the consolation you offered another person: "Let your-self be contented with the grace of God."

Stop now a moment, lest everything—thought and discourse and language—be confused, lest everything be confused because the relation certainly continues but only like this—that it is reversed in such a way that that man is the one who has consolation, and you are the one who needs it; that that man is the rich one, and you are the needy one, although it was completely turned around until you heard the little incantation that transformed everything. Perhaps you did not even notice it yourself. For many a saying is sidestepped in this way, just as the child does with a momentous saying, without discov-ering in it the sting of the thought that wounds unto death in order to save life.

To be contented with the grace of God! God's grace is, indeed, the most glorious of all. Surely we shall not fight about this, because it is basically every human being's deepest and most blessed cer-tainty. But he very rarely summons the thought about it. And even-tually, when he really wants to be honest, then he quietly applies—without, however, being clear about what he is doing—to this idea that old saying: "Everything in moderation." If he were to think the thought in its eternal validity, then it would immediately take deadly aim at all his worldly thought, poetry, and aspiration. It would turn everything around on him, and he cannot endure this for long. Then he goes back to the nether regions of the worldly, to his customary ways of talking and thinking. And, indeed, the older a person becomes, the more difficult does it become for him to learn a new language, especially one that is so extremely different. He notices this now and then—that the way in which he uses this saying does not hang together properly amid all his worldly discourse. He gets a bad conscience about the saying and obtains no blessing from it. Yet God's grace is, indeed, the most glorious of all.

But, now, if a person owned what is certainly not so glorious—owned all of the earth's treasures—and you said to him: "Now, let yourself be contented with this"—then he would smile at you, no doubt. If he himself said to you: "I will be contented with this, then," it would probably shock you. For what more could he need, and what nerve to want to be *contented* with the *most*. After all, that which one is contented with must be a little. But to be contented with the most glorious of all seems a peculiar way to talk. And that this consoling suggestion is made by a person who himself does not understand it is again peculiar, as if someone—not without sympathetic concern—gave a little coin to the needy person, admonishing him to be content with it, even as, however, this coin made the recipient into the owner of the whole world. For would it not be peculiar if the giver himself could think so poorly about the gift he offered that he would pair it with an admonishment about being contented! Or would it not be like a man, who, personally invited by a powerful person, went to the place of banquet and met a poor person, to whom he said in order to offer him a kind of consolation: "Let yourself be contented with having a table in the kingdom of heaven!" Or if the poor person himself was eloquent and said: "Alas! I was not invited by the powerful person and, therefore, cannot accept his invitation either, since I am invited elsewhere and must be contented with having a table in the kingdom of heaven." Would this not be a strange way of talking?

The more one thinks about it, the more peculiar earthly life and human language become. For amid all the earthly and worldly difference, which is jealous enough in itself, the God-difference is thoughtlessly interfered with—indeed, even in such a way that it is basically shut out. To come in the king's name opens every door for a person, but to come in God's name is the last thing that a person should attempt. And the one who can be contented with that must be contented with little. If he came to the door of the powerful, if the servant did not even understand from whom he brought greetings, if the powerful person impatiently went out himself and saw the poor man who was to greet him on behalf of God in heaven—perhaps the door would be closed for him.

Still, the discourse does not want to catch you off guard, my listener, or to produce a sudden effect. When the words say, "to be *contented* with the grace of God," then the reason is certainly that God's grace does not express itself like a human being would like to understand it; rather, its speech is more difficult. In other words, as soon as God's grace gives the human being what he wants and desires, then he is contented not only with grace but is happy with what he receives and, according to his own reckoning, easily understands that God is gracious to him. Now, that this is a misunderstanding, which no one should be in a hurry to denounce, is obvious enough. But that is why one ought not to forget to practice at the opportune time understanding what is more difficult and true. That is to say, if a human being can be assured of God's grace without needing temporal evidence as a middleman or as an interpreter of what he sees as beneficial changes, then it is indeed certain to him that God's grace is the most glorious of all. And then he will endeavor to be gladdened by it in such a way that he is not only contented with it; he will endeavor to give thanks for it in such a way that he is not "contented" with grace. He does not grieve over that which was denied, does not grieve over the linguistic difference that was between God's eternal reliability and his childish little faith, which now, however, no longer exists, since now "his heart is strengthened by grace and not by food" (Heb 13:9).

If a needy person dared to enjoy the friendship of a powerful person, but this powerful man could do nothing for him (this is, after all, the corresponding point to the fact that God's grace does not allow earthly evidence to materialize)—still, the fact that he had such a friendship was already very much. But here, perhaps, lies the difficulty. For, of course, the needy one could be convinced that such a powerful man was actually incapable of doing anything for him, but, ultimately, how could he be convinced that God cannot? He is, after all, almighty! From this it indeed is shown that the thought of impatience constantly insists, as it were, that God can surely do it. And that is why—because human beings are so impatient—that is why language says: "To be contented with the grace of God."

In the beginning, when impatience is most vociferous, then it can scarcely understand that it is a praiseworthy contentment.

Inasmuch as it is slowed and calmed down in the quiet incorruptibility of the inner human being, then it understands this better and better, until the heart is moved and at least occasionally sees the divine glory that had taken on a lowly form. And if this glory again disappears for the human being, so that he is back to being needy—something he also was while he saw the glory—then it seems to him again that contentment still belongs to being contented with the grace of God. Then, in shame, he himself surely admits that God's grace is worth being contented with. Yes, it alone is worth coveting; yes, to possess it is the lone blessed thing.

Then, in a beautiful sense, the human heart will gradually become more and more discontented, because God's grace is never taken with violence. That is to say, in order to know that grace is certain, the heart will gradually become more and more eager, more and more full of longing. And, see, now everything has become new, everything has been changed! In relation to the earthly, it is a matter of needing little, and, to the extent that one needs less, the more perfect one is to that same extent. A pagan[2]—who, indeed, only knew how to talk about the earthly—has said that the deity is blessed, because he needs nothing, and next to him is the wise man, because he needs little. In the human being's relation to God, it is reversed: the more he needs God, the deeper he understands that he needs God and, the more perfect he is, the more he pushes forward to God in his need. That is why the saying about being contented with God's grace will not only comfort a person—and then comfort him again every time earthly privation and need make him, in earthly terms, need comfort—but when he has become properly attentive to the saying, then it calls him aside where he no longer hears the earthly mother tongue of the worldly mind. He no longer hears the speech of human beings, the noise of the shopkeepers, but where the words explain themselves to him, they entrust to him the secret of perfection: that to need God is nothing to be ashamed of but is perfection

---

2. Here Kierkegaard is referring to Diogenes the Cynic, active during the fourth century BCE, who so observed simplicity that he slept in an empty storage barrel. See, e.g., William Desmond, *Cynics* (New York: Routledge, 2014), esp. 19ff. (Tr.)

itself, and that it is the saddest thing of all if a human being goes through life without realizing that he needs God.

So, then, we want to clarify for ourselves this upbuilding thought:

To Need God Is the Human Being's Highest Perfection.

That it is true that needing God is a perfection—on this subject, a circumstance that is well known to all seems to remind everyone with at least a passing admonition. Indeed, in the churches of various lands, the king and the royal house are prayed for after the sermon. That prayers are offered for those who are sick and sorrowful cannot prove that to need God is a perfection, for, after all, these are suffering persons. But the king is a powerful man—yes, the most powerful. And yet, prayers are offered for him in particular, but for the sick and the sorrowful only in general, although the Church hopes and trusts in the fact that God in heaven will understand this prayer particularly—that he thinks of each definite thing in its distinctiveness, while the Church does not even think of any definite thing. And if it is otherwise with God's understanding, if his cares of governing likewise only allow him to concern himself with the individual in general—yes, then God help us! But, alas, this is the last thing a person says in his misery. Even when he cannot endure this last thought—that God would care for the individual only in general—even then he says: "God help me to endure this thought." And, in this way, he nevertheless gets God to concern himself with him in particular.

But why, now, are prayers offered especially for the king? Is it because he has earthly power and holds the fate of many in his hands? Is it because his well-being determines that of countless others? Is it because every "shadow of adversity" that passes over the king's house also passes over the whole nation? Is it because his sickness brings the activity of the state to a standstill, his death disrupts its life? Such a purely worldly worry can certainly keep many people occupied, and not in an ungraceful way either. But, still, it will scarcely bring anyone to pray in any other way than with the restraint that is necessary when we pray for worldly goods. For, in that case, a king indeed becomes such an earthly good. In this sense, then, the intercession would also become more and more heartfelt, inasmuch as the personal life of the one praying is connected more and more closely to him, until, at last, the prayer is no more an intercession than the wife's prayer for her husband is an intercession. But, of course, the Church cannot pray in this way just because it makes an intercessory prayer. Yet, it surely does this because it is convinced that the higher a person stands, the more he needs God.

However, even though prayers are offered in all churches for a king, it admittedly does not follow from this that the king for whom a prayer is offered personally understands that to need God is the human being's highest perfection. And if the individual in the church tacitly gives his consent to the intercession, and, alas, if the many who do not visit the church nevertheless have no objection to the intercession, it admittedly does not follow from this that these persons understand it in godly fashion—that, indeed, the higher one climbs in earthly power and might, the closer one comes only to intercessory prayer. To take it in vain is, for the mighty, only all too easy; to say it in vain is, for the one praying, only all too easy. On the other hand, what is right for earnestness to want to understand is already not understood earnestly enough, when one will seek this consciousness oneself rather than leave it to God, who knows best how to scare all self-confidence out of a person and to keep him— when he wants to sink into his own nothingness—from maintaining the diver's connection [*Dykkerens Forbindelse*] with the earthly itself. What is right for earnestness to want to understand makes life difficult; we do not deny it. Let us just admit it, without thereby becoming so disheartened or cowardly that we want to sleep our way to what others have had to work for. Let us not take it in vain when the believer enthusiastically says that all his suffering is brief and short, that the yoke of self-denial is so easy to bear. But do not let us doubt either that the yoke of self-denial is beneficial, that the cross of suffering ennobles a person in the end, and let us hope to God that, should we come so far one day, we also could speak with enthusiasm. Still, let us not ask for this too early, lest the believer's enthusiastic talk make us disheartened, because it will not be an immediate success. It often goes like this for a person: he fixes in his memory a particularly powerful saying; now, when suffering comes to his house, then he is reminded of the saying and thinks that he should be immediately victorious in the joy of the words. But even an apostle does not always speak with powerful words. He, too, is weak at times; he, too, is uneasy and thereby makes us understand that powerful words are costly and never possessed in such a way that one can again have an opportunity to make certain how costly they are.

But, now, even if this understanding makes life more difficult—not only for the frivolity of the fortunate person and for the many whose aspiration is to become like him, but also for the unfortunate, since this understanding really does not work like magic, does not work in any externally decisive way—should we therefore questionably puff it up or covet it double-mindedly? And yet, it is certainly a worrying matter that what is offered as consolation in life begins by making it more difficult in order—yes, in order—to make it truly easier. For so it is with every one of truth's miracles, as it was with that miracle at the wedding in Cana: the truth bestows the poor wine first and saves the best until last, whereas the deceitful world bestows the best wine first.

Just because a person became unhappy ("infinitely unhappy," as he himself says), it does not at all follow from this that the understanding that conditions the consolation—the understanding that he himself is capable of nothing at all—has matured in him yet. Hence, if he believes that he only lacks the means, then he still believes in himself. If he believes that if he were given this power or the admiration of other persons or the possession of his wish; if he thinks that the complaint contains a justifiable demand for something temporal, which becomes more justifiable the more vehement the complaint becomes—then, humanly speaking, he still has a bitter cup to drink before the comfort comes. It is, therefore, always a difficult matter for one human being to offer another such comfort. For when the worried person turns to him, and then he wants to say: "I certainly know where to find comfort, an indescribable comfort; yes, what's more, it changes itself little by little in your soul into the highest joy"—then the worried one will listen attentively, won't he? But when there is added: "However, before this comfort can come, then one must understand that one is nothing at all oneself. Then one must cut off the bridge of probability, which wants to connect desire and impatience and demand and expectation with the object desired, demanded, and expected; then one must forsake the worldly mind's association with the future; then one must withdraw into oneself, not as into a fortress—which still defies the world, while the withdrawn person really has his most dangerous enemy with him in the fortress, while, in fact, he may have followed the enemy's advice when he withdrew into himself in this way—but withdraw into oneself, sinking into one's own nothingness, giving oneself over to grace and disgrace." Then the worried person would surely go away distressed like that rich young man, who had many possessions. And yet, even if he did not have many possessions, he would resemble him nonetheless, so much so that one could not distinguish them. Or if the worried one had run wild and run fixedly into deliberation so that he was unable to act, because an equal case could be made from both sides, and then another person would say to him: "I know a way out, and you will certainly be victorious. Abandon desire. Act, act in the conviction that, even when the very opposite of your wish takes place, you have still prevailed." Then there would surely be one who would turn away impatiently, because such a victory would seem like a defeat to him, and because such a way out would seem even more burdensome than the multifaceted unrest of his doubting soul.

What, after all, is a human being? Is he just one more ornament in the string of creation? Or does he have no power? Is he himself capable of nothing? And what, then, is this power? What is the highest that he is able to will? How does the answer to this question go, when the audacity of youth unites itself with the power of adulthood in order to ask it, when this glorious union is willing to sacrifice everything in order fulfill great things, when burning with zeal it says: "Even if no other person in the world has reached it before, I will reach it nonetheless; if millions were corrupted and forgot the task, I will strive nonetheless...but what is the highest?" Well, now, we do not want to defraud the highest of its price; we do not conceal the fact that it is seldom reached in the world. For the highest is this—that a human being is fully convinced that he himself is capable of nothing at all, nothing at all. Oh, what rare might, albeit not rare in the sense that only one individual is born to be king, since everyone is born to it! Oh, what rare wisdom, albeit not in the sense that it is offered only to a few, since it is really offered to all! Oh, what wonderful rarity, which is not degraded by being offered to all and by being able to be held by all! Yes, when the human being wants to turn outward, then it probably seems as if he were capable of doing something more astonishing, something that would satisfy him in an entirely different way, something around which jubilant admiration would flock. For that rare sublimity is no good to admire. It does not tempt the sensual person, since, on the contrary, it judges that the admiring person is a fool, who does not even know what he admires, and orders him to go home. Or it judges that he is a deceitful soul and orders him to think better of what he is doing.

It is true that, according to external consideration, the human being is the most glorious created thing, but all his glory is still only in the external and for the external. For does not the eye aim its arrow outward, every time passion and desire tighten the bowstring? Does not the hand grab outward? Is not the human being's arm stretched out? Is not his ingenuity conquering? But if he nevertheless does not want to be like an instrument of war in service to inexplicable urges—yes, in service to the world, because the world itself, for which he longs, awakens the urges; if he nevertheless does not want to be like a stringed instrument in the hands of inexplicable moods or, rather, in the hands of the world, because his soul's movement is in relation to the way that the world plucks the strings; if he does not want to be like a mirror in which he captures the world or, rather, in which the world is reflected; if he does not want this, if he himself—before the eye takes aim at something in order to conquer it—first wants to capture the eye so that it might belong to him and not he to the eye; if he grabs the hand before it grasps after the external, so that it might belong to him and not he to the hand; if he wants this so earnestly that he is not afraid to take out the eye, to cut off the hand, to shut the window of sense, if it should be made necessary—yes, then everything is changed. The power and the glory are taken from him.

He does not struggle with the world but with himself. Observe him now. His powerful figure is held enfolded by another figure, and so firmly are they locked in an embrace that they oppress one another in equally supple and equally strong fashion. Thus the wrestling cannot even begin, because, in that moment, the one figure would overwhelm him. But this other figure is himself. In this way, he is capable of nothing at all. Even the weakest person, who is not tried in this struggle, is capable of far more than he.

And this struggle is not only exhausting but very terrible as well (if it is not really he himself who has ventured out in this on his own idea, and, if that is so, then he is not tried in the struggle about which we are talking) when, by God's governance, life casts a human being out in order to be strengthened in this annihilation that knows no letdown, permits no evasion, facilitates no self-deception that he would be capable of something more under different circumstances. For when he struggles with himself, circumstances cannot determine the result. This is a human being's annihilation, and the annihilation is his truth. He shall not slip out of this knowledge, since, after all, he is his own witness, his accuser, his judge. He himself is the only one who is capable of consolation, since he understands the distress of annihilation, and the only one who cannot console, since he himself is indeed the instrument of annihilation. To comprehend this annihilation is the highest that a human being can do. To brood over this understanding because it is a good entrusted to him—namely, from God in heaven, who entrusted it to him as truth's secret—is the highest and the most difficult thing that a human being can do. For deception and forgery are easily done, so that he himself becomes something at the expense of truth. This is the highest and most difficult thing a human being can do; however, what I am saying is that he cannot even do this. At most, he is capable of wanting to understand that this scorching fire only consumes until the ardor of God's love ignites the flame in what the scorching fire could not consume.—In this way, the human being is a helpless creature, for every other understanding by which he understands that he can help himself is only a misunderstanding, even if in the eyes of the world he was regarded as brave...by having courage to remain in a misunderstanding, that is, by not having courage to understand the truth.

But in heaven, my listener, there lives the God who can do everything, or, rather, he really lives everywhere, even if human beings do not notice it. "Yes, O Lord, if you were like a powerless, lifeless body that withers like a flower, if you were like a brook that flows past, if you were like a building that falls in time, then people would pay attention to you, then you would be a suitable object for our base and brutish thoughts." But, now, it is not like this, and your very greatness renders you invisible. In your wisdom, you are too far away from human thought to be seen, and, in your omnipresence, you are too near to be observed. In your goodness, you hide yourself from human beings, and your omnipotence makes it so that you cannot be seen, since then he himself would become nothing. But God in heaven is capable of everything and the human being nothing at all.

Now, my listener, is it not the case that these two—God and the human being—correspond to one another? Yet, if they correspond to one another, then, of course, there is only the question about whether or not you will be happy about the wonderful fortune that you two correspond to one another or, rather, whether you will be the sort of person who does not at all correspond to God, the sort of person who himself is capable of something—and therefore does not entirely correspond to God. For, after all, you cannot change God, and you really do not want to change God, lest he should be incapable of all things.

To become nothing seems hard—oh, but we speak differently even in human affairs. If misfortune taught two human beings that they corresponded to one another in friendship or in love, how trifling the distress caused by misfortune would really seem in comparison with the joy that misfortune also brought—that these two correspond to one another! And if two persons did not understand until death that they corresponded to one another for all eternity—oh, then, what would death's brief though bitter moment of separation be in comparison with an eternal understanding!

In this way, the human being is great and at his highest when he corresponds to God by being nothing at all himself. But let us not carelessly admire or take the admiration in vain. Did not Moses go as the Lord's emissary to a vicious people in order to free them from themselves—their slavish mentality—and from their slavish condition under the yoke of a tyrant? Hence, what is even the greatest deed of a hero in comparison with what one calls the works of Moses? For what is it to level mountains and to fill rivers against letting a darkness fall over all of Egypt? Yet, after all, these were only Moses's so-called works, for he was capable of nothing at all, and the work was the Lord's. See the difference here. Moses: he does not come to decisions, does not formulate plans while the council of good sense listens attentively because its leader is the wisest. Moses is capable of nothing at all. If the people would have said to him, "Go to Pharaoh, since your word is powerful, your voice triumphant, your eloquence irresistible," then he presumably would have answered, "Oh, you fools! I am capable of nothing at all, not even of giving up my life for you, if the Lord does not will it. I am only capable of entrusting everything to the Lord." Then he appears before Pharaoh, and what is his weapon? It is the weapon of the powerless—prayers. And even when the last word of his prayers has reached heaven, he still does not know what will happen, even if he believes that whatever happens still happens for the best. Then he returns home to the people, but, if they were to praise and to thank him, then he would doubtless answer: "I am capable of nothing." Or when the people are thirsting in the desert and perhaps turn to Moses and say, "Take your staff and order the rock to give water," then Moses would likely answer, "What is my staff other than a stick?" And if the people continued, "But in your hand the staff is mighty," then Moses would have to say, "I am capable of nothing. But since the people are asking for it, and since I myself cannot bear the sight of the misery of this languishing people, I will strike the rock, even if I myself do not believe that water will spring from it"—and the rock would not give water. Therefore: whether the staff he holds in his hand is to be the finger of the Almighty or the stick of Moses, he does not know, not even in the moment when the staff is already touching the rock. He only knows it after the fact, just as he only ever sees the Lord's back.

Oh, humanly speaking, the weakest person in Israel is capable of more than Moses, for, after all, this means that there is something he can do. But Moses is capable of nothing at all. In one moment, as it were, to be stronger than the strongest, than all human beings, than the whole world, insofar as the miracle occurs by his hand; in the next moment—yes, in the same moment—to be weaker than the weakest, insofar as this one still constantly thinks that there is something he can do. Such greatness will not experience the craving of vanity, insofar as it gives itself time to understand what constitutes greatness. Otherwise, in its disgusting cowardice, it would immediately be ready to wish to be in Moses's place.

But if this view—that to need God is the human being's highest perfection—makes life more difficult, then it only does so because it wants to look at the human being according to his perfection and to bring him to look at himself in this way. For, in and by this consideration, *the human being learns to know himself.* And the person who does not know himself, his life is indeed a fraud in a deeper sense. Yet, such a fraud is seldom due to a person not discovering which abilities have been entrusted to him, not seeking to develop these abilities as much as possible in accordance with the life circumstances that have been given to him. Then he rightly puts deep roots into existence. He does not behave carelessly like the fortunately talented child, who does not understand how much has really been entrusted to him, like the careless rich youth, who does not understand the significance of gold—and so it is, after all, that we also speak of a person's self just like the value of money. And the one who knows himself, he knows down to the least how much he is worth and knows how to invest himself so that he gets full value out of it. If he does not do this, then he does not know himself, and he is cheated.

What the sensible person will be sure to say to him—and say to him step by step as life goes forward—is that he is not delighted by life in the springtime of today, that he is not asserting himself for what he actually is, that he does not know that people take a person for what he purports himself to be, that he has not known how to make himself important and thereby to give life meaning for himself. Alas, but even if a person knew himself ever so well in this sense, even if he knew ever so well how to get himself exposed to profit in life as advantageously as possible, I wonder if he would therefore know himself? But if he did not know himself, then, in a deeper sense, his life would indeed be a fraud. Now, would it then be rare that, in these sagacious times, a human being be responsible for such a fraud? That is to say, what would that sagacious self-knowledge be other than this—that he knew himself in relation to something else, but did not know himself in relation to himself. In other words, all his self-knowledge was downright vague, despite its apparently reliability, since it only concerned the relation between a doubtful self and a doubtful other. For this other could be changed so that another became the strongest, the most beautiful, the richest, and this self could be changed so that he himself became poor, became ugly, became powerless. And this change could set in at any moment. Only now this other is taken away, so he is cheated after all, and, if this something is such that it can be taken away, he is indeed cheated even if it is not taken away, because his entire life's meaning was grounded in something else. It is, namely, no fraud if that which can cheat does cheat but, rather, a fraud when it stops doing so.

Such self-knowledge is, then, imperfect and far from considering the human being according to his perfection. For, after all, it would be an odd perfection about which one must finally say, perhaps after having praised it in the strongest terms: "Is it a fraud as well?" Along this road, one does not come to consider the human being according to his perfection, and, in order to begin on this, one must begin by tearing oneself away from any such consideration, which is just as difficult as tearing oneself away from a dream, so that one does not make a mistake and continue the dream: dreaming that one is awake. In a certain sense, this is sure to be drawn out, because a human being's actual self seems to him to lie so far away that the whole world lies much closer to him; this is sure to be terrible, because deeper self-knowledge begins with what the one who does not want to understand it has to call the alarming deception: to receive himself instead of the whole world; to become the one in need instead of the master; to be capable of nothing at all instead of being capable of everything. Alas, how difficult that here one does not fall into dreams again and dreams that one does this by his own power.

When, then, the human being turns toward himself in order to understand himself, he steps in the way of that first self, as it were, halts that which was turned outward in craving for and hankering after the surrounding world—which is its object—and calls it back from the external. In order to move the first self to this withdrawal, the deeper self lets the surrounding world become what it is—become doubtful. It is, indeed, like this too. The world around us is unstable and, at every moment, can be changed into the opposite. And not one person can be found who, by his power or by his wish's incantation, can force this exchange. The deeper self now shapes the deceitful flexibility of the surrounding world in such a way that it is no longer desirable to that first self. The first self, then, either must look to kill the deeper self—to have it forgotten, whereby the whole thing is dropped—or it must concede that the deeper self is right. For to want to predicate constancy about that which constantly changes is indeed a contradiction, and, as soon as one confesses that it changes, it admittedly can change in that same moment. However much that first self shrinks from this, there has never been found any chatterbox so clever or thought-forger so cunning that he can invalidate the deeper self's eternal claim. Only one way out is given: to bring the deeper self to silence by letting the roar of inconstancy drown it out.

Now, what has happened? The first self is halted and cannot move at all. Alas, in real life, the surrounding world can be so favorable, so tangibly trustworthy, so apparently unswerving, that everyone will vouch for fortunate progress if one just begins. This does not help. The person who is a witness to that struggle in his heart [*Indre*] must admit that the deeper self is right: this very minute everything can be changed, and the one who does not discover this constantly runs into the dark. Never in the world has there been a tongue so quick that it could enchant the deeper self as soon as it was allowed to speak. Ah, it is a painful situation: the first self sits and looks at all the beckoning fruits, and it is indeed so clear that, if only one jumps at the chance, everything will succeed. Every person will admit that. But the deeper self sits there earnestly, thoughtfully, like the doctor at the sick person's bedside, albeit with transfigured gentleness as well, because it knows that this sickness is not unto death but unto life. The first self really has a specific craving. It is conscious that it is in possession of the conditions. As it understands it, the surrounding world is as favorable as possible; they are just waiting for one another, as it were: the happy self and the favors of fortune—ah, what a pleasant life! But the deeper self does not yield; it does not bargain, does not give its consent, does not reconcile. It only says: "Still, this very moment everything can certainly be changed." Nevertheless, people help that first self with an explanation. They call to him; they explain that it goes like this in life—that there are some persons who are fortunate, and they are to take pleasure in life, and he is one of them. Then the heart throbs; he wants to take off....

That a child who has a strong father must stay at home—one must put up with that. For, after all, the father is the strongest. But surely the first self is no child, and that deeper self is indeed himself. And yet, it seems stricter than the strictest father. One cannot curry favor with him in the least. Either he will speak with candor, or he will not speak at all. Then there is danger. Both the first self and the deeper self notice it. And then the latter one sits worried like an experienced pilot, while a secret council is held about whether it would not be best to cast the pilot overboard, since he is causing a headwind. That, however, does not happen, but what is the result? The first self cannot move from the spot, and yet...yet it is clear that the moment of joy hurries, that fortune already is in flight. For, indeed, persons say that when one does not immediately take advantage of the moment, then it is soon too late. And who, then, is guilty in this? Who else but that deeper self? But even this outcry does not help.

Really, what kind of unnatural condition is this? What does it all mean? When such a thing goes on in a person's soul, does this not mean that his mind is beginning to grow feeble? Alas, no, it means something entirely different. It means that the child has to be weaned. For, of course, one can be thirty years old and more, forty years old and still but a child—yes, one can die as an old child. But to be a child is so delightful! So one sleeps at the breast of temporality in the cradle of finitude, and probability sits by the cradle and sings for the child. If the wish does not come true, and the child becomes restless, then probability calms the child and says: "Now, just lie still and sleep, so I can go out and buy something for you, and next time it will be your turn." Then the child falls back asleep, and the pain is forgotten, and the child glows again in the dream of new wishes, although he believed that it would be impossible to forget the pain. Now, obviously, if he had not been a child, he surely would not have forgotten the pain so easily, and it would have become apparent it was not probability who had sat by his cradle, but the deeper self who had sat with him at the deathbed in self-denial's hour of death, when it itself rose up to an eternity.

When, then, the first self succumbs to the deeper self, then they are reconciled and go on together. Then, I suppose, the deeper self says: "In our great struggle, it is true that I had nearly forgotten what it was now that you so fervently wished. I do not believe at this time that there is anything to hinder the fulfillment of your wish, if only you do not forget the little secret we two have with one another. Now, you see, now you can be gratified, can't you?" Perhaps the first self answers: "Well, now I do not care about it in that way. No, I will never be as joyful as before—oh, as the time when my soul craved it, and you actually do not understand me." "I do not believe so either, nor would it be desirable, I suppose, that I understand you in such a way that I craved just as much as you. Still, have you lost something by not caring about it in that way? Consider the other side. What if the surrounding world really had deceived you? You know that it indeed could have. More I did not say. I only said that it is possible, whereby I, rightly enough, also said that what you regarded as a certainty was actually only a possibility. What then? Then you would have despaired, and you would not have had me to rely on. For you recall well enough that the ship's council was almost of a mind to cast me overboard. Now, would you not be better off having lost some of that burning desire and won the fact that life cannot deceive you? To lose in this way, is it not to win?"

"That little secret we two have with one another"—the deeper self spoke in this way. What do you suppose this secret is, my listener? What else but that a human being is capable of nothing at all in relation to the external. If he wants to seize upon the external immediately, then it can be changed in the same moment, and he can be deceived. On the other hand, he can take it with the consciousness that it also could be changed, and he is not deceived, even if it is changed. For he has the consent of the deeper self. If he wants to act immediately in the external, to do something, then everything can become nothing in the same moment. On the other hand, he can act with this consciousness, and even if it came to nothing, he is not deceived, because he has the consent of the deeper self.

Still, even if the first self and the deeper self are reconciled in this way, and even if the common mind is turned away from the external, then this is indeed only the condition for coming to know oneself. But if he actually is to know himself, there are new struggles and new dangers. Do not let the struggling person simply be terrified and deterred by the thought, as if needing were an imperfection, when the discourse is about needing God; as if needing were a shameful secret that one preferably would hide, when the discourse is, after all, about needing God; as if needing were a sad necessity that one would seek to compel to a more gentle side by enunciating it oneself, when the discourse is still about needing God. By a deeper self-knowledge, one learns precisely that one needs God. Yet, at first glance, the depressing thing in this would deter one from beginning, if one would not be aware of and be enthusiastic about the thought that this is just the perfection, since it is far more imperfect and only a misunderstanding that one should not need God.

Even if a person had accomplished the most glorious feats, if he nevertheless thought that it was all by his own power, if by overcoming his mind he became greater than one who captured a city, if he still thought that it was done by his own power, then his perfection was essentially only a misunderstanding. Yet, after all, such a perfection would not be very praiseworthy. On the contrary, the one who realized that he was not capable of the least thing without God, not even to be joyful over the most joyful event: he is closer to perfection. And the one who understood this and found absolutely no pain in it but only an overflow of bliss; the one who hid no secret wish that still would rather be joyful on one's own; the one who felt no shame that people noticed that he himself was capable of nothing at all; the one who put no conditions on God, not even that his weakness should be kept hidden from others, but in whose heart joy constantly prevailed by, so to speak, jubilantly casting himself into God's arms in inexpressible wonder over God, who is, after all, capable of all things—yes, he was the perfect one that the Apostle Paul describes better and more concisely: he "boasts of his infirmities" and has not even had so many and ambiguous experiences that he knows how to express himself with more detail. Of course, people say that not knowing oneself is a deception and an imperfection, but they often do not want to understand that the one who actually knows himself precisely comprehends that he is capable of nothing.

In the external, he was capable of nothing. But is he not capable of anything in the internal either? If an ability is actually to be such, then admittedly it must have opposition, because if it has no opposition, then it is either omnipotent or a fantasy. Yet, if he is supposed to have opposition, where shall this come from? After all, in the internal, the opposition can only come from himself. So, then, he struggles with himself internally, not as before, when the deeper self struggled with the first self in order to prevent it from worrying about the external. If a person does not discover this struggle, then he is in a misunderstanding, and his life is therefore imperfect. Yet, if he does discover it, then he will again understand that he himself is capable of nothing at all.

It seems curious that this is what a person is to learn from himself. Why, then, praise self-knowledge? And yet, this is how it is, and a person cannot learn from the whole world that he is capable of nothing at all. Even if the whole world united to crush and to annihilate the weakest, he could still constantly hold onto a quite faint conception that he himself would be capable of something under other circumstances, when the superior force was not as great. He can only discover by himself that he is capable of nothing at all. And whether he is victorious over the whole world or whether he stumbles over a straw, it is still the case that, by himself, he knows or can know that he himself is capable of nothing. If someone wants to explain it differently, then, of course, he has nothing to do with the others but only with himself, and every excuse is seen through. People think that it is so difficult to know oneself, especially when one is very gifted and has multiple aptitudes and abilities and now is to know about all these. Oh, the self-knowledge that we are talking about is not really detailed, and every time one rightly comprehends this brief and pithy truth—that one is capable of nothing at all—then one has recognized oneself.

But can one, then, not overcome oneself by oneself? That is certainly said at times, but I wonder if the one who says that has tested and understood himself in what is said. How can I be stronger than myself? I can be stronger than the weakest, and perhaps a person lives or has lived about whom one had to say that he was stronger than all others. But no one was ever stronger than himself. When, then, one talks about overcoming oneself on one's own, one is actually thinking of the external; in this way, the struggle is not equal. Hence, when the one who is tempted by worldly honor overcomes himself in such a way that he no longer stretches his arm out after it; when the one who feared life's dangers chases fear to such an extent that he does not flee the dangers; when the one who had lost free-spiritedness overcomes himself to the point that he remains still and does not fall back from the place of decision: then we do not want to degrade this; on the contrary, we praise him. But if he will take care not to save his soul in a new vanity and to drive out the devil with the devil's help, then he will simply confess that he is not capable of overcoming himself in his innermost being. By no means, however, does he think this as if the evil one had gotten power over him once and for all. No, but he is only capable of so much and this—that he can resist himself, which, after all, is not to overcome himself—only by extreme exertion. In his innermost being, he fashions temptations of honor and temptations of fear and temptations of despondency and temptations of pride and of defiance and of pleasure greater than the ones that meet him in the external world, and precisely for that reason he struggles with himself. Otherwise, he struggles with an occasional degree of temptation, and the victory proves nothing with respect to what he would be capable of in a greater temptation. If he is victorious in the temptation that his surroundings put before him, then this does not prove that he would be victorious when the temptation appeared as terrible as he can imagine it. But only when it seems too great, only then does he actually come to know himself. Just now it appears so very great to him in his inner being, and therefore he knows in himself what he perhaps did not get to know in the world—that he is capable of nothing at all.

Surely, my listener, you do not believe that these are the gloomy thoughts of a "heavy-blooded" [*tungblodet*] person. Do you not ever thank God that you are not plagued by such depression [*Tungsindighed*]? If it were depression, is this the way one ought to love God and human beings? That one thanks God for preferential love, which, of course, is to deceive him and to give him to understand that, if something more onerous happened, then one could not believe in his love (for, with this confession, it is indeed something entirely different to thank God that one was not tried in the most severe strife)? That one shuns the depressed person, as you call him; that one does not wish to know that, after all, he is a human being as well, and you dare not say that he is a criminal—therefore, that he is an unhappy person, therefore a person who needed your very sympathy, which you show him by asking him to wander out among the graves like a leper, while you do not dare acknowledge him as a fellow human being? But if someone regarded talking about such a self-understanding as the dark thoughts of a heavy-blooded person, then surely it would have to be regarded as a folly inseparable from his depression—that he thought this perspective considered the human being according to his perfection and an even greater folly that he would rejoice in his perfection.

And, really, why should he not be glad? For, after all, a person is always made happy by the perfect, and his joy did not consist in a thoughtless agreement with God's preferential love for one individual, and his joy did not flee from the sight of the sorrowful one. On the contrary, he would love every sorrowful person. And truly this is the way it is, and you, my listener, surely would not call him depressed. Far from it, since he alone is the happy person. For the one who is happy in and about God rejoices, and, again I say, he rejoices. For what reason, I wonder, does the Apostle Paul—who has given this beautiful injunction: "Rejoice, and, again I say, rejoice"—for what reason, I wonder, does he pause? For what reason, I wonder, does he stop before he bids the believer to be glad a second time? Because, in that space, he has given himself time, as it were, to hear everything terrible that may be said—the terrible thought that a human being is capable of nothing at all—in order to let the joy be totally victorious: "Again I say, rejoice."

The view that to need God is the human being's highest perfection certainly makes life more difficult, but it also considers life according to what is perfect. And, in this view, the human being comes to learn *to know God* by the piecemeal experience that is the right understanding with God.

Insofar as a human being does not know himself in such a way that he knows that he himself is capable of nothing, he actually does not notice in a deeper sense that God exists. Even if one mentions his name at times, calls on him occasionally, perhaps thinks to see him in major decisions, is moved, since it is indeed an impossibility to catch even a glimpse of God without being moved, one is nevertheless somewhat piously deceived, if one therefore believes that it is evident that God exists or that God's existence should not have another distinctness in earthly life, whose meaning is, after all, constantly confused if God is not inferred. We say that it is a pious deception; we call it as beautiful a name as possible. We do not intend to rush in with heated speech against it, even though we wish for everyone that it would become evident to him that God exists with an otherwise decisive certitude.

The person who himself is capable of nothing at all cannot do the least thing without God's help—therefore cannot do the least thing without noticing that there is a God. At times one talks about coming to know God from the history of past ages; one gets out the chronicles and reads and reads. Well, now, that may succeed. But how much time is lost, and how doubtful is often the benefit, how near the misunderstanding that is the sensual person's wonder over what is ingenious!

On the other hand, the one who himself knows that he is capable of nothing at all, he has the desired and indisputable opportunity to experience every day and every moment that God lives. If he does not experience it often enough, then he knows well why that is— namely, that he is in a misunderstanding and believes that he himself is capable of something. When, then, he goes into the Lord's house, he surely knows that God is not there, but he knows as well that he himself is capable of nothing at all, not even of inducing prayer. Therefore, if he is actually moved, God must be there after all.

Alas, there are many who remain otherwise unconcerned about God but who still do not neglect to come into the Lord's house. What a peculiar contradiction: there gather the ones who say, "God is not here, for he does not dwell in a house built by human hands." Then they go home, but God is not at home whatsoever. In contrast, the one who knows himself in the way mentioned knows well that God does not dwell in temples, though he also knows that God is with him at night, when sleep refreshes and when he wakes up in an anxious dream; in the day of need, when, to no avail, he is on the lookout for comfort; in the noise of thoughts, when he listens in vain for a salvific word; in mortal danger, when the world does not help; in anxiety, when he is afraid of himself; in the moment of despair, when he is working out his soul's salvation in fear and trembling. He knows that God is with him in the moment when anxiety, with its lightning-quick swiftness, rushes at him when it already seems too late, and there is no time left to go up to the Lord's house. Then God is with him, faster than the light that pierces the darkness, faster than the thought that drives away the fog, present—ah, yes, present as quickly as only one can be who, indeed, was already present. And if it were not this way, where would the express messenger actually be found, who would go to the worry quickly enough to fetch the Lord? Yet, before he came, more time again would pass! But this is not the case. Only the one who believes that he is capable of something thinks that way.

It is surely true that one can come to know God on the day of joy in exactly the same way, if one otherwise understands that one is capable of nothing at all. But to hold fast to this on the day of joy is just so difficult. When one is most happy, the thought is suddenly tempting: would it not be even more glorious if one were capable of everything oneself? Then the joy takes a false turn, so that it does not work itself up to God but away from him and then…then it is a sign that one needs more practice. Hence, when everything is reeling again, when thought is confused, when memory wants to terminate its service, when what has been experienced approaches one only disturbingly in the form of terror, when even the most honest thought becomes dishonest to oneself through the treachery of anxiety, then one understands again that one is capable of nothing at all. Yet, in and with this understanding, God is immediately present as well. He rules over the confusion and remembers everything that was entrusted to him, for the person being tried has surely done this. In the whirl of spiritual trial, whose outcome seems to be more terrible than death, he has confided in God with the greatest haste what lay especially on his mind—what would eternally annihilate him and transform his life's content into a frightful disappointment, if he himself would forget it and if God in heaven would forget it as well.

He has surely entrusted it to God, until, through God, he fought through the terrors again, resigned himself, and won calmness in trusting God.

If a person whose life was tried in some critical difficulty has a friend, and now, at a later juncture, he cannot manage to retain the past clearly; if anxiety gives rise to confusion; if accusing thoughts work against him with all their might, while he fights back; then he would probably go to his friend and say, "My soul is sick, so that nothing will become clear to me, but I entrusted everything to you; you remember it, so explain the past to me again." Yet, if a person has no friend, then surely he goes to God, provided that he has entrusted something to him, provided that he called God to witness in the hour of decision, since no one else understood him. And, at times, the one who went to his friend was perhaps not understood, perhaps he was what is even more oppressive—disgusted with himself by discovering that the one to whom he had confided his distress had not understood him at all. Even though he had listened to him, he did not sense what was making him anxious but, with mere curiosity, concerned himself with his strange collision with life.

This would never happen with God. Who would dare to venture to think this about God, even if he, because he dares not think it about God, is cowardly enough to prefer to forget God—until he stands before the judge, who condemns him but not the one who truly has God as a witness. For where God is the judge, there is, after all, no judge when God is the witness.

Nevertheless, because a human being comes to know God in this way, it by no means follows that his life becomes easy. On the contrary, it can become very hard and, as stated, become more difficult than the despicable ease of sensual human life. Yet, in this difficulty, his life also acquires ever deeper and deeper meaning. Or should it perhaps have no significance for him that he constantly has God before his eyes? That, while he himself is capable of nothing, he is capable of ever more and more through God—that he is capable of overcoming himself? For, after all, he is capable of this by God's help! Should it have no meaning for him that, ever more and more, he learns to die to the world? That, less and less, he learns to consider the external—what life gives and takes, what is granted to him to accomplish in the external—but to trouble himself over the internal all the more, over an understanding with God, over having to remain in it and, in that, over having to come to know God as one who lets everything serve the good for a person when he loves God? And should this not even have meaning for him by making life's hardship lighter, since, indeed, it is always true that the one who has something to think about and, in turn, is prevented from being occupied with sorrow finds it lighter? Finally, should it not have meaning for him and be a blessed reward that, quite vividly and convincingly, he understood that God is love, that God's goodness surpasses all understanding, and that he is not content with the testimony of others or with a view of the order of the world and of the course of history? For this is probably much greater, but the question is also how one understands it in such a way that one truly benefits from it.

We are not saying that to know God like this—or a kind of sinking into a dreaming admiration and a visionary contemplation of God—should be the only glorious thing. God does not let himself be taken in vain in this way. Just as knowing oneself in one's own nothingness is the condition for knowing God, so is knowing God in this way the condition for a human being to be sanctified by God's assistance and according to his determination. Where God is in truth, there he is always creating. He does not will that, in spiritual softness, a person shall bask in the contemplation of his glory, but, in becoming known by the human being, he wants to create in him a new human being.

Now, if it were the case—let us assume it—that a human being could be improved and developed just as much by himself without knowing God, then I will ask you, my listener, on this assumption: would knowing God not, in and of itself, have the highest meaning? And if a choice could be conceived—that a human being could go just as far by himself as by knowing God—what would you choose? Even in human terms, you would probably choose the latter. For if you could be developed just as much in solitariness, if that were possible, as by coming to know a human being to whom you were drawn by your whole soul, then the fact that you came to know him would, indeed, have the most beautiful meaning in and of itself.

The most beautiful meaning? Alas, no, you surely know that it is otherwise, at least when we talk about God. For to know God is the decisive thing, and, without this knowledge, a human being would become nothing at all, yes, perhaps would scarcely be able to comprehend the first mystery of truth—that he himself is nothing at all, and then, even less, that to need God is his highest perfection.

Chapter Five

WHAT WE LEARN FROM THE LILIES IN THE FIELD AND FROM THE BIRDS OF THE AIR[1]

PRAYER

Father in heaven! From you come only good and perfect gifts. It must also be beneficial to follow the guidance and teaching of whomever you appoint as a teacher to human beings, as a guide to the worried. So, then, grant that the worried may truly learn from the divinely appointed teachers: the lilies in the field and the birds of the air! Amen.

I

This holy gospel is written by the evangelist Matthew, 6th chapter, 24th verse to the end:

No one can serve two masters: for either he will hate the one, and love the other; or else he will hold to the one, and despise the other. You cannot serve God and mammon. Therefore I say unto you, Take no thought for your life, what ye shall eat, or what ye shall drink; nor yet for your

---

1. From Niels Jørgen Cappelørn et al., eds., *Søren Kierkegaards Skrifter*, vol. 8 (Copenhagen: Gads Forlag, 2004), 258–307.

body, what ye shall put on. Is not the life more than meat, and the body than raiment? Behold the birds of the air: for they sow not, neither do they reap, nor gather into barns; yet your heavenly Father feeds them. Are you not much better than they? Which of you by taking thought can add one cubit unto his stature? And why take ye thought for raiment? Consider the lilies of the field, how they grow; they toil not, neither do they spin: and yet I say unto you, That even Solomon in all his glory was not arrayed like one of these. Wherefore, if God so clothe the grass of the field, which today is, and tomorrow is cast into the oven, *shall he* not much more *clothe* you, O you of little faith? Therefore take no thought, saying, What shall we eat? or, What shall we drink? or, With what shall we be clothed? (For after all these things do the Gentiles seek:) for your heavenly Father knows that you have need of all these things. But seek you first the kingdom of God, and his righteousness; and all these things shall be added unto you. Take therefore no thought for tomorrow: for tomorrow shall take thought for the things of itself. Sufficient unto the day *is* the evil thereof.

Who has not known this holy gospel from earliest childhood and often rejoiced at the happy message! And yet, in this, it is not simply a happy message; it has an essential quality that really makes it into a gospel—namely, that it is addressed to those who are worried. Yes, in every line of the compassionate gospel, it is recognizable that the words are not for the healthy, not for the strong, not for the happy, but for the worried. Oh, it is thus recognizable that the cheerful message itself is doing what it says that God does: it receives the worried and cares for them—in the right way. Ah, this is certainly rendered necessary, for every person who has sorrow, and especially the deeper and the longer it penetrates into the soul or the longer it penetrates deeply into it, perhaps he is also tempted impatiently not to want to hear human talk about comfort and hope. Perhaps the sorrowful one is in the wrong; perhaps he is too impatient when it occurs to him that no person can fittingly talk to him about his sorrow. The happy person does not understand him. The strong person, just as he comforts him, seems to rise over him. For the worried person, sorrow merely increases by what he says about it. Therefore, when this is the case, it is best to look around for other teachers, whose talk does not cause misunderstanding, whose encouragement contains no secret reproach, whose glance does not judge, whose comfort does not disturb instead of calm.

The compassionate gospel refers the sorrowful to such teachers, to the lilies in the field and to the birds of the air. With these inexpensive teachers, whom one pays neither with money nor with humiliation, no misunderstanding is possible, because they are silent—out of care for the worried person. And, of course, all misunderstanding results from speech—to be more precise, speech that contains a comparison, especially conversation—as when the happy person says to the worried one: "Be glad." Surely the statement implies as well: "As I am glad." And when the strong person says: "Be strong," then it is implied: "As I am strong." But silence honors the worry and the worried one, like Job's friends, who, out of respect, sat silent with the suffering one and held him in honor. And yet, admittedly, they did look at him! But that—that one person looks at another—again implies a comparison. The silent friends did not compare Job with themselves, not at first. Then they violated the honor (in which they silently had held him) and broke the silence in order to attack the suffering one with speech. But their presence caused Job to compare himself with himself. No person, even if he is silent, can be present in this way—that his presence means nothing at all in terms of comparison. At best, this can be done by a child, who, after all, also has a certain likeness to the lilies in the field and with the birds of the air. How often has not a suffering person experienced and touchingly felt that, when a child is present, no one is really present. And now the lily in the field! Even if it is comfortably off, it does not compare its wealth with anyone's poverty; even if it is carefree in all its beauty, it compares itself neither with Solomon nor with the most wretched. And even if the bird springs lightly into the sky, it does not compare its easy flight with the worried person's heavy gait; even if the bird, richer than the one whose barns are full, does not gather into barns, it does not compare its rich independence with the needy one who gathers in vain. No, where the lily blooms beautifully—in the field; where the bird is freely at home—in the heavens, whose comfort is sought: there is unbroken silence; there is no one present; there everything is sheer persuasion.

Yet, after all, this is only true if the sorrowful one actually pays attention to the lilies and the birds, forgets himself over them and their life, while in this self-surrender before them he, unobserved, learns something about himself by himself—unobserved, for there is, of course, sheer silence, no one present, the worried one exempt from every consciousness except God's, his own—and that of the lilies.

In this discourse, then, let us consider how the worried person, by properly looking at the lilies in the field and at the birds of the air, learns:

to be content with being a human being.

"*Consider the lilies in the field,*" look at them—that is to say, pay close attention to them, make them into an object, not of a cursory sight in passing, but of your contemplation. For that reason, the expression used is one like the priest is in the habit of using in the most earnest and most solemn connection, when he says: "Let us in this time of worship contemplate this and that." So solemn is the call and the invitation. Perhaps many live in the big city and never see the lilies; perhaps many live in the country and indifferently go past them everyday. Alas, how many are there who properly look at them according to the gospel's instructions?

"*The lilies in the field,*" for nothing is said about the rare plants that a gardener raises in his garden and that are eyed by experts. No, go out in the field, where no person cares for the abandoned lilies and where it is ever so recognizable that they are not abandoned. Should this request not be inviting to the worried one, alas, he is also like the abandoned lily, abandoned, misunderstood, overlooked, without human care, until he—by rightly looking at the lily— understands that he is not abandoned.

So the worried one goes out in the field, and he stops beside the lilies. Not like a happy child, or a like childish adult probably does, running about to find the most beautiful one in order to satisfy his curiosity by finding what is rare. No, with quiet solemnity he contemplates them, as they stand there in numerous, multicolored quantity, the one just as good as the other—"*how they grow*." Now, he actually does not see how they grow, for it is indeed as the proverb says: one cannot see the grass grow, but he does, after all, see *how* they grow. Or just because how they grow is inconceivable to him, he sees that there must be one who knows them just as intimately as the gardener knows the rare plants—one who looks after them every day, morning and evening, just as the gardener looks after the rare plants; one who gives them growth. Presumably this is also the same one who gives growth to the gardener's rare plants, except that these plants so easily occasion misunderstanding because of the gardener's help. On the other hand, the abandoned lilies, the common lilies, the lilies in the field, do not occasion any misunderstanding in the observer. For there, where the gardener is conspicuous, where no trouble or no expense is spared in order to urge on the rich man's rare plants, it seems perhaps rather splendid to understand that they grow. But in the field, however, where no one, no one, no one cares for the lilies, how can they grow there? And yet, they do grow.

But then, I suppose, the poor lilies themselves must work all the harder. No, "*they toil not*." It is only the rare flowers that are associated with so much work in order to get them to grow. There, where the carpet is more costly than in the halls of kings, there is no work. As the observer's eyes are amused and refreshed by the sight, his soul shall not be worried by the thought of how the poor little lilies have to toil and to slave in order to make the carpet so beautiful. Only in relation to the products of human ingenuity is it the case that the eyes, while dazzled by the fineness of the work, are filled with tears at the thought of the sufferings of the poor lace maker.

The lilies "*toil not, neither do they spin*." They actually do nothing other than adorn themselves or, even more correctly, be adorned. Just as in the passage from the gospel mentioned earlier, where it is said about the birds, "They sow not, neither do they reap, nor gather into barns," it is referred to man's work in order to provide for himself and his own, so do these words about the lilies (they toil not, neither do they spin) contain a reference to woman's work. The woman remains in the house; she does not go out in order to seek the necessaries of life. She remains at home, sews and spins, tries to keep everything as neat as possible. Her daily pursuit, her diligent work is, after all, closest in relation to adornment. Thus the lily as well: it remains at home; it does not leave the place. But it does not work; it does not spin. It only adorns itself or, even more correctly, it is adorned. Should the lily have any worry, then this would not be about a livelihood, which the bird really could seem to have, since it flies so far and wide around and gathers food. No, in a feminine way, the lily's worry might stand in relation to whether it was very lovely and was adorned. But it is without worry.

For adorned it is; that is certain. Yes, the observer cannot leave it be. He bends down to a particular lily, taking the first that comes along: "*I say unto you, That even Solomon in all his glory was not arrayed like one of these.*" Thus he considers it carefully and closely. And if his mind was restless—alas, as a human mind can be restless— and if his heart was beating violently—alas, as a human heart can beat—he finds rest just in contemplating this lily. The closer he looks, the more he marvels at its beauty and its ingenious formation. For only in relation to products of human ingenuity is it true that, by looking much closer, a person discovers deficiencies and imperfections. It is true that, if you sharpen your sight with a manufactured cut lens, then you see the coarse threads even in the finest human fabric. Alas, it is as if the human being to his own humiliation has made the discovery of which he is proud: when he discovered how to manufacture cut glass so that it magnifies the object, then he discovered, with the help of the magnifying glass, that even the finest human work is coarse and imperfect. But the discovery that humiliated the human being honored God, for no one has ever discovered with the help of a magnifying glass that the lily became less beautiful, less ingenious. On the contrary, it turned out to be more and more beautiful, more and more ingenious. Yes, the discovery honored God, as every discovery must, for only in relation to a human artist is it true that the one who knows him intimately, close at hand and in daily practice, sees that he is not great after all. In relation to the artist who weaves the carpet of the field and effects the beauty of the lily, it is true that wonder rises with proximity, that the distance of worship increases by proximity to him.

So, then, the worried one who went to the lilies with his sorrow stands among them in the field, astonished at the beauty of the lily he is contemplating. He has picked the first that comes along; he has made no choice. It does not occur to him at all that there should be any single lily, no more than any grass in the field, about which it would not be true that not even Solomon in all his glory was clothed as one of them. If the lily could talk, would it not speak to the worried one like this: "Why are you so surprised at me? Should being a human being not be just as glorious? Should it not hold good that all of Solomon's glory is nothing in comparison with what every human being is by being human? Hence, in order to be the most glorious thing he is and to be conscious of this himself, Solomon must strip off all his glory and just be a human being! Should what is true of poor me not be true of being a human being, who, after all, is the wonder of creation!" However, the lily cannot talk, but just because it cannot talk, just because there is sheer silence out there and no one present, that is exactly why the worried one—if he talks and if he talks with the lily—talks with himself. Yes, little after little, he discovers that he is talking about himself, that what he says about the lily he says about himself. It is not the lily who says something; it cannot talk. It is not any *other* person who says something to him, for, after all, with the *other* person the restless thoughts of comparison come so easily and directly. Among the lilies the worried one is only a human being and—is content to be a human being.

For entirely in the same sense as the lily is a lily, so in just the same sense is the person—despite all his worries as a human being—a human being. And entirely in the same sense as the lily, without working and without spinning, is more beautiful than Solomon's glory, so in the same sense is the person—without working, without spinning, without meriting anything—more glorious than Solomon's glory just by being human. Indeed, it does not say in the Gospel that the lily is more glorious than Solomon. No, it says that it is better clothed than Solomon in all his glory. But, alas, in recurring dealings with people, in manifold dissimilarity and its different points of contact, one forgets through the busy or the worried inventiveness of comparison what it is to be a human being. One forgets it due to the dissimilarity between one person and another. But in the field with the lilies, where the sky arches high as over a ruler, free as breathing is out there, where great thoughts about the clouds scatter all pettiness: there the worried one is the *only* person and learns from the lilies what he perhaps could not learn from any *other* person.

"Consider the lilies in the field." How brief, how solemn, how impartial is this language about the lilies. There is not a trace of an intimation. Not in the least is it hinted that there could be any difference among the lilies themselves. All of them, and each single one of them, are talked about. All of them are talked about equally: the lilies. Perhaps one will also think that, after all, it would be odd and too much to expect that human language should involve itself with the difference among the lilies themselves and their potential worries occasioned by the difference. Perhaps one will think: "Such differences and such worries are not worth paying attention to." Let us understand one another. Is this the point—that for the lilies it is not worth paying attention to such worries, in other words, that the lilies ought to be sensible enough not to pay attention to such things? Or is this the point—that it is beneath the human being's dignity to care about the potential worries of the lilies, because the human being is a human being and not a lily? That is to say: are such worries foolish in and of themselves, and therefore not worth paying attention to? Does it not matter who has them, either the simple lilies or the sensible human beings? Or is essentially the same worry something other when the lily has it than when the human being has it, so that it is bad of the lily to worry about such things but not bad of the human being? If, that is, the lilies actually had such worries—and the one speaking was of the opinion that essentially the same worry had great significance in relation to a human being—then of course it would not be wisdom and sympathy but human self-love that could speak so curtly and so dismissively about the poor lilies, so aristocratically about the petty cares of the lilies, so aristocratically by calling them petty cares that are not worth paying attention to. Now suppose that there were differences among the lilies themselves, which, in their little world, corresponded to human differences. Suppose these differences occupied and worried the lilies, just as much as human beings, and then suppose that what was said was really true—that such differences and such worries are not worth paying attention to.

Let us consider this question more closely. And since the worried one who went out to the lilies in the field precisely wished to avoid all comparison with other people, since he was so reluctant that any *other* person should talk to him about his worry, the discourse will respect his worry. I shall not talk about any human being, or about any worried human being, but I prefer to talk *about the worried lily*.

There was once a lily. It stood in an out-of-the-way place by a little stream and was well known by some nettles as well as a couple of other small flowers there in the vicinity. The lily was, according to the gospel's truthful description, more beautifully clothed than Solomon in all his glory, as well as carefree and glad all day long. Imperceptibly and blessedly the time slipped by, like the stream that hums and fades away. But then one day it happened that a little bird came and visited the lily. It came again the next day, was then away for several days, until it came again once more, which seemed peculiar and inexplicable to the lily—inexplicable that the bird did not stay in the same place like the small flowers, peculiar that the bird could be so whimsical. Yet, as it so often goes, so it also went with the lily: it loved the bird more and more precisely because it was whimsical.

This little bird was a bad bird. Instead of putting itself in the lily's place, instead of rejoicing over its loveliness and being happy in its innocent blissfulness, the bird would make itself important by fancying its freedom and by letting the lily feel its lack of freedom. And not only this, but the little bird was also talkative and now talked fast and loose, truthfully and untruthfully, about how in other places there were entirely different splendid lilies in great number, where there was delight and cheerfulness, a fragrance, a flamboyance, a birdsong that surpassed all description. The bird talked in this way, and it liked to end its story with a humiliating remark for the lily— that in comparison with such glory the lily looked like nothing, yes, that it was so insignificant that whether or not it actually could be called a lily was a question.

So the lily became worried. The more it listened to the bird, the more it became worried. No longer did it sleep restfully at night, and no longer did it wake up cheerful in the morning. It felt imprisoned and bound; it found the babbling of the water dreary and the day long. Now, in self-concern, it began to occupy itself with itself and with the circumstances of its life—all day long. "It can, indeed, be nice enough," it said to itself, "now and then, for variety's sake, to listen to the babbling of the brook, but always to hear the same thing day in and day out: that really is all too dreary." "It can, perhaps, be pleasant enough," it said to itself, "now and then to be in an out-of-the-way place and solitary, but like this, throughout one's life, to be forgotten, to be without a community or in community with stinging nettles, which surely are not a community for a lily: that is not to be endured." "And then to look as simple as I do," the lily said to itself, "to be as insignificant as the little bird says I am: oh, why have I not yet come to exist in another place, under other circumstances, oh why have I not yet become a Kaiser's Crown!" For the little bird had related that, among all lilies, the Kaiser's Crown was seen as the most beautiful and was the object of envy for all other lilies. The lily noticed that, badly enough, the worry exhausted it. But then it talked sensibly to itself, albeit not so sensibly that it knocked the worry out of mind, but in such a way that it convinced itself that the worry was right. "After all," it said, "my wish is not some senseless wish. After all, I do not ask for the impossible, to become what I am not—a bird, for example. My wish is only to become a magnificent lily or perhaps even the most magnificent."

During all this, the little bird flew to and fro. With its every visit and its every separation, the lily's unrest was nourished. At last it completely confided in the bird. One evening they agreed that, on the next morning, a change should take place that would put an end to the worry. The little bird came early the next morning. With its beak it pecked the soil away from the lily's root so that it could become free. When this was successful, the bird took the lily under its wing and flew away. The decision was that the bird would fly with the lily to where the magnificent lilies bloomed; after that, the bird would again help it to be planted there. If only by the change of place and the new environment, the lily was supposed to succeed in becoming a magnificent lily in community with the many others or perhaps even a Kaiser's Crown, envied by all the others.

Alas, the lily withered on the way. Had the worried lily been content with being a lily, then it would not have become worried; had it not become worried, then it would have remained standing where it stood—where it stood in all its beauty; had it remained standing, then it would have been the very lily about which the priest talked on Sundays, when he repeated the words of the gospel: "Consider the lily; I say to you that not even Solomon in all his glory was clothed like it." For, after all, one cannot well understand the gospel otherwise, whereas it is lamentable—yes, almost horrifying if true—that an interpreter of Holy Scripture, like the little bird, has found occasion in the text about the lilies to state that the Kaiser's Crown grows wild in that area—as if one could then better understand that the lily surpasses Solomon in beauty, as if one could then better understand the gospel, which, accordingly, does not pertain to the unimpressive lily.

So this is how things turned out for the worried lily, whose worry was to become a magnificent lily or even a Kaiser's Crown. The lily is the human being. The bad little bird is the restless thought of comparison, which wanders far and wide, unceasingly and capriciously, and gathers the unhealthy knowledge of difference. And just as the bird did not put itself in the lily's place, so does comparison do the same by putting the person either in another's place or another in his place. The little bird is the poet, the seducer, or the poetic and seductive in the human being. The poetic is like the bird's speech, true and untrue, fiction and truth. In particular, it is true that difference exists and that there is much to say about it, but the poetic is that passionate difference is the highest, whether in despair or in jubilation. And this is eternally untrue.

In the worry of comparison, then, the worried one ultimately goes so far that, due to difference, he forgets that he is a human being. Then, in despair, he considers himself to be so different from other persons that he even considers himself different from being human, as, indeed, the little bird also thought that the lily was so unimpressive that it became a question whether or not it actually was a lily. But the supposedly sensible answer to the worry is always this: one, after all, does not demand something unreasonable—for example, to become a bird—but only to become this particular thing that one is not, even if this particular thing in turn seems totally insignificant to other worried persons. When, then, comparison with the bird's movement to and fro has incited worry's passion and gotten the worried one torn loose from the ground—that is, from wanting to be what he is intended to be—then it looks out for a moment in which comparison would really come in order to fetch the worried one to the desired goal. But it comes right enough and fetches him, yet only as death fetches a person. It lets the worried one perish in the drifting of despondency.

Now, if the person, not without smiling, can think about the lily's worry about becoming a Kaiser's Crown, think about how it died on the way: oh, then may that person bear in mind that, on the other hand, it is proper to weep when a human being is worried just as foolishly. But, no, how dare I leave this undecided in this way. How dare I earnestly accuse the divinely appointed teachers—the lilies in the field—in this way. No, the lily is not worried like this; that is precisely why we ought to learn from it. And, so, when a human being, like the lily, is content with being a human being, then he does not become sick with temporal worry. And when he does not become temporally worried, then he remains in the place he is assigned. And when he remains there, then it is truthful that he, by being a human being, is more glorious than Solomon's glory.

What, then, does the worried one learn from the lilies? He learns to be content with being a human being and not to be worried about the difference between one person and another person. He learns to talk just as concisely, just as solemnly, just as inspiringly about being a human being as the gospel concisely talks about the lilies. And this is, after all, also human custom and usage precisely on the most solemn occasions. Let us think about Solomon. When he puts on the royal purple, when he sits majestically on his throne in all his glory—now, yes, there is solemn speech in such a way that the one speaking says: "Your Majesty." But when, in the eternal language of earnestness, the most solemn is to be spoken, then it is said: "Human Being!" And we say just the same thing to the lowest person when he, like Lazarus, lies almost unrecognizable in poverty and misery; we say: "Human Being!" And in the decisive moment of a person's life, when the choice of difference is demanded, we say to him: "Human Being!" And in death's decisive moment, when all differences are abolished, we say: "Human Being!" All the same, we are still not talking contemptuously. On the contrary, we say the highest because to be a human being is not lower than the differences but is raised over them. For the essentially equal glory among all human beings is surely not death's sad equality, as little as it is not the essential equality among lilies, which is precisely an equality in beauty.

All *worldly* worry has its basis in the fact that a human being will not be content with being a human being, in the fact that, through comparison, his worried craving is for difference. However, one does not dare to say simply and as a matter of course that *earthly* and *temporal* worry is comparison's invention. That a human being, in the actual moment of need, requires food and clothes is not discovered through comparison. The one who lived alone among the lilies in the field would also discover it. Alas, financial difficulty[2]—or as it is commonly called in a sad plural, financial difficulties—are not exactly an invention of comparison. Still, whether or not comparison, in countless ways, ambiguously works to determine what is to be understood by financial difficulty is something else, whether, after all, there should not be…but, no, the worried one is, indeed, very reluctant that any *other* person should talk to him on the subject, precisely in order to avoid comparison. Well, now, then let us put it in this way: should one still not be able to learn much from the birds pertaining to this care?

---

2. Kierkegaard's word here is *Næringssorgen*. In contemporary Danish, it means "financial difficulty," though it is a more nuanced term than that. The noun *næring* can be translated as either "food" or "business" or "trade," as in the terms *næringsmiddel* ("foodstuff") and *næringsfrihed* ("freedom of trade"), respectively. Hence, when Kierkegaard speaks of *Næringssorgen*, he is alluding to *sorg* ("worry") about putting food on the table and *sorg* about earning a living. Given this ambiguity, one might translate *Næringssorgen* as "worry about sustenance," and I have chosen to do so in certain contexts. At the same time, the contemporary Danish meaning of "financial difficulty" is often sufficient (not to mention fitting in modern English) to encompass the significance of *næring*. After all, the one who has financial difficulties must face the question of providing for the next meal. (Tr.)

We will now consider this: *how the one whom financial difficulty causes worry learns to be content with being a human being by rightly paying attention to the birds of the air.*

"*Behold the birds of the air.*" Look at them, that is to say, pay close attention to them—in the way the fisherman comes in the morning and looks at the line that has been out in the night; in the way the doctor comes and looks at the one who is sick; in the way the child stands and looks when the adult does something that the child has never seen before. Hence, not with a divided mind and distracted thoughts, but with total attention and contemplation—with wonder, if possible—one must pay close attention to the birds. If someone were to say: "One has seen a bird so often; surely that is not remarkable," then he has not understood the invitation in the gospel about the birds of the air.

"*The birds of the air,*" or, as it is said in another place, "the birds under heaven." One sees well the birds down near the earth, sees them on the ground. Yet, if one is to truly benefit from looking at them, one must see them under heaven or yet continually keep in mind that they are home under heaven. If anyone, by always seeing a bird on the ground, could forget that it was a bird of the air, then he would have hindered himself in understanding the gospel about the birds of the air.

"*They sow not, neither do they reap, nor gather into barns.*" How are such things even to be done where the birds find refuge—under heaven, where they live without the foresight of temporality, unacquainted with time, in the moment. The provident person on earth learns from time to take advantage of time, and when he has a full barn from a *past* time and is provided for in the *present* time, then he still takes care to sow again for a future harvest so that he can always have the barn full for *future* time. For that reason, three words are used in order to signify the work of foresight. It is not said concisely, as it is about the lilies: "They toil not." By these three words are indicated the rule of time, which lies at the basis of foresight.

"*Yet your heavenly Father feeds them.*" The heavenly Father, yes, clearly it must be him, if the observer looks at the birds—under heaven. For where the farmer, morning, midday, and evening, comes out and calls the birds together and gives them food, there the observer can easily see the wrong way and believe that it is the farmer who feeds the birds. But where there is no farmer—in the field, where there is no storeroom; under heaven, where the carefree birds soar lightly over forest and lake without sowing, without harvesting, without gathering into barns, and without financial difficulties—surely there it must be the heavenly Father who feeds them.

"He feeds them," or should we perhaps foolishly say what many a foolish farmer has certainly said: "The birds steal," so it is still actually the farmer who feeds the birds because they steal from him. Alas, if a person's mind had sunk so deeply into miserable wretchedness that, in annoyed seriousness, he could think anything like that, how should he well be able to learn loftiness from the birds of the air, how should it help him to look at the birds of the air! And yet, it assuredly should help him, if he only would *look at them*, that is to say, pay close attention to them, learn once again, learn to forget the miserable sensibleness that inhumanly made his soul small. No, the heavenly Father feeds the birds and does so in spite of the fact that they do not sow and harvest and gather into barns. That is to say, the heavenly Father also feeds the creatures that sow and harvest and gather into barns, and therefore the one who supports himself is to learn from the birds of the air that it is, after all, the heavenly Father who feeds him. But the one who owns nothing, nothing at all, on earth; the one who also lives "under heaven" in this way; the one who sadly feels that he is very near in cheerful kinship with the birds of the air: he learns that the heavenly Father feeds them.

"Behold the birds of the air—your heavenly Father feeds them." How concise, how solemn, how impartial is this speech. All the birds are referred to. Not a single one is forgotten in the discourse, which clarifies that the heavenly Father does not forget a single one, he who opens his gentle hand and fills everything that lives with blessing. In the gospel's language about the birds, there is not the least hint of any difference—that one perhaps got plenty, the other scantily; that one perhaps had provision for a little longer time, the other necessities for only a moment; that now and then one had to wait, wait in vain, had to perhaps go to bed hungry. No, only the birds and that the heavenly Father feeds them are talked about.

154

Yet perhaps one says: "If a bird now and then got too little as well, if a bird starved to death too, that would not be such a big deal." How should a human being have the heart to talk in this way about the birds? And is the worry about a livelihood not essentially the same whether it is a bird who has it or a human being? Should a person aristocratically ignore this worry, if it was only the bird who knew it and the human being was exempted? Or was it unreasonable of the bird to be worried about such trivialities, but it was not unreasonable of the reasonable human being to be worried about the same trivialities? Suppose the life of birds was not unfamiliar with difference as regards to livelihood, which, for the worse, is in force among human beings. Suppose this difference occupied and worried the birds in the same way that it worries human beings?

Correspondingly, when this is assumed, then the discourse can indeed avoid what the worried one does with such reluctance—let *another* person talk to him about his worry. Then the discourse can remain out in the field with the birds and talk about the *bird's worry*.

There was once a wood pigeon. In the scowling forest, where wonder lives shuddering among the upright solitary trees, it had its nest. But not far away, where smoke rises up from the farmer's house, lived some of its more distant relatives—some tame pigeons. It met with a couple of these more often. That is, it sat on a branch that bent out over the farmyard; the two tame ones sat on the ridge of the roof, yet the separation was not so great that they could not exchange their thoughts with one another in conversation. One day they talked together there about the days' events and about making a living. The wood pigeon said, "Until now I have my livelihood in such a way that I let each day have its trouble, and in that way I go through the world." The tame pigeon had listened closely, not without feeling a certain indulgent movement through its whole body called strutting. Then it answered, "No, we do otherwise. With us—that is to say, with the rich farmer with whom we live—one's future is made secure. When harvest time comes, then I or my mate, one of us, sits up on the roof and looks out. Then the farmer carts in one load of seed after the other, and when he has carted in so many that I cannot count any longer, then I know that there is store enough for a long time. I know that by experience." When it had spoken like this, it turned, not without a certain arrogance, to its mate sitting by, as if it would say: "Is it not true, my little mate, that we two have our future guaranteed?"

Then the wood pigeon came home. It thought further about this situation. Immediately, it occurred to it that it would be a great comfort to *know* in this way that one's livelihood had been made secure for a long time. On the other hand, it really was miserable to constantly live in uncertainty, so that one never dares to say that one *knows* one is provided for. Therefore it thought, "It would be best to see if it should not be possible to collect a greater supply, which you could have lying in one or another well-secured place."

The next morning it woke earlier than usual and now was so busy gathering things together that it scarcely had time to eat or to eat its fill. But it was as if a fate hung over it, so that it could not get leave to accumulate wealth. For every time it had accumulated a little supply and stashed it in one or another of the supposedly safe places, it was gone when the wood pigeon came to look for it. In the meantime, there was no essential change with regard to making a living. Every day it found its food as before, and so far as it took a little less for itself, then it was because it wanted to accumulate and because it did not give itself time to eat. Otherwise it had its ample livelihood as before. And yet, alas, it had undergone a great change. It far from suffered actual need, but it had gotten a *notion* of need in the future. Its restfulness was lost—it had gotten *worry about sustenance*.

From now on the wood pigeon worried. Its feathers lost their play of colors; its flight lost its lightness. Its day passed in a fruitless attempt to accumulate wealth; its dreams were the impotent plans of the imagination. It was no longer happy. Indeed, it was almost as if the wood pigeon became envious of the rich pigeons. Each day it found its food, had enough to eat, and yet it was as if it did not have enough to eat, because it hungered for a long time in its worry about sustenance. It had trapped itself in a snare in which no fowler could trap it—in the idea, wherein only the free can be trapped. "Very true," it said to itself, "very true, each day when I get as much as I can eat, then admittedly I have my livelihood. The great supply I want to accumulate I could never eat at one time, and in a certain sense one cannot eat more than one's fill. Yet, after all, it would be a great comfort to be freed from this uncertainty in which one becomes so dependent." "It may well be," it said to itself, "that the tame doves pay dearly for their secure livelihood; it may even be that, in the end, they have many worries, which I have been free from until now. However, this security for the future is constantly on my mind. Oh, why did I ever become a poor wood pigeon and not one of the rich pigeons!" Then it realized that worry was exhausting it, but then it talked sensibly to itself, albeit not so sensibly that it banished worry from its thoughts and put its mind at rest. Rather, it talked in such a way that it convinced itself that its sorrow was justified: "Of course, I am not asking for something unreasonable," it said, "or for something impossible. Indeed, I am not asking to become like the rich farmer, but only like one of the rich pigeons."

At last it devised a scheme. One day it flew over and sat on the ridge of the farmer's roof between the tame pigeons. Then it noticed that there was a place where the two flew in. It flew in as well, for surely the storeroom had to be there. But then the farmer came in the evening and shut the pigeon cote; immediately he discovered the strange pigeon. It was then placed in a little compartment until the next day, when it was killed—and freed from worry about sustenance. Alas, the worried wood pigeon had not only trapped itself in worry, but it also trapped itself in the pigeon cote—unto death.

Had the wood pigeon been content with being what it was—a bird of the air—then it would have had its livelihood. Then the heavenly Father would have fed it. Then, on the terms of uncertainty, it would have remained where it came from, there where the upright solitary trees are in melancholy harmony with the cooing trill of the wood pigeon. Then it would have been the one about whom the pastor spoke on Sunday, when he repeated the words of the gospel: "Behold the birds of the air: for they sow not, neither do they reap, nor gather into barns; yet your heavenly Father feeds them."

The wood pigeon is the human being—but, no, let us not forget that the discourse has only allowed the wood pigeon to be picked on out of respect for the worried person. Yes, as when a princely child is brought up and there is a poor child who is punished instead of the prince, so has the discourse let the wood pigeon suffer everything. And it has willingly put up with it, for it very well knows that it is one of the divinely appointed teachers, from whom we are to learn. But at times a teacher also does this so that he himself shows the error he wants to warn against. The wood pigeon itself is carefree; indeed, it is actually what the gospel talks about.

Therefore the wood pigeon is the human being. When he, like it, is content with being a human being, then he understands what he learns from the bird of the air—that the heavenly Father feeds him. Yet, if the heavenly Father feeds him, then he is, of course, without worry about sustenance. Then he lives not only like the tame pigeons with the rich farmer, but he lives with the one who is richer than all. He actually dwells with him, for then heaven and earth are God's house and property. In this way, the human being dwells with him indeed.

This is the point: to be content with being a human being, to be content with being the lowly one, the creature who can just as little support himself as create himself. In contrast, if the human being wants to forget God and sustain himself, then we have worry about sustenance. It is certainly praiseworthy and pleasing to God that a person sows and reaps and gathers into barns, that he works in order to find food. Yet, if he wants to forget God and to think that he sustains himself by his work, then he has worry about sustenance. The richest man who has ever lived—if he forgets God and thinks that he sustains himself, then he has worry about sustenance. For let us not talk foolishly and pettily by saying that the rich one is free from worry about sustenance, the poor one not. No, only that person is free who, content with being a human being, understands that the heavenly Father feeds him. And, of course, the poor can do this just as well as the rich.

Worry about sustenance is, therefore, the trap in which no external power, no *actuality*, can trap a person but in which only he—the rich as well as the poor—can trap himself when he will not be content with being a human being. That is, if he will not be content with this, then what is the more he demands? The more is: to be himself his own providence for all his life or perhaps only for tomorrow. And if he wants that, then he goes—*ingeniously*—into the trap, the rich just as well as the poor. Thus he wants to wall himself, as it were, in a little or large area, which is not to be an object of God's providence and the supportive care of the heavenly Father. Perhaps he does not notice, before it is too late, that he lives in this walled security—in a trap. He is doing to himself what the farmer did to the wood pigeon: he locks the cage and believes that now he is secure, yet, on the contrary, he is now trapped. Or, what can also be said in another way, he is now certainly locked out from the care of providence and abandoned to worry about sustenance. For only the one who has locked himself in with his many or few goods is trapped and locked out in the thought of supporting himself. And only that person is free and without worry about sustenance who—with many or few goods, indeed, in poverty—understands that the heavenly Father feeds him. And the one who, with presumptuous reason, has ingeniously locked himself and thereby trapped himself has, just like the wood pigeon, trapped himself unto death in a spiritual sense.

Already, then, it emerges that worry about sustenance arrives by comparison—here, namely, in the terrible way that the human being does not want to be content with being a human being, but wants to compare himself with God, wants to have security by himself, which no human being dares to have. And, therefore, a security that is precisely—worry about sustenance.

Yet, in other ways, it also emerges that worry about sustenance arrives by comparison, insofar as worry about sustenance is not today's actual need, but the idea of a future one. Comparison, then, always arrives when the human being does not want to be content with being a human being. After all, the poor bird of the air compared himself with the rich birds; by this comparison it discovered worry about sustenance. What it is to hunger and to find food—it had known that for a long time. But worry about sustenance it had not had before. And now since these classifications—rich and poor—are not separated from one another by an engulfing abyss, then they, on the contrary, touch one another in continual association and constant disagreement about borders. And, further, since the different consideration comparatively changes the classification, then this third thing of comparison can, therefore, be extremely different. In the worry about sustenance, then, the worried one will not be content with being a human being, but wants to be or wants to have difference, wants to be rich, wealthy, well-off, fairly secure, and so on. He does not look, namely, at the bird of the air—away from the difference of human life—but he looks at others in comparison, at difference, and his worry about sustenance is a relation of comparison.

And even if, in comparison, the worried person does not fix his attention on degrees of difference in this way and call *that* worry about sustenance which is more a worldly worry (for, after all, to be worried about having just as much as this one and that one is not worry about sustenance)—even if this is not the case, comparison nevertheless lies at the root of worry about sustenance, insofar as this is not the expression for actual but imagined need. Why is it that the bird does not have worry about sustenance? From this— that it does not compare one day with the other, that it lets each day have its own trouble in accordance with the word of the gospel. But even if the worried one does not compare his circumstances with any other person's and, in this sense, "keeps himself untainted by the world" (alas, comparison is perhaps one of the most pernicious kinds of defilement)—however, when he anxiously compares the one day with the other, when, on the day he has a rich livelihood, he says: "But tomorrow!" And when, on the day he has hardly a thing, he says: "Tomorrow it will be even worse"—indeed, then he compares.

Alas, if such a worried person were to read this, would he not become impatient with the speaker! Gladly would I do as a pagan wise man did out of respect for the object of his discourse: he veiled his countenance. Out of respect for the worry, I would gladly cover my face in this way, so that I see no one but only talk about the bird of the air. After all, it was by this kind of comparison that the wood pigeon discovered worry about sustenance in worry's sorrowful interaction with itself from day to day. It certainly confessed that it had its livelihood, but uncertainty saddened it. It seemed that it became so dependent—on God. It grieved over the fact that it never dared to talk about the next day with certainty. Oh, but let us not forget that, in a godly sense, it dared to talk with certainty when it said: "The heavenly Father will surely feed me tomorrow." Let us not forget that it talked with greatest certainty about tomorrow if, with true sincerity, it limited itself to only giving thanks for today! Is this not the way it is? If there was a loving girl whom the beloved came and visited, if she then said to him, "Will you also come again tomorrow?"—then there really was some worry in her love. But if, without mentioning tomorrow, she threw her arms around his neck and said, "Oh, thank you for coming today"—then, indeed, she would be entirely at peace about today. Or if there were two girls, and one said to the beloved, "Will you also come again tomorrow?" and the other said, "Oh, thank you for coming today"—which of these two would be most convinced that the beloved would come again tomorrow?

A useless and perhaps vain dispute is conducted often enough in the world when the poor person says to the rich one: "Yes, you are a lucky fellow; you are free from worry about sustenance." I wish to God that the poor person would really understand how the gospel thinks so much better of him, equally and more lovingly. The gospel truly does not let itself be deceived by the illusion of visible difference, does not let itself be deceived by taking sides with any person against any other person, with the rich against the poor or with the poor against the rich. Not having to worry about sustenance is, in truth, a pleasing thing in God's eyes. Should, then, the rich have this advantage as a matter of course and the poor be shut out? Ah, no. If the poor person would really be content with being a human being, and learn from the birds of the air to be without worry about sustenance, then he would simply elevate himself over apparent difference. At times, perhaps, he would be prompted to say: "That poor rich person, he has financial difficulties after all." For what person can rightly and truly say these words: "I have no financial difficulties"? If the rich person points to his riches as he says that, I wonder if there is a trace of sense in his words! Does he not outrageously contradict himself in the same moment—he who holds fast to his worry about sustenance while he holds it away by his treasures and, because of his worry about sustenance, closely attends to his treasures and adds to them! Yes, if the rich person would give away all of his possessions, cast his money and worry about sustenance away and really say, "I have no financial difficulties"—only then would there be sense in his words. And, of course, this is the poor person's situation, when he, who owns nothing and thus has nothing to give away, casts worry about sustenance upon God and says, "I have no worry about sustenance." Is it not the case that the riches must go away, if it is to be at all possible for his words to make sense? If one who owned an expensive collection of glorious medications that he used every day were to say while he pointed at the medications, "I am not sick"—would this not be an outrageous contradiction!

Often enough in the world, the strife of discontented comparison about dependence and independence, about the happiness of being independent and the difficulty of being dependent, is carried on between one person and another person. And yet, neither human language nor thought has ever devised a more beautiful symbol of independence than—the poor bird of the air. And yet, no speech can be more strange than to say that it must be so heavy to be—as light as the bird! To be dependent on one's treasures is dependence and heavy slavery; to be dependent on God, entirely dependent, is independence. The worried wood pigeon badly feared to become entirely dependent on God. Therefore it ceased to be independent and to be the symbol of independence; it ceased to be the poor bird of the air, which is entirely dependent on God. Dependence on God is the only independence, because God has no weight. Only earthly things, and especially earthly treasures, have that. Thus the one who is entirely dependent on him, he is light. It is the same with the poor person, when he, content with being a human being, looks at the bird of the air, looks at it—under the heavens. Indeed, the praying one always looks up; the praying one—no, he, the independent person, is indeed one who gives thanks.

To be content with being a human being. The discourse was about this and about how the worried one learns this from the lilies in the field and from the birds of the air—how, on the other hand, comparison caused worldly worry and how it caused worry about sustenance. It is certainly a human being who has spoken, but, aided by the lilies and the birds, he has spoken about the lilies and the birds. That he is the one speaking, then, implies no comparison with any other human being, as if he had any advantage by being the speaker. No, here again is equality in relation to the divinely appointed teachers: the lilies in the field and the birds of the air.

II

If it is the case that care and worry—especially the longer and the deeper they penetrate into the soul, or the longer they penetrate deeply into it—also become fixed all the more firmly, then it is certainly beneficial to think of a diversion for the worried one, albeit not in the sense that, often enough and foolishly enough, the world recommends: the wild hurrying or noisy anesthetization of vain diversion. When, then, the worried one feels forsaken and yet, by a self-contradiction in his cares, does not want sympathy, because, pinching and pressing, this comes too near to him, so that he winces almost just as much at the sympathy as at the pain—then one leads him into the surrounding country, where nothing reminds him of his cares, not even of sympathy, where sympathy, as it were, is and yet is not; surrounding country that has sympathy's touching nearness, insofar as it is somewhat present, and sympathy's soothing distance as well, insofar as it is not sympathy after all.

In this way, the gospel read earlier leads the worried one out into the field, into the surrounding country, which will weave him into the great common life and win him for the great fellowship of existence. Yet, since worry has now become firmly fixed in him, the important thing is to do something to get his eyes and mind away from it. For this purpose, the gospel recommends two useful movements. Because when the worried one "looks at the lily" at his feet, then he looks *down*; and when he looks down at the lily, then he does not see the worry. It is certainly possible that, in his cares, he also normally walked bent over, looked down, and saw his worry. However, if he looks down in order to see the lily, then he looks away from the worry.

And when he, in accordance with the gospel's directions, looks at the bird of the air, then he looks *up*; and when looks up at the bird, then he does not see his worry. It is certainly possible that, in his cares, he also looked up at times, when he sent a worried sigh up to God and, with the gaze of worry, looked after it. Yet, if he looks up to see the bird of the air, then he looks away from the worry. Because worry has fixed itself in a person's soul, how else should one signify it than by saying that it is like when the eyes *stare*. When the eyes stare, then they look out ahead without changing, look constantly at one thing, and yet actually do not see, because, as science explains, they see their own seeing. But then the doctor says: "Move your eyes." And thus says the gospel: "Divert your mind, look down at the lily, and stop staring at the worry; look up to the bird and stop staring at the worry." Hence, when the tears cease while the eyes look down at the lily, is it not as if it were the lily who is wiping away the tears! When the wind dries the tears from the eyes that watch the bird, is it not as if it were the bird who is wiping away the tears! Even when the loved one sits with a person and wipes the tears away if the worried one keeps on crying, is this actually wiping the tears away? But the one who gets the worried one to stop crying—he wipes the tears away.

This is what one dares to call a *godly diversion*, which does not excite impatience and feed worry like the worldly and vain diversion, but it diverts, calms, persuades the more one devoutly gives oneself over to it. Human shrewdness has invented so much in order to entertain and to divert the mind, and yet the law for this kind of invention defies this fruitless endeavor by a self-contradiction. The art is itself in the service of impatience. More and more impatiently it teaches to condense the many diversions into the transitory moment. The more this shrewdness increases, the more it works against itself, since it turns out that the diversion will continually cover a shorter and shorter time as the art increases. Let us take an example, where the vain and worldly diversion rightly shows itself as flimsy and self-contradictory as it is. The pyrotechnist, to be sure, wants to entertain the eyes and to divert the mind by lighting the artificial blazing evanescence in the darkness of night. And yet, if it only is to last an hour, then the onlooker becomes tired; if it is to be only a little moment between each new ignition, then the onlooker becomes tired. The task of shrewdness is, therefore, to finish it off faster and faster; the highest, the most perfect thing will be to burn the whole lot in a few minutes. But if diversion is determined to pass the time, then, to be sure, the self-contradiction shows itself clearly: the diversion, when it has become most perfect in its art, can only while away a couple minutes—the more frightfully it becomes very clear how long the time is. For a fee, then, one buys admission to be able to wait, in the tension of impatience, for the entertainment's beginning, and in the same moment it is over. As that conjuring flare shines and, in a moment, vanishes into nothing, so must be the soul of the person who only knows such diversions: he despairs over the length of time in the minute of diversion.

Ah, how different it is with the godly diversion! For have you ever seen the starry sky, and have you really found any more reliable sight? It costs not a thing, so there is no urge of impatience. Nothing is said about tonight, still less about 10 o'clock on the dot. Oh, no, it waits on you, if, in another sense, it does not wait on you—as the stars now shine sparkling in the night, so have they, unchanged, endured for millennia. As God makes himself invisible—alas, perhaps that is why there are many who never really become aware of him—so does the starry sky make itself just as insignificant—alas, perhaps that is why there are many who never really see it. The divine majesty refuses the visible, the falsely prominent. The solemnity of the starry sky is more than unassuming; oh, but if you stand still, if you perhaps go out there without purpose, where it is visible year in and year out, unappreciated, if you by chance came to a stop and looked upward—then you surely have experienced it. The persuasion rises with each moment. More and more movingly it tricks you out of the temporal; what should be forgotten sinks into deeper and deeper oblivion with each moment that you continue to contemplate it. Oh, godly diversion, you do not faithlessly and treasonously call yourself a diversion, while, with empty noise and with hurrying impatience, you really are in league with boredom, into which you plunge a person deeper and deeper—by means of diversion. No, you are in league with the eternal, and therefore only the beginning is difficult. When it is made, then the stillness of diversion grows and, with it, the persuasion.

So it is with everything in nature. It seems insignificant and yet is so infinitely rich. If you, therefore, go hastily on your way on an important errand, and the way leads you along the seashore, then be on your guard. Well, true, there is no one who calls out to you; no invitation is heard, neither the advertiser's voice nor the cannon's thunder as with human entertainment. And yet, be careful; hurry, lest you—by standing still a moment—perhaps discover the persuasion of monotony in the waves of the sea. And so it is too with the lily in the field and with the bird of the air. If you quickly go "to your farm, to your business, to your wife," and a bird flies past you, then do not look after it. For if you look after it, then perhaps you are bound to stand far too long to watch the bird. If it is time for work, wherein one is to attend to his labor, if the harvester nimbly sharpens his scythe and swings it against the grain, then let him not look to the lily at his feet, lest it persuade him so that both the lily and the harvester remain standing.

But the worried one, he is not warned. On the contrary, the gospel encourages him to go out in the field and to stand still there in order to contemplate the lily and the bird, so that the godly diversion can bring the gazing eyes to move, can divert the mind in which worry has become fixed. Contemplate the lily; see how it stands lovely at your feet. Do not refuse it. After all, it waits for you to delight in its beauty! See how it moves to and fro, shakes off everything in order to continue being lovely! See how it is refreshed by the wind, exercises as it were, so that it—calm once again—might rejoice in its happy existence! See how gentle it is, always willing to joke and to play, while it nevertheless conquers and endures the most violent storm by giving in! Contemplate the bird of the air; see how it flies. Perhaps it comes from far away, from distant, distant happier parts of the country—so they do exist, after all. Perhaps it flies away, far away to distant, distant parts of the country—so let it take your worry with it! And this it does without noticing the burden, if only you continue to look after it. See how it now stands still. It takes a rest—in that infinite space; therefore it takes a rest where no rest seems possible! See how it finds its way, and yet what way through all the hardships and adversities of human life is as difficult, as incomprehensible as "the bird's mysterious way through the air"! Accordingly, where no way seems possible, there is a way and a way to be found.

However, since all diversion is not only to pass the time, but is to serve primarily to give the worried one something else to think about, then we will now consider how the worried one—who looks at the lily and at the bird, with the help of the godly diversion, which disperses the mists—gets to think about something else than worry, how he, by forgetting the worry in the diversion, is led to consider:

how glorious it is to be a human being.

"Wherefore, if God so clothe the grass of the field...shall he not much more clothe you, O you of little faith?" Thus God clothes the grass, or the grass is clothed. The stalk's beautifully formed frame, the delicate lines of the blades, the lovely shades and mixtures of colors, the whole richness, if I dare say so, of ribbons and bows and frills—all of this belongs to the lily's clothing, and it is God who clothes it in this way. "Shall he not much more clothe you—you of little faith?" *"You of little faith."* This is the admonition's gentle reproach; when love does not have the heart to talk severely to the one who is wrong, this is how it talks. It wags the finger reproachfully at him and says, "You of little faith," but says it so gently that the reproach does not hurt, does not sadden, does not dishearten, but instead elevates and makes one bold. If a disheartened child came to an adult and asked for something that the child had anyway and had had for a long time but was not aware of it and therefore thought that it ought to ask for it in order to get it instead of giving thanks for having it, I wonder if the adult, gently reproaching, would not say: "Yes, my dear child, you will be sure to get it tomorrow, you of little faith!" That is to say, when you come to understand better one day, then you will be sure to appreciate that you have it, that you have had it forever, and that it therefore was a kind of indiscretion—although forgivable, indeed, charming for a child—that you asked for what you had.

But if this is the meaning of the words, then, indeed, it is said in the gospel not only that the human being is clothed like the grass but that he is clothed far more gloriously. With the help of the added reproach ("you of little faith"), it is actually said: would God not *have* clothed you much more? Thus the words are not about the new dress one would like to have for Sunday or about the new tailcoat one needs so greatly, but about the indiscretion that would forget how gloriously the human being is clothed from God's hand. Would there not even be an inconsistency in the words, if the first was that the lily is more gloriously clothed than Solomon, and the last is: "Shall God not much more clothe you?" Would there not be an inconsistency, if the last part was to be understood as referring to the few pieces of clothing a person may need?

Indeed, let us consider this matter correctly. It is said that the lily is clothed, but, after all, this is not to be understood in this way—that the lily's existence is one thing and that to have clothes is something else. No, its clothing is to be a lily. Now, in this sense, would not the human being be far more gloriously clothed? Or would the human being, out of worry about articles of clothing, be allowed to entirely forget its first clothing? O you of little faith, you misguided person with your imaginary need, O you worried one, even if your need was so great that you totally would forget how God has clothed you—learn from the ant to become wise but learn from the lily how glorious it is to be a human being, how gloriously you are clothed, you of little faith!

Worldly worry always seeks to lead a person out into the petty unrest of comparison, away from the sublime rest of simple thoughts. To be clothed means, then, to be a human being—and thus to have good clothes on. Worldly worry occupies itself with clothes and with a multiplicity of clothes: is it, then, not like the sorrowful child who comes and asks for what it has and to whom the adult says with a gentle reproach: "You will be sure to get it tomorrow, you of little faith!" Really, the gospel first wants to remind even a needy person not to forget how gloriously he is clothed by God. And, in the next place, we are all admittedly a long way from being needy in a serious and more strict sense; yet, on the other hand, we are all perhaps only too inclined to be worried about clothes and ungrateful enough to forget the first thoughts—and the first clothing. But by contemplating the lily the worried one is reminded to compare his clothing to the lily's—even if poverty has clothed him in rags.

Should not, then, the invitation to learn from the lilies be welcome to everyone, just as the reminder is useful to him! Alas, in the weekday and worldly life of comparison, those great, uplifting, simple thoughts—those first thoughts—are more and more forgotten, perhaps entirely. The one human being compares himself with others; the one generation compares itself with the other. And, in this way, the heaped-up pile of comparisons rightly overwhelms an actual human being. As ingenuity and the pressure of business increase, there come to be more and more in each generation who tiresomely work their whole lives far down in the low, underground regions of comparison. Indeed, just as miners never see the light of day, so do these unhappy ones never come to see the light—those uplifting, simple thoughts, those first thoughts, about how glorious it is to be a human being. And up there on the high places of comparison, smiling vanity plays its false game, deceiving happy persons so that they get no impression of those sublime, simple thoughts, those first thoughts.

To be a ruler—yes, what conflict is not carried on about that in the world, now about ruling over kingdoms and lands, over thousands, or yet about having one person to rule over—besides oneself, which no one is worried about ruling over. But out in the field with the lilies, where every person who quietly and solitarily nurses on the milk of those first thoughts, is what every person is according to divine purpose: he is a ruler. Indeed, no wants to be a ruler out here! To be a prodigy—ah, what efforts are made in the world in order to reach this envied status, and how envy bends over backwards in order to hinder it! But out in the field with the lilies, where every person is what God has made him to be, is the marvel of creation. Yes, no one wants to be the prodigy out there! The better individual would probably smile; the crowd's strident laughter would mock the fool who could talk about being a ruler and a prodigy in this sense.

And yet, what can the Preacher mean by the words: "that God separated the human being in order to see if he would regard himself as a beast"? For the one who, having been isolated, does not want to be calmed, comforted, upbuilt, uplifted by the absolute nature of those first thoughts, the one who wants to abandon himself to disappearing and perishing in the meaningless service of comparisons: he regards himself as a beast, whether or not he was distinguished or lowly in terms of comparison. Therefore God singled out the human being, made every human being into this distinct entity, who is encompassed by the absolute nature of the first thoughts. The individual animal is not isolated, is no absolutely distinct entity; the individual animal is a number and belongs under what the most famed pagan thinker[3] has called the animal category: the herd. And the human being, who, in despair, turns away from those first thoughts

---

3. This is a reference to Aristotle. (Tr.)

in order to plunge himself into the herd of comparisons: he makes himself into a number; he regards himself as a beast, whether or not he was distinguished or lowly in terms of comparison.

However, the worried one is isolated with the lilies, far away from all human or, perhaps rather, inhuman comparisons between person and person. Yes, not even the one who has turned his back on the greatest city in the world has left behind such a motley crew, such a confused, immense multiplicity, as the one who turned his back on inhuman comparisons—in order to compare, like a human being, his clothing with the lily's.

By clothing, then, must be understood what it is to be a human being, as has been shown. Already a pagan[4] has been aware of this. He did not know to attribute everything to God, but, as he ingeniously says, he thought that it was the soul itself that like a weaver wove the body—which is the human being's clothing. And now he praised the ingenious creation of the human body in perfect wonder, its glory, with which surely no plant and no animal could sustain any comparison. In this thought, he let it, as it were, grow into what is the human being's distinction: the upright walk. And while he imitated it by thinking, his mind was uplifted. He wondered over the ingeniousness of the human eye and even more over its look, for an animal has an eye but only the human being has a look. Therefore, in the beautiful mother tongue of that man of wonder, the human being is called the upright one, albeit in such a way that a twofold meaning is suggested—first, that the human being's figure is upright like a straight tree trunk and next that the upright one accordingly directs his look upward. Even if the straight tree trunk rises higher, the upright one, with this help of vision, proudly lifts his head higher than the mountains. Thus the human being stands upright—commanding. And that is why it seemed so glorious to that man of wonder that the human being was the only creature that has hands, for, after all, the ruler holds out his hands when he gives orders.

And so again, in many ways, that man of wonder knew how to speak gloriously about the human being's glorious clothing. Perhaps

---

4. Here, and on into the next paragraph, Kierkegaard is referring to Socrates. (Tr.)

many have talked more learnedly, more insightfully, more scientifically about this, but, amazingly enough, no one has talked with more
wonder than that noble wise man, who did not begin with doubting
everything but, on the contrary, when he had become older, when he
had seen and heard and experienced much, he properly began to
wonder, to wonder over that *simple first thought*, which otherwise no
one cares about in this way, not even the scholars and the scientists,
because, after all, they are not occupied with this subject—as an
object of wonder. But this language about wonder really is imperfect
insofar as it assigns clothing to the soul. Indeed, most imperfect of all
is the foolish talk that entirely forgets that solemn first thought, so
that it, without further ado, thoughtlessly takes being a human being
as if it were nothing, takes it in vain and immediately begins the foolishness about pieces of clothing, about trousers and jackets, about
purple and ermine. Yet, the talk that is certainly aware of that first
thought but not truly aware of God is also imperfect. No, if the
human being is to compare himself with the lily, then he must say:
"All that I am by being a human being—that is my clothing; none of
it is caused by me, but it is glorious."

Now, how should we talk about this glory? It could be talked
about a long time without finishing, but this is not the place for that.
Instead, then, let us talk briefly and gather everything into one simple phrase, which Scripture itself uses with authority: *God created the
human being in his own image*, but, again, for the sake of brevity let
us only understand this verse with regard to one thing.

God created the human being in his own image. Should it not
be glorious to be clothed in this way! In order to praise the lily, the
gospel says that it surpasses Solomon in glory: should it not be
infinitely more glorious to be like God! The lily does not resemble
God; no, it does not do that. It bears a little hint by which it reminds
one about God; it is a witness, since God, after all, has not let himself
be without witness in any created thing. But the lily is not like him.

When the human being sees his image in the mirror of the
ocean, then he sees his own image. But the ocean is not the human
being's image, and when he moves away, the image is gone: the ocean
is not the image and cannot even hold on to the image. What is the
cause of this, except that the visible figure, precisely by its visibility, is

powerless (just as the bodily presence makes it impossible to be omnipresent). Thus it cannot reproduce itself in another so that this retains the image when the figure is gone. But God is spirit, is invisible, and the image of invisibility is, again, obviously invisible. In this way, the invisible creator reproduces himself in the invisibility that is the definition of spirit, and God's image is exactly the invisible glory. If God were visible, well, then there would be no one who could be like him or be his image. For the image of everything visible *does not exist* and among everything visible there is nothing, not even a leaf, that is like another or is its image. If that were the case, then the image would be the object itself. But since God is invisible, then no one can *visibly* be like him. That is just why the lily is not like God, because the lily's glory is the visible, and therefore the pagan really spoke imperfectly about the human being even as he spoke most perfectly about the glory of the human body, yet said nothing about the fact that the invisible God created each human being in his own image.

To be spirit is the human being's invisible glory. When, then, the worried one stands out in the field surrounded by all the witnesses, when every flower says to him, "Remember God!" then he answers, "I will be sure to do that, little children; I will worship him—something you poor little ones cannot do." The upright one is, therefore, a worshiper. The upright walk was the distinguishing mark, but to be able to kneel down in worship is even more glorious. And the whole of nature is like the great staff of servants who remind the human being, the ruler, about worshiping God. It is this that is expected, not that the human being is to come and to take control, which is also glorious and assigned to him, but that the human being is to praise the creator in worship—something nature cannot do, because it can only remind the human being about doing that. To be clothed like the lily is glorious; to be the upright ruler is even more glorious; to be nothing by worshiping is most glorious!

To worship is not to rule, and yet worship is precisely that by which the human being is like God, and to be able to worship in truth is the virtue of the invisible glory above all creation. The pagan was not aware of God and, therefore, sought likeness in ruling. But the resemblance is not like this. No, on the contrary, then it is taken in vain. Truly, it is only within the infinite difference, and, for that reason, to worship is likeness with God, since it is the virtue above all creation. The human being and God are not literally like one another, but inversely like one another: not until God has infinitely become the eternal and omnipresent object of worship and the human being always a worshiper, not until then are they like one another. If the human being wants to be like God by ruling, then he has forgotten God, then God has gone away, and the human being pretends to be a ruler in his absence. And so it was in paganism; it was the human being's life in the absence of God. That is why paganism was really like nature, and the most grim thing that can be said about it is: it could not worship. Even that noble, simple wise man, he could fall silent in wonder, but he could not worship. But to be able to worship is no visible glory; it cannot be seen. And yet, nature's visible glory yearns; it pleads with the ruler. Without ceasing, it reminds the human being that he finally must not forget—to worship. Oh, how glorious to be a human being!

Truly, then, the worried one, in his diversion among the lilies, got something entirely different to think about than worry. He came to properly consider how glorious it is to be a human being. If, in worldly fashion, he forgets it again in the crossroads of comparisons and the collision of differences between one human being and another, then it is not the fault of the lilies. On the contrary, then it is because he also has forgotten the lilies, forgotten that there was something he should learn from them and something he finally must remember to do for them. That is, if one were to characterize worldly worry with a single word, then must one not say: it is a worry about clothes, a worry about how things look. Just for that reason, the highest exaltation over worldly worry is the upbuilding by the invisible glory—that to worship is the glory and also a service that is shown to the lily.

So it is with the instruction of the lilies. Now we will contemplate how the worried one learns from ***the bird*** how glorious it is to be *a human being*.

"*The bird sows not, neither does it reap, nor gather into barns.*" The bird is without worry about sustenance. But is this, then, actually a perfection? Is it a perfection to be carefree in danger, when one does not know it, does not know it exists? Is it a perfection to take certain steps—because one is walking blindly? Is it a perfection to walk securely—because one is sleepwalking? No, to be more truthful, one must surely say that it is a perfection to know danger, to confront it, to be awake—that it is a perfection *to be able* to have worry about sustenance precisely in order to overcome this fear, thereby letting faith and trust drive out the fear. Then one is truly without worry about sustenance in the carefreeness of faith. For only faith's carefreeness is, in a divine sense, the gliding whose beautiful yet imperfect symbol is the easy flight of the bird. After all, that is why we even talk about rising on the wings of faith, and this stroke of the wings is, in a divine sense, the perfect one. The bird's wing-stroke is only a faint and pictorial hint. Yes, as when the weary bird with flagging wing-strokes slowly sinks to the earth, so is the proudest flight of even the most daring bird only an earthly and temporal feebleness in comparison with the high gliding of faith—a slow sinking in comparison with faith's easy rising.

We will consider this more closely. Why does the bird not have worry about sustenance? Because it only lives in the moment. Therefore nothing eternal is in the bird. But is this really a perfection? On the contrary, how does the possibility of worry about sustenance come to light? In this way—that the eternal and the temporal touch one another in consciousness or, rather, that the human being has consciousness. In consciousness, he is eternally far, far beyond the moment. No bird flew so far away, and yet precisely thereby he becomes aware of the danger that the bird does not suspect. Because eternity came into existence for him, tomorrow came into existence too. Through consciousness, he discovers a world that the most traveled bird does not know: the future, and when this future is taken back into the moment by consciousness, then the worry that the bird does not know is discovered. For however far away it flew and from however far it flew back, it never flew to the future, nor did it ever return from there.

Since, then, the human being is consciousness, he is the place where the eternal and the temporal touch one another, where the eternal breaks into the temporal. That is why time can seem long to a human being, because he is conscious of the eternal and measures

174

the moments with it. But time never seems long to the bird. The human being, therefore, has a dangerous enemy that the bird does not know: time, an enemy, yes, an enemy or a friend, whose demands and whose dealings the human being cannot evade, because he is conscious of the eternal and, accordingly, must measure it. The temporal and the eternal can painfully touch one another in many ways in the human consciousness, but one of the points of contact that the human being especially shrinks from is, of course, worry about sustenance. Its distance from the eternal seems so infinite; there is not talk about filling up time with some glorious feat, some great thought, some uplifting feeling, as in the hours that one says are being lived for eternity. Alas, no, there is only talk about lowly work in hours that, quite literally, are lived for temporality—the poor work to procure the condition for temporal existence. But to be able to have worry about sustenance is a perfection and is but depression's expression for the loftiness of the human being. For as high as God raises up, he also presses down as deep. But, then, that means that to be pressed down deep is also to be raised up high. And as God lifted the human being high over the bird by consciousness of the eternal, so again he pressed him down, if you will, under the bird by his acquaintance with care, the earthly, lowly care that the bird does not know. Oh, how dignified it seems that the bird does not have worry about sustenance—and yet, how much more glorious to be able to have it!

From the bird, then, the human being can certainly learn. He can also call the bird his teacher, but not in the highest sense. Just as the bird lacks worry about sustenance, so, by the way, is a child like that too. Ah, who would not gladly learn from a child! And when the imaginary or the actual need in the worry makes a person despondent, dejected, downcast: oh, then he will gladly be soothed, gladly learn from a child, gladly call the child his teacher in his calm, grateful mind. But if the child were to begin to speak and to talk didactically, then the adult would gently say: "Yes, my dear child, that is something that you yourself do not understand." And if the child were not silent, then the adult would say that he was a naughty child, and perhaps not hesitate to paddle—the teacher, and perhaps rightly do so. Why? Because the adult is the child's teacher in an earnest sense, while the child is the adult's teacher only in the beautiful sense of playful earnestness. But, then, it is truly a perfection to be able to have worry about sustenance, and the human being is by far the superior, even if he gladly learns from the bird in accordance with the gospel's instructions and calls the bird his teacher in his calm, grateful mind.

Hence, since it lacks worry about sustenance, the bird certainly serves as an example for the human being, and yet the human being, in being able to have worry about sustenance, is far more perfect than the example. That is why the human being never dares to forget that the one who sent him to the bird of the air—as if for a first, a childlike education—that precisely he is the actual example in earnestness and in truth, that precisely he serves as the true, the essential example of human perfection. For when it is said that the birds have nests and the foxes have holes, but the Son of Man has no place to lay his head, a state that is indeed more helpless than the bird's is being talked about, and it is conscious of this as well. But then, with the consciousness of being without a nest, without a place to reside, yet—to be without a care. Indeed, this is the divine example of the exalted creation; this is the human being's divine example. This example does not exist for the bird, nor for the child. But, for that reason, it is a perfection to be able to have worry about sustenance. Is that not the case? Do we really say that it is a perfection in woman that, as the weaker sex, she does not go into war; that it is a perfection in the prisoner that he cannot come out and risk his life; that it is a perfection in the person sleeping that he sleeps through the danger! Or do we really say that it is a perfection to be excluded from daring to call the exalted one his example! But why, then, is worry about sustenance talked about in another way, as if the woman were happier because it is rather the man who must acquire things; as if the prisoner were happy because the state provides for him; as if the one who slept himself into wealth were happy; or as if the one who perhaps by wealth was prevented from calling the God-man his example were happiest of all!

Yet, the worried person cannot speak this way out there with the bird. He looks at the bird; he entirely forgets his imagined worry. He even forgets the actual need for the moment. He is relieved; yes, he is upbuilt. But if the bird dared to say a didactic word, then he would certainly answer: "My little friend, this is something you do not understand." That is, he would become aware that it is a perfection to be able to have worry about sustenance.

"The bird sows not, neither does it reap, nor gather into barns." In other words, the bird does not work.

But, then, is this a perfection—to not work at all? Is it a perfection to steal the day's time in the sense that sleep steals the night's? For it is true that the bird wakes early to sing, and yet...yet, when it has slept, it actually wakes in order to dream. Even its most beautiful song is, after all, a dream about an unhappy love. And, in this way, it sleeps and dreams life away—a happy or a melancholy jest. But is this really a perfection? Is it a perfection in the child that it plays and becomes tired—like the man of work—and sleeps and plays again! It is lovable in the child—ah, who would not gladly learn from a child! And when, at times, the adult does his work well but receives no joy from it, yes, is perhaps even annoyed: oh, then he would gladly be comforted by the child, gladly learn from it, gladly call the child his teacher in his calm, grateful mind. But, if necessary, he would not hesitate to reprimand—the teacher. And the adult would do that with justification. Why? Because the adult is the child's teacher in an earnest sense, and the child is the adult's teacher only in the beautiful sense of playful earnestness.

The bird does not work. In an innocent sense, its life is vain, and, in an innocent sense, it even takes its life in vain. Is this a perfection? Then, I suppose, it is also an imperfection in God that he works, that he works up to now! Is it a perfection in the bird that, in hard times, it sits and starves to death and knows nothing at all about what to do, that, confused, it lets itself fall to the earth and die? Of course, we do not normally talk in this way. When the sailor lies down in his boat and lets things take their course in the storm and knows nothing at all about what to do, we do not talk about his perfection. But when the brave sailor knows how to steer, when he works against gale and storm through ingenuity, strength, and perseverance, works himself out of danger, then we admire him. When, late in the morning, one person sees another who gets up late, sluggish and yet hungry, waiting to get food by chance, we do not praise this, do we? But when, early in the morning, we see the good worker, or when we do not see him but see that he has already been there early in the morn-ing, that the fisherman has already been out to his nets, that the cat-tleman has already moved the cows, then we praise the fisherman and the cattleman. To work is the human being's perfection. By working the human being is like God, who, after all, also works. And so when a human being works for food, then we would not foolishly say that he feeds himself. Rather, precisely in order to recall how glo-rious it is to be a human being, we would say that he works with God for food. He works with God; therefore, he is God's coworker. See, the bird is not that. The bird gets enough food, but it is not God's coworker. The bird gets food just as a wanderer subsists out in the country, but the master calls the servant who works for food his coworker.

The bird does not work—and yet it gets food. Is this a perfec-tion in the bird? After all, we normally say that the one who will not work does not get food either, and God says this as well. Hence, when God makes an exception for the bird, it is because the poor bird can-not work. The poor bird cannot work: we do not talk like this about a perfection, do we? To work, then, is a perfection. It is not, as one inadequately represents it, that it is a hard necessity to have to work in order to live. Oh, no, it is a perfection not to be a child all one's life, not to have parents who always care for one, both while they are liv-ing and when they are dead. The hard necessity—which, at the same time, still precisely acknowledges the perfection in the human being—is needed only in order to force the one who will not freely understand that it is a perfection to work and, therefore, will not gladly go to work. That is why, even if there was not a so-called hard necessity, it would still be an imperfection if a person were to cease to work.

It is said that, with regard to royal medals, some wear the medal to honor themselves, others honor the medal by wearing it. So let us refer to a great example, who rightly can be said to have honored work in actuality: the Apostle Paul. If anyone else was bound to have wished the day was twice as long—then surely it was Paul. If anyone else could have easily allowed himself to be supported by the congregations—then surely Paul. And yet, he preferred to work with his own hands! Just as he humbly thanked God that he enjoyed the honor of being scourged, persecuted, insulted; just as he, humble before God, proudly calls his fetters a point of honor, so he found it also an honor to work with his own hands—an honor so that, in relation to the gospel, he dared to say with the beautiful modesty of a woman and the holy modesty of an apostle: "I have not earned a cent from preaching the word; I have not married money in becoming an apostle"; an honor so that, in relation to the lowliest human being, he dared to say: "I have not been exempted from any of life's hardship, nor have I, through favor, been barred from any of its advantages; I also have had the honor of working with my own hands!"

Oh, in the despairing, glittering or utterly miserable wretchedness of worldly comparisons, where one knows just as little about what honor is as about what perfection is, there one talks cravenly or treacherously in another way. But out with the bird, there the worried one understands how glorious it is to work or, in doing so, how glorious it is to be a human being. For it does not make a difference whether or not one works for riches, another for bread, one in order to gather an abundance, another to defend himself against poverty. No, what makes a difference is—that the bird cannot work.

Hence, in this diversion with the bird, the worried one did, after all, get something entirely different to think about than his worry. He came to rightly consider how glorious it is to work, how glorious it is to be a human being. If he forgets it again during work, oh, then perhaps that sweet teacher, the bird, will fly by him and remind him about what he forgot...if only he looks at the bird.

III

If it is the case that care and worry, especially the longer and the deeper they penetrate into the soul, or the longer they deeply penetrate into it, also give the strength of worry, then it is indeed likely that the consoling friend is bound to get the worst of it in the struggle. That is to say, it is like a struggle that is conducted between worry and consolation; they look at one another as enemies in the same sense as sickness and medicine. They cannot tolerate, cannot stand one another, at least not immediately. And who has not experienced what powers worry can give a human being, how he both cunningly and powerfully knows to defend himself against consolation, how he can do what no leaders can otherwise do: in the same moment that worry's defense is disarmed, to lead the very defense freshly into battle at the same time! Who has not experienced how the passion in worry can give a human being strength in thought and in expression, of which the consoling person is almost afraid. Who has not experienced that scarcely anyone desiring something can talk as seductively in order to win over another as a worried person can persuasively talk in order to convince himself—and the person consoling him— that once again there is no consolation! But when this is so, when a worried person has become the stronger—perhaps at times only by what appears to be obstinacy, at times, alas, actually the stronger by the magnitude of sorrow—is there nothing at all to do then? To be sure. One seeks then to persuade the worried one to familiarize himself with another's suffering. And the one who himself will not receive consolation from another person is often willing to take part in another's sorrow, to become worried about another and on another's behalf. Thus is the struggle forgotten. While the worried one wistfully suffers with another, the mind is appeased. The one who armed himself against consolation is now disarmed; the one who was like a fortified city is now like a city that has surrendered. By grieving with another he finds consolation for himself.

In this way, the abovementioned gospel leads the worried one out to the field, and he who—alas, at once weak and strong—thought of himself as victor over all human consolation now stands in an entirely different environment. Consider the grass, *"which today is, and tomorrow is cast into the oven."* Ah, what a fleeting life, oh sheer vanity! And even if it is not cast into the oven, "the sun is no sooner risen with a burning heat, but it withers the grass, and the flower thereof falls, and the grace of the fashion of it perishes." So the grass withers, and no one knows its place anymore. No, no one, no one knows its place anymore; no one asks about, and if anyone asked, it would, after all, be impossible to find it. What a miserable existence—to be, to have been, and then to be forgotten in this way!

Consider the bird! *"Are not two sparrows sold for a penny?"* Alas, one sparrow has no value at all; there must be two if the buyer is to give a penny. What a change—so cheerful, so happy...and now not worth a penny! This is how the bird dies! Oh, how hard to die in this way! And then, when the first swallow comes again in the spring, all will greet it with joy, but whether it is the same one who was here last year—indeed, no one knows that. No one knows it, and therefore no one can recognize it either!

Oh, in nature, there is certainly beauty, and there is youthfulness and loveliness; there is certainly a manifold and teeming life, and there is delight and jubilation. But there is also something like a deep, inscrutable sorrow, which not one of them out there ever suspects. And just this—that no one suspects it—is the sadness in the human being. To be so lovely, to blossom in this way, to flutter about so, to build with the beloved in this way: to live in this way—and to die in this way! Is this life, or is it death? When the sick person is at the decisive moment of his illness, one asks: is it life or death? But, then, one admittedly sees the perilousness as well; one sees it before one's eyes and sees it with a shudder. But, in nature, where everything smiles invitingly and seems secure! And yet, the life of nature is always in this tension: is it life or death? Is it life, which, eternally young, renews itself? Or is it corruptibility, which insidiously hides itself so that it will not be seen for what it is—the corruptibility that precisely thereby swindles with the charm of the lily and field, with the carefreeness of the bird, while, underneath, it only waits to reap the deception with insidiousness. Thus is the life of nature: short, rich with song, blossoming, but death's prey in every moment. And death is the stronger.

So the worried person sinks into sadness. It grows dark before his eyes. The beauty of nature fades. The bird's song becomes as silent as the grave. Corruptibility wants to swallow everything— and yet he cannot forget the bird and the lily. It is as if he would save them from death by his recollection, save them for a longer life by recollecting them. The sadness lies just in this. But is death's earnest reminder of death really more gripping than that of sadness, which is contained in this expression: is it life or death? What death says is more terrible: it is finished. But what sadness says is more gripping: is this life or death? The shape of death is more horrifying—he, the pale reaper. Yet, when death is clothed like the lily in loveliness, it is more gripping. Thus the worried one, gripped by sadness, is weakened like a woman, pacified like a city that has surrendered—and consolation finds a way in.

Now, then, let us bear in mind how the worried one, through his sadness with the lily and the bird, in an earnest sense gets something to think about other than worry, how he is led to rightly consider:

What blessedness is promised in being a human being.

"No one can serve two masters: for either he will hate the one, and love the other; or else he will hold to the one, and despise the other. You cannot serve God and mammon." But are these also the words of the gospel? Certainly. The abovementioned gospel about the lilies in the field and about the birds of the air begins in this way. But is such talk, then, directed to a worried person? Certainly. It is a worried person to which a high value is ascribed; the language is stern for just that reason. The sterner the authoritative person speaks to a worried person, the more he concedes to him as well; the more he demands of the worried person, the more he concedes to him as well: the sternness and the demand are precisely the concession. Is this not how it is? When the doctor sees that it is over for the sick person, then one can immediately hear it in the doctor's voice. He speaks in passing, in an undertone, evasively. Yet, on the other hand, when the doctor sees that there is much to do, especially that the sick person can do much himself, then he speaks sternly: the sternness is precisely the concession. What is heard at times is, therefore, by no means doubtful—that a person, instead of begging for gentleness, has said, "Oh, just speak to me sternly." And the gospel's stern language, is it not like when an earnest father says to the child: "I want to hear no whining"? Is, then, the earnest father lacking in sympathy for the child's worries? Far from it. He just wants the worries to be legitimate, while he is like a consuming fire toward foolish worries. So also with the gospel. The lilies and the birds can be talked about in many ways. They can be talked about gently, movingly, ingratiatingly, affectionately, almost like a poet. And a person even dares to talk in this way, dares to persuade the worried one. Yet, when the

gospel speaks authoritatively, then it speaks with the earnestness of eternity, then there is no more time to be suspended dreamily over the lily or to look at the bird with longing—a brief, instructive allusion to the lily and the bird, but then the eternal demand of earnestness. And as it is true about diversion—that, in an alleviating sense, it gives the worried one something else to think about—so is it true about the stern talk of earnestness, which, in earnestness and in truth, gives the worried one something else to think about than to worry.

"*No one can serve two masters.*" And here there can be no doubt about which two are being talked about. Therefore the worried one was led out into the field, where there can be no talk about human relations, about serving a ruler as an assistant or about serving a wise person as a devotee, but only about serving God or the world. Nature does not serve two Gods; there is no vacillation or double-mindedness. The poor bird of the air and the humble lily of the field do not serve two masters. Even if the lily does not serve God, it is nevertheless in service to God's honor alone; it does not spin, does not work. It does not want to be anything at all itself or to have something for itself, to have it as spoils. The bird does not serve two masters. Even if it does not serve God, it exists for God's honor alone, sings to his praise, does not demand at all to be anything itself. Thus is everything in nature. This is its perfection but also its imperfection, because for that reason there is no freedom. The lily, which stands in the open, and the free bird of the air are, nevertheless, bound in necessity and have no choice.

"*Either he will hate the one, and love the other; or else he will hold to the one, and despise the other.*" Therefore love of God is hatred of the world, and love of the world is hatred of God. Therefore this is the immense point of contention—either love or hate. Therefore this is the place where the most terrible struggle conducted in the world is to be fought, and where is this place? In a person's heart. Perhaps that is why the one who sensed the struggle in his own heart often came to a standstill; he stood and sought a diversion by contemplating the raging of the elements and the battle of nature, because he felt that this struggle is really like a game, since it does not matter if either the storm or the sea wins. Yes, why do the storm and the sea actually quarrel, and over what do they actually fight! It is different with the terrible struggle in a person's heart. Whether the fight is over millions or a penny, the fight is about this—that a human being will lovingly prefer it to God. The most terrible struggle is the one that struggles over the highest. The penny seems to be nothing; the struggle seems to be about nothing—about a penny—and yet there is a dispute over the highest. And everything is at stake. Or is it more offensive to a girl that the beloved prefers a thousand talents, rather than a penny, to the possession of her?

Now, is not the sadness forgotten over the terribleness of the struggle? But then we come to the glorious thing—*that the human being is granted a choice*. What blessedness is not promised hereby for the one who chooses rightly!

A choice. My listener, if you talked year in and year out, do you know how to express anything more glorious in a single word, how to name anything more glorious than a choice, to have choice! For it is certainly true that the sole blessing is really to choose rightly, but, to be sure, choice itself is ultimately the glorious condition. What does the girl care about a list of all her fiancé's excellent qualities when she herself may not choose? And, on the other hand, whether others praise her beloved's many perfections or name his many flaws, what more glorious thing does she know to say than when she says: "He is my heart's choice!"

A choice—yes, it is the glorious treasure, but it is not intended to be buried and hidden. For an unused choice is worse than nothing, is a snare in which the person trapped himself like a slave who did not become free—by choosing. It is a good that you can never get rid of again; it stays with you, and, if you do not use it, it is like a curse. A choice, not between red and green, not between silver and gold—no, a choice between God and the world. Do you know anything greater to place together for a choice! Do you know any more overwhelming and humbling expression for God's complaisance and indulgence toward the human being than that, in a certain sense, he puts himself in the straight line of choice with the world, just so that the human being can choose. That God, if language dares to put it this way, proposes to the human being, that he—the eternally strong one—proposes to the weak human being. For, after all, the strong one always proposes to the weaker one. Yet, how insignificant is even the girl's choice between suitors in comparison with this choice between God and world. A choice, or is it perhaps an imperfection in the choice under discussion that the human being not only *can* choose but *must* choose? Would it not, then, be to the young girl's benefit if she had an earnest father who said, "My dear girl, you have your freedom; you may choose yourself, but you must choose." Would it be more useful to her that she had the choice but coyly picked and picked and never came to choose!

No, the human being *must* choose. For, in this way, God holds himself in honor, while he also has fatherly solicitude for the human being. If God has humbled himself to be the one who *can be chosen*, *so must* the human being choose as well—God does not let himself be mocked. Therefore it is truly like this—that if a human being avoids choosing, then this is the same as the presumption of choosing the world.

The human being is to choose *between God and mammon*. This is the choice's eternally unchanged condition; there will be no way out—not in all eternity. No one will be able to say: "God and mammon, they are not so unconditionally different; one can unite both parts in the choice." This is not to choose. When there is a choice between two things, then wanting to choose both is precisely "to draw back unto perdition" from the choice. No one will be able to say: "One can choose a little mammon and then God too." No, oh no, it is presumptuous blasphemy if someone dares to think that only the one who requires much money chooses mammon. Alas, the one who requires a penny without God, who wants to have a penny for himself, he chooses mammon. One penny is enough; the choice is made; he has chosen mammon. That it is little makes no difference, after all. If one rejects one girl and chooses another, and this other one is as nothing in comparison with the first one, who was like the Queen of the Orient—has he therefore not rejected the girl? If one buys a toy with the money with which he could buy the highest, has he therefore not refused to buy the highest? Is this really an excuse—that, instead of buying the highest, he has bought what is nothing at all, even in the sense of nothingness! If anyone does not understand this, then it is because he does not want to understand that, in the moment

185

of the choice, God is present, not in order to look on, but in order to be chosen.

Therefore, it is deceitful talk if someone wants to say that God is so sublime that he cannot stoop to being chosen, since then the choice is abolished. And if the choice is abolished, because God is not present as the object of choice, then mammon is not an option either. It is precisely God's presence in the choice that posits the choice between God and mammon. And God's presence in order to be chosen is that which gives eternal earnestness to the decision of the choice, for it is never to be forgotten what has been granted to a human being, nor how he chose. But that kind of talk is blasphemy, which would prevent God from letting himself be chosen on account of sublimity, which seeks to get God set aside in a polite way, which haughtily wants to be knowledgeable about the difference that, so to speak, should be involved with being God, instead of being content with what God wills. To place a crown of thorns on his head and to spit on him is blasphemy, but to make God sublime in such a way that his existence becomes a fancy, becomes meaningless—that is blasphemy as well.

Therefore the human being must choose. Terrible is the struggle, the struggle in a human being's heart between God and the world. To have the choice is the glorious perilousness of the condition. But what, then, is the blessedness that is promised when one chooses rightly? Or, to say the same thing, what is the human being to choose? He is to choose God's kingdom and his righteousness. He is to give up everything for this. It does not matter at all if this everything is either millions or a penny, for even the one who chooses a penny instead of God chooses mammon. Only when the human being, although he works and spins, is nevertheless entirely like the lily, who does not work and does not spin, only when the human being, although he sows and reaps and gathers into barns, is entirely like the bird, who does not sow and does not reap and does not gather into barns, only then does he not serve mammon.

"Seek first the kingdom of God, and his righteousness; and all these things shall be added unto you."

The kingdom of God is, therefore, the name of the blessedness that is promised to the human being. It is at this name and before this name's glory that all of nature's beauty and its peace fade and vanish. While sadness, bent over, sees nature sink into corruption, the eyes of faith aspire to the invisible glory. Just as Noah, saved, saw a world's destruction, so does sadness see the destruction of the visible world, sees everything founder whose life is united with visibility. But faith, saved, sees the eternal and the invisible.

Seek first the kingdom of God—"*which is above in heaven.*" The bird does not seek anything. However far it flies, it is not seeking. It is migrating and being drawn; its longest flight is a migration. But the one in whose soul the eternal is lodged—he seeks and aspires. If visibility does not deceive him, as the one who grasps the shadow instead of the form is deceived; if temporality does not deceive him, as the one who constantly waits for tomorrow is deceived; if the temporary does not deceive him, as the one who delays on the way is deceived; if this does not happen, then the world does not quiet his longing. Only repulsively, then, does it help him to seek further, to seek the eternal, the kingdom of God, which is above in heaven. The bird never reached so high; the one who flies highest still flies under heaven.

Seek first the kingdom of God—"*which is within you.*" The flower does not seek anything. Should it get something, this something must come to it. It waits, and even this is without longing. But the one whom visibility did not deceive by anesthetization; the one whom temporality did not lull to sleep by monotony; the one whom the temporary did not bewitch by fantasy—the world does not satisfy him. It only helps him by painfully keeping him awake and waiting, to seek, to seek the eternal, the kingdom of God, which is within a human being. The flower does not know such an invisible, inner glory. What it has, it must give away immediately; the bud quickly breaks the silence, gives away the glory, which is also soon gone.

Seek *first* the kingdom of God. This is the order, but it is also the order of inversion, for that which first presents itself to the human being is precisely everything visible and corruptible, which tempts and allures, indeed, wants to imprison him in this way—that he comes to seek God's kingdom last or perhaps never. But the right beginning begins with seeking God's kingdom first; therefore it begins just by letting a world come to an end. Oh, difficult beginning!

We cannot specifically profess how this earthly life begins for a human being; it is begun unnoticed, and the human being evades the difficulty of the beginning. But living for the eternal begins with first seeking God's kingdom. There is no time to accumulate wealth beforehand, no time to think over this question; there is no time to lay up a penny beforehand, for the beginning is: to seek God's kingdom first. If a human being has something that he knows must be done first each morning, then he also knows that there can be no thought about anything else that could be done beforehand; he knows that, even if he did what was prescribed at another time of day, it would be wrong, since this should be done first. And yet, it would certainly be possible that such an earthly task could even be done at another time of day, but, in relation to seeking the kingdom of God, it holds true that it must be done first. That is unconditionally the only way in which it can be done. The one who will think to do it at some other time of day, at some other hour, has not even come to the beginning, which, after all, is to seek it first. The one who does not seek it first does not seek it at all. It does not matter—it absolutely does not matter—whether he goes and seeks a penny or millions.

"*The kingdom of God, and his righteousness.*" The first term is described by the last, for the kingdom of God is "righteousness, peace and joy in the Holy Spirit." Here, then, is no talk about setting out on a quest in order to find the kingdom of God, for the kingdom of God is righteousness. If you had every aspiration of desire in describing, if you could calm the world's otherwise busy capital city, because all listened to your discourses, you have not thereby come to the kingdom of God, not a single step closer, for the kingdom of God is righteousness. You can live so hidden in the great mass of people that not even the authorities know your name and your whereabouts; you can be the only one, the absolute ruler over all kingdoms and lands: you have not thereby come to the kingdom of God, not a single step closer, for the kingdom of God is righteousness.

But what, actually, is righteousness? It is to seek the kingdom of God first. Righteousness is neither extraordinary abilities, for when righteousness is demanded of you, it is precisely of such abilities that righteousness will call you to an accounting; nor is it earthly obscurity, for no human being is so lowly that he can do no wrong. And just as no coin is too little to bear the image of the emperor, so is no human being too lowly to bear God's image. Neither is righteousness power and might, for no human being stands so high that he is higher than righteousness, so that he would need to lay down his crown in order to find occasion to practice righteousness. Righteousness is to seek the kingdom of God first. If you give all persons their due but forget God, are you then practicing righteousness? Is this way of practicing righteousness not like when the thief does what is right and just with the money he has stolen? To forget God—is this not like stealing your whole existence? But if you seek God's kingdom first, before anything else you do, then you will not practice unrighteousness toward any person, and you will not forget God either. For how would one be able to forget that which is constantly the first thing one seeks.

The beginning is to seek the kingdom of God first, and righteousness is to seek the kingdom of God first. See, that is why we said that setting out on a quest to find the kingdom of God is not the point. On the contrary, you remain in the place where you are and that is assigned to you; every search away from this place is already unrighteousness. And if it were the case that you first should seek somewhere else before you begin to seek the kingdom of God, then, after all, it would not be true that you *first* should seek the kingdom of God. While, then, the world of visibility founders and sinks into corruption, you nevertheless remain in your place, and the beginning is to seek the kingdom of God first. From an earthquake the human being runs away to safer places; before a forest fire the human being flees to areas without vegetation; from a flood the human being makes for higher points. Yet, if it were the case that the world of visibility wholly sank into corruption, then, of course, the human being would have no other place to which he could flee. And that is precisely why he remains on the spot and seeks the kingdom of God first. If the whole world of visibility does not founder, then, for him, the kingdom of God would be like another place upon the earth. Then he would set out on a quest to find the kingdom of God, and, in his fruitless and self-contradictory search, he would either realize that he is not finding it, or he would be deceived if he has found it.

But when a human being seeks the kingdom of God first—*"then all these things shall be added unto to him."* They shall be *added* unto him, for there is only one thing that is to be *sought*: the kingdom of God. Neither the thousands of wealth nor the penny of poverty is to be sought; this shall be added unto you.

"All these things," or as another gospel writer has it—"the rest." Oh, what blessedness the kingdom of God really must be! For if you take everything that the bird and the lily have, everything that glorious nature has, and think of all this together, then it is included in the saying: "the rest," "all these things." Therefore, God's kingdom must be valued so highly that, in relation to it, one can talk about that in this way—with so little esteem, so negligently, so sublimely. When a man has gathered a very big fortune but perhaps still has some outstanding debts that he could claim, then he says: "No, the rest doesn't matter." When a man called to a high position in a foreign land travels away and takes everything that is dear and important to him, but there are still many things behind, then he says: "No, I will not take all of these things with me." Alas, all of what the bird has is this "rest"; all of the lily's glory is "all these things." Oh, what blessedness the kingdom of God must be!

Yet, in his sadness, the worried person indeed went out with the lily and the bird to think about something other than worry; he came to consider what blessedness is promised in being a human being. So he let the lily wither and its loveliness become unrecognizable; let the leaf fall to the ground and the bird fly away; let it get dark over the fields: the kingdom of God does not change with the changes of the year. So let the rest be needed for a long or a short time; let it come abundantly or scarcely. Let all these things have their moment when they are discarded or possessed, their moment as a subject of conversation until, in death, they are eternally forgotten: the kingdom of God is still that which is to be sought first but also that which is to endure through all eternities until the end. And "if that which is done away *was* glorious, much more that which remains *is* glorious." And if it was hard to live in want, then, after all, to die to want is only an easier separation!

Chapter Six[1]

1 CORINTHIANS 8:1

"But Love Upbuilds"[2]

All human speech about the spiritual, even the divine speech of Holy Scripture, is essentially figurative speech. And this is quite in order or in the order of things and of existence, since the human being—even if he is spirit from the moment of birth—nevertheless does not become conscious of himself as spirit until later and, in this way, has previously lived out a certain part of his life in material-mental fashion. But this first part, then, is not to be cast away when the spirit awakens, just as little as the spirit's awakening—as opposed to the material or the material-mental—announces itself in a material or a material-mental way. On the contrary, the first part is taken over by the spirit and, used in this way, provides a basis; *it becomes the figurative [det Overførte]*.

Therefore, in a certain sense, the spiritual person and the material-mental person say the same thing. And yet, there is an infinite difference, since the latter does not intuit the mystery of figurative words, while he nevertheless uses the same words, albeit not figuratively. There is a world of difference between the two: the one has made the transition or let himself be *carried over [føre over]* to the other side, while the other remains on this side. But there is a connection between them—that both use the same words. The one

1. From Niels Jørgen Cappelørn et al., eds., *Søren Kierkegaards Skrifter*, vol. 9 (Copenhagen: Gads Forlag, 2004), 212–26.
2. In this case, I have significantly departed from the King James Version ("But charity edifieth"), so as to bring the opening quotation (*Men Kjerligheden opbygger*) in line with the rest of Kierkegaard's text.

in whom the spirit has awakened does not therefore forsake the visible world; although conscious of himself as spirit, he is still constantly in the sensible world and is himself visible to the senses. In this way, he also remains in the language, except that his language is the figurative kind. But, of course, figurative words are not brand-new words; they are, on the contrary, words that are already given. Just as the spirit is invisible, so is its language a secret as well, and the secret lies just in this—that it uses the same words as the child and as the simple one but uses them figuratively, by which the spirit refuses to be the material or the material-mental but does not refuse that in a material or a material-mental way. The difference is by no means a striking difference. Therefore we rightfully look on it as a sign of false spirituality to flaunt a striking difference—which is just materiality. In contrast, the spirit's essence is the quiet, whispering secret of the figurative—for the one who has ears to hear.

One of the figurative expressions that Holy Scripture frequently uses figuratively is: *to upbuild* [*at opbygge*]. And it already is—yes, it is very upbuilding to see how Holy Scripture has not grown tired of this simple saying, how it does not brilliantly seek after variety and new expressions but, on the contrary, renews thinking in the same saying. This is the true nature of spirit. And it is—yes, it is very upbuilding to see how Scripture succeeds in signifying the highest with that simple saying and in the most profound way. It is almost like that miracle of the feeding with the limited supply, which, by the blessing, nevertheless stretched out amply and left an abundance. And it is—yes, it is upbuilding, if someone prospers by humbly being content with the word of Scripture, instead of being busy with making new discoveries that will busily supplant the old; by gratefully and profoundly assimilating what has been handed down by the fathers, in order to establish a new acquaintance with…the old acquaintance. As children, we all surely have often played the game of "Stranger." In truth, just this is earnestness: spiritually understood, to be able to continue this upbuilding jest in earnestness, to play "Stranger" with the old acquaintance.

To upbuild is a figurative expression. But now, with this secret of the spirit in mind, we will see *what this saying means in plain speech*. "To upbuild" is formed from "to build" and the adverb "up," on which the accent therefore must fall. Everyone who upbuilds does build, but not everyone who builds upbuilds. When, for instance, a man builds a wing on his house, then one does not say that he upbuilds a wing but that he builds *on*. This "up," therefore, seems to indicate the direction in height, the direction upwards. Yet this is not the case either. If, for instance, a man raises a building that is sixty feet high even twenty feet higher, then we still do not say that he upbuilt the house twenty feet higher; we say that he built *on*. Here, already, the saying's meaning begins to become remarkable. For it is seen that it is not the height that matters. If, on the other hand, a man constructed a house, even if quite low and small, from the ground up, then we say that he built up a house. To upbuild, therefore, is to construct something in stature *from the ground up*. This "up" certainly indicates the direction as upward, but only when, conversely, the height is also depth do we say "to upbuild." From this it appears that, if a man builds up in height and from the ground, but the depth does not properly correspond to the height, then we surely say that he built up but also that he built up poorly, whereas by to "build poorly" we understand something different.

In this way, the emphasis in relation to upbuilding lies especially on this: to build from the ground up. Certainly we do not call building into the ground "to upbuild"; we do not say that we upbuild a well. Yet, if there is to be talk about upbuilding, then—no matter how high or how low the building becomes—the work must be *from the ground up*. Thus we could say about a person: "He began to build up a house, but he did not finish." On the other hand, if it was not done from the ground up, we could never say about a person who added ever so much in height to the building: "He built up." How strange! In the word "to upbuild," this "up" indicates height, but it indicates height inverted as depth. For to upbuild is to build from the ground *up*.

For that reason, the Scripture also says that the foolish man "built without a foundation." Yet, about the man who hears the word for true upbuilding or, in the words of Scripture, who hears the word and acts accordingly—about him it is said that he is like a person who built a house "and dug deep" (Luke 6:48). When, therefore, a rush of water came and the storm pounded on this securely built-up house, then we all rejoiced at the upbuilding sight that the storm could not rock it. Ah, as said, with respect to the upbuilding it especially depends on building into the ground. It is praiseworthy that, before he begins, a man mulls over "how high he can construct the tower," but if he is to build up, then be sure to have him take care to dig deeply. For even if the tower reached up to the sky—if such a thing were possible—it would not really be built up if it lacked a foundation. To build up completely without a foundation is impossible, for it is building into the air.

That is why, in linguistic terms, one rightly says "to build castles in the sky." One does not say "to build up castles in the sky," which would be a careless and erroneous use of language. For even in the expression for something insignificant, there must be an agreement between the respective words. There is none between "in the sky" and "to build up," since the former takes away the foundation and the latter refers to this "from the ground up." The combination would, therefore, be a false exaggeration.

In this way, with the expression "to upbuild" in plain speech, we now call to mind that it is a figurative expression and then pass on to the object of this deliberation:

Love upbuilds.

Yet, spiritually understood, is "to upbuild" such a singular modifier of "love" that it simply and solely belongs to it? After all, it is normally the case with a modifier that many objects are given that equally—even if in varying degrees—have a right to one and the same modifier. If this is the case with "to upbuild," then it would be wrong to accentuate it so particularly in relation to love as this deliberation does. It would indeed be an attempt based on a misunderstanding to attribute arrogance to love, as if it wanted to be alone or to arrogate to itself what it shared with others—and, after all, love is absolutely willing to share with others, since it "never seeks its own" (1 Cor 13:5). Still, it is truly the case that "to upbuild" is exclusively characteristic of love; yet, on the other hand, this upbuilding quality has, in turn, the characteristic that it can give itself up to everything, can take part in everything—just like love. In this way, one sees that, in this characteristic quality, love does not isolate itself, nor does it act spitefully in any independence and being-for-itself in line with another but gives itself entirely. The characteristic is just that it exclusively has the quality of giving itself entirely.

After all, there is nothing, nothing, that cannot be done or be said in such a way that it becomes upbuilding. Yet, whatever it is, if it is upbuilding, then love is there. Therefore, just where love itself admits the difficulty of giving a specific rule, the admonition goes, "Do everything for upbuilding." It could just as well have gone, "Do everything in love," and it would have expressed precisely the same thing. One person can do the very opposite of another person, but, if each one does the opposite...in love, then the opposite becomes upbuilding.

There is no word in language that, in and of itself, is upbuilding, and there is no word in language that, after all, cannot be said in an upbuilding way and become upbuilding when love is there. For that reason, it is so very far (alas, it is just an unloving and quarrelsome delusion) from being the case that the upbuilding ought to be something that is an *excellence* of gifted individuals—like knowledge and literary talent and beauty and other such things—that, on the contrary, exactly every human being by his life and course of life, by his conduct in daily life, by his dealings with regular people, by his words, by his expression, he ought to and could build up, and would do so if love were truly in him.

We ourselves notice this too, for we use the word "upbuilding" to the widest extent. But what we perhaps do not account for ourselves is that we still use it only wherever love is present. But this is the right use of language: to be adamant about not using this word except where love is present and in turn, by this limitation, to make its range limitless. For everything can be upbuilding in the same sense that love can be present everywhere.

Hence, when we see a single person get along frugally with little by praiseworthy modesty, then we honor and praise him. We rejoice, and we are confirmed in the good by this sight. But we do not actually say that it is an upbuilding sight. In contrast, when we see how a housewife, who has many to care for, lovingly knows how to place a blessing on little by modesty and wise thriftiness, so that enough still

195

remains for everyone, then we say that it is an upbuilding sight. The upbuilding lies in the fact that—at the same time that we see modesty and thriftiness, which we honor—we see the housewife's loving care. On the other hand, we say that it is not a very upbuilding sight, a sinister sight, to see the one who, in a way, is starving in abundance and who still has nothing at all left over for others. We say that it is an appalling sight; we are disgusted by his extravagance; we shudder at the thought of the frightful revenge of loving pleasure: to starve in abundance. But that we seek in vain for the least expression of love is decisive for us, because we say that this is not very upbuilding.

When we see a large family squeezed into a little apartment, and yet we see it inhabit a cozy, friendly, spacious apartment, then we say that it is an upbuilding sight, because we see the love that must be in each and every individual, since, after all, one unloving person would already be enough to occupy the whole place. We say that because we see that there actually is room where there is room in the heart. Or, on the other hand, it is not so very upbuilding to see a restless soul inhabit a palace without finding rest in a single one of its many rooms and yet without being able to afford or to be without the smallest cubbyhole.

Yes, what cannot be upbuilding in this way! One would not think that to see a person sleeping could be upbuilding. And yet, if you see a child sleep on its mother's breast—and you see the mother's love, see that she has, so to speak, waited on and now makes use of the moment, while the child is sleeping to really rejoice in it because she hardly dares to let the child notice how inexpressibly she loves it: then it is an upbuilding sight. If the mother's love is not visible, if you seek in vain to discover the least expression of maternal love's joy or care for the child in her eyes or countenance, if you only see apathy, indifference, which is happy to get rid of the child for so long: then the sight is not upbuilding either. Just to see the child sleeping is a friendly, pleasant, calming sight, but it is not upbuilding. If you want to call it upbuilding anyway, then it is because you still see love present; it is because you see God's love hover over the child.

To see the great artist complete his masterpiece: that is a glorious, an uplifting sight, but it is not upbuilding. Suppose this masterpiece was a wonder. Now if, out of love for a person, the artist smashed it into pieces—then this would be an upbuilding sight.

Wherever the upbuilding is, love is. And wherever love is, the upbuilding is. That is why Paul says that a human being without love, even if he spoke with the tongue of men and of angels, is like a sounding brass and a tinkling cymbal. To be sure, what is even less upbuilding than a tinkling cymbal! Worldly things, however glorious and however vociferous, are without love and therefore not upbuilding; the most insignificant word, the slightest deed, with love or in love is upbuilding. Knowledge, then, puffs up. And yet, you see, knowledge and the communication of knowledge can be upbuilding as well. But, if they are, it is because love is there. To praise oneself hardly seems upbuilding, and yet this, after all, can be upbuilding too. Does not Paul do it at times? But he does it in love and therefore, as he himself says, "for upbuilding." It would, then, be the most inexhaustible discourse of all discourses—the one about what is able to be upbuilding. For everything can be that. It would be the most inexhaustible discourse, alas, just as it is the most grievous lament that can be raised against the world—that one sees and hears so few upbuilding things.

If, namely, it is rare to see riches, that is neither here nor there; we prefer to see ordinary prosperity. If it is rare to see a masterpiece—now, in a certain sense, it surely makes no difference, and, in this respect, it makes no difference to most persons. It is different with the upbuilding. After all, at every moment, there lives the countless number of human beings. It is possible that everything that each human being undertakes, that each human being says, can be upbuilding—and yet, alas, it is so rare to see or to hear something upbuilding!

Love is upbuilding. Now, let us consider what was developed in the introduction, whereby we immediately guarded against the discourse losing its way by choosing an overwhelming task, insofar as everything can be upbuilding. To upbuild is to construct something from the ground up. In simple talk about a house, a building, everyone knows what is meant by the ground and the foundation. But, now, what is the ground and foundation—spiritually understood—of the life of the spirit, which is to support the building? It is just love. Love is the source of everything, and, spiritually understood, love is the deepest ground of the life of the spirit. In every person in whom love exists, the foundation, spiritually understood, is laid. And again the building that, spiritually understood, is to be constructed is love, and it is love that upbuilds. Love is upbuilding, and this means: it builds up love.

The task is defined in this way. The discourse does not scatter itself in particularities and multiplicities; it does not confusedly begin something that, completely arbitrarily, it must break off somewhere in order to still have an ending. No, it centers itself and its attention on what is essential, on one and the same thing in all the manifold-ness. From start to finish, the discourse remains about love, precisely because to upbuild is love's ownmost determination. Love is the ground; love is the building; love upbuilds. To upbuild is to build love up, and it is love that upbuilds. At times, we do indeed talk in a more ordinary sense about upbuilding; we talk—in contrast to the corruption that only wants to tear down, or in contrast to the confusion that can only tear down and disperse—about the fact that the competent person builds up, is the one who knows how to guide and to lead, is the one who knows how to effectively teach in his field, is the one who is a master in his art. Any such person builds up rather than tears down. Yet, insofar as it does not build up love, all this upbuild-ing—in knowledge, in insight, in skill, in uprightness, etc.—is still not upbuilding in the deepest sense. For, spiritually, love is *the ground*, and to upbuild is indeed to construct from *the ground up*.

When, therefore, the discourse is about the work of love in upbuilding, then *either* this must mean that the loving person places love in the heart of another person, *or* it must mean that the loving one presupposes that love is in the heart of another person and, pre-cisely by this presupposition, builds up love in him—from the ground up, provided, of course, that he lovingly presupposes it in the ground. To upbuild must be one of the two. But, I wonder, if one person can place love in the heart of another person? No, this is a suprahuman relation, an inconceivable relation between human beings. In this sense, human love cannot upbuild. It is God, the Creator, who must place love in every human being—he who himself is love.

Admittedly, then, it is exactly unloving and by no means upbuilding if someone presumptuously imagines that he wants and is able to create love in another person. In this regard, all busy and conceited zeal neither builds up love nor is itself upbuilding. The first relationship of upbuilding would then be inconceivable; therefore, we must contemplate the second relationship. In this way, we have gained the explanation of what it is that love builds up, on which we want to dwell: *the loving one presupposes that love is in the heart of the other person, and, just by this presupposition, he builds love up in him—from the ground up, provided, of course, that he lovingly presupposes it in the ground.*

The discourse, then, cannot be about what the loving person— who wants to build up—is now to do in order to transform the other person or in order to force love from him; rather, it is about how the loving person constrains himself in upbuilding. See, this is already upbuilding to think about: the loving person upbuilds by constraining himself. Only the unloving person imagines that he is to upbuild by coercing the other. The loving person constantly presupposes that love is present; he upbuilds precisely in this way. A builder thinks little about the stones and the gravel he is to use for the building, and a teacher presupposes that the pupil is ignorant; a disciplinarian presupposes that the other person is corrupted. But the loving person who upbuilds has only one practice—to presuppose love. What is to be further done can constantly only be to constrain himself to presuppose love always. Thus he elicits the good; he loves love into view. He upbuilds. For love can and will only be treated in one way—by being loved forward.

Yet, after all, to love it forward is precisely to presuppose that it is present in the ground. That is why being a builder, a teacher, a disciplinarian can tempt a person, because it seems to be ruling over others. But to upbuild as love does cannot tempt, for it is precisely to be the one who serves. Only love, then, has the desire to upbuild, because it is willing to serve.

The builder can point to his work and say: "That is my work." The teacher can point to his pupil. But love, which upbuilds, has nothing to point to; after all, its work just consists in presupposing alone. Again, this is very upbuilding to bear in mind. Suppose the loving person is successful in building up love in another person: in that case, when the building is standing there, then the loving person stands off by himself and, humbled, says: "Indeed, I have constantly presupposed that." Alas, the loving person gets no credit at all. The building is not like a monument to the builder's skill or, like a pupil, a remembrance of the teacher's instruction. After all, the loving person has done nothing; he has only presupposed that love was in the ground. The loving person works so quietly and so solemnly, and yet the strength of eternity is in motion. Just when it works the most, love humbly makes itself unnoticeable. Yes, you see, its work is as if it did nothing at all.

Ah, for busyness and worldliness, this is the greatest foolishness—that, in a certain sense, to do nothing at all should be the most difficult work. And yet, it is so. For it is more difficult to command one's mind than to capture a city and more difficult to upbuild—as love does it—than to carry out the most astonishing work. If, in relation to oneself, it is difficult to master one's mind, then how difficult, in relation to another person, to annihilate oneself entirely and yet to do everything and to suffer everything. Truly, if it is normally difficult to begin without presuppositions, to begin to upbuild with the presupposition that love is present—and to end with the same presupposition—is most difficult of all. Then, after all, one's entire work is made into almost nothing beforehand, because, namely, the presupposition is self-denial first and last. The builder is hidden and is as nothing.

For that reason, we can only compare love's upbuilding with the hidden working of nature. While human beings sleep, the forces of nature sleep neither night nor day; no one thinks about how they continue—while everyone is delighted in the loveliness of the meadow and the fruitfulness of the field. Love conducts itself in this way. It presupposes that love is present, like the germ in the grain, and if it is successful in bringing it to fruition, then love has hidden itself, as it was hidden while it worked early and late. Yet, after all, this is precisely what is upbuilding in nature: you see all this glory, and then, when you come to think about the singular fact that you cannot at all see the one who produces it, it grips you in upbuilding fashion. If you could see God with bodily eyes—if he, I daresay, stood beside nature and said, "It is I who have produced all this"—then the upbuilding is lost.

Love upbuilds by presupposing that love is present. In this way, the loving one upbuilds the other, and surely here it is easy enough to presuppose love where it is obviously present. Alas, at the same time, love is still never perfectly present in any human being, insofar as it is indeed possible to do something other than presuppose it, to discover one or another fault or frailty in it. And when, therefore, someone has unlovingly discovered this, then perhaps he wants—as it is said—to take it away, to take the splinter away in order to properly build love up. But love upbuilds. To the one who loves much, much is forgiven. But the more perfect the loving person presupposes the love to be, the more perfect a love does he love forward. Among all the relationships in the world, there is no relationship where there is such a like for like, where the result corresponds so exactly to what was presupposed. One raises no objection; one does not appeal to experience. For, after all, this is precisely unloving—to arbitrarily set a day where the result is now to appear. Love does not understand such things; it is eternally certain of the presupposition's fulfillment. If this is not the case, then love is beginning to decline.

Love upbuilds by presupposing that love is present in the ground. Therefore, love also upbuilds where, humanly speaking, love seems to be lacking, and where, humanly understood, it seems first and foremost necessary to tear down—in truth, not for the sake of desire but for the sake of salvation. The opposite of upbuilding is tearing down. This opposition never shows itself more clearly than when the discourse is about the fact that love upbuilds. For any other connection in which upbuilding is talked about still has a resemblance to tearing down—that it involves doing something to another. Yet, when the loving person upbuilds, then it is just the opposite of tearing down. For the loving person does something to himself: he presupposes that love is present in the other person—which, to be sure, is just the opposite of doing something to the other person. To tear down gratifies the sensuous person only all too easily; likewise, to upbuild in the sense that one does something to the other person can gratify the sensuous person. But to upbuild by overcoming oneself—that is gratifying to love alone. And yet, this is the only way to upbuild. However, in the well-intentioned zeal to tear down and to build up, one does forget that no person is finally capable of placing the ground of love in the other person.

See, here it is seen just how difficult the art of building is—the art that love practices and that is described in that celebrated passage by the Apostle Paul (1 Cor 13). For what is said *there* about love is simply more definite stipulations about how love manages to upbuild. "*Love suffers long.*" That is how it upbuilds. For, after all, long-suffering is essentially perseverance in presupposing that love really is in the ground. The one who judges, even if this happened slowly, the one who judges the other person to be lacking in love—he takes the foundation away. He cannot upbuild. But love upbuilds by patience. Therefore "*it does not envy*" or "*think evil,*" because envy and malice would deny love in the other person and, in doing so, consume the foundation, if that were possible. But love, which upbuilds, bears the other person's misunderstanding, his ingratitude, his anger. That is already enough to bear. How, then, should love be able to carry envy and malice too! In the world, things are distributed in this way: the one who allows envy and malice, he does not in turn bear the other person's burdens; however, the loving one, who does not allow envy and malice, he bears the burdens. Each one bears his burden—the envious person and the loving person. In a certain sense, they both become martyrs. For as a pious man has said: "The envious person, too, is a martyr—but the devil's."[3]

"*Love does not seek its own.*" Therefore it is upbuilding. For, after all, the one who seeks his own must get everything else out of the way. He must tear down in order to get a place for his own, which he wants to build up. But love presupposes that love is present in the ground. That is why it upbuilds.

"*It does not rejoice in iniquity.*" But the one who wants to tear down or at least wants to become important by the idea that it is necessary to tear down—he must certainly be said to rejoice in iniquity,

---

3. Here Kierkegaard is quoting (and, indeed, translating) the German Augustinian monk, Abraham a Sancta Clara (1644–1709), who once wrote, "Der Neidige ist ein Martyrer, aber des Teufels." See *SKS* 18, JJ:449, as well as *Abraham a St. Clara's sämmtliche Werke*, vol. 10 (Passau, Lindau: 1835–54), 392.

or else there would be nothing to tear down. On the other hand, love rejoices in presupposing that love is present in the ground. That is why it upbuilds.

"*Love bears all things.*" For what is it to bear all things? It is ultimately to find in everything the love that is presupposed in the ground. When we say about a person who has a very strong constitution that he can bear everything in relation to eating and drinking, then we mean by this that his health derives nourishment even from what is unhealthy (just as the sick person is damaged even from healthful food); we mean that he derives nourishment from what seems least nourishing. Love bears all things in this way, constantly presupposing that love really is present in the ground—and, by this, it upbuilds.

"*Love believes all things.*" For, indeed, to believe all things is to presuppose—even though it is not seen, yes, though the opposite is seen—that love is still present in the ground...even in the misguided, even in the corrupted, even in the most hateful. Mistrust takes away the very foundation by presupposing that love is not present. That is why mistrust cannot upbuild.

"*Love hopes all things.*" But, indeed, to hope all things is to presuppose—even though it is not seen, yes, though the opposite is seen—that love really is present in the ground and that it will be sure to show itself in the one who errs, in the misguided, even in the loss. See, the father of the prodigal son was perhaps the only one who did not know that he had a prodigal son, because the father's love hoped all things. The brother knew immediately that he was hopelessly prodigal. But love upbuilds, and the father won back the prodigal son precisely because he, who hoped all things, presupposed that love was present in the ground. Despite the son's errors, there was no break from the father's side (and a break is, after all, just the opposite of upbuilding). He hoped all things. Therefore he truly upbuilt by his fatherly forgiveness, just because the son felt very intensely that fatherly love had stuck with him. Thus there had been no break.

"*Love endures all things.*" For to endure all things is just to presuppose that love is present in the ground. When we say that the mother puts up with all the child's naughtiness, do we then say by this that, considered as a woman, she patiently suffers evil? No, we say something else—that she, as a mother, constantly goes on remembering that this is a child and, therefore, by presupposing that the child still loves her and that it will surely show itself. Otherwise, after all, we would talk about how patience endures all things, not how love endures all things. For patience endures all things and is silent, and, if the mother endured the child's naughtiness in this way, then we would actually say that the mother and the child nevertheless had become strangers to one another. But love endures all things, is patiently silent—yet presupposes in perfect silence that love still is present in the other person.

Love upbuilds in this way. *"It is not puffed up; it does not behave itself unseemly; it is not easily provoked."* It is not puffed up by the idea that it should create love in the other person; it is not easily provoked and unseemly, impatient, almost hopelessly busy with what it first must tear down in order to then build up again. No, it constantly presupposes that love is present in the ground. That is why it is unconditionally the most upbuilding sight to see love upbuild—a sight by which even angels are upbuilt. And that is why it is unconditionally the most upbuilding thing if a person succeeds in speaking properly about: how love is upbuilding. There is many a friendly, many a charitable, many an enchanting, many a gripping, many an uplifting, many a captivating, many a persuasive sight and so on; however, there is only one upbuilding sight—to see love upbuild. Therefore, whatever you have seen of horror or abomination in the world—which you wanted to be able to forget, because it will break down your courage, your confidence, give you a distaste for life and a disgust at living—just bear in mind how love upbuilds, and you are built up in order to live. There are very many different subjects to talk about, but there is only a single upbuilding one: how love upbuilds. Whatever, then, can be done to you so embittering that you could wish never to have been born and, the sooner the better, to fall silent in death: just bear in mind how love upbuilds, and you are built up in order to speak again. There is only one upbuilding sight and only one upbuilding subject; however, everything can be said and done in an upbuilding way. For wherever the upbuilding is, love is; and wherever love is, the upbuilding is; and as soon as love is present, it upbuilds.

Love upbuilds by presupposing that love is present. Have not you experienced this yourself, my listener? If some person has ever talked in such a way to you or acted in such a way toward you that you truly felt yourself upbuilt by it, then it was because you very vividly perceived how he presupposed love to be in you. Or, in your mind, how should the person who could truly upbuild you be? Is it not true that you would like him to have insight and knowledge and talent and experience? But you still would not consider that it decisively depended on this but, rather, on the fact that he was a reliable, loving person—that is, truly a loving person. Accordingly, you think that upbuilding decisively and essentially depends on being loving or having love to such an extent that one can rely on it.

But, now, what is love? Love is to presuppose love; to have love is to presuppose love in others; to be loving is to presuppose that others are loving. Let us understand one another. The qualities that a person can have must either be qualities he has for himself—even if he makes use of them against others—or qualities for others. Wisdom is a being-for-itself quality; power and talent and knowledge, and so on are likewise being-for-itself qualities. To be wise does not mean to presuppose that others are wise; on the contrary, it can admittedly be very wise and true if the truly wise person assumes that far from all persons are wise. Yes, because "wise" is a being-for-itself quality, there is nothing in the thought to prevent the assumption that there could live or have lived a wise person who dared to say that he took all others to be unwise.

There is no contradiction in that thought (to be wise—and to assume that all others are unwise). In the actuality of life, such an expression would be arrogance, but in the thought simply as such there is no contradiction. On the other hand, if one were to think that he was loving but also that all others were not loving, then we would say: "No, stop, here is a contradiction in the thought itself." For to be loving is, after all, precisely to assume, to presuppose, that others are loving.

Love is not a being-for-itself quality but a quality by which or in which you are for others. In everyday language, while we enumerate a person's qualities, we say rightly enough that he is wise, sensible, loving—and we do not notice what a difference there is between the last quality and the first ones. He has his wisdom, his experience, his sensibleness for himself, even if he is useful to others with them. Yet, if he is truly loving, then he does not have love in the same sense as he has wisdom; rather, it is precisely his love to presuppose that we others have love. You praise him as the loving person; you mean that it is a quality he has, as it also is. You feel upbuilt by him, just because he is loving, but you do not notice that the explanation is that his love signifies that he presupposes love in you and that, precisely by this, you are upbuilt [*opbygges*]—that, precisely by this, the love in you is built up [*bygges op*].

If it actually were the case that a person could be loving without this love signifying the presupposing of love in others, then, in the deepest sense, you would not feel yourself upbuilt either, no matter how plausible it was that he was loving. You would not feel yourself upbuilt in the deepest sense, just as little as you are upbuilt in the deepest sense, no matter how plausible it is that he is wise, sensible, experienced, learned. If it were possible that he truly could be loving without this love signifying the presupposing of love in others, then you could not completely rely on him either, for the reliability of the loving person is precisely that—even when you doubt yourself, even when you doubt whether there is love in you—he remains loving enough to presuppose it. Or, rather, he is the loving one who presupposes it.

But, after all, you insisted that a person should be truly loving in order to truly upbuild. And to be loving has now shown itself to mean: to presuppose love in others. So, indeed, you are saying exactly the same thing that the discourse has developed.

In this way, the deliberation turns back to its beginning. To upbuild is to presuppose love; to be loving is to presuppose love; only love is upbuilding. For to upbuild is to construct something from the ground up, but, spiritually, love is the ground of everything. No human being can place the ground of love in another human being's heart. Still, love is the ground, and one can only upbuild from the ground up. Therefore, one can only upbuild by presupposing love. If you take love away, then there is no one who upbuilds and no one who is upbuilt.

Chapter Seven[1]

THE SICKNESS UNTO DEATH IS DESPAIR

A

To Despair Is the Sickness unto Death

A

Despair is a sickness of the spirit, of the self, and can thus be threefold: in despair not to be conscious of having a self (figurative despair); in despair not to want to be oneself; in despair to want to be oneself.

The human being is spirit. But what is spirit? Spirit is the self. But what is the self? The self is a relation that relates itself to itself, or, in the relation, it is that the relation relates itself to itself. The self is not the relation but that the relation relates itself to itself. The human being is a synthesis of infinitude and finitude, of the temporal and the eternal, of freedom and necessity—in short, a synthesis. A synthesis is a relation between two entities. Considered in this way, the human being is still not a self.

In the relation between two entities, the relation is the third entity as a negative unity, and the two entities relate to the relation and in the relation to the relation. Hence, under the category "soul," the relation between soul and body is a relation. If, on the other hand,

---

1. From Niels Jørgen Cappelørn et al., eds., *Søren Kierkegaards Skrifter*, vol. 11 (Copenhagen: Gads Forlag, 2006), 129–33.

the relation relates itself to itself, then this is the positive third entity, and this is the self.

Such a relation that relates itself to itself—a self—must either have composed itself or been composed by another.

If the relation that relates itself to itself is composed by another, then the relation is certainly the third entity. But, then, this relation—the third entity—is yet again a relation and relates itself to what has composed the whole relation.

The self of the human being is such a derived, composed relation—a relation that relates itself to itself and, in relating itself to itself, relates itself to another. From this it follows that there can be two forms of despair proper. Had the self of the human being composed itself, then there could only be talk about one form—that of not wanting to be oneself, of wanting to get rid of oneself. But there could not be talk about wanting to be oneself in despair. That is to say, this formula is the expression for the dependence of the whole relation (of the self)—the expression for the fact that the self cannot come to or be in balance and rest by itself, but only, in relating itself to itself, by relating itself to that which has composed the entire relation. Yes, it is so far from the case that this second form of despair (to want to be oneself in despair) merely denotes a peculiar kind of despair that, on the contrary, all despair can ultimately be dissolved into and traced back to it. If, as he considers it, a despairing person is aware of his despair and does not talk meaninglessly about it as if it were something that happens to him (almost like when, in a nervous delusion, the one who suffers from dizziness talks about a weight on his head or that it is like something has fallen down on him, etc., the weight and the pressure are still not something external but an inverse reflection of the internal)—and now with all his power wants to extract the despair by himself and by himself alone: then he is still in despair and, with all his supposed effort, only works himself deeper into a deeper despair. Despair's misrelation is not a simple misrelation but a misrelation in a relation that relates itself to itself and has been composed by another. Thus the misrelation in that relation that is for itself also reflects itself infinitely in the relation to the power that composed it.

This is, namely, the formula that describes the state of the self when despair is entirely rooted out: in relating itself to itself, and in wanting to be itself, the self is grounded transparently in the power that composed it.

B

The Possibility and Actuality of Despair

Is despair a virtue or a defect? Purely dialectically, it is both. If one were to stick to the abstract idea of despair, without thinking of someone in despair, then one would have to say: it is an immeasurable virtue. The possibility of this sickness is the human being's virtue over against the animal, and this virtue distinguishes him in an entirely different way than walking upright. For it suggests the infinite uprightness or loftiness—that he is spirit. The possibility of this sickness is the human being's virtue over against the animal; to be aware of this sickness is the Christian's virtue over against the natural human being; to be healed from this sickness is the Christian's blessedness.

Therefore it is an infinite virtue to be able to despair, and yet to be in despair is not only the greatest unhappiness and misery—no, it is perdition. The relation between possibility and actuality is not normally like this. If it is a virtue to be able to be this or that, then it is an even greater virtue to be that. In other words, being is a step up in relation to being able to be. As for despair, on the other hand, being is like a step down in relation to being able to be. As infinite as the virtue of possibility is, the fall is just as deep. Hence, in relation to despair, to not be in despair is a step up. Again, however, this categorization is ambiguous. Not being in despair is not the same as not being lame, blind, etc. If not being in despair means neither more nor less than not being that, then it is precisely to be in despair. Not being in despair must mean the annihilated possibility of being able to be in despair; if it is to be true that a person is not in despair, he must annihilate the possibility in every moment. The relation between possibility and actuality is not normally like this. For thinkers certainly say that actuality is annihilated possibility, but that is not

SØREN KIERKEGAARD

entirely true: it is the completed, the active possibility. Here, on the other hand, the actuality (not to be in despair) is the impotent, annihilated possibility, which, for that reason, is a negation as well. Normally, actuality is a corroboration in relation to possibility; here it is a denial.

Despair is the misrelation in the relation of a synthesis that relates itself to itself. But the synthesis is not the misrelation; it is only the possibility. Or the possibility of the misrelation lies in the synthesis. Were the synthesis the misrelation, then despair would not exist at all; then despair would be something that lies in human nature as such. That is, it would not then be despair; it would be something that happened to the person—something he suffered, like a disease into which the person falls or like death, which is the lot of all things. No, to despair lies in the human being as such. Yet, if he were not a synthesis, he could not despair at all, and, if the synthesis were not originally from the hand of God in the proper relation, he could not despair either.

From where, then, does despair come? It comes from the relation in which the synthesis relates itself to itself, because God, who made the human being into the relation, lets it go from his hand, as it were—that is, inasmuch as the relation relates itself to itself. And therein—that the relation is spirit, is the self—therein lies the responsibility for all despair and for every moment that it exists, however much the person in despair talks about his despair as bad luck and however ingeniously he deceives himself and others by a confusion like that previously mentioned case of dizziness, with which despair, even if qualitatively different, has much in common. For, under the category "soul," dizziness is what despair is under the category "spirit" and is pregnant with analogies to despair.

Hence, when the misrelation of despair has set in, is it then a matter of course that it continues? No, it is not a matter of course. If the misrelation continues, it does not follow from the misrelation but from the relation that relates itself to itself. That is to say, for every time the misrelation manifests itself, and in every moment it exists, it must be directed back to the relation. See, one talks about the fact that a person catches a sickness, for example, through carelessness. So, then, the sickness sets in, and from that moment it makes itself

210

felt and is now an *actuality*, whose origin becomes more and more *past*. It would be both cruel and inhumane if one were to keep on saying again and again: "You, the sick person, are catching this sickness in this moment." It would be as if one wanted, in every moment, to dissolve the sickness's actuality into its possibility. It is true that he caught the sickness himself, but he did that only one time. The continuance of the sickness is a simple result of the fact that he once caught it himself; its progress cannot be ascribed to him as cause in every moment. He caught it himself, but one cannot say: "He *is catching* it himself."

It is different with despair. Every actual moment of despair leads back to possibility; every moment he is in despair, he *is catching* it himself. It is constantly the present tense; in relation to actuality, nothing is done in the past. In every actual moment of despair, the despairing person bears in possibility all the past as something present. This is due to the fact that despair is a category of "spirit" and relates itself to the eternal in the human being. But he cannot get rid of the eternal—no, not in all eternity. He cannot throw it away once and for all; nothing is more impossible. In every moment that he does not have it, he must have thrown it or is throwing it away...but it comes again. That is, every moment he is in despair, he is catching despair. For despair does not follow from the misrelation but from the relation that relates itself to itself. And a person can get rid of the relation to himself as little as he can get rid of himself—what, incidentally, is one and the same thing, since the self is indeed the relation to oneself.

C

Despair Is: "The Sickness unto Death"

This concept of "the sickness unto death" must be taken in a particular way. It literally means a sickness whose end, whose outcome is death. Thus the expression "deadly sickness" is used synonymously with "sickness unto death." Despair cannot be called the sickness unto death in that sense. Yet, Christianly understood, death itself is a passage into life. No earthly, bodily sickness is, as far as it goes, a sickness unto death from a Christian point of view. For death is undoubtedly the end of the sickness, but death is not the last thing. If there is to be talk about a sickness unto death in the strictest sense, it must be one where the last thing is death and where death is the last thing. And just this is despair.

Still, in another sense, despair is even more definitely the sickness unto death. That is to say, it is as far as possible from one literally dying from this sickness or from this sickness ending with bodily death. On the contrary, the agony of despair is precisely not to be able to die. In this way, it has more in common with the condition of the critically ill person, when he lies and is being drawn into death and cannot die. Thus to be sick *unto* death is to be unable to die, yet not as if there were hope about life. No, the hopelessness is that even the last hope of death is not there. When death is the greatest danger, one hopes for life. But when one comes to know the even more horrifying danger, one hopes for death. So, when the danger is so great that death has become the hope, then despair is the hopelessness of not even being able to die.

Despair, then, is the sickness unto death in this last sense—this agonizing contradiction, this sickness in the self, to die eternally, to die and yet not to die, to die death. For dying means that it is past, but to die death means to experience that dying. And if this is experienced for one single moment, then that is to experience it forever in turn. If a person were to die of despair like one dies of a disease, then the eternal in him—the self—would have to be able to die in the same sense as the body dies of disease. But this is an impossibility. The dying of despair constantly transforms itself into living. The despairing person cannot die. "As little as the dagger can slay thoughts" can despair consume the eternal—the self—that lies at the foundation of despair, whose worm does not die and whose fire cannot be extinguished. After all, despair is precisely a *self*-consuming, albeit a powerless self-consuming that cannot do what it wants to do. But what it wants is to consume itself—something it cannot do—and this impotence is a new form of self-consumption, in which despair is yet again unable to do what it wants: to consume itself. This is an intensification or the law of intensification. This is the infuriating thing, or it is the cold fire in despair—this gnawing, whose movement is constantly within, deeper and deeper into powerless self-consumption. That despair does not consume him is very far from being any comfort to the person in despair. It is just the opposite. This comfort is precisely the agony, is precisely what keeps the gnawing alive and life in the gnawing. For it is precisely over this issue—rather than over having despaired—that he despairs. But he does despair that he cannot consume himself, cannot get rid of himself, cannot become nothing. This is the intensified formula for despair, the rising fever in this sickness of the self.

A person in despair despairs over *something*. It looks like this for a moment, but it is only a moment. In the same moment, true despair shows itself, or despair in its truth shows itself. While he despaired over *something*, he actually despaired over *himself* and now wants to get rid of himself. Hence, when the power-hungry person, whose motto is "either Caesar or nothing at all," does not become Caesar, he despairs over that. But this means something else—that he now cannot stand to be himself, precisely because he did not become Caesar. Therefore he does not actually despair over the fact that he did not become Caesar, but over himself that he did not become Caesar. This self, if it had become Caesar, would have satisfied his every desire (which, by the way, is just as despairing in another sense)—this self is now the most intolerable of all to him. In a deeper sense, what is intolerable to him is not that he failed to become Caesar; rather, what is intolerable to him is this self, which did not become Caesar. Or, even more correctly, what is intolerable to him is that he cannot get rid of himself. If he had become Caesar, then he would get rid of himself in despair. But now he did not become Caesar and cannot get rid of himself in despair. In essence, he is equally in despair. For he does not have his self; he is not himself. After all, in becoming Caesar, he would not have become himself but gotten rid of himself, and, by not becoming Caesar, he despairs over not being able to get rid of himself. It is, therefore, a superficial observation (from one who has probably never seen a person in despair, not even himself) when one says about a person in despair: "He is consuming himself"—as if this were his punishment. For that is precisely what he is in despair, and that is precisely what he cannot do to his agony, because something in the self that cannot burn or cannot be burned has caught fire from despair.

For that reason, to despair over something is still not actually despair. It is the beginning, or, as the physician says about a disease, it has still not declared itself. The next type is the despair that declares itself: to despair over oneself. A young girl despairs of love; therefore, she despairs over the loss of the beloved—that he died or that he was unfaithful to her. This is no declared despair; no, she despairs over herself. This self of hers—which she would have gotten rid of or would have lost in the most blissful way, if it had become "his" beloved—this self is now a torment to her, if it is to be a self without "him." This self would have become her treasure (which, by the way, is just as despairing in another sense)—this self has now become a repulsive emptiness to her, since "he" is dead, or it has become a repulsion to her, since it reminds her that she has been deceived. Now, try it; say to such a girl: "You are consuming yourself." And you will hear her answer: "Oh, no, the agony is precisely that I cannot do that."

To despair over oneself, to will to get rid of oneself in despair, is the formula for all despair. So, then, the other form of despair (to will to be oneself in despair) can be traced back to the first one (not to want to be oneself in despair), as we previously dissolved the form "not to want to be oneself in despair" into the one "to want to be oneself in despair" (cf. A). The one who is in despair wants to be himself in despair. But if he wants to be himself in despair, then, after all, he does not want to get rid of himself. Yes, it seems like that. However, if one looks closer, one nevertheless sees that the contradiction is the same. The self that he wants to be in despair is a self that he is not (for to want to be the self that he is in truth is, to be sure, just the opposite of despair). That is to say, he wants to detach his self from the power that composed it. Yet, in spite of all despair, this he cannot do. In spite of despair's every effort, that power is the stronger and compels him to be the self he does not want to be. In this way, however, he actually wants to get rid of himself, to get rid of the self he is in order to be the self he has made up himself. To be the self that he wants to be would satisfy his every desire, even if it would be just as despairing in another sense. But to be compelled to be the self that he does not want to be is his agony—in other words, that he cannot get rid of himself.

Socrates demonstrated the soul's immortality from the fact that the soul's sickness (sin) does not consume the soul as the body's sickness consumes the body. Thus one can also demonstrate the eternal in a human being by the fact that despair cannot consume his self, that just this is the agony of contradiction in despair. If there were nothing eternal in a human being, then he could not despair at all. Yet, if despair could consume his self, then no despair would exist anyway.

Despair—this sickness in the self, the sickness unto death—is like this. The person in despair is critically ill. In an entirely different sense than applies to any sickness, this sickness has attacked the most valuable parts, and yet he cannot die. Death is not the last thing of the sickness, but death is incessantly the last thing. To be saved from this sickness by death is an impossibility, for this sickness and its agony—death as well—is precisely not to be able to die.

This is the state of despair. However much the person in despair avoids it, however much the person in despair succeeds in having entirely lost his self (which, then, especially applies to the kind of despair that is ignorant of being despair) and lost it in such a way that it is not noticed in the least: eternity will then nevertheless make it manifest that his condition was despair and will nail his self to him. Then the agony really becomes that he cannot get rid of his self, and it becomes obvious that it was a fantasy that he succeeded in doing so. And eternity must do it in this way, because to have a self—to be a self—is the greatest, the infinite concession made to the human being. Yet, it is eternity's claim upon him as well.

B

The Commonality of This Sickness (of Despair)

As the physician must rightly say that perhaps not one single living person is entirely healthy, one who truly knows humanity must likewise say that not one single living person is without a little despair, is without an unrest deep down, is without discord, is without disharmony, is without anxiety about an unknown something or about a something he does not even dare to become acquainted with—an anxiety about some possibility in existence or an anxiety about himself, so that, just as the physician talks about going around with a bodily disease, he goes around with a sickness, goes on and is carrying a spiritual sickness that, in and with an inexplicable anxiety, once in a while betrays that it lies inside. And, in any case, no human being has lived, and no human being outside of Christendom lives, without despairing. And insofar as anyone in Christendom is not a true Christian, and insofar as he is not entirely a true Christian, he is still somewhat in despair.

For many persons, this observation will certainly seem like a paradox—an exaggeration from a dark and depressing point of view. But it is nothing of the sort. It is not dark; on the contrary, it seeks to cast light on what one generally leaves in a certain darkness. It is not depressing; on the contrary, it is uplifting, since it considers every human being under the purpose of the highest claim on him: to be spirit. Nor is it a paradox; on the contrary, it is a thoroughly consistent foundation-view and, therefore, really no exaggeration either.

On the other hand, the common view of despair stops at what seems to be the case and thus is a superficial view—that is, no view at all. It assumes that, after all, each human being himself must know best whether or not he is in despair. The one, then, who says himself that he is that: he is considered to be in despair. But the one who does not consider himself to be that: he is therefore not regarded as that either. As a result, despair becomes a scarcer phenomenon, instead of being quite a common thing. That one is in despair is not a rare occurrence. No, what is rare, very rare, is that one is truly not in despair.

But the crude view understands despair very poorly. Hence, among other things, it entirely overlooks (to name just this, which, rightly understood, nevertheless brings thousands and thousands and millions under the category of despair), it entirely overlooks that it is precisely a form of despair not to be in despair, not to be conscious that one is in despair. In a far deeper sense, the crude view in relation to understanding despair works at times like that in relation to determining whether or not a person is sick—in a far deeper sense. For the crude view is still a far inferior judge of what spirit is (and without that one cannot understand despair either) than of sickness and health. In general, one assumes that a person is in good health, if he himself does not say he is sick (not to mention if he himself says he is healthy). The doctor, on the other hand, views sickness differently. And why? Because the doctor has a defined and developed conception of what it is to be healthy, and he examines a person's condition according to this conception. The doctor knows that, just as there is a sickness that is only an illusion, it is also this way with health. In the latter case, that is why he first takes measures to get the sickness to become evident. On the whole, the doctor—just because he is a doctor (one who is well-informed)—does not have unconditional trust in the person's assertion about his state of health. If it were the case that what every person said about his health—whether he is healthy or sick, about where he is suffering, etc.—was to be unconditionally relied on, then being a doctor would be an illusion. For a doctor does not only have to prescribe treatments but, first and foremost, to recognize the sickness and therefore (again, first and foremost) to recognize whether the supposedly sick person actually is sick or whether the supposedly healthy person perhaps is actually sick.

This is how it is with the person knowledgeable about the soul and his relation to despair. He knows what despair is; he recognizes it and therefore is content neither with a person's assertion that he is not in despair nor with his assertion that he is in despair. For it must be noted that, in a certain sense, those who claim to be in despair are not even always in despair. After all, one can affect despair, and one can confound and confuse despair—which is a spiritual category— with all sorts of transitory states of gloom and discord that once more pass without developing into despair. At the same time, the person knowledgeable about the soul rightly regards even these as forms of despair; he sees very well that they are affectation—but just this affectation is despair. He sees very well that this state of gloom, etc. does not have great significance. But just this—that it does not have and does not acquire great significance—is despair.

The crude view still overlooks the fact that, compared with a sickness, despair is dialectically different from what one usually calls a "sickness," because it is a sickness of the spirit. And this dialectic, rightly understood, again brings thousands in under the category of despair. That is, if a physician has convinced himself in a given moment that someone is healthy—and, subsequently, that person becomes sick in a later moment—then the physician is right that this person *was* in good health at that time. Now, on the other hand, he *is* sick.

It is different with despair. As soon as despair appears, it shows that the person was in despair. Really, at no point can one decide anything about a person who is not saved by having been in despair. For when that which brings him to despair sets in, then, in the same moment, it becomes manifest that he has been in despair all of his preceding life. In contrast, when one gets a fever, one cannot at all say that it is now manifest that he has had a fever his whole life through. But despair is a category of the spirit, is related to the eternal, and therefore has something of the eternal in its dialectic.

Despair is not only dialectically different from a sickness, but, in relation to despair, all symptoms are dialectical, and that is why the superficial view is so easily frustrated regarding whether or not despair is present. For example, not to be in despair can precisely signify to be in despair, and it can signify being saved from being in despair. Peace of mind and restfulness can signify being in despair; precisely this peace of mind, this restfulness, can be the despair. And it can signify having overcome despair and having won peace. Not being in despair is not like not being sick. For, after all, not being sick cannot be the same as being sick, but not being in despair can be the very same as being in despair. With a sickness, to feel unwell is the sickness; despair is not like that. By no means. Again, to feel unwell is dialectical. To have never perceived this sick feeling is precisely to be in despair.

This means and has its basis in the fact that, viewed as spirit (and if one is to talk about despair, one must view the human being under the category of "spirit"), the human being's condition is ever critical. One talks about a crisis in relation to sickness but not in relation to health. And why not? Because bodily health is an immediate category, which first becomes dialectical in the condition of sickness, where talk about a crisis then emerges. But spiritually—or when the human being is viewed as spirit—both health and sickness are critical. No immediate spiritual health is given.

As soon as one does not view the human being under the category of "spirit" (and if not, neither can one talk about despair) but only as a mental-physical synthesis, then health is an immediate category, and the sickness of the mind or of the body is first the dialectical category. But despair is precisely that the person himself is unconscious of being defined as spirit. Even what, in human terms, is the most beautiful and most lovable of all things—a feminine youthfulness, which is sheer peace and harmony and joy—is nevertheless despair. In other words, this is good luck, but good luck is not a category of spirit. And deep, deep inside, at the far end of good luck's most secret hiding place, there too resides anxiety—which is despair. It certainly wants permission to remain there, for it is despair's most cherished, most select place to live: at the far end of good luck. Despite its illusory peace of mind and rest, all immediacy is anxiety and thus, quite consistently, is most anxious about nothing. One does not make immediacy as anxious by the most hideous description of the most terrible something as by a subtle, almost slapdash, but— with the certain, calculating aim of reflection—nevertheless casually observed allusion to an indefinite something. Yes, one makes immediacy most anxious by slyly insinuating that it knows very well what it is one is talking about. For, surely enough, immediacy does not know it. But reflection never traps as certainly as when it fashions its snare out of nothing, and reflection is never so much itself as when it is…nothing. It takes eminent reflection—or, rather, it takes great faith—to be able to endure nothing—that is, infinite reflection. That is why even the most beautiful and most lovable of all things—a feminine youthfulness—is still despair, is good luck. Nor is it very successful, therefore, to slip through life in this immediacy. And if this good luck is successful in slipping through—well, it helps only a little, for it is despair. That is, just because it is wholly dialectical, despair is the sickness about which it is true that it is the greatest misfortune never to have had it: to get it is a true godsend, even if it is the most dangerous sickness of all when one does not want to be healed from it. Normally, however, there can only be talk that it is good fortune to be healed from a sickness; the sickness itself is the misfortune.

This is, therefore, as far as possible from the crude view, which assumes that despair is a rare thing. On the contrary, despair is entirely ordinary. This is as far as possible from the crude view, which assumes that everyone who does not think or feel himself to be in despair is not in despair either, and that only the one who declares himself to be in despair is in despair. On the contrary, the one who, without affectation, declares himself to be in despair is, however slightly, dialectically closer to being healed than all those who are not considered as such and who do not consider themselves as being in despair. But I think the person knowledgeable about the soul will agree with me precisely on this point—that, in general, most human beings live without truly becoming conscious of being determined as spirit...and from this all the so-called peace of mind, satisfaction with life, etc., etc., which is just despair. In contrast, those who declare themselves to be in despair are ordinarily either those who have such a very deep nature that they are bound to become conscious of themselves as spirit or those whom difficult events and terrifying decisions have helped in becoming conscious of themselves as spirit. It is either one or the other. For the one who is not in despair is, I dare say, very rare.

Oh, there is so much talk about human need and misery. I try to understand it and have intimately known quite a lot of things about it. There is so much talk about wasting a life, but only that person's life was wasted who lived in such a way that, deceived by life's joys or by its sorrows, he never became conscious as spirit, as a self, in eternal and decisive fashion. Or, what is the same thing, he never became aware and, in the deepest sense, got the impression that God exists and that "he," he himself, his self, exists before this God, which is the reward of infinity never attained except through despair. Alas, and this misery—that so many live in this way, swindled of the most blessed of all thoughts; this misery—that one is occupied with or occupies the human masses with everything else, using them to supply the forces in the drama of life but never reminding them of this blessedness; this misery—that one gathers them and yet deceives them, instead of splitting them up so that each individual may win the highest, the only thing worth living for and sufficient to live in for an eternity.

It seems to me that I could cry an eternity over the fact that this misery exists! Oh, and in my mind, an additional expression of terror for this the most terrible sickness and misery of all lies in its hiddenness: not only that the one who suffers from it may wish to hide it and is capable of doing so; not only that it can dwell in a person in such a way that no one, no one can discover it; no, that it can be so hidden in a person that he himself does not know it! Oh, and some day when the hourglass has run out, the hourglass of temporality; when the noise of the secular world has died down and the restless or ineffective bustle has come to an end; when everything around you is still, as it is in eternity; then—whether you were a man or a woman, rich or poor, dependent or independent, fortunate or unfortunate; whether you bore the radiance of the crown in royalty or bore only the pain and heat of the day in lowly obscurity; whether your name shall be remembered for as long as the world stands (and therefore is remembered as long as it stood) or you, without a name, run as one nameless among the innumerable crowd; whether the glory surrounding you surpassed all human description or the most severe and most dishonorable human judgment befell you—then eternity asks you, along with every individual among these millions and millions, only one thing: whether you have lived in despair or not; whether you have despaired in such a way that you did not know that you were in despair or in such a way that you secretly bore this sickness in your heart of hearts as your gnawing secret, as a fruit of sinful love under your heart; or whether you have despaired in such a way that you, a terror to others, raged in despair.

And if so, if you have lived in despair, whatever you won or lost besides, then everything is lost for you. Eternity does not acknowledge you. It never knew you, or, even more terrible, it knows you as you are known. It chains you to yourself in despair!

Part Three

Jesus Christ

INTRODUCTION
TO PART THREE

Part 3 of this volume concerns the figure who may very well lie at the heart of Kierkegaard's life and authorship—Jesus Christ. Of course, at this point, it should come as no surprise that Kierkegaard's interest in Jesus is neither historiographical nor doctrinal. That is to say, he refuses to engage in modern scholarly debates about "the historical Jesus" and thus effectively presupposes the New Testament account of Jesus's birth, ministry, death, resurrection, and ascension. Moreover, he does not occupy himself with ecclesial-cum-academic debates about the finer points of christological doctrine, and he thus adheres to the basics of Chalcedonian Christology: Jesus Christ is the Son of God, one divine person in two natures, truly human and truly divine. Hence, as with the topics of "God" and "Creation," Kierkegaard's principal focus is on what Jesus means in and for human existence, though he addresses this problem in various ways throughout his authorship.

To be sure, in early pseudonymous works such as *Fear and Trembling* (1843) and *Philosophical Fragments* (1844), Kierkegaard explores the nature of "faith in the incarnate Christ,"[1] albeit by way of a subtle and unique fusion of philosophy and literature. But the writings that succeeded Kierkegaard's public row with *The Corsair*—a quarrel that began late in 1845 and erupted into a *cause célèbre* during the first few months of 1846—adopt a different approach.[2] In them,

---

1. George Pattison, *Kierkegaard and the Crisis of Faith* (London: SPCK, 1997), 116.

2. *The Corsair* was a sardonic yet fashionable weekly paper, and Kierkegaard's dispute with it—the so-called *Corsair* Affair—was discussed in the general introduction. Also see, e.g., Joakim Garff, *Søren Kierkegaard: A Biography*, trans. Bruce H. Kirmmse (Princeton, NJ: Princeton University Press, 2005), esp. 375–428.

Kierkegaard increasingly views the Christian faith "in terms of being willing to share with [Christ] the experience of rejection and of going with him on the way to the cross."[3] With this newfound focus, he slowed (but did not stop) his production of pseudonymous writings and, little by little, intensified his polemics against the Danish state church, arguing that its political function had led it to neglect the very foundation of Christianity—that the Christian believer is to live, or at least always *strive* to live, in conformity with the example [*Forbillede*] of the humble and suffering Jesus.

Nevertheless, even this later stress on *imitatio Christi* is far more nuanced than often assumed.[4] It is neither a straightforward equation of Christianity and martyrdom nor the inexorable endpoint of a jaded outsider. In fact, Kierkegaard's writings about Jesus are not haphazard musings but are rooted in his lifelong interest in Catholic mystical and Pietist literature, as well as in his upbringing among Denmark's Moravian community.[5] Thus they betray a familiarity with and a sensitivity to the challenges they raise, even as they register a variety of emotions and perspectives on the significance of Jesus—a variety that is reflected in the four pieces included in this section, each of which belong to the period following the *Corsair* affair.

The first selection might be seen as inaugurating Kierkegaard's turn to the *imitatio* motif. Entitled "What the Thought of Following Christ Means and What Joy Lies Therein," it stands as the opening discourse of *The Gospel of Sufferings: Christian Discourses*, which itself constitutes the third and final part of *Upbuilding Discourses in Various Spirits*. Here the larger title *The Gospel of Sufferings* is already indicative of Kierkegaard's task in the piece included here. According to Kierkegaard, the decision to follow Christ is likewise a choice to suffer, for following means precisely to live in the manner that Christ lived—namely, as one who serves others in humble self-denial. And yet, the upshot of this suffering is not misery but joy, inasmuch as the

---

3. Pattison, *Kierkegaard and the Crisis of Faith*, 116.
4. I have written extensively on this topic. See, e.g., Christopher B. Barnett, *Kierkegaard, Pietism and Holiness* (Farnham, UK: Ashgate, 2011), esp. 169–212.
5. See Barnett, *Kierkegaard, Pietism and Holiness*, esp. 3–107.

follower has made the blessed choice to walk in the footsteps of the Son of God, both in this world and in the next.

The second piece in this section belongs to another one of Kierkegaard's Anti-Climacan writings—namely, *Practice in Christianity* (1850). It is, indeed, a kind of sequel to *The Sickness unto Death*, presupposing its predecessor's psychological analyses of despair and sin and, in turn, attending to "the healing of the sin-conscious self and the indicative ethics gratefully expressive of the redemptive gift."[6] Thus *Practice in Christianity* has an exhortative, encouraging tone—indeed, Kierkegaard had pondered entitling it *The Ultimate Cure: Christian Healing/The Atonement*[7]—and this tenor is clear from the outset. The book comprises three major sections, each of which is based on a New Testament passage that encapsulates some aspect of Jesus's life or teaching. The two short pieces reproduced here are taken from the first section, "Come unto Me, All *You* That Labor and Are Heavy Laden, and I Will Give You Rest." After a brief "Editor's Preface," which is ascribed to Kierkegaard himself, the book opens with a brief "Invocation" followed by a section called "The Invitation." The purpose of the "Invocation" is to petition and to recall Jesus, not as a triumphant Savior, but as the poor and humble figure who lived on earth—a key theme in *Practice in Christianity* and in many of Kierkegaard's later writings. "The Invitation," meanwhile, is a tripartite meditation on the manifold implications of Jesus's desire to bestow "rest" (*Hvile*) on weary humanity.

Part 3's third selection is taken from *For Self-Examination*, which Kierkegaard published in September 1851 in the midst of another remarkable period of productivity. Roughly a month earlier, the Dane had issued a pair of short treatises, *On My Work as an Author* and *Two Discourses at the Communion on Fridays*, and he was working on another text alongside *For Self-Examination*, namely, *Judge for Yourself!*, which came out posthumously in 1876. Of course, these works also bear an overarching relation to the Anti-Climacan

---

6. Howard V. Hong and Edna H. Hong, "Historical Introduction," in Søren Kierkegaard, *Practice in Christianity* (Princeton, NJ: Princeton University Press, 1991), xiii.

7. *SKS* 20, NB4:76, my translation.

writings, which appeared in 1849 and 1850, respectively. As Howard and Edna Hong explain, "The tone and aim of *For Self-Examination* link it retrospectively to *Practice in Christianity*," inasmuch as it "shares the high ideality of *Practice* as well as the implied critique inherent in that ideality."[8] The phrase "high ideality" here broadly refers to Kierkegaard's insistence that Christian discipleship is a venture, entailing various temptations and trials, including suffering at the hands of the other people. More specifically, however, it indicates the emphasis on *imitatio Christi* that animates much of Kierkegaard's later output—an emphasis that permeates the second discourse in *For Self-Examination*, "Christ Is the Way."

Of course, "Christ Is the Way" is a somewhat self-explanatory title, though here Kierkegaard gives the *imitatio* motif an intriguing contemporary application. The discourse is based on Acts 1:1–12, which describes Jesus's glorious ascension into heaven. Kierkegaard concedes that the glory of the ascension might seem to contradict his own longstanding stress on Christ's hard and narrow way. Moreover, he acknowledges that a doctrine such as the ascension, which is doggedly supernatural, has engendered skepticism in the modern era. But why? Kierkegaard returns to the problem of imitation. The ascension, as an object of faith, presupposes a life of committed discipleship; it is a promise to and a hope for those who are willing to pass through "the narrow way." He argues, then, that modern people tend to doubt Christ's ascension (and other aspects of Christian teaching), not because modernity is intrinsically superior to earlier historical epochs, but because it is an era that cowers before Christ's demand to follow his way.

The final selection of Part 3 was written during Kierkegaard's notorious "attack upon Christendom."[9] Kierkegaard's polemics against the Danish state church began in December 1854, when he published a critical rejoinder to the claim that Jakob Peter Mynster,

---

8. Howard V. Hong and Edna H. Hong, "Historical introduction," in *For Self-Examination/Judge for Yourself!*, ed. Howard V. Hong and Edna H. Hong, *Kierkegaard's Writings 21* (Princeton, NJ: Princeton University Press, 1990), xi.
9. For more information, see the general introduction. Also see, e.g., Garff, *Kierkegaard*, 727–81.

the recently deceased bishop of Zealand, should be remembered as a "witness to the truth" (*Sandhedsvidne*). Kierkegaard rejected this characterization for a number of reasons, but his fundamental objection was that Mynster, both in his life and in his teaching, supported the symbiosis of church and state in Denmark—a symbiosis that Kierkegaard feared had reduced Christianity to an insipid bourgeois humanism on the one hand and the church to a mere branch of the state on the other. Kierkegaard's diatribes first appeared in the Danish periodical *The Fatherland* (*Fædrelandet*), but he soon began publishing his own paper, *The Moment* (*Øieblikket*). Several editions of *The Moment* were issued between May 1855 and September 1855, when he fell ill. Then, after a fairly rapid decline, Kierkegaard died on November 11, 1855.

In a sense, then, *The Moment* served as the conclusion of Kierkegaard's authorship, but, intriguingly, he also published a few writings separate from *The Moment* during the summer of 1855. One of these pieces has already been encountered in this volume, namely, "The Unchangeableness of God." Another one composes the last chapter of this section. Entitled "What Christ Judges of Official Christianity," it came out in June 1855, bearing all the hallmarks of Kierkegaard's "attack upon Christendom"—the biting satire, the black humor, and the relentless disparagement of the Danish state church. What distinguishes this treatise, however, is that it draws even more heavily from the New Testament, applying, often quite literally, Christ's condemnation of the scribes and Pharisees to the ecclesiastical leaders of his day. Thus Kierkegaard's "attack upon Christendom" becomes Christ's as well, effectively completing the christological turn taken by Kierkegaard in the mid-1840s and epitomizing Kierkegaard's notion that Christian discipleship involves imitating (or, indeed, "re-presenting") Christ even in the midst of modern society.

Chapter Eight[1]

WHAT THE THOUGHT OF FOLLOWING CHRIST MEANS AND WHAT JOY LIES THEREIN

PRAYER

You who once wandered the earth yourself, leaving behind footprints that we are to follow; you who still look down from your heaven on each person who wanders, strengthen the weary, encourage the faint-hearted, restore the erring, comfort the struggling; you who shall come again at the end of time in order to judge each person individually, whether he followed you: our God and our savior, let your archetype stand very clearly before the eyes of the soul in order to dissipate the fog, strengthen in order to have this alone unchanged before our eyes, so that, by resembling you and by following you, we may find the right way to the judgment. For, after all, every human being ought to be brought before the judgment—oh, but may we also be brought by you to blessedness with you in the next life. Amen.

Luke 14:27: Whoever does not bear his cross, and come after me, cannot be my disciple.

Guidance is offered surely enough on life's way, and, no wonder, since every error passes itself off as guidance. Yet, even if errors are many,

---

1. From Niels Jørgen Cappelørn et al., eds., *Søren Kierkegaards Skrifter*, vol. 8 (Copenhagen: Gads Forlag, 2004), 319–30.

the truth is still only one, and there is only one who is "the way and the life," only one guidance that truly leads a person through life to life. Thousands upon thousands bear a name by which it is indicated that they have chosen this guidance—that they belong to the Lord Jesus Christ, after whom they call themselves Christians; that they are his subjects, whether they are masters or servants in other respects, slaves or freepersons, men or women.

They call themselves *Christians*, and they also call themselves by other names, which all designate a relation to this single guidance. They call themselves *believers* and by this signify that they are wanderers, strangers, and aliens in the world. Yes, a wanderer is not known as certainly by the staff in his hand (after all, many could also bear a staff, without being a traveler) as calling oneself a believer obviously testifies that one is on a journey. For faith just means this: what I am seeking is not here; that is precisely why I believe it. Faith just means the deep, strong, blessed unrest [*Uro*] that drives the believer, so that he cannot settle down [*ikke kan slaae sig til Ro*] in this world. Thus the one who did settle down also ceased being a believer. For a believer cannot sit still like one sits with a walking stick in one's hand; a believer wanders ahead.

They call themselves "*the communion of saints*" and by this signify what they should be and ought to be, what they hope to become at some point, when faith is given up and the walking stick laid down. They call themselves *cross-bearers* and signify by this that their way through the world is not as light as a dance but is heavy and laborious, though, to them, faith is still also the joy that overcomes the world. For just as the sailboat, which easily proceeds before the wind, deeply cuts its heavy path through the sea at the same time: so also the way of the Christian is easy when one looks at the faith that overcomes the world, yet hard when one looks at the laborious work at bottom. They call themselves "*followers of Christ*," and it is now on this name that we want to dwell, as we bear in mind:

*What the Thought of Following Christ Means and What Joy
   Lies Therein*

When the bold warrior presses forward courageously and receives all the enemy's arrows with his breast, yet also defends his squire who is following behind: can one then say that this assistant follows him? When the loving wife thinks that—in what she holds dearest in the world, in her husband—she has the beautiful example that she wished to attain in life, and she then femininely (for, after all, the woman was taken from the side of the man) wanders with him side by side, leaning on him: can one then say that this wife follows her husband? When the undaunted teacher stands calmly in his place, surrounded by ridicule, plotted against by envy; when every attack is directed only at him but never takes aim at the follower who becomes attached to him: can one then say that this follower follows him? When the hen sees that the enemy is coming and therefore spreads out her wings to cover up the chicks that are walking behind her: can one then say that these chicks follow the hen?

No, one cannot talk in this way; the relation must be changed. The bold warrior must fall out, so that it now can become manifest whether his squire will also follow him, follow him in the actuality of danger, when all the arrows are aimed at his breast, or whether he will cowardly turn back from the danger, lose courage, because he lost the courageous one. The noble husband—alas, he must step aside, go away from her, so that it now can become manifest whether the grieving widow, without his support, will follow him or whether she, deprived of his support, will let his example go. The undaunted teacher must hide himself or must be hidden in a grave so that it now can be revealed whether the follower will follow him, will hold out in that place surrounded by ridicule, plotted against by envy, or whether he, while alive, will relinquish the place in shame because the teacher honorably abandoned it in death.

To follow, then, means to go on the same path that was taken by the one whom one is following. Therefore it means that he no longer goes visibly in front. And thus it was necessary, after all, that Christ had to go away, had to die, before it could become manifest whether the disciple would follow him. It is many, many centuries since this happened, and yet, even now, it always happens in this way. For there is a time when Christ almost visibly walks by the child's side, goes in front of the child, but then a time also comes when he is taken away from the eyes of the sensory imagination, so that now, in the earnestness of decision, it can become manifest whether the adult will follow him.

When the child gets permission to hold onto its mother's dress: can one then say that the child goes the same way *just* as the mother does? No, one cannot say that. The child must first learn to go individually, to go alone, before it can go the same way as the mother and go just as she does it. And when the child learns to go individually, what, then, is the mother to do? She must make herself invisible. That her tenderness remains the same anyway, remains unchanged—yes, that it almost certainly increases in the time since the child has learned to go individually: of course, we know that well, whereas the child perhaps cannot always understand it.

But what it means for the child to have to learn to go individually and to go alone—in spiritual terms, that is the task assigned to the one who is to be one's follower. He must learn to go individually and to go alone. Ah, how strange! Almost jokingly and always with a smile we talk about the child's worry when it must learn to walk by itself. And yet, perhaps language has no stronger or more gripping or truer expression for the deepest grief and suffering than this: to go individually and to go alone. That, in heaven, solicitude is unchanged—indeed, if it were possible, heaven is even more concerned in this dangerous time—we know that well, of course. But perhaps it cannot always be understood while one is learning.

To follow, then, means to go individually and to go alone on the way that the teacher went. It means to have no visible person with whom one can consult, to have to choose oneself, to scream in vain as the child screams in vain (for the mother dares not help in overt fashion), to despair in vain (for no one can help, and heaven dares not help in overt fashion). But to be helped invisibly is precisely to learn to go individually, because it is to learn to transform one's mind into the likeness of the teacher's mind, who, however, is not visibly seen. To go alone! Yes, there is no one, no human being, who can choose for you or, in a final and decisive sense, give you counsel about the only important thing, decisively give you counsel about the matter of your salvation. And, even if ever so many were willing to do so, it would, after all, only be to your harm.

Alone! For when you have chosen, you will surely find fellow wanderers. But in the decisive moment, and every time there is mortal danger, then you are alone. No one, no one, hears your ingratiating prayer or heeds your fierce complaint—and yet there is help and willingness enough in heaven. But it is invisible. To be helped by it is precisely to learn to go alone. This help does not come from the outside and grip your hand; it does not support you like a loving person supports a sick person. It does not lead you back by force when you have gone astray. No, only when you completely give in, give up your will altogether, and give yourself away with your whole heart and mind: then the help comes invisibly. But then you have indeed gone alone.

One does not see the powerful instinct that leads the bird on its long course. The instinct does not fly in front and the bird behind it; it looks as if it were the bird who found the way. Likewise, one does not see the teacher but only the follower who resembles him, and it looks as if the follower himself were the way, precisely because he is the true follower, who goes alone by the same way.

This is what is implied in the thought of following someone. But to *follow Christ*, to take up his cross, or as it is put in the text in question: "to bear his cross." To bear his cross means to deny oneself, as Christ explains when he says: "If anyone will come after me, let him deny himself, and take up his cross, and follow me" (Matt 16:24). Or it was: "Let this mind be in you, which was also in Christ Jesus: who, being in the form of God, thought it not robbery to be equal with God: but made himself of no reputation, and took upon him the form of a servant, and was made in human likeness: and being found in fashion as a man, he humbled himself, and became obedient unto death, even the death of the cross" (Phil 2:5ff.). The archetype was like this; the imitation must also be like this, even if it is a *slow and difficult task* to deny oneself, a heavy cross to take up, a heavy cross to drag, and one that, according to the archetype's direction, is to be borne in obedience unto death, so that the follower resembles the archetype in dying "with the cross on," even if he does not die on the cross.

One good deed, one noble resolution, is not to deny oneself. Alas, perhaps one does learn this in the world, because even this is seen so rarely that, on the rare occasion, it is then seen with astonish-ment. But Christianity teaches otherwise. Christ did not say to the rich young man: "If you would be perfect, then sell all your goods and give it to the poor." Even this demand alone would seem exagger-ated and eccentric to many persons, wouldn't it? Perhaps one would not even admire the young man if he did such a thing, but smile at him as if he were an oddball or pity him as a fool. However, Christ is saying something else. He says: "Go your way, sell whatever you have, and give to the poor, and come, take up the cross, and follow me" (Mark 10:21). Therefore, to sell one's goods and to give to the poor is not to take up the cross. Or, at most, it is the beginning, the good beginning, in order to take up the cross and to follow Christ.

To give everything to the poor is the first step; it is (since, after all, the language allows an innocent cleverness) *to take up the cross*. The next step is the protracted continuation: to *bear one's cross*. It must take place everyday, not once and for all, and there must indeed be nothing, nothing, that the follower would be unwilling to give up in self-denial. It makes no essential difference at all whether it is a trifle (as one says) that he would not deny himself or whether it is something big. For even the trifle becomes infinitely significant as a guilt in relation to the required self-denial. Perhaps there was one who was willing to do what the rich young man failed to do, hoping thereby to attain the height of perfection, and who nevertheless did not become a follower, because he remained standing, "turned around and looked back"—at his great achievement. Or, if he went ahead, he still did not become a follower, because he thought he had done something so great that trifles did not matter.

Alas, why is it that to deny oneself in trifles is the most difficult thing of all? I wonder if it is not because a certain enhanced self-love is apparently capable of denying itself in great things. But the lesser, the more insignificant, the more petty the requirement is, the more offensive it is to self-love, because it is completely abandoned by its own and by the pompous notions of others in relation to such a task. However, that is just why self-denial is the more humble.

Why is it that denying oneself when one lives alone and as if in a backwater is the most difficult thing of all? I wonder if it is not because a certain enhanced self-love is also capable of apparently denying itself—when many are looking on admiringly. But just as little as it makes any difference (whatever the difference is) in what the individual person denies himself in relation to his circumstances—unconditionally, then, a beggar can deny himself as well as a king—so it makes no essential difference either (whatever the difference is) in what a person cannot deny oneself. For, in the end, self-denial is precisely the inwardness to deny oneself. And this is a hard and difficult task. For it is true that self-denial entails casting off burdens and could seem easy enough as far as it goes. But, of course, it is still hard to cast off the very burdens that self-love would carry so gladly, yes, so gladly that even now it is very difficult for self-love to understand that they are burdens.

To follow Christ, then, means to deny oneself and therefore means to *go the same way* as Christ went in the lowly form of a servant—poor, abandoned, mocked, not loving the world and not loved by it. And that means, consequently, *to go alone*. For the one who, in self-denial, gives up the world and all that belongs to the world forsakes every relation that otherwise tempts and imprisons. "So he does not go to his field, nor does he bargain or take a wife either." The one who, if necessary, surely does not love father and mother, sister and brother less than before but loves Christ so much more that he can be said to hate these others: certainly he goes alone, goes alone into the entire world. Yes, in the crisscrossing busyness of life, it seems like a difficult, an impossible task to live in this way; already it seems impossible to judge whether anyone is actually living in this way. But let us not forget that eternity is to judge how the task was carried out, and that eternity's earnestness will command that embarrassment be silent in relation to everything worldly, about which there is perpetual talk in the world.

For in eternity you will not be asked about how great a fortune *you are leaving*; the *survivors* ask about that. Nor will you be asked about how many battles you won, how clever you were, how powerful your influence; that, of course, becomes your *reputation in the future*. No, eternity will not ask about what *worldly* things remain *behind you* in the world. But it will ask about what riches you have gathered in heaven; about how often you have conquered your mind; about what control you have exercised over yourself, or whether you have been a slave; about how many times you have mastered yourself in self-denial, or whether you have never done it; about how often you, in self-denial, have been willing to offer a sacrifice for a good cause, or whether you have never been willing; about how often you, in self-denial, have forgiven your enemy, whether probably seven times or seventy times seven times; about how often you, in self-denial, bear insults patiently; about what you have suffered, not for your own sake or for the sake of your self-interested purposes, but what you, in self-denial, have suffered for God's sake.

And the one who is to ask you, the judge from whose verdict you cannot go to anyone higher: he was not an army commander who conquered kingdoms and lands, with whom you could talk about your earthly achievements; on the contrary, his kingdom was not of this world. He was not a person clothed in purple, with whom you could seek dignified company; for he only wore purple in indignity. He was not powerful through his influence, so that he could wish to be initiated into your worldly secrets; for he was so despised that the distinguished person dared visit him only under the cover of darkness.

Oh, it really is always a comfort to meet with like-minded people—when one is cowardly, then not to have to be brought before a court of warriors; when one is selfish and worldly-minded, then not to have to be judged by self-denial. And this judge not only knows what self-denial is; he knows not only to judge in such a way that no fraud can hide itself. No, his presence is the judging that lets everything die down and fade that, to the worldly, looked so good out in the world, that was heard and seen with admiration. His presence is the judging, for he was self-denial. He who was equal to God took on the form of a lowly servant. He who could rule over legions of angels—yes, over the origin and the end of the world—went around defenseless. He who had everything in his power gave up all power and could not even do anything for his beloved disciples but simply demand the same lowly and despicable conditions of them. He who was the Lord of creation constrained nature itself to keep quiet, for it was not until he had given up his spirit that the curtain split and the graves opened and the forces of nature betrayed who he was. If this is not self-denial, what, then, is self-denial!

This is what is implied in the thought of following Christ. But let us now bear in mind the *joy in this thought*.

My listener! If you imagine a young man who stands on the threshold of his life, where many paths open up before him, asking himself which track he would like to set foot on: is it not true, then, that he would closely inquire into where each particular path leads? Or, in what amounts to the same thing, would he not seek to get to know who had gone by that path previously? Then we mention to him the famous, the prized, the glorious names of the ones whose remembrance is preserved among persons. Perhaps at first we name many persons, so that the choice can stand in relation to the young man's possibility; thus the wealth of instruction offered can be abundant. But then he himself, driven by a desire in his gut, narrows the choice, and, at last, there remains for him only one, a single one, which in his eyes and from his heart is the most excellent of all. Then the young man's heart beats violently when he enthusiastically mentions this name—the only name to him—and says: "I want to go this way, because he went this way!"

Now we would not want to divert attention or waste time by naming such names. For, after all, there is still only one name in heaven and on earth, a single name, and therefore only one path to choose—if a person is to choose in earnest and to choose correctly. That is to say, there must be many ways, since a person is to choose; but, additionally, there must be just one to choose, if the earnestness of eternity is to rest upon the choice. A choice about which it is true that one can just as well choose one thing as another does not have the eternal earnestness of the choice. In the choice there must unconditionally be everything to win and everything to lose, if the choice is to have the earnestness of eternity, even though, as said, there must be a possibility of being able to choose something else, so that the choice actually can be a choice.

There is only one name in heaven and on earth, only one way, only one archetype. The one who chooses to follow Christ chooses the name that is higher than all names, the archetype that is highly exalted above all heavens, but still also human in such a way that it can be an archetype for a person, so that it is named and shall be named in heaven and on earth—in both places—as the highest. For there are archetypes whose names are mentioned on earth, but the highest one, the only one, must indeed have just this excluding quality—that it is named both in heaven and on earth—whereupon it is again perceived as the only name.

This name is the name of our Lord Jesus Christ. But, then, is it not joyous to dare to choose to go the same way that he went! Alas, in the world's confused and confusing talk, sometimes the simple and the earnest almost sound like a joke. The person who has probably experienced the greatest power that has ever been experienced in the world calls himself proudly the successor [Efterfølger] of Peter. But to be the follower [Efterfølger] of Christ! Yes, that does not tempt the pride of a person. It is permitted equally to the most powerful and to the most lowly, to the wisest as well as the most simple, which, again, is the very blessed thing in the end.

And is it really so glorious to become *the* excellent person, which no other person can become? Is it not more like hopelessness? Is it so glorious to eat on silver, when others are hungry? To dwell in palaces, when so many do not have shelter? To be the scholar that no ordinary person can become? To have a reputation in the sense that thousands upon thousands are excluded? Is that so glorious? And if this—the *envious* dissimilarity of *earthly life*—was the highest, would it then not be inhuman! And would not life be unbearable for the fortunate!

How different, on the other hand, when the only joy is to follow Christ. After all, a higher joy than this cannot be given: to be able to become the highest. And this sublime joy cannot be made more bold, more blessed, more secure than it is by the joyful, by the *merciful* thought *of heaven*—that every person can do this.

So, then, the one who chose to follow Christ goes forward on the path. And when he too must get to know the world and what is in it, the world's strength and his own weakness; when the fight against flesh and blood becomes anxiety-ridden; when the way becomes hard, the enemies many, the friends none: then the pain surely wrings this sigh from him: "I am going alone." My listener, if a child starting to learn to walk were to come crying to the adult and say: "I am walking by myself"—would not the adult then say: "That is precisely what is glorious, my child!" And following Christ is also like this. On this way it is not only the case, as is usually said, that when the need is greatest, the help is nearest. No, here—on this way—the height of suffering is nearest to perfection. Do you know of any other way on which this is the case? It is the opposite along any other way: if sufferings come there, then the weight is predominant— yes, even predominant in such a way that it can mean that one chose the wrong way.

In contrast, on the way along which a person follows Christ, the height of suffering is the most glorious. As the person wandering sighs, he accurately counts himself blessed. See, when a person sets foot on any other path, then doubtless he must make himself familiar in advance with the risks on the way. Perhaps it can go well and without a difficult accident, but, in like manner, perhaps so many hindrances can pile up that he cannot press his way forward. On the other hand, there is eternal safety on the road that is the way of self-denial, of following Christ. The "signs" of suffering are on this way—the joyous signs that one is going ahead on the right path. But what joy is even greater than daring to choose the best way, the way to the highest. And so, in turn, what joy is as great as this, except the joy that, in all eternity, the way is certain!

Even still, there is a final blessed joy contained in the thought of following Christ. For, as was explained, surely Christ does not go with the follower, nor does he go visibly before him. Rather, he has gone *ahead*, and this is the follower's joyful hope: that he is to follow him. After all, it is one thing to follow him on the way of self-denial— and even this would be joyous—but something else to follow him into eternal blessedness. When death has separated two lovers, and then the survivor dies, then we say: "Now she has followed him; he went ahead." Christ went ahead in this way, and not only in this way, for he went ahead *in order to prepare a place for the follower*.

When we are talking about a human predecessor, then perhaps it holds true that, by going ahead, he has made the way easier for the one who follows him. And when the way that we are talking about concerns the earthly, the temporal, the imperfect, then it may be the case that the way has even become quite easy for the follower. This is not true in relation to the Christian or about the perfect way of self-denial. In essence, this way is always equally difficult for every follower. But, then, that Christ went ahead is true in an entirely different sense: he did not prepare the way for the follower by going ahead, but he went ahead in order to prepare a place for the follower in heaven. At times, a human predecessor can say with justification: "Now it is easy enough to go behind, since the way has been paved and prepared and the gate wide." Christ, on the other hand, must say: "Look, everything is prepared in heaven—if you are prepared to go in by the narrow gate of self-denial and along its straitened path."

Amid the world's busyness, perhaps this place in the hereafter seems very uncertain. But, after all, the one who renounced the world and himself in self-denial must have convinced himself that such a place exists. Indeed, the one who exists must be somewhere; he must take refuge somewhere. Yet, he cannot have his place in the world that he has given up. That is why there must be another place; yes, there must be, so that he is able to give up the world. Oh, how easy this is to understand for a person, if he actually has denied himself and the world! And it is also easy to test his life in this respect, how far one actually is assured that there is such a place in the next world, whether one actually has his life eternally assured.

The Apostle Paul says (1 Cor 15:19): "If in this life only we have hope, we are the most miserable of all." This is even certain, because the one who forsakes all the world's goods and bears all its evils for the sake of Christ—if there were no eternal blessedness in the next world, he is deceived, awfully deceived. If there were no eternal blessedness in the next world, it seems to me that it must come into existence, simply out of compassion for such a person. If, then, a person does not hanker after earthly things and halcyon days, does not strive after earthly advantage, does not even grasp it when it is offered; if he chooses trouble and difficulty and the thankless task, whatever it may be, because he chose the best cause; if he, when he must do without earthly things, does not even have the consolation of knowing that he has done his very best to win them: then he is indeed a fool in the eyes of the world. He is the miserable one in the world. If, then, there were no eternal blessedness in the next world, then surely he would be the most miserable of all persons. His very self-denial would make him miserable—he who had not even tried to acquire earthly things but voluntarily gave them up.

On the other hand, if there is an eternal blessedness in the next world, then he—the miserable one—is really the richest of all. For it is one thing to be the most miserable in the world, if the world is thought to be the highest; it is another thing to be the most miserable in the world, if there is eternal blessedness, or to be that if there were no eternal blessedness. The proof that this eternal blessedness exists is conveyed by Paul most gloriously. For there can be no doubt about the fact that, without it, he would have been the most miserable of all. In contrast, if a person seeks to assure himself in this world, seeks to assure himself of the advantage of this world, then his assurance that there is an eternal blessedness in the next world is just not convincing. It hardly convinces others; it has hardly convinced him himself. However, no one is to judge about this, or each person himself alone. For even to want to judge another person in this respect is an attempt to assure oneself in this world. Otherwise, after all, he would realize that both judgment and eternal blessedness belong to the other world.

Alas, over the course of time, it often has been repeated—and the repetition continues—that someone goes ahead after whom another person longs, whom he wishes to follow. But never has any person, never any loved one, never any teacher, never any friend gone ahead—in order to prepare a place for the follower. Just as Christ's name is the only one in heaven and on earth, so also is Christ the only forerunner who has gone ahead in this way. Between heaven and earth, there is only one way: to follow Christ. In both time and eternity, there is only one choice, one single choice: to choose this way. On earth, there is but one eternal hope: to follow Christ into heaven. In life, there is one blessed joy: to follow Christ. And, in death, there is one final blessed joy: to follow Christ to life!

Chapter Nine[1]

"COME UNTO ME, ALL YOU THAT LABOR AND ARE HEAVY LADEN, AND I WILL GIVE YOU REST"

INVOCATION

It is true that it has been eighteen hundred years since Jesus Christ wandered here on the earth, but, after all, this is not an event like other events, which pass over into history as soon as they are done and then pass over into oblivion as distant past. No, his presence here on earth never becomes a thing of the past and therefore not more and more past either—if, at that time, faith is otherwise found on earth. For, if not, even in that same moment it is a long time since he lived. On the other hand, as long as there is a believer, this person—in order to have become that—also must have been and, as a believer, must be just as contemporary with Christ's presence as his contemporaries. This contemporaneity is the condition of faith, and, more accurately defined, it is faith.

Lord Jesus Christ, would that we also might become contemporary with you in this way, might see you in your true form and in the actual surroundings in which you walked here on earth, rather than in the form into which an empty and meaningless or a thoughtless-romantic or a historical-talkative remembrance has twisted you, since that is not the form of degradation in which the believer sees

---

1. From Niels Jørgen Cappelørn et al., eds., *Søren Kierkegaards Skrifter*, vol. 12 (Copenhagen: Gads Forlag, 2007), 17–33.

you, and it cannot possibly be the form of glory in which no one has seen you yet. Would that we might see you as you are and were and will be until your second coming in glory, as the sign of scandal and the object of faith, the lowly human being but the savior and redeemer of the human race, who came to earth out of love in order to seek the lost, in order to suffer and die, and yet out of concern—alas, for every step you took on earth, for every time you called to those who are in error, for every time you reached out your hand to do signs and wonders, and for every time you, defenseless, suffered the opposition of people without raising a hand—again and again had to repeat: "Blessed is *he*, who shall not be offended in me." Would that we might see you in this way, and that we, then, might not be offended at you!

THE INVITATION

Come unto me, all you that labor and are heavy laden,
and I will give you rest.

How wonderful, wonderful that the one who has help to bring is the one who says: "Come here!" What love! It is already loving when one is able to help, then to help the one who asks for help. But to offer the help oneself! And to offer it to everyone! Yes, and precisely to all those who could not help in return! To offer it—no, to shout it out, as if it were the helper himself who needed the help, as if he who can and wants to help everyone were still a needy person himself in one respect—that he feels need, and really needs to help, needs those who suffer in order to help them!

I

"Come here!"—Yes, there is nothing strange when the one who is in danger and needs help—perhaps needs quick and immediate help—shouts: "Come here!" And there is nothing strange either when a huckster begins shouting: "Come here! I have the cure for every sickness." Alas, in relation to the huckster, the untruth that it is the doctor who needs the sick is only all too true. "Come here, all you

who are able to pay dearly for the cure—or really the drugs. Here is medicine for everyone—who can pay. Come here, come here!"

But normally it is the case that the one who can help must be sought out. And when one has found him, he is perhaps still hard to talk to. And when one has talked to him, one must perhaps still plead with him for a long time. And when one has pleaded with him for a long time, perhaps he lets himself be persuaded at long last—that is, he makes himself expensive. And at times, just when he will not take money or when he magnanimously forgoes it, this is but an expression for how infinitely expensive he sees himself.

In contrast, he who gave himself up, he gives himself up here as well. He himself is the one who seeks those who have need of help; he himself is the one who goes around—and calling, almost pleading— says: "Come here." He—the only one who can help and help with the one thing needful, who is able to save from the only life-threatening sickness in the truest sense—he does not wait for anyone to come to him. He comes by himself, without being called. For, after all, he is the one who calls on them. He offers help—and what help!

Yes, that simple wise man of antiquity was just as infinitely much in the right as most persons when they do the opposite, when they are wrong, in that he neither made himself nor his teaching expensive (even if, in another sense, he thereby expressed the dissimilar value with noble pride). But he was not so concerned out of love that he implored anyone to come to him—should I now say "although," or should I say "because"?—he was not entirely certain about what his help would mean. For the more certain one is that his help is the only help, the more reason, humanly speaking, to make it expensive, and the less certain, the more reason to offer his possible help with greater readiness, in order to do something after all. But he who calls himself the Savior and knows himself to be that, he says out of concern: "Come here."

"Come here, *all of you!*"—Wonderful! That a person, who perhaps cannot help one single person in the end, says too much and thoughtlessly invites everyone—that is not so wonderful, considering that people are the way they are. But when a person is entirely certain that he can help, and when he also is willing to help, when he is willing to expend all his time in this way and with every sacrifice: even so he usually reserves one thing for himself—to make a choice. However willing one is, one still does not want to help everyone; one will not abandon oneself in this way.

But he—the only one who in truth can help and in truth can help everyone, the only one therefore who in truth can invite everyone—he makes no condition at all. This saying, which seems to have been designed for him from the beginning of the world, he says it as well: "Come here, all of you." Oh, human self-sacrifice, even when you are most beautiful and most noble, when we admire you the most, here is still one sacrifice more—to sacrifice every determination of one's own self. Consequently, in the willingness to help, there is not even the least partiality. Oh, love, thus to set no determination of price at all upon oneself, to forget oneself completely, so that one is someone who helps, entirely blind to who it is one is helping, seeing with infinite clarity that, whoever he is, he is a sufferer. Thus to want to help everyone unconditionally—alas, therein different from everyone!

"Come here *to me!*" Wonderful! For, after all, human sympathy also willingly does something for those who labor and are heavy laden. One feeds the hungry, clothes the naked, makes charitable donations, starts charitable foundations, and, if the sympathy is more heartfelt, one probably also visits those who labor and are heavy laden. But to invite them to come to one, that cannot be done; then one's entire household and way of life would have to be changed. To live and to reside in a house together in a common life and in day-to-day dealings with the poor and the miserable, with those who labor and are heavy laden, is not acceptable, even when living in abundance or, at any rate, in peace and joy.

In order to be able to invite them to come to one in this way, one must live exactly in the same manner oneself—poor as the poorest, esteemed as lowly as the lowly man among the people, familiar with life's sorrow and agony, totally belonging to the same condition as those one invites to come to one, those who labor and are heavy laden. When a person wants to invite the sufferer to come to him, he must either change his condition in conformity with that of the sufferer or change the sufferer's condition in conformity with his own. For, if not, the dissimilarity only becomes greater in contrast. And if a person wants to invite all suffering persons to come to him (for, after all, he can make an exception for an individual and change his condition), it can only be done in one way—by changing his condition in conformity with theirs, if it is not already originally so designed, as was the case with him who says: "Come unto me, all you who labor and are heavy laden." He says that, and those who lived with him saw and see that there is truly not the slightest thing in his way of life that contradicts it. With the silent and truthful eloquence of action that his life expresses—even if he never would have said these words—his life expresses: "Come unto me, all you who labor and are heavy laden." He stands by his word, or he himself is his word. He is what he says: in this sense, too, he is the Word.

"All you who labor and are heavy laden." Wonderful! The only thing he is worried about is that there might be one person who labored and was heavy laden who did not get to hear this invitation. That many persons might come is not his concern, since he is not afraid. Oh, where there is room in the heart, there is indeed always room. But where was there room in the heart, if not in his heart! How the individual will understand the invitation, he leaves that to the individual. His conscience is free; he has invited all those who labor and are heavy laden.

But what is it, then, to labor and to be heavy laden? Why does he not explain it more meticulously, so that one can know with certainty what he means? Why is he so sparing of words? Oh, you nitpicker, he is so sparing of words in order not to be nitpicking; you narrowhearted person, he is so sparing of words in order not to be narrowhearted. It is precisely love (for "love" is for everyone) that holds him back, lest there be a single person who can be made anxious by brooding over whether he is among the invited as well. And the one who would call for a more meticulous definition—would it not be a form of self-love that calculated that especially this would take care of and be suitable for him, without considering that the more such stricter and stricter definitions there were, the more inevitable that, in turn, there might be individuals and individuals for whom it would become increasingly harder to define whether they were invited.

Oh, human being, why does your eye only look to your own interest? Why is it evil, because he is good! The invitation to all opens the inviter's arms, and, in this way, he stands as an eternal image. As soon as a meticulous definition appears, which perhaps would help the individual to another kind of certainty, then the inviter looks different, then a shadow of change, as it were, hovers over him.

"I will give you rest." Wonderful! For, then, surely that saying "come *unto me*" must be understood in this way: "Remain with me; I am the rest, or to remain with me is rest." Thus it is not as it usually is—that the helper who says, "Come here," next must say, "Now go back," while he then explains to each individual where the help he needs is to be found, where the pain-killing herb grows that can heal him, or where the quiet place is where he can unwind from his labor, or where the more fortunate part of the world is where one is not heavy laden. No, he who opens his arms and invites everyone—oh, if all, all who labor and are heavy laden would come to him, then he would gather them all in his arms and say: "Now remain with me, for to remain with me is rest."

The helper is the help. Oh, wonderful, he who invites all and wants to help all, his way to treat the sick is precisely as if it were intended for each individual, as if in each sick person he had, he only has this one sick person. Normally, a doctor must divide himself among his many patients, who, however many there are, are still very far from being everyone. He prescribes the medication; he says what needs to be done, how it is to be used; and then he goes—to another patient; or if the patient has been with him, he lets the patient go. The doctor cannot sit all day with a single patient, even less have all his patients at home with him and yet sit the entire day with one patient—without neglecting the others. That is also why the helper and the help are not one and the same thing. The help that the doctor prescribes is kept by the patient all day for the sake of regular use, while the doctor looks in on him only now and then, or the patient sees the doctor only now and then. But if the helper is the help, then, after all, he must remain with the sick person or the sick person with him the entire day—how wonderful, then, that this helper is the very one who invites everyone!

II

Come unto me, all you who labor and are heavy laden,
and I will give you rest.

What immense diversity, what almost boundless dissimilarity among those invited. For a human being, a lowly human being, certainly can try to give an account of some particular differences—the inviter must invite all, even each one separately or as an individual.

So, then, the invitation goes out along the highways and the byways, and along the loneliest way—yes, where there is a way so lonely that only one person, one solitary person knows it (otherwise no one does), so there is only one trail—that of the unhappy person, who fled down that way with his misery (or else no trail and no trail by which one can come back along this way): there, too, the invitation fights its way. It finds the way back itself easily and safely, most easily when it leads the runaway with it to the inviter. "Come here, come here all of you, and you, and you, and you as well, you the loneliest of all those who run away!"

The invitation goes out in this way, and, wherever there is a crossroad, it stands still and calls. Oh, just as that soldier's bugle call turns to all four corners of the world, so does the invitation resound wherever there is a crossroad, and not with an uncertain sound—for who, then, would come!—but with the reliability of eternity.

It stands at the crossroad—there where temporal and earthly suffering placed its cross—and calls. "Come here, all you poor and wretched, you who must slave in poverty in order to secure for yourselves—not a carefree but a toilsome future." Oh, bitter contradiction: to have to slave in order to *secure* what one sighs under, what one *flees from*.

"You who are looked down upon, you who are overlooked, whose existence no one, no one cares about, not even as much as a domestic animal, which has more value!—You sick, lame, deaf, blind, crippled, come here!—You bedridden, yes, you come here too. For the invitation dares to invite the bedridden…to come!—You lepers!" For the invitation disrupts all differences in order to gather all; it wants to make good again what difference is guilty of: to assign to one person the position as ruler over millions, in possession of all the goods of fortune, and to another a place out in the desert—and why (what cruelty!), because (oh, cruel human conclusion!) *because* he is miserable, indescribably miserable, and so then because he needs help or compassion, and so then because human compassion is a despicable invention that is cruel where the greatest need is to be compassionate and only compassionate where it really is not compassion in truth!

"You who are sick at heart, you who only through pain got to know that a human being has a heart in a different sense than an animal and what it means to suffer there and what it means that the doctor can be right that a person is heart healthy and nevertheless heartsick; you whom faithlessness deceived and whom human sympathy (for human sympathy rarely keeps one waiting) then made a target for mockery; all you mistreated and injured and violated and abused; all you noble ones who—as everyone knows to say to you, after all—deservingly harvested the reward of ingratitude, for why would you be stupid enough to be noble, why foolish enough to be loving and unselfish and faithful; all you sacrifices to cunning and deceit and slander and envy, whom baseness picked out and cowardice left high and dry, whether you are sacrificed in some out-of-the-way and lonely place after having gone away to die, or whether you are trampled down by the human throng, where no one asks about what right you have, no one asks about what wrong you suffer, no one asks about where it aches or how it might be painful, while the throng tramples you into the dust with beastly vigor: come here!"

The invitation stands at the crossroad, where death comes between death and life. "Come here, all you sorrowing ones, you who labor and are heavy laden in vain!" For there is certainly rest in the grave. But to sit by a grave or to stand by a grave or to go to a grave is, after all, not yet to lie in the grave. And again and again to read silently one's own writing, which one can do by heart, the inscription that one put there oneself, and one best understands oneself who it is who lies buried *here*: that, of course, is not the same as lying buried oneself. In the grave there is rest, but *by* the grave there is no rest. It is said: up to here and no further, so you can go home again. But however often you come back to *that* grave day after day, in thought or on foot—you come no further, not from the spot. And this is very trying and does not convey rest. "Therefore come here." Here is the way by which one goes further; here is rest by the grave, rest from the pain of privation. Or there is rest in the pain of privation—through him, who eternally reunites those separated more firmly than nature unites parents and children, children and parents—alas, they were separated in the end; more fervently than the priest unites husband and wife—alas, separation indeed entered in; more indissolubly than the bond of friendship unites one friend and another—alas, it was undone, after all. Everywhere separation pierced through to bring pain and unrest. But here is rest!

"You, too, come here. You whose whereabouts are consigned among the graves, regarded as dead by human society but not missed, not lamented—not buried yet dead, that is, neither belonging to the living nor to the dead—alas, you to whom human society cruelly shut itself, and for whom still no grave has opened out of mercy: you, too, come here. Here is rest, and here is life!"

The invitation stands at the crossroad, where the way of sin swerves from the fence of innocence—oh, come here, you are so close to him. A single step along the other way, and you are so infinitely far away from him. It may well be that you still do not need to rest, do not understand what that truly means, but follow the invitation so that the inviter may save you from what is so hard and dangerous to be saved from. Thus saved, you may remain with him, who is the Savior of all, even the Savior of innocence. For even if it were possible that perfectly pure innocence was found somewhere: why should it not also need a savior who could keep it safe from evil!

The invitation stands at the crossroad, where the way of sin swerves more deeply into sin. "Come here all you who have stumbled and gone astray, whatever your error and sin was, be it more excusable in human eyes and yet perhaps more terrible, or be it more terrible in human eyes and yet perhaps more excusable, whether it became manifest here on earth or whether it is hidden and yet known in heaven—and even if you found forgiveness on earth but still not rest on the inside, or found no forgiveness because you did not seek it or because you sought it in vain: oh, turn back and come here; here is rest!"

The invitation stands at the crossroad, where the way of sin swerves for the last time and vanishes before one's eyes—into perdition. "Oh, turn back, turn back, come here." Do not shudder at the difficulty of retreat, no matter how hard it is. Do not be afraid of the burdensome path of conversion, however laboriously it leads to the Savior, whereas sin leads onward with winged speed, with rising velocity—or leads downward so easily, so indescribably easily, even as easily as when the horse, completely exempt from pulling, still cannot stop the wagon with all his might, so that it runs into the abyss. Do not despair over every relapse, which the God of patience has the patience to forgive and under which a sinner really should have patience to humble himself. No, fear nothing and do not despair. He who says, "Come here," is with you on the way; from him are help and forgiveness on the way of conversion, which leads to him. And with him is rest.

"Come here, all, all, all of you." With him is rest. And he makes no difficulty; he does only one thing: he opens his arms. He will not first ask you, you suffering one—alas, as righteous persons do, even when they want to help: "You are not yourself to blame for your misfortune, are you? You have nothing to reproach yourself for, have you?" It is so easy, this human tendency to judge according to appearance, according to the result: when one is a cripple, is deformed, has an unprepossessing appearance, then to judge that *ergo* he is an evil person; when one is unfortunate enough to suffer badly in the world, so that he amounts to nothing or so that it hit rock bottom for him, then to judge that *ergo* he is a bad person. Oh, and it is such an exquisitely invented kind of cruel pleasure to want to feel one's own righteousness just opposite a person who is suffering, by explaining his suffering as God's punishment upon him, so that one therefore does not even dare to help him, or by laying that disapproving question before him, which flatters one's own righteousness before one helps.

But he will not ask you in this way; he does not want to be your benefactor in a cruel way. And if you are conscious of yourself as a sinner, he will not ask you about it; he will not break the bruised reed even more but will raise you up when you join him. He will not point you out by contrast, as he places you apart from himself, so that your sin becomes even more terrible. He will give you a hiding place with himself, and, hidden in him, he will hide your sins. For he is the sinner's friend. When one is talking about a sinner, then he does not simply stand still, open his arms, and say, "Come here." No, he stands—and waits, as the father of the prodigal son waited. Or he does not stand and wait; he goes to seek the sinner, as the shepherd sought the strayed sheep, as the woman sought the lost penny. He goes—still no. He has gone, but infinitely farther than any shepherd and any woman. After all, he went the infinitely long way from being God to becoming a human being; he went that way in order to seek sinners!

III

Come unto me, all you who labor and are heavy laden,
and I will give you rest.

"*Come here!*" For he assumes that those who labor and are heavy laden are sure to feel the burden heavy, the labor heavy, and now stand there perplexed and sighing: one, with a glance, looking all around to find help, another with downcast eyes because he saw no comfort, a third staring upward, as if it might still come from heaven—but all searching. Therefore he says: "Come here." The one who ceased to seek and to sorrow, he does not invite.

"*Come here!*" For he, the inviter, knows that just this is part of true suffering, to go to a secluded place by oneself and ponder in quiet hopelessness, without courage to confide in anyone, still less to dare to hope for help with boldness. Alas, that man possessed by a demon was not the only one beset by a dumb spirit; any suffering that does not begin by making the suffering person speechless does not mean much, as little as erotic love when it does not make one silent. Suffering persons whose quick tongues run effortlessly with their stories of suffering neither labor nor are heavy laden. See, that is why the inviter does not dare to wait for those who labor and are heavy laden to come to him; he himself calls them lovingly. Perhaps all his willingness to help would not really help, if he did not say these words and thereby take the first step. For in the calling of these words ("Come unto me") he certainly comes to them.

Oh, human sympathy, at times perhaps it is still respectable self-control, even perhaps at times true and heartfelt compassion, when you refuse to ask the one whom you suspect is going and brooding over a hidden suffering. But, to be sure, it is often a shrewd-ness as well, which does not wish to get to know too much! Oh, human sympathy, how often it was still only curiosity, not sympathy, that you dared to venture into a suffering person's secret, and how you felt it as a burden, almost as a punishment of your curiosity, when he followed the invitation and came to you! But he who says these freeing words, "Come here," he does not deceive himself as he says these words. Nor will he deceive you when you come to him in order to find rest by casting your burden on him. He follows his heart's prompting in saying that, and his heart follows the words—if, then, you follow these words, then they follow you back again to his heart. It is a matter of course that the one follows from the other—oh, that you would only follow the invitation.

"Come here!" For he assumes that those who labor and are heavy laden are so weary and exhausted and fainting that they, as if sedated, have become oblivious to the fact that there is comfort. Or, alas, he knows that it is just all too true that there is no comfort and help, if it is not sought in him. That is why he must call out to them, "Come here!"

"Come here!" For, after all, every society has a symbol or something by which it is known that one belongs to it. When a young woman is spruced up in a certain way, one knows that she is going to a dance. "Come here, all you who labor and are heavy laden." "Come here!" You do not need to wear an external and conspicuous sign of distinc-tion. Come with only an anointed head and washed face, when you labor and are heavy laden in your heart alone.

"Come here!" Oh, do not stand still and think twice. No, consider, consider, that for every moment you stand still after having heard the invitation, the next moment you will hear its call more faintly and, in

this way, distance yourself, even if you remain on the spot. "*Come here!*" Oh, however tired and weary you are of the labor or of the long, long, and yet previously futile running after help and rescue, even if it seems to you that could not gain one step more, could not hold out one moment longer without dropping: oh, even now, just one step. Here is rest! "*Come here!*" Alas, but if there was one who was so miserable that he could not come—oh, a sigh is enough. That you sigh after him—even a sigh is to come here.

Chapter Ten[1]

CHRIST IS THE WAY

PRAYER

Lord Jesus Christ, you who knew your destiny in advance and yet did not draw back; you who then let yourself be born in poverty and in lowliness and thereafter bore the world's sin in poverty and in lowliness; a sufferer, hated, abandoned, mocked, spat upon, finally even forsaken by God, until you bowed your head in that ignominious death: oh, but you lifted it up again, you eternal victor—you who, in life, certainly did not conquer your enemies but, in death, even conquered death; you lifted up your head again, forever victorious, you who ascended into heaven![2] Would that we might follow you!

Christ is the way. These are his own words, so it certainly must be the truth.

And this way is *narrow*. These are his own words, so it certainly must be the truth. Yes, even if he had not said it, it would still be the truth. Here you have an example of what it is to "preach" in the highest sense. For even if Christ had never said, "Strait *is* the gate, and narrow *is* the way, which leads unto life," look at him and you immediately see: the way is narrow. But this is, after all, an entirely different constant and penetrating proclamation of the fact that the way is

---

1. From Niels Jørgen Cappelørn et al., eds., *Søren Kierkegaards Skrifter*, vol. 13 (Copenhagen: Gads Forlag, 2009), 80–92.
2. Elsewhere Kierkegaard specifies that this discourse is based on Acts 1:1–12, which concerns Jesus's ascension in heaven.

narrow—that every single day, every hour, every moment his life expresses that the way is narrow—than if his life had not expressed it, and he then had proclaimed a few times: "The way is narrow." In addition, here you see that the proclamation of what is Christian for half an hour, by a man whose life expresses the opposite every day, every hour of the day, every moment, is the greatest possible distance from the true proclamation of Christianity. Such a proclamation transforms what is Christian into its very opposite.

In that old hymn ("O great God, we praise you"), which names the various proclamations of the Word, there is no mention of the kind of proclamation that is an invention of a later time—"when Christianity has conquered completely." It is said in the hymn that "the prophets made you (God) known"; they were the first in time. Next "the apostles proclaimed you." They are the extraordinary ones: prophets and apostles. Now comes a whole host, a swarm of human beings—then both you and I are included, I can imagine—yes, now listen: "And the host of martyrs praised you solemnly in the hour of death." And then it is over. This is the true proclamation of the doctrine that the way is narrow. The proclaimer does not mock himself, as would be the case if the way he himself went was easy, while he (perhaps touched, convincing, perhaps not without tears—though perhaps weeping also comes easily to him!) nevertheless proclaims that "the way" is narrow—that is, the way he does not go by.

No, the life of the proclaimer expresses the teaching: the way is narrow. There is only one way—the one by which the proclaimer goes, proclaiming that "the way" is narrow. There are not two ways, one easy, smooth, by which the proclaimer goes, proclaiming that "the way" is narrow—that is, the true way, the way he does not go by—so that his proclamation invites persons to follow Christ along the narrow way, while his life (and, naturally, it exerts much greater force) invites them to follow the proclaimer on the easy, smooth way. Is this Christianity? No, in Christian terms, life and proclamation are to express the same thing, this very thing: "the way" is narrow.

And this way, which is Christ, this narrow way is *narrow in its beginning.*

He is born in poverty and wretchedness. One is almost tempted to think that it is not a human being who is born here. He is born in a stable, swaddled in rags, laid in a manger, yet, amazingly enough, already as an infant plotted against by those in power, so that his poor parents must flee with him. That is, in truth, even a particularly narrow way. For, when one is highborn (for example, as an heir to the throne), yes, then it can very well happen that one becomes an object of persecution by the mighty. But to be born in a stable and swaddled in rags—that is destitution and poverty that can be urgent enough. But then one usually is exempt from the persecutions of the mighty.

But just as he does not seem destined for highness by his birth, so did it also remain about like it was at the beginning: he lives in poverty and in lowliness; he does not have a place where he can lay his head.

To be sure, this would already be just about enough so that, humanly speaking, it might be said that a way is narrow. And yet, this is doubtless the easiest part on the narrow way.

The way is narrow in an entirely different sense, and from the very beginning. For his life is a story of temptation from the very start. It is not only a particular chapter of his life—the forty days—in which there is a story of temptation. No, his life (which is also a story of suffering) is a story of temptation. In every moment of his life, he is tempted—that is to say, he has this possibility in his power, to take his calling, his task, in vain. It is Satan who is the tempter in the desert, or else it is others who execute the role of the tempter, now the people, now the disciples, perhaps even at one time, especially in the beginning, the powerful tried to tempt him to make his calling and his task worldly—and then, in one way or another, he would have become something great in the world, a king and a ruler, his beloved disciples' only wish. Then, after all, he could be tempted to give in a little for their sakes, instead of having to make them, humanly speaking, as ill fated as possible. Just as others, then, fight hard from the very beginning in order to become a king, a ruler, so has he from the very beginning had to guard with an infinitely greater effort against being made a king and a ruler.

What a narrow way! Narrow enough when the suffering is unavoidable, when there is no way out; a narrower way when in every moment of suffering (alas, and every moment was suffering!) is this—frightful!—possibility that almost is imposed on him, this possibility of so easily being able to obtain more than relief—victory and everything that a mortal heart could desire! Narrow way, which still so many a true follower has had to travel, even if on a smaller scale! The universally human is to aspire to becoming looked upon as someone great; and the universal forgery is to pretend to be something more than one is. Religious suffering begins differently. Through the relation to God, the one who is called feels powerful in this way—that he is simply not tempted by the aspiration of being looked upon as more. No, but in the same moment a mortal dread runs through him, because he understands that this kind of gift usually means certain downfall. And then the temptation is to say less about himself than what is true. No one, no one but God will be able to know it, and, if he does it, then joy and jubilation and glory are in store for him. For then he is victorious—therefore he precisely must guard against being victorious. Narrow way!

The way is narrow from the very beginning, because, from the very start, he foreknew his destiny. Oh, fearful weight of suffering right from the beginning! There was many a one, many a one, who went undauntedly, almost jubilantly, into battle with the world. He hoped that he would be victorious. It did not turn out that way; the situation took a different turn. Yet, even in that moment—when downfall seemed unavoidable most of all—even in that moment perhaps there was still in him a human hope that even now it could take a turn toward victory or a god-fearing hope that even now everything could take a turn toward victory, since all things are possible for God.

But Christ knew his destiny from the beginning, knew that it was unavoidable—after all, he himself willed it; after all, he himself went into it freely! Fearful knowledge from the very start! When the people, in the beginning of his life, shout at him with joy, he knew in that moment what it means: it is this people who will yell, "Crucify!" "Why, then, does he want to have anything to do with the people?" You dare to talk so presumptuously to the Savior of humankind! Once again, he now does a work of love for these people (and his entire life was nothing but a work of love), but, at the same moment, he knows what it means—that even this work of love is part of bringing him to the cross. Had he loved himself and stopping doing works of love, then perhaps his crucifixion would have become doubtful. "But, then, he certainly could have stopped doing that work!" You dare to talk so presumptuously to the Savior of humankind! Oh, narrow way! Narrow way, which still so many a true follower has had to travel, even if on a smaller scale!

For a human heart, it is a joyous feeling to be sure of the powers that have been granted to one. Thus there is a moment in the beginning when "the one who is called" tries out his strength, as it were, happy and thankful as a child for what has been granted to him. And, like a child, he perhaps asks for even more, albeit humbly, and it is given to him. And still more, which is given. He himself is almost overwhelmed; he says, "No, now I do not ask for more." But it is as if there was a voice that said to him, "Oh, my friend, that is only a small part of what is granted to you." Then he turns pale, the one who is called, he nearly collapses in a faint; he says, "Oh, my God, I do understand it. So, then, my destiny is already decided, my life dedicated to suffering, to be sacrificed. And by now I must be able to understand that!" Narrow way!

Yes, the way is narrow from the very beginning, because he knows from the very beginning that his word is to work against himself. Oh, the way can certainly be narrow where you still get permission to use all your strength in order to prevail while the opposition is outside yourself. Yet, when you are to use your strength in order to work against yourself, then it seems infinitely too little to say that the way is narrow. Indeed, if anything, it is impassable, blocked, impossible, mad! And yet, it is the way about which it holds true that Christ is the way; it is narrow in just this way. For the true, the good, that he wills—if he does not let it go, if he works for it with all his might, then he is working himself into certain downfall. And, on the other hand, if he inserts the whole truth too quickly, then his downfall will come too soon. Thus he, working against himself, must seem to enter into illusions for a time in order to secure the downfall all the more deeply. Narrow way! To go by this way is immediately, at the beginning, like dying! Omnipotently to try out, as it were, the powers of omnipotence, to be a human being and, in this way, fit to be able to suffer through all human sufferings—and then to have to use these powers

261

of omnipotence in order to work against oneself, to know it right from the start—oh, a narrow way from the very beginning!

And this way, which is Christ, this narrow way, then becomes narrower and narrower as it progresses, until the end, until death.

It becomes narrower. Therefore, it does not become easier little by little. No, a way that becomes easier little by little—that Christ is the way does not hold true about it. Human shrewdness and common sense go along such a way. One perhaps has more shrewdness, has a greater intellect than another person, therefore is capable of venturing further and holding out longer, but it constantly holds true that common sense and shrewdness can calculate that when suffering and exertion are endured for a longer or shorter time, then the way becomes easier, and one is still victorious in life. On the other hand, a way that becomes narrower and narrower until the end: shrewdness and common sense never go along that way—"that would be madness, after all."

Yet, whether it is madness or shrewdness, it is like this: the narrow way becomes narrower.

"I am come to send fire on the earth; and what will I, if it be already kindled!" That is a sigh—the way is narrow. A sigh! What is a sigh? A sigh means that there is something shut up inside, something that wants out but that still cannot or must not come out, something that wants to get air. A person sighs, then, and gets something off his chest (in order not to die) while he gasps for air in order not to die. "I am come to send fire on the earth; and what will I, if it be already kindled!" How shall I describe this suffering! Let me try it, but right away let me recall the attempt beforehand and say that it is only a powerless nothing if it is to describe Christ's suffering.

Imagine, then, a ship, but you can indeed imagine it infinitely greater than anything seen in actuality. Imagine—in order to say something anyway—that it could carry a hundred thousand people. It is wartime, in battle—and the battle plan requires that it must be blown up. Imagine the commanding officer who must ignite this fire! And this is really only a poor, meaningless illustration. For what are a hundred thousand persons compared with the human race, and what is being blown up all at once compared with the terror of the fire that Christ would ignite, which, exploding, would divide father and son, son and father, mother and daughter, daughter and mother, mother-in-law and daughter-in-law, daughter-in-law and mother-in-law—and where the danger is not that of death but of the loss of eternal blessedness! "I am come to send fire on the earth; and what will I, if it be already kindled!" The moment, after all, is not here yet, the terrible moment, while it really is not less terrible, the moment beforehand, when one sighs: "Oh, if only it would happen!"

"O faithless generation, how long shall I be with you? How long shall I suffer you?" That is a sigh. It is like when the sick person—not on his sick bed but on his death bed (for it is no mild illness; he has been given up!)—rises up a bit, lifting his head from the pillow and says: "What time is it?" Death is the certainty; the question is just: "How far off is it? What time is it?" The moment, after all, has not come yet, the terrible moment, while it really is not less terrible, the moment beforehand, when the suffering person sighs: "How long do I still have to hold on?"

For the last time, then, he is gathered with his apostles for the meal that, with all his heart, he had longed to eat with them before he dies. As always, he is defenseless. Defenseless. Yes, for he certainly could have defended himself in one respect. He could—and it would have been a kindness that, by now, we human beings would have had to admire immensely—he could have said to Judas: "Stay away; do not come to this meal; the sight of you is painful to me." Or he could have asked one of the apostles—without really saying to him what he knew about Judas—to tell Judas that he should not come. But no! They are all assembled. Then he says to Judas: "What you are going to do, do quickly." That is a sigh. But quickly! Even the most horrifying is less horrifying: but quickly! A sigh that breathes deeply and slowly: but quickly! It is as when one who has an immense task to shoulder, tired almost beyond his strength, nevertheless feels that he still has energy remaining for the next moment—"One more moment and perhaps I am incapacitated, no longer myself"—and therefore: but quickly! "What you are going to do, do quickly."

So he rises from the table and goes out into the Garden of Gethsemane; there he sinks down—oh, that it would happen soon! He sinks down, destined to die—yes, was he actually any more a dying person on the cross than in Gethsemane! If the suffering on the cross was a fight to the death—oh, this spiritual warfare was even in life. Nor was it without blood, for his sweat fell like drops of blood to the earth.

Then he rises, strengthened: "Your will be done, Father in heaven!"

Then he kisses Judas—have you heard the like of it!—then he is seized, accused, condemned! It was an ordinary legal proceeding; it was human justice! There was a people whom he had done well by; truly he had willed nothing for himself. Every day of his life and every thought was sacrificed for this people—those who shout, "Crucify him; crucify him!" Then there was a prefect, who feared the emperor, a cultured man who therefore did not neglect the importance of "washing his hands"—and then he was condemned. Oh, human justice! Yes, in calm weather, when everything is going its smooth way, then a little bit of justice may take place. But every time the extraordinary arrives—oh, human justice! Oh, human culture, to what extent are you actually different from what you most abhor—rudeness, the coarseness of the masses? That you do the same as the crowd, but you are careful with the form, not to do it with unwashed hands—oh, human culture!

Then he is nailed to the cross—and so only one sigh more, then it is over. One sigh more, the deepest, the most terrifying: "My God, my God, why have you forsaken me?" This humiliation is the last of the suffering. You will find weak suggestions of the same thing in his followers—in the stricter sense, the blood witnesses. They have appealed to God and for God's assistance; abandoned by all, they have been strong and felt strong through God's assistance—yes, what a miracle! Then comes a moment at the end, and the sigh goes: "God has forsaken me." "Therefore you are right, my enemies; now shout with joy. All that I have said was not true; it was a fantasy. Now it is revealed: God is not with me; he has forsaken me." Oh, my God! And indeed he—he had claimed to be the Father's only begotten Son, one with the Father. One with the Father—but if they are one, how then can the Father forsake him at any moment! And yet, he says: "My God, my God, why have you forsaken me?" Therefore it was not true that he was one with the Father, after all. Oh, an extremity of super-human suffering. Oh, a human heart would have broken a little sooner. Only the God-man must suffer this suffering in full. Then he dies.

Now remember, my listener, what it was we said at the beginning: this way is narrow—is it not?

Still we go further; and *Christ is the way*. Christ is the way: he climbs the mountain; a cloud takes him away from the disciples' sight; he ascends into heaven—and he is the way!

Perhaps you are saying, "Yes, and there should have been talk about this today, not what you have talked about, almost as if it were Good Friday." Oh, my friend, are you the kind of person that can get into a certain mood precisely on the hour and date? Or do you assume that it is Christianity's intention that we should be like that or, even better, that we should combine the various things of Christianity as far as possible? That he is the narrow way ought to be recalled precisely on Ascension Day. For otherwise we could easily take the Ascension in vain. Remember, the way was narrow until the end; death comes in between—then the Ascension follows. It was not midway that he ascends into heaven; it was not even at the end of the way. For the way ends on the cross and in the grave. The Ascension is not a simple continuation of what came before, truly no! And a narrow way, which even in this life becomes easier and easier, it never soars so high—even when it soars highest to victory—never so high that it becomes an Ascension. But every living person is indeed—if he is on the right way at all, and not on a wrong way—he is indeed on the narrow way.

That is why the Ascension, and that Christ is the way, certainly should be talked about. Oh, but with the Ascension it is so easy to surpass, if only we reach there, and we reach there least of all by only wanting to think about the Ascension, even if you also let yourself be uplifted by the thought of his Ascension.

He ascends into heaven: never has anyone been victorious in this way! A cloud took him away from their sight: never has any triumphant person been lifted up from the earth in this way! They saw him no more: never has the end for anyone else been such a triumph! He sits at the right hand of power—so does the triumph not end with the Ascension? No, it begins with it: never has anyone triumphed in this way! He is coming again with a host of angels—so does the triumph not end with him taking the place at the right hand of the Almighty? No, it was only the end of the beginning: oh, eternal conqueror!

My listener, along which way are you going in life? Keep in mind what I say to myself—that it is not valid of every narrow way that Christ is that way, nor that it leads to heaven.

A pious man has said that it costs a human being just as much or even more hardship to go to hell as to come into heaven. Therefore perdition's way is a narrow way. But Christ is not that way, and it does not lead to heaven either. There is sufficient unrest and anxiety and agony on this way. As far as it goes, this way is truly narrow, the way to perdition, the way that—unlike the other ways we have talked about (the way that is narrow in the beginning and becomes easier and easier; the narrow way that becomes narrower and narrower)—is recognizable in that it seems so easy at the start but becomes more and more terrible. For it is so easy to step to the dance of desire, but, when it is further along, and it is desire that dances with the person against his will: that is an onerous dance! And it is so easy to give rein to the passions—daring speed, one can hardly follow with the eye!—until the passions, after having taken the reins given to them, sweep him away with even more daring speed! The person himself hardly dares to see where they are leading! And it is so easy to allow a sinful thought to creep into the heart—no seducer was as skillful as a sinful thought! It is so easy. Here it does not hold true as usual—that it is the first step that costs. Oh, no, it costs nothing at all. Just the opposite: the sinful thought pays for itself in costly decisions. It costs nothing at all—until the end, when you have to pay dearly for this first step that did not cost anything at all. For if the sinful thought enters in, it exacts a terrible payment. Most often sin enters into a person like a sycophant, but, when the person has become the slave of sin, it is the most terrible slavery—a narrow, an exceedingly narrow, way to perdition!

Again, there are also other narrow ways about which it does not unconditionally hold true that Christ is that way or that they lead to heaven. There are human sufferings enough, only all too many—sickness and poverty and being unappreciated, and who can name all these sufferings! Of course, everybody who goes along such a way also goes along a narrow way. Truly we should not talk in lofty tones, as if these sufferings amounted to nothing—oh, but you, my friend, certainly do know what Christianity is, and let me simply remind you about it. That which distinguishes the Christian narrow way from the common human narrow way is the voluntary. Christ was not one who coveted earthly goods but who had to be content with poverty; no, he chose poverty. He was not one who craved human honor and esteem but who had to be content with living in lowliness or perhaps unappreciated and slandered; no, he chose debasement. This is the narrow way in the strictest sense. The common human sufferings are not the narrow way in the strictest sense, yet the way truly can be narrow enough, and you also can strive to go along this narrow way of human sufferings in a Christian manner. If you go along it in a Christian manner, it really does lead to heaven, where he went, he the one who ascended.

Still, it is true that people have doubted the Ascension.

Yes, who has doubted? I wonder if any of their lives have borne the marks of "imitation"? I wonder if any of them have forsaken all things in order to follow Christ? I wonder if any of them were marked by persecution—and when "imitation" is a given, persecution follows. No, not one of them. But when people abolished "imitation" and in turn rendered persecution an impossibility, which, however, in the thieves' jargon that we human beings mutually speak did not sound like an accusation against an erring century's declining Christianity (God forbid!)—no, it sounded like a tribute to an enlightened century's matchless advance in tolerance; when they so reduced being Christian that being Christian almost became nothing—and so there was not anything to persecute either: then all sorts of doubts came up in that idleness and smugness. And doubt and who doubts became important, and people themselves became important by doubting—just as one formerly became important by giving all of one's goods to the poor (what we truly do not approve of but nevertheless understand better). In this way, one now became (presumably in order to establish the true concept of "the meritorious" in place of the misunderstanding of the Middle Ages, which one piously detested) self-important by doubting. And while one doubted everything, one thing was still beyond all doubt: by this claim ("We must doubt everything") one secured oneself a—nothing less than doubtful, no, an extremely firm—position in society, as well as great honor and esteem among persons.

Accordingly, some doubted. But then, in turn, there were some who sought to disprove doubt by reasons. In fact, the connection is surely this: first, people tried to prove the Christian with reasons or to apply reasons in relation to the Christian. And these reasons— they gave birth to doubt, and doubt became the stronger. That is, the proof for what is Christian really lies in "imitation." People took that away. Then they felt a need for "reasons," but these reasons, or that there are reasons, is already a kind of doubt—and so doubt rose up and lived on reasons. People did not notice that the more reasons one brings in, the more one nourishes doubt, and the stronger it becomes, so that to present reasons to doubt in order to kill it is just like offering a hungry monster one wishes to destroy the tasty food it loves most. No, one should not present reasons to doubt—at least not if one's intention is to kill it—but, as Luther did, one should command it to shut up and, to that end, keep quiet and include no reasons.

On the other hand, those whose lives were marked by "imitation" have not doubted the Ascension. And why not? In the first place, because their lives were too strained, too devoted in daily sufferings, to be able to sit in idleness and consort with reasons and doubt, playing odds and evens. For them, the Ascension stood firm; however, perhaps they came to think about or to dwell on it even more rarely—because, on the narrow way, their lives were so active. It is as with a soldier, who owns a magnificent uniform. He knows well that he has it, but he almost never looks at it, because his whole life is passed in daily combat and valor, and therefore he wears a daily uniform in order to move around properly.

See, in this way, those whose lives were marked by imitation were convinced that their Lord and Master ascended into heaven. And, again, it was imitation that contributed to this conviction. That they had to bear all these daily agonizing sufferings, that they had to give all these sacrifices, all this opposition, scorn and mockery and sneering and bloody cruelty of human beings, all this forced on "the imitator," the need that, just as the Ascension disrupts or conflicts with the laws of nature (that, after all, is doubt's objection), disrupts the merely human grounds of comfort (how should these even be able to comfort the one who must suffer because he is doing the good!), needs another kind of comfort, needs the Ascension of their Lord and Master, and faithfully presses through to the Ascension.

It is always like this with need in a human being. From the one eating comes something to eat: where the need is, there it itself generates, as it were, that which it needs. And the imitators truly needed his Ascension in order to endure the life they led—indeed, that is why it is also certain. But one who sits in idleness through good days or busily is on the go in busyness from morning to night but has never suffered anything for the sake of truth, he actually has no need. It is more like something he imagines, or something he lets himself imagine for money; he occupies himself with this Ascension almost as with a curiosity—and so, naturally, he doubts. He has no need either. Or he thinks up some reasons, or another person is so good to let him have three reasons—yes, his need really is not very great either!

And now you, my listener, what are you doing? Are you doubting the Ascension? If so, then do as I do; say to yourself: "Yes, one should not make a fuss over such a doubt; I know from where it comes and of what it comes—namely, that I must have spared myself concerning 'imitation,' that my life is not strenuous enough in this direction, that I am too much in clover, that I spare myself the dangers that are bound up with witnessing for truth and against untruth." Just do that! But, above all, do not become self-important by doubting. There is—I assure you!—not any basis for it either, since all such doubt actually is self-implicating. No, make a confession to yourself and to God, and, you will see, one of two things will happen: either you will be moved to venture further out in the direction of "imitation"—and then certainty about the Ascension comes immediately; or you will humble yourself, confess that you have spared yourself, that you have become a pushover of a preacher, and then at least you will not allow yourself to doubt but humbly will say: "If God wants to be so gracious to treat me like a child, who almost entirely is spared from the sufferings of 'imitation,' then I at least will not be a naughty child, who doubts the Ascension on top of that."

Oh, when you live admired, flattered, esteemed, in abundance, you are tempted to say many a word and to take part in much that you perhaps really would rather stop doing and that you (remember this!) still have to make an accounting for——and, moreover, the Ascension so easily slips out of your mind. When you think about it at some point, perhaps you even doubt and say: "An Ascension, after all, goes against all laws of nature, against the spirit in nature—but only the nature spirit!" But when it is for a good cause—for otherwise it does not help, and, if it is like that, the circumstances are indeed also in conflict with all merely human notions: to suffer because one does good, because one is in the right, because one is loving—when it is for a cause that you live forsaken, persecuted, derided, in poverty: you will see that you do not doubt his Ascension, because you need it.

And not even that much is needed in order to bring doubt to a standstill. For if you do humble yourself before God because your life is not marked as that of an imitator in the stricter sense, if you humble yourself under that, then you will not make so bold as to doubt. How should you be able to set about reporting with a doubt, when the answer would have to be: first, go and become an imitator in the stricter sense. Only an imitator has the right to speak up—and not one of these has doubted.

Chapter Eleven[1]

WHAT CHRIST JUDGES OF OFFICIAL CHRISTIANITY

It might seem strange that only now do I move forward with this, because Christ's judgment is surely decisive, however inconvenient it appears to the clerical guild of con men, which has seized the firm "Jesus Christ" and made brilliant profits under the name of Christianity.

At the same time, it is surely not without reason that only now do I bring what is decisive to light, and the one who attentively has followed my entire authorial activity cannot fail to notice that there is a certain method in the way I go about it, that it is characterized *both* by what I say—that the whole thing with "Christendom" is a criminal case corresponding to what people usually recognize as forgery, swindling, only that here it is religion that is used in this way—*and* of the fact that I actually am, as I put it, a police talent.

Just consider, then, so that you can follow the trail of the case. I started by posing as a poet, subtly taking aim at what I thought was the truth of official Christianity, that the difference between the freethinker and official Christianity is that the freethinker is an honest man, who literally *teaches* that Christianity is fiction, poetry; official Christianity is a forgery, which ceremoniously assures that Christianity is something else entirely, solemnly declaims against freethinking and, with the help of this, covers up that it is itself actually *making* Christianity into poetry, doing away with the imitation of Christ, so that one relates oneself to the archetype only through

---

1. From Niels Jørgen Cappelørn et al., eds., *Søren Kierkegaards Skrifter*, vol. 13 (Copenhagen: Gads Forlag, 2009), 17–181.

the imagination, even lives in entirely different categories, which is to relate oneself poetically to Christianity or to transform it into poetry, no more binding than poetry is. And, at last, the end comes, when one completely casts the archetype away and lets what one is—mediocrity—nearly hold true of the ideal.

In the name of being a poet, I then brought forward some ideals, recited what—yes, what 1,000 royal officials are bound to by oath. And these good men, they noticed nothing at all; they were perfectly secure, to the extent that, in Christian terms, everything was mindlessness and worldliness. These good men did not at all suspect that something was hiding behind this poet—that the procedure was police-intelligence, in order to make the men in question feel secure, what the police use precisely to get an opportunity to obtain a deeper insight.

Time passed in this way. I was even on quite good terms with these oath-bound men—and, in total silence, I both managed to plant the ideals and to get acquainted with those with whom I was having to deal.

And yet, these good men eventually grew impatient with this poet; he became too offensive to them. This happened by way of the article against Bishop Martensen regarding Bishop Mynster.[2] Perfectly secure as they were, they now (one will remember it from the time) stressed that "much too great a measure was applied here," etc.—perfectly secure.

Then this poet was suddenly transformed. He (if I dare say so) tossed aside his guitar and took out a book called "The New Testament of Our Lord and Savior" and with—yes, it was with the eye of a policeman—he let these good, oath-bound teachers, "witnesses to the truth," understand: is it not this book to which they are bound by an oath, this book whose measure is a good bit greater than the one he had used?

As we know, silence set in from that moment. So impudent they were, so good to declaim as long as they thought they not only could get away but could act important in this way: "We have a poet before

2. For more on this article and on Kierkegaard's relation to Mynster and Martensen, see the general introduction.

us; his ideals are exaggerated; the measure is much too great." Then they became silent from the moment this book and the oath came into play.

This is precisely what happens in police business. One first makes the person in question secure, and if, by the way, a police agent possesses all other gifts, he is not any "definite police talent" if he is not a virtuoso in the art of being able to make one feel secure. In that condition, the opposing party turns the whole relationship around; he and only he is the upright man, and it appears certain that it was the police agent who got into trouble. But when, then, the latter has gotten to know what he wants to know by making the other feel secure in this way, he changes the procedure, proceeds in completely direct fashion—and then suddenly the opposing party becomes silent, bites his lip, and probably thinks like this: "That was a nasty business."

That is why I took out the New Testament and most deferentially allowed myself to call to mind that these honored witnesses to the truth are bound by an oath to the New Testament—and then the silence set in. Was this not odd?

Meanwhile, for some time longer, I considered it most proper to keep them unclear, if possible, about how well informed I am and to what degree I have the New Testament on my side—something I managed to do, but it did not occur to me to boast about it.

Next I spoke in my own name, more and more decisively to be sure, since I indeed saw that they still rejected the fact that I first presented the case for the opposing party as favorably as it was possible for me to do it. And, at last, I took it upon myself to say in my own name that it is a guilt, a great guilt, to take part in the official worship of God as it now is. That was in my own name. Obviously, then, to escape from me in that way—to say that I am a poet, so it is indeed the others who display the truth—well, now, that was no longer possible. But it is still always somewhat reassuring that I speak in my own name, and therefore, in view of this reassurance, I yet again arrived at making the opposing party feel a little secure, so as to get an opportunity to get to know them even better: whether they intended to harden themselves against the charge. For, no doubt, conscience still must have struck the oath-bound men by hearing these all-transforming words: "It is a guilt, a great guilt, to take part in the official worship of God as it now is, because this is the greatest possible distance from being the worship of God."

Yet, as stated, it was reassuring that I spoke in my own name. For even if it is the case that, with God, I know that I have spoken truthfully and spoken as I should speak; and even if what I have said is true and should be said; if also there were no words from Christ himself: then, after all, it is always good that we learn from the New Testament how Christ judges official Christianity.

And we know that from the New Testament; his judgment is found there. But, of course, I remain perfectly convinced that, whoever you are, if you do not know anything else about what Christianity is than from the Sunday sermons of "the witnesses to the truth," then, year in and year out, you can go into three churches every Sunday and hear, ordinarily, any of the royal officials—and you will never have heard the words of Christ to which I refer. The witnesses to the truth presumably think like this: "The proverb says, 'One should not talk about rope in the house of a hanged man'; so, too, it will be madness to bring these words from God's Word—which loudly witness against the pastor's catchpenny acting—to light in the churches."

Yes, I could be tempted to make the following demand, which, so moderate and simple, is really the only punishment of the pastors that I want: unearth certain sections from the New Testament, and the pastor is obligated to read them aloud before the congregation. Naturally, I would have to reserve one thing—that it would not be that, as is customary, the pastor would lay aside the New Testament after having read such a passage in order to "lay out" what was read. No, thank you! No, what I could be tempted to propose is the following church service: the congregation is gathered; a prayer is offered at the church door; a hymn is sung; then the pastor mounts the pulpit, takes out the New Testament, calls on God's name, and loudly and clearly reads the determined passage before the congregation—after that he has to fall silent and to remain silent for five minutes in the pulpit, and then he can go.

I would regard this as extremely beneficial. To get the pastor to blush does not occur to me. The one who consciously wants to understand by Christianity what he understands by Christianity, who has been able to take an oath on the New Testament without blushing—one does not easily get him to blush. And it probably ought to be said as well that part of properly being able to be an official pastor is that one, first and foremost, has weaned oneself from the childishness of youth and innocence—to blush and the like. But I assume that the congregation would come to blush on the pastor's behalf.

* * *

And now to the words of Christ that I am talking about.

They are found in Matthew 23:29–33, Luke 11:47–48, and read as follows:

> **Matthew 23:29–33.** (29) Woe unto you, scribes and Pharisees, hypocrites! because you build the tombs of the prophets, and garnish the sepulchres of the righteous, (30) and say, If we had been in the days of our fathers, we would not have been partakers with them in the blood of the prophets. (31) Wherefore you be witnesses unto yourselves, that you are the children of them which killed the prophets. (32) Fill you up then the measure of your fathers. (33) *You* serpents, *you* generation of vipers, how can you escape the damnation of hell?

> **Luke 11:47–48.** (47) Woe unto you! for you build the sepulchres of the prophets, and your fathers killed them. (48) Truly you bear witness that you allow the deeds of your fathers: for they indeed killed them, and you build their sepulchres.

But, now, what is "Christendom"? Is Christendom not the greatest possible attempt in the direction of: rather than following Christ, to suffer for the doctrine, as he has demanded; therefore instead to worship God by "building the tombs of the prophets, and garnishing the sepulchres of the righteous, and saying, 'If we had been in the days of our fathers, we would not have been partakers with them in the blood of the prophets'"?

I have said about this kind of divine worship that, compared with the Christianity of the New Testament, it is playing at Christianity. This expression is entirely true and perfectly characteristic. That is, if one thinks about how the words must be understood in this connection, what does it mean to play? It means to counterfeit, to mimic a danger where there is no danger, and in such a way that the more art one puts in, the more deceptively can one pretend as if danger were there. The soldiers play at war like this on the commons. There is no danger; one simply pretends as if there were, and the art consists in making everything truly deceptive, entirely as if it were a matter of life and death.

And Christianity is played this way in "Christendom." Dramatically costumed, the artists step forward in artistic buildings—in truth, there is no danger, not in the least. The teacher is royal official, gradually advancing, making a career—and now he plays at Christianity in dramatic fashion. In short, he is performing a comedy. He declaims about renunciation, but he himself is gradually advancing; he teaches one to despise worldly titles and rank, but he himself is making a career; he depicts the glorious ones ("the prophets") who were put to death, and the refrain is constantly: "If we had lived in the time of our fathers, we would not have taken part with them in the blood of the prophets—we who, after all, are building their tombs and garnishing their sepulchers." Accordingly, they will not even at least be so honest (as I constantly, urgently, and pleadingly have suggested) as to confess that they are not at all better than those who killed the prophets. No, they want to take advantage of this situation—that they are not contemporary with them after all, lying to themselves about being much, much better than those who killed, about being entirely different creatures than those monsters. Indeed, they are building the tombs and garnishing the sepulchers of those so unjustly put to death.

Nevertheless, to play at Christianity—however significant this expression can be, the person in authority cannot use such a phrase. He speaks about it differently.

Christ calls it—oh, pay attention!—he calls it: "Hypocrisy." And not only this, but he says—shudder!—he says that this guilt of hypocrisy is just as great, precisely just as great a crime as that of killing the prophets, therefore: blood-guilt. Yes, if one could ask him, perhaps he would answer that the guilt of this hypocrisy is a greater guilt than the guilt of those who killed the prophets in a blazing fury, just because it is so pompously hidden and slowly carried on through a whole life.

Therefore this is the judgment—Christ's judgment on Christendom, on the worship of God on Sunday, on official Christianity. Shudder, for otherwise you are still caught in it. It is so deceptive: "Are we not nice persons, true Christians, we who build the tombs of the prophets and garnish the sepulchers of the righteous? Are we not nice persons, and especially compared with the monsters who killed them? And, besides, what are we to do? After all, we cannot do more than be willing to give our money in order to build churches, etc., not to be sparing on the pastor, and then to listen to him ourselves." The New Testament answers: "What you are to do is this—you are to follow Christ, to suffer, suffer for the doctrine. The worship of God that you want to arrange is hypocrisy and equal to blood-guilt. What 'the pastor,' along with his family, lives on, exists on, is that you are a hypocrite, or on making you into a hypocrite and keeping you in being a hypocrite."

"Your fathers killed them, and you build their sepulchres. Truly you bear witness that ye allow the deeds of your fathers." Luke 11:48.

Yes, indeed, Sunday-Christianity and the immense guild of pastors who are tradesmen have to become furious at such talk, which, with one single word, closes all their boutiques, scraps the whole of this royally authorized industry, and not only that, but warns against such worship of God as against blood-guilt.

After all, this is Christ who is speaking. So deeply, then, does hypocrisy hang together with being human that, just when the natural human being feels best of all, just when he gets the worship of God set up properly in accordance with his taste, Christ's judgment resounds: "This is hypocrisy, is blood-guilt." It is not the case that, while your life on weekdays is worldliness, there is still this good in you—that, on Sunday, you attend church with the official Christianity. No, no, the official Christianity is much worse than all the worldliness of your weekdays, is hypocrisy, is blood-guilt.

At the foundation of "Christendom" lies the truth: the human being is a born hypocrite. The Christianity of the New Testament was the truth. But the human being shrewdly and roguishly invented a new kind of Christianity, one that builds the tombs of the prophets and garnishes the sepulchers of the righteous and says: "If we had lived in the time of our fathers." And this is what Christ calls blood-guilt.

What Christianity wants is: imitation [*Efterfølgelse*]. What the human being does not want is to suffer, least of all the kind of suffering that is genuinely Christian—to suffer because of people. So he takes imitation away and suffering with it, the particularly Christian; then he builds the tombs of the prophets. That is the one thing. And then he lies to God, to himself, to others—that he is better than those who killed the prophets. That is the other thing. Hypocrisy first and hypocrisy last—and according to Christ's judgment: "Blood-guilt."

* * *

Imagine when people are gathered in a church in Christendom, that then—Christ suddenly stepped into this assembly: what do you think he would do?

Now, after all, you can read in the New Testament what he would do.

He would direct himself against *the teachers*—for, I suppose, he would judge *the parishioners* as in former times: they are misled. He would direct himself against those "in long robes," the merchants, the entertainers, who have transformed God's house, if not into a den of thieves, then into a boutique or into a booth, and he would say, "You hypocrites, *you* serpents, *you* generation of vipers," and, as before, he probably would fashion a whip of cords in order to chase them out of the temple.

You who are reading this—I am totally prepared for this—if you know nothing else about Christianity than from the blather on Sundays, you will be shocked at me. It will seem to you as if I were guilty of the most dreadful blasphemy at representing Christ in this way, "to put words in his mouth such as: serpents, generation of vipers; it is certainly frightful; they are certainly words that one never hears in the mouth of any cultured person; and to have him repeat them several times—it is certainly so terribly vulgar; and to make Christ into a person who uses force!"

My friend, you can consult the New Testament, after all. But when a comfortable, pleasure-filled life in an esteemed occupation is to be achieved by proclaiming and teaching Christianity, then the image of Christ must be changed somewhat. Finery, no, there will be no sparing of gold and diamonds and rubies, etc. No, the pastors regard it with pleasure and make people believe that it is Christianity. But the rigorousness, the rigorousness, that is inseparable from the earnestness of eternity—that has to go. Christ then becomes a languorous figure, nothing but a Mr. Goodman, so that the plate can go around during the sermon and so that the congregation can have a desire to spend something and to cough up a good amount, whereas the Christianity of the New Testament is: in fear of God to suffer for the doctrine because of people.

But "woe unto you because ye build the tombs of the prophets" (teaching people that this is the Christianity of the New Testament) and "garnish the sepulchres of the righteous" (constantly joining money and Christianity) and say, "If we"—yes, if you had lived at the same time as the prophets, then you would have killed them. That is to say, you secretly would have let the people do it and bear the guilt, as it indeed happened. In vain, however, do you hide yourselves in "Christendom." Ultimately, what is hidden there will be revealed when the truth judges: "Truly you bear witness that you allow the deeds of your fathers: for they indeed killed them, and you build their sepulchres." In vain do you act holy; in vain do you, simply by building the tombs of the righteous, mean to show how different you are from the ungodly people who killed them. Oh, the powerlessness of hypocrisy to hide itself. You are seen through. Just building the tombs of the righteous and saying, "If we," just this is: to kill them. It is to be the authentic children of those ungodly people, to do the same as they did, to attest to the deeds of the fathers, to consent to them, "to fill the measure of the fathers"—therefore, to do what is even worse.

Part Four

The Church

⚮

INTRODUCTION
TO PART FOUR

Kierkegaard's "attack upon Christendom" ensured that his relation to the church would remain famously uncertain. After all, while he was denigrating a particular instantiation of the Christian *ekklesia*, he was doing so for the greater good of Christianity and the church. Such, at any rate, has been the argument of commentators such as Howard A. Johnson, who claims that, in attacking the Danish state church, Kierkegaard was "attacking something to which he was devoted."[1] Vernard Eller agrees, albeit in a different sense. For him, Kierkegaard's "attack upon Christendom" discloses his association with "classic Protestant sectarianism,"[2] meaning that Kierkegaard's ecclesiology best corresponds to the churches of the Radical Reformation. Still others wonder if Kierkegaard might not have been closest to Roman Catholicism toward the end of his life,[3] while some even argue that Kierkegaard sought to jettison the notion of "the church" from Christian thinking altogether.[4]

---

1. Howard A. Johnson, "Kierkegaard and the Church: A Supplement to the Translator's Introduction," in *Kierkegaard's Attack upon "Christendom" 1854–1855*, trans. Walter Lowrie (Princeton, NJ: Princeton University Press, 1968), xxv.
2. Vernard Eller, *Kierkegaard and Radical Discipleship: A New Perspective* (Princeton, NJ: Princeton University Press, 1968), 231.
3. See, e.g., Erich Przywara, *Das Geheimnis Kierkegaards* (Munich: Verlag R. Oldenbourg, 1929), esp. 102ff. While Przywara's suggestion is speculative, there are some intriguing connections between Kierkegaard and the Catholic tradition. See, e.g., Christopher B. Barnett and Peter Šajda, "Catholicism: Finding Inspiration and Provocation in Kierkegaard," in *A Companion to Kierkegaard*, ed. Jon Stewart (Oxford: Wiley Blackwell, 2015), 237–49.
4. See, e.g., Bruce Kirmmse, "'But I am almost never understood...' Or, Who Killed Søren Kierkegaard?" in *Kierkegaard: The Self in Society*, ed. George Pattison and Steven Shakespeare (Basingstoke, UK: Macmillan, 1998), 173–95.

Given such widely divergent appraisals, it seems safe to say that Kierkegaard's relation to the church will remain a topic of debate. At the same time, however, the church endures as an important category in Kierkegaard's authorship, one to which he devoted both direct and indirect attention. For that reason, it would be inadequate to neglect the church in a volume such as this one, even if limited space dictates that it will be a smaller section than its predecessors.

As with the other themes explored thus far, Kierkegaard principally thinks of the church in terms of its significance for existential authenticity or, more specifically, in terms of its potential to facilitate or to encumber individual upbuilding. Indeed, it is striking that Kierkegaard argued that the church is a community that *presupposes* personal commitment and, with it, the goal of personal edification. As he puts it in an 1835 journal entry, "With regard to the Church [*Kirken*], the subjectivity that I think must come first…*is* already exemplary in this fact—that the most objective part of the creed begins in this way: "I believe."[5] In 1851, Kierkegaard returned to this point by way of the Lutheran Augsburg Confession (1530), noting that its articles describe the church as "the Communion of Saints" (*de Helliges Samfund*), but that this tendency "in the direction of the existential" has been underemphasized in relation to doctrinal teaching and sacramental administration.[6] According to Kierkegaard, this is an essential omission, since the very heart of Christian life involves the believer's decision to follow Christ. Consequently, a church that lacks this existential urgency "is really paganism."[7]

For Kierkegaard, then, the church should not be thought of as a thing unto itself; it is not a public that exists apart from the individuals who compose it, lest "Christians go on holiday behind this abstraction [*Abstraktum*]."[8] On the contrary, to belong to the church signifies either that one follows Christ or that one is striving constantly to follow Christ. Thus the task of the one who would write about the church is to spur the church's members to pursue Christian

5. *SKS* 27, *Pap.* 91, my translation.
6. *SKS* 24, NB24:7, my translation.
7. *SKS* 24, NB24:7, my translation.
8. *SKS* 26, NB35:40, my translation.

holiness—a task that Kierkegaard epitomizes in the two texts included in this section.

The first selection, "Watch Your Step When You Go to the House of the Lord," is taken from *Christian Discourses*—a four-part volume, published in April 1848, in which Kierkegaard ponders (rather than pronounces on)[9] various aspects of the Christian life. In particular, "Watch Your Step" opens the third section of *Christian Discourses*, which is entitled "Thoughts That Wound from Behind— for Upbuilding." But what, exactly, does it mean to "wound from behind"? According to Kierkegaard, this phrase indicates the irony latent in various biblical texts, whereby an ostensibly ordinary pericope directs a critical question at the reader. As he puts it, "In the following discourses, the text is to be chosen in this way—that it looks like a gospel, and is that too, but then comes the sting."[10] Thus there is a "satirical"[11] (*Satiriske*) element in Scripture, which underlines the discrepancy between what is expected of Christians and what most persons erroneously assume, thereby exposing the deception and falsehood of Christendom. To become aware of this irony is to experience "an assault of thoughts,"[12] though its pain is the precondition for personal renewal or "upbuilding."

"Watch Your Step" is an excellent example of this strategy. Its title is taken from Ecclesiastes 5:1, which warns persons to be careful about making empty sacrifices in "the house of God." And yet, Kierkegaard begins, most people in Christendom assume that time in God's house, amid "the beauty of the [ecclesial] surroundings,"[13] is supposed to be soothing and self-gratifying. Here, then, is "the sting": it *is* a blessing to spend time in church, but not because it gives one a pleasant feeling; rather, the blessing comes from a terrifying encounter with the living God, since in this encounter one faces the truth of God's majesty and of the human being's frailty. Hence, those who would invite persons to enter the church are responsible for making

9. *SKS* 20, NB:120, my translation.
10. *SKS* 20, NB4:5, my translation.
11. *SKS* 20, NB4:5, my translation.
12. *SKS* 20, NB4:5a, my translation.
13. *SKS* 10, 175, my translation.

sure that they do not enter under false pretenses. The dialectical tension between blessing and terror must always be maintained, for it is the very nature of Christian faith.

The second piece in this section again comes from the pen of Anti-Climacus. More specifically, it is the fifth of seven "expositions" (*Udviklinger*) of John 12:32[14]—an exegetical series that constitutes the third and final part of *Practice in Christianity*. Accordingly, Anti-Climacus names this third part "From on High He Will Draw All to Himself," and, as a unit, it deals with "the relation between [Christ's] lowliness and his loftiness,"[15] not only with regard to Christ himself, but also with regard to those who claim to be followers of Christ. Indeed, the fifth exposition, which is otherwise untitled, hones in on what Jesus's life of hardship and suffering means for the church. Many people, especially those in Christendom, assume that to be a Christian no longer involves self-denial and persecution, since the church has become an established part of Western culture. And yet, Anti-Climacus argues, the church can never lose sight of its mission to imitate Christ in the world and thus to imitate him in humble service to God and to humanity. Of course, this is scarcely the first (or the last) time Kierkegaard would invoke the theme of *imitatio Christi*. What distinguishes this piece is that Kierkegaard relates the *imitatio* motif to the doctrinal categories of the "militant church" (the pilgrim church on earth) and the "triumphant church" (the church in heaven), thereby implying that his thought is indeed compatible with traditional ecclesiology.

And yet, if this approach is distinctive, it should not be surprising. Kierkegaard never claimed to be an innovator as a Christian theologian. His task, as has been seen, was to stimulate upbuilding so as to elicit an encounter with the challenging yet loving Christ of the New Testament. As he once put it, "I want to apply the Christian demand, imitation [*Efterfølgelsen*], in all its infinity, in order to press in the direction of grace."[16]

---

14. The pericope is a quotation from Jesus: "And I, if I be lifted up from the earth, will draw all *men* unto me" (AKJV).

15. *SKS* 21, NB7:4a, my translation.

16. *SKS* 25, NB27:87, my translation.

WATCH YOUR STEP WHEN YOU GO TO THE HOUSE OF THE LORD[2]

How still, how secure, everything is in the house of God. To the one who enters, it is as if he had come, with a single step, to a distant place, infinitely far away from all clatter and screeching and noisiness, from the terrors of existence, from the storms of life, from scenes of dreadful events or their debilitating expectation. And wherever you turn your eyes in there, everything will make you secure and restful. The high walls of the venerable building, they stand so firm; they protect so reliably this secure place of refuge, under whose mighty vault you are free from every stress. And the beauty of the surroundings, its magnificence, will make everything friendly for you, so inviting. The holy place wants to ingratiate itself with you, as it were, by likewise recollecting what indeed must be presupposed— good and tranquil times that have favored these undertakings of peace.

See, the man who cut these images into stone, he took a long time to do it. And in all this long time, his life must have been protected and made secure so that no one jolted him and nothing happened to him that in any way could make his hand or thought unsteady. As an artist, he needed the deepest quiet of peace—what he

---

1. From Niels Jørgen Cappelørn et al., eds., *Søren Kierkegaards Skrifter*, vol. 10 (Copenhagen: Gads Forlag, 2004), 175–86.
2. The expression comes from Ecclesiastes 5:1, which reads in the King James Version: "Keep thy foot when thou goest to the house of God." Since this wording is quite awkward in contemporary English, I have modified it accordingly. (Tr.)

produced therefore also reminds us about this quiet. See, the one who has woven this velvet with which the pulpit is adorned, he must have had quiet to sit still at this work, at the work that thrives in times of peace and is not needed in times of war. And the woman who sewed the gold on it, she must have been allowed to sit undisturbed and diligent in her work, solely occupied with it and with the thought of doing each stitch with equal care.

How calming, how soothing—alas, and how much danger in this security! And therefore it really is true that, strictly speaking, only God in heaven can preach very effectually to human beings in life's actuality. For he has the circumstances, has the destinies, has the situations in his control. And the circumstances—and when *you* are in them, when they surround *you* as the person in question: yes, their eloquence is penetrating and awakening. I suppose you, too, have experienced that. If you yourself were the sick person, who lay sleepless on the sick bed in the midnight hour; or if you alone were the one who sat by the sick person's painful bed in the midnight hour and with alarming clarity counted every stroke of the clock and every sigh of the sick person, but without finding the relief of monotony or of the counting—if, then, you were to hear that devotional song, "Our Savior Was Born in the Midnight Hour," do you believe that all speakers together would be capable of producing this effect? And why not? Because the sick bed and the nighttime hour preach more powerfully than all speakers; they understand this secret, talking to you in such a way that you come to feel that it is you, just *you*—not the one who is sitting beside you, not those out there—but just *you* who is being addressed, you who feels alone, alone in the whole world, alone in the midnight hour by the sick bed.

Or if a person is at death's door, and one frankly and honestly has not concealed from him what in these times one will conceal from the dying person, what is the most important thing for him to know—that it is over: do you not believe that a simple, comforting word from the most limited person will produce an entirely different effect than all the most famous speakers on the person who—healthy and fresh, even spiritually sound in his own mind—sits securely in the magnificent temple and listens and perhaps evaluates the address? And why will that simple word produce an entirely different effect?

Because death knows how to make itself understood, finding the one to whom it relates; it knows how to let you understand that is *you*, that you are the person concerned, that it is no one else, not your next-door neighbor or your opposite neighbor or another person in the city, but that it is *you* who is to die.

It is this way in the actuality of life, where, with the help of circumstances, God is the one who preaches for awakening. But it is in God's house, in the magnificent house of God, where the pastor preaches—for comfort. Especially if he would strive to satisfy human demands or what people then call the demands of the times. For while people in these times become more and more fearful, more and more afraid to actually experience themselves the terror implicit in the violence of circumstances, they are becoming more and more finicky in coveting the vanity of eloquence on the other hand. People do not want to hear anything in earnest about that which is terrible; they want to play at it, almost like soldiers in peacetime (or rather non-soldiers, I suppose) play at war. Artistically, people want to demand everything with respect to the beauty of their environment, and they artistically demand everything of the speaker. Yet, in a worldly and ungodly way, they themselves want to sit in perfect security in God's house, because, after all, they know well that no speaker has the power—the power that only Providence has—to grip a person, to cast him into the force of circumstances, to let the vicissitudes and ordeals and spiritual trials preach in earnest to him for awakening.

Oh, there is so much in the usual course of life that will lull a person to sleep, teach him to say "peace and no danger." That is why we go into God's house in order to be awakened from sleep and in order to break the spell. But when, in turn, there is sometimes so much in God's house that will lull us to sleep! Even what is awakening in and for itself—thoughts, meditations, ideas—can lose meaning entirely by the force of habit and monotony, just as a spring can lose the tension by which, after all, it really only is what it is. Hence, in order to come closer to the subject of this discourse, it is indeed right and proper, is a plain duty to invite persons again and again to come into the Lord's house, to call on them. But people can become so accustomed to hearing this invitation that it loses its meaning.

Thus one ultimately stays away, and it ends with the invitation preaching the church empty. Or people can become so accustomed to hearing this invitation that it develops false notions in those who do come, makes us important in our own minds, so that *we* are not like those who stay away, makes us self-satisfied, secure, because it entangles us in an illusion—as if it were God who needed us since we are invited so urgently, as if it were not we, on the contrary, who in fear and trembling should think about what he can demand of us, as if it were not we who sincerely ought to thank God that he will have anything to do with us at all, that he will put up with us and permit that we may approach him ourselves, tolerate that we presume to believe that he cares about us, that he unashamedly wants to be known, to be called our God and our Father.

So, then, let us now talk in a different way about this matter, while we discuss this saying from Ecclesiastes:

Watch Your Step When You Go to the House of the Lord

Watch your step when you go to the house of the Lord. For it is an exceedingly responsible matter to go up into the Lord's house. Remember that he who is present there is he who is in heaven—and you are on the earth. But do not imagine that he is far away in his sublimity. Just this is indeed earnestness and responsibility—that he, the infinitely sublime one, is quite close to you, closer than the people you have about you on a daily basis, closer than your most intimate friend before whom you feel entirely able to show yourself as you are. Sublimity and distance seem to correspond to one another, so that the one who is sublime is also distant from you; equality and closeness seem to correspond to one another, so that the one who is near is also your equal. Yet, when sublimity is quite near to you and is still sublimity, then you are in a difficult position. In his sublimity, God himself—the infinitely sublime one—is really quite close to you in the Lord's house. For it is not with God as with a human being, who, after all, basically becomes less sublime when he comes close to and has dealings with you, the lowly one. No, God can come quite near to the lowliest one and yet remain in his infinite sublimity.

Watch Your Step When You Go to the House of the Lord

Oh, the earnestness of eternity; oh, what a difficult position! For is it not true that, normally if a stranger alone is present where you are, then you are somewhat changed, and if the most powerful and most lofty person in the land is present, then you are much changed, because he is so lofty, and because you see him so rarely. But God in heaven is lofty in an entirely different way, and yet, when you go up into the house of the Lord, then God—in his infinite sublimity—is quite close to you, closer than you are to yourself, since he understands and discovers even your thoughts that you do not understand yourself. Oh, what an immense weight of responsibility—that the infinitely sublime one, the one for whom you perhaps would prefer to show yourself in your best form, that he is quite close to you in his sublimity, sees you, and yet sees you absolutely close at hand in his sublimity, as not even the one who is around you every day sees you. Even if you—in view of the fact that you are presenting yourself before the Most High—would try to appear different than you are, you cannot do it: he is too infinitely sublime for that. Yes, and now it comes again: he is too close to you for that. If a person can lose his composure and forget what he wanted to say when he is placed right before His Royal Majesty: oh, how terrible to be placed right before God. For His Royal Majesty is neither as lofty as God, nor can he come as close to you.

Be on guard, then, when you go to the house of the Lord. What do you want there? You want to call on the Lord your God, to exalt and to praise him. But now, in all honesty, is that actually your earnest intention? As you know, language has no more solemn expression with respect to demanding honesty than when one says to a person: "Is that your conviction, your opinion, before God?" And, after all, you are *before* God in the house of the Lord. Accordingly, is your invocation that calls upon God honestly meant before God? And what is honesty before God? It is that your life expresses what you say. We human beings must be content with less, with the one person solemnly assuring the other person that this or that is what he sincerely means. But God in heaven—the infinitely sublime one or (yes, here it comes again) God the knower of hearts, who is absolutely close to you—God will only understand one kind of honesty: the honesty that a person's life expresses what

291

he says. All other honesty, all other solemnity, all mere assurance that one means what he says: it is a deception, an untruth, before God. Such an invocation is a presumption against him.

Be on guard, then, that your invocation is not presumptuousness toward God, instead of being able to please God. Be on guard that you—deceived by your own self, because you do not understand yourself—do not presume to deceive God, as if you had in your heart the pious feelings that nevertheless do not have power over you to change your life, to let your life be the expression for these feelings. Oh, we human beings often complain over the fact that we lack the words and expressions for our feelings—that the language will not aid us, that we must hunt for words and perhaps in vain. Nothing like that will worry you before God, if only your life expresses that you have these feelings. Yes, then you are sincere before God and that loquacious honesty utterly superfluous.

Or perhaps you go up into the Lord's house in order to pray to God for help and assistance. Be on guard for what you ask. Have you rightly, have you before God, realized yourself whom you are calling upon for help, what it means to call upon his help, what it commits you to? If it is perhaps worldly matters, childish worries, trifles, on account of which you want to call upon his help—and not in order that he might help you to forget them but in order to occupy yourself with them—then if it is on account of trivialities (which, after all, you perhaps will have forgotten tomorrow and, with them, also this by no means trifling thing, that you called upon the assistance of the Most High): then you indeed have mocked God. And he does not forget that you called upon his help.

If a physician becomes impatient (and certainly with justification) when childish parents send word to him for every trifle, so that the whole thing is over when he comes, and they have nearly forgotten why they sent for him: then should God, the omnipotent one, be willing to be treated in this way? Or do you dare hazard to think that it is God who is to serve you, that he, the most exalted one, should be ready to hear your prayers and to fulfill your wishes right away? Oh, if you involve yourself with him, then you are the one who thereby is unconditionally bound to obey and to serve. And if you do not understand this, then it is a presumption to have a relationship with him, a presumption to call upon his help.

Yes, he certainly is the omnipotent one and can do everything that he wills. It looks almost tempting, as if you only needed to wish. But be on guard. No thoughtless word is so avenged as a thoughtless prayer to God, and no prayer is so binding as the prayer that invokes God for help. For it now binds you unconditionally to let God help you as he wills. You can ask a human being for help, and you may have forgotten it when he comes with the help. You can ask a human being for help, and, if he does not want to help you as you desire, then you can say, "That was not what I asked for." Yet, if you have prayed to God for help, then you are bound, bound to accept the help as he sees fit. Oh, how often a cry for help is heard, and this cry is that there is no help. In truth, there is always help enough. But the human heart is so cunning and keeps its word so little that when the help turns out to be what one had most feared, then one says, "But that is no help, is it?" And yet, if this help is from God, and if you have prayed to him for help, then you are bound to accept the help and, in faith and with gratitude, to call it help.

Or perhaps you go up to the house of the Lord in order with a vow to commit yourself to a purpose, to a resolution for the future. But be on guard for what you do. Have you rightly understood what it means to promise God something, that what you promise God is something a human being can and dares to promise, that it is not something that we human beings are able to be fooled into promising one another, that it is something God will permit you to promise him. Otherwise it is indeed a presumption. And have you rightly understood how a promise to God binds you? They say that "a promise is a snare"—and a promise to God, yes, if it is what it is supposed to be and becomes what it should become, then surely it is as far as possible from being a snare, then it is a saving leading-string. But if it is not! If you do not understand yourself in what you promise God, if you do not have the true conception of what you can and dare to promise God: then you lose God; you pamper your soul into handling God and God's name light-mindedly and vainly. And if you do not keep what you promise to God, then you lose yourself. Oh, and really there is always one whom a person cannot escape: oneself. And then one more: God in heaven!

Be on guard, then, when you go to the house of the Lord. Take the words of the Preacher into consideration: "Be not rash with your mouth, and let not your heart be hasty to utter *any* thing before God: for God *is* in heaven, and you upon earth: therefore let your words be few. For a dream comes through the multitude of business; and a fool's voice *is known* by multitude of words. When you vow a vow unto God, defer not to pay it; for *he has* no pleasure in fools: pay that which you have vowed. Better *is it* that you should not vow, than that you should vow and not pay."

Watch your step when you go to the house of the Lord. For perhaps you should get to know much more than you really wish to know after all, and perhaps you will receive an impression that you later will seek to get rid of in vain. So be on guard with fire; it burns.

It is heard again and again; it is regarded in the world as a done deal: human beings would like to know the truth, if only they had ability and time for it, and then if one could make it obvious to them in proper fashion. What a superfluous worry; what an ingeniously concocted excuse! In truth, every human being has sufficient ability to know the truth—surely God in heaven would not be so inhuman as to have treated anyone unfairly! And truly every human being, even the most occupied, also has sufficient time to come to know the truth. Nothing is more certain, since he *shall* have time. That the busy person has just as little time as the loafer for it is surely by no means a refutation! And since every person has sufficient ability and time, then, of course, neither can it be so difficult a matter to make it obvious in proper fashion—if a person himself *wants* to have it made obvious. But herein lies the very difficulty: it is so easy to shove the blame onto the lack of ability, onto the lack of time, and onto the obscurity of truth, and then, on the other hand, it looks so neat and is so comfortable that one would very much like to recognize the truth.

Truly, truly, this is not so. The one who only knows himself to a degree knows the answer from his own experience; it is rather that, deep down, the person has a secret dread of and reserve toward the truth, a fear of getting to know too much. Or do you actually believe that it is every human being's sincere wish to get to know fully what self-denial is, to get it made so clear that every excuse, every evasion, every mitigation, every retreat to the untrue but favorable opinion of others is to be cut off for him! Do you believe that? Yes, I need not wait for your answer. For if it were the case, then every human being would truly have self-denial, since just this is the principal form of self-denial. Oh, but even the better person who really has overcome the initial shudder at the truth and does not shrink in an entirely worldly way from getting to know it—even he, or rather precisely he, will no doubt confess that he often and often enough suspects himself with reason, that he still hides from the truth like Adam among the trees, that he still steals away from something and still creeps to something, that sometimes he still wants to slip into darkness, where there is only twilight, than have the truth make it all too bright around him.

Be on guard, then, when you go up to the house of the Lord. For there you will get to hear the truth—for upbuilding. Yes, it is true, but watch out for the upbuilding. There is nothing, nothing as gentle as the upbuilding, yet there is nothing as domineering either. The upbuilding is vague talk least of all; there is nothing so binding. And in God's house you get to know the truth—not from the pastor (whose influence, after all, you easily can evade and even in a certain sense should evade) but from God or before God. This is the very earnestness of truth, is the truth—that you get to know it before God. What it especially depends on is this: before God. In God's house, there is one present who, with you, knows that you—precisely you— have gotten to know the truth. Be on guard for this shared knowledge. You will never be able to slip back into ignorance from this shared knowledge. That is to say, you will not slip back without guilt, and you will not slip away from the consciousness of this guilt either.

Be on guard, then, that you do not get to know too much, that you do not get to know that the assurance—which made you comely in your own eyes, agreeable in the eyes of others, while your life went on pleasantly under it—the assurance that you very much wished to get to know the truth: this is a fancy or, even worse, an untruth. Be on guard that, in God's house, you do not get to know—but, of course, you do know it. In all your knowledge, perhaps you raise yourself above the simple speakers, who want to talk about such outdated things, which every child knows—but nevertheless be on guard that, in God's house, you do not get to know in such a way that you have to understand it: that you can be required, in self-denial, to give up everything in which the natural human being has life, pleasure, and pastime.

Have you considered what it means to have a distaste for life? That a distaste for life appears just when everything finite is taken from a human being, while one is still allowed to hold onto life, so that then everything around him becomes desolate and empty and undesirable. Then time becomes so indescribably long; yes, it is to him as if he were dead. Now, indeed, self-denial calls it to die to [*at afdøe*]—and the truth teaches that a human being is to die to finitude (its pleasures, its occupations, its games, its pastimes), is to go through this death to life, is to taste (to taste death, as it is said) and to grasp how empty is that with which busyness fills up life, how insignificant is that which is the eye's desire and the carnal heart's demand. Alas, the natural human being understands the matter in the just the opposite way. He believes that the eternal is what is empty. There is probably no instinct as strong in a human being as that with which he clings to life—when death comes, we all pray that we may be allowed to live, but the dying to [*Afdøen*] of self-denial is just as bitter as death. And you get to know the truth in the house of the Lord—that you are to die to the world. And if God has gotten to know that you got to know it (which, after all, is inevitable), then no escape will help you in all eternity. Be on guard, then, when you go to the house of the Lord.

Watch your step when you go to the house of the Lord. For even if you came from the most horrifying thing that can happen to a person in the world, even if you entered into God's house running away before the horror out there: you really are coming to something even more terrible. Here, in God's house, there is essentially discourse about a danger that the world does not know—a danger in comparison with which everything that the world calls danger is child's play: the danger of sin. And here, in God's house, there is essentially discourse about a terror that has never happened either before or after, in comparison with which the most terrible thing that can happen to the most unfortunate of all persons is a trifle: the terror that the human race crucified God.

Why, then, are you going into God's house? Is it poverty or sickness or other hardships—in short, any earthly need and misery? This is not spoken about in God's house, at least not at first. Sin is spoken about first and must be spoken about first—about the fact that you are a sinner, that you are a sinner before God, that you in fear and trembling are to forget your earthly need before this thought. It is a peculiar way to comfort, is it not? Instead of sympathetically asking about your health, instead of giving you advice and tips…if you had recourse there for that reason, then you have indeed made a mistake. After all, you are coming to something even more terrible. For instead of having sympathy for your earthly misery and busily remedying it, an even heavier weight is put on you: you are made a sinner. That there is salvation for sinners, comfort for the repentant, is what is spoken about—and truly for upbuilding.

But perhaps all this does not concern you, you who, solely occupied with your earthly suffering, fled here. And yet, it does concern you. In vain would you say that it does not concern you; in vain would you leave again. It is said to you, and God knows with you that it was said to you—and that you heard it!

Why, then, are you going into God's house? Perhaps you have suffered wrong. It is possible that you are the innocent one, the lovable one, and yet perhaps people treacherously deceived you. It is possible that you are the noble one, the good one. It is possible that, one day, you will even be counted among the benefactors of this generation, and yet, yet, perhaps people ostracized you from their community as a reward, mistreated, insulted, mocked you, indeed plotted against your life—and you flee into God's house in order to seek comfort. Whoever you are, you are making a mistake. You are coming to something even more terrible!

Here, in God's house, the talk is not, at least not at first, about you and me, about what we human beings could suffer in the world for a little injustice, which, in another way, we still have richly earned. No, in God's house, here the talk is first and foremost about the terror, whose equal was never seen and never shall be seen later in the world's confusion; about the injustice, crying to heaven, which was never committed before and never shall be later; about that rebellion, more terrible than the ocean's wildest, when the human race rebelled against God—not with the usual powerlessness but, as it were, victoriously—grabbed and crucified him. Therefore the one who flees in here from the terror outside really is making a mistake—is fleeing to something even more terrible!

Really, the talk shall be about that first and foremost. His figure, that of our Lord Jesus Christ, is to be evoked—not in the way that the artist finds and takes his time to portray it, not in the way that it is taken out of the environment of terror and is made an object for calm observation. No, he must be remembered in the moment of danger and terror, when the calm spectator doubtless would prefer to remain home, since it would have been suspicious if anyone would have looked upon him worshipfully or merely lovingly, when there was nothing to see except this "Behold the man," when there was not even time to look upon him, because the terror averted one's eyes and drew them on oneself, staring. And Christ's suffering is not to be remembered as something bygone—oh, save your sympathy! No, as this terror is depicted, it is a present thing, and you are present, and I am at a present thing—and as an accomplice!

But then, after all, you did make a mistake when you went to the house of the Lord. Instead of getting to hear the comfort that could comfort you in whatever injustice you are suffering, instead of proving to be right against people who are doing wrong to you, so instead you are shown to be wrong, you, precisely you, the innocently persecuted, insulted, wronged one! You get a guilt, a guilt that cries to heaven, laid upon your conscience—that even you are an accomplice in his innocent suffering and death. Oh, what hard words of comfort! Who can listen to them? O, rigorous way to divert your dark and mournful thoughts—to give you something even more terrible to weep over!

Watch your step when you go to the house of the Lord—and why? Just because the only saving thing, the most blessed comfort, is offered to you in God's house; the highest thing—friendship with God, his grace in Christ Jesus—is offered to you. That is why we still should not abandon inviting persons to come into God's house; we should always be willing to pray for others as for ourselves that our visit to God's house may be blessed. But therefore, precisely therefore, we should not hesitate to cry out to people: for the sake of God in heaven, be on guard, watch for everything, so that you worthily make use of what is offered to you—just because there is everything to win, that is why *there* is everything to lose too.

Use it in faith! There is no conviction as heartfelt, as strong and as blessed as that of faith. But faith's conviction is not something one is born with, the confidence of a youthful, cheerful mind. Still less is faith something one pulls out of the air. Faith is the conviction, the blessed conviction, which is in fear and trembling. When faith is seen from its one side—the heavenly—then one only sees the reflection of eternal blessedness in it. But seen from its other side—the human side alone—one sees nothing but fear and trembling. Yet, in that case, the discourse that continually and never in any other way than invitingly, enticingly, winningly wants to talk about the visit to God's house is indeed also untrue. For, seen from the other side, it is horrifying. The discourse is also untrue, then, that finally ends by frightening people away from coming into the house of the Lord. For, from the other side, it is blessed. One day in God's house is better than a thousand elsewhere.

Oh, and that is why it is a difficult matter to steer the right way, and surely that is why only very rarely is a person successful in doing it—and yet always in frailty. For it is easy to win people enticingly; it is also easy to frighten them away forbiddingly. But to invite them to come, if possible, with a fervor that no one could resist, and moreover with a terror that could teach even the bravest to shudder, to cry out: "Be on guard!"—yes, that is difficult. In other words, what the speaker argues is what applies to him. For it is said to the speaker: "Use every ability granted to you, ready for every sacrifice and compliance in self-denial; use it to win human beings—but woe to you if you win them in such a way that you leave out the terror. Therefore use all the ability given to you, ready for every sacrifice in self-denial; use it to terrify persons—but woe to you if you do not use it, after all, to win them for the truth."

Chapter Thirteen[1]

FROM ON HIGH HE WILL DRAW ALL TO HIMSELF

Exposition V

Lord Jesus Christ, it is certainly from on high that you draw a person to yourself, and it is to victory that you call him. But this is indeed to say that you call him to conflict and promise him victory in the strife to which you call him from on high, you, the great victor. Just as you keep our souls from all other error, so also keep us from this one—that we imagine ourselves to be members of a church already triumphant here in the world. After all, your kingdom was not and certainly is not of this world. Your church's place is not here in the world; there is only a place for it if it will struggle and by struggling secure itself a place to exist. But if it will struggle, then it will never be driven out by the world either; you will vouch for that. On the other hand, if it imagines that it is supposed to triumph here in the world—alas, then indeed it has itself to blame that you withdrew your assistance. Then it has foundered; then it has confused itself with the world.

So, then, be with your militant [*stridende*] church, so that it would never happen that it—and, of course, this is the only way in which it could happen—would be obliterated from the earth by becoming a triumphant church.

John 12:32: **And I, if I be lifted up from the earth, will draw all unto me**.

---

1. From Niels Jørgen Cappelørn et al., eds., *Søren Kierkegaards Skrifter*, vol. 12 (Copenhagen: Gads Forlag, 2007), 198–226.

"Yes, this is easy to understand; he has been victorious. We have only to go along with him in order to share the victory with him. Just no delays or hairsplitting; then the matter is entirely simple." Hardly anyone, I hope, would express himself quite this way in words, but perhaps there was still such and such a person who thought like this in secret. And what, then, do we have to say from our side?

One could point out that, even if nothing else was a hindrance, it cannot be done easily, because in one sense Christ's life stands outside a direct relation to each individual in the human race, so that he as the God-man [*Gud-Mennesket*], though a true human being [*Menneske*], is still so heterogeneous with the individual human being that it cannot be done very directly without further ado, to want to go alongside him like this in a kind of impudent tactlessness. One could point out that Christ's (the God-man's) heterogeneity with all individual human beings is also expressed by the doctrine of his second coming. For it is not with him as with another human being, who has lived at one time, perhaps has won one or another great victory, whose consequences we appropriate as a matter of course, whereas nothing is heard from him, still less that he could come again to settle accounts with us, to judge us by demanding his due or in turn demanding ourselves of us.

With Christ it is different. He lived here on the earth; this, his life, is the archetype. After that, he enters into exaltation, and then he says, as it were, to the generation: "Now you begin." And what is it they are supposed to begin? To live in conformity with the archetype—but, he adds, I am coming again some day at the end of time. Accordingly, if I dare to put it like this, this form of existence makes the church's whole existence here on the earth into a parenthesis or into something parenthetical in Christ's life. The contents of the parenthesis begins with Christ's ascension into exaltation and closes with his second coming. Here, therefore, it does not end in one thing, as is usual in the historical relation between an individual and the others who profit from his victory as a matter of course. For neither is such an individual the archetype, nor is such an individual the one who will come again. Christ alone is the one who can make his life into the test for all persons. As he ascends into heaven, the time of examination begins. It has now lasted for 1,800 years; perhaps it shall last for 18,000. But (and just this is part of the fact that the intervening time is an examination) he is coming again. And when this is the case, then all direct connection to him in order to profit from his victory as a matter of course is more impossible than in relation to any other person.

Here, however, we will not detain ourselves further; we prefer to advance another consideration: is *truth* such that, in relation to it, one may believe that one can appropriate it with the help of another, just like that? Just like that, in other words, without starting to want to be developed in a similar way oneself, to be tried, to fight, to suffer like the one who acquired the truth for him? Is it not just as impossible as sleeping or dreaming oneself into the truth, just as impossible as appropriating it just like that, however wide awake one is? Or if one is wide awake, is this not just a fantasy when one does not understand or does not want to understand that, in relation to the truth, no cutback is given that leaves out acquiring it and, in relation to acquiring it from generation to generation, no essential foreshortening—so that every generation and every person in the generation essentially must begin from the beginning?

For what is truth? And in what sense was Christ the truth? As is well known, Pilate asked the first question, and another question is whether he actually cared to get this question answered. In any case, his question in one sense was absolutely on the spot and in another sense missed the mark as much as possible. Pilate asks Christ this question: "What is truth?" But Christ was indeed the truth; therefore the question is quite in order. Yes—and yet in another sense, no. That in the moment it can occur to Pilate to question Christ in this way just proves that he has no eye for the truth at all. That is, Christ's life was the truth, and therefore Christ himself says (as he more precisely explains the words: "My kingdom is not of this world: if my kingdom were of this world, then would my servants fight, that I should not be delivered to the Jews"): "To this end was I born, and for this cause came I into the world, that I should bear witness unto the truth." Christ's life on the earth, every moment in this life, was the truth.

In what, then, lies the basic confusion in Pilate's question? It lies in the fact that it can occur to him to question *Christ* in this way. For as he questions Christ like this, he informs against himself, you see.

He reveals about himself that Christ's life has not explained to him what truth is. But how, then, should Christ verbally be able to enlighten Pilate about the truth, when that which is the truth—Christ's life—has not opened Pilate's eyes to what truth is! It appears that Pilate had an inquiring mind, was willing to learn, but truly his question is as foolish as possible. Not that he asks, "What is truth?" but that he asks Christ about it, whose very life is the truth and so, in every moment, demonstrates what truth is by his life more powerfully than all the most long-winded lectures of the sharpest thinkers. Every other human being—a thinker, a teacher of science, etc.; yes, it absolutely does not matter, every other human being, a farmhand, a postman, etc.—there really is a kind of point in asking him: "What is truth?" But to ask Christ, who stands alive and kicking before one, to ask Christ about it is the most complete possible confusion. Should Christ answer this question, he would have to appear, falsely, as if he were not the truth for a moment. No human being but Christ is the truth. In relation to every other human being, the truth is something infinitely higher than his being, and that is why it is natural to ask, "What is truth?" and to reply to this question. Pilate is obviously of the opinion in relation to Christ that Christ, too, is a human being such as others, and therefore he falsely makes him into whatever he wishes by his question (a kind of thinker) and asks him—I suppose almost in the character of a highly distinguished man who basically sees thought as something that does not have a home anywhere but, with aristocratic condescension and for the sake of curiosity, takes pleasure in dealing with this man for a moment—in this way Pilate asks Christ: "What is truth?" And Christ *is* the truth!

Poor Pilate. After all, your pitying words about him, the crucified one, are preserved: "Behold the man!" But regarding this your question, there is surely reason to say about you: "Behold the fool!" For this your question, even if you could not understand it this way, is unconditionally the most foolish and most confusing question ever posed in the world. The question is just as foolish, precisely just as foolish, as if someone were to ask a man he stood and talked with: "I have to ask you: do you exist?" For Christ is the truth. And what should that man probably answer? "If one cannot be convinced that I exist by standing and talking with me, then my assurance cannot help at all, because it is indeed something far inferior to my existence." And it is also like this with Christ in relation to Pilate. Christ is the truth. "If my life cannot open your eyes to what truth is," he might say, "then to say it to you is the most impossible of all for me. My difference from all other human beings lies in this. It is certainly never quite true what any other person states in order to answer the question, 'What is truth?', but I am the only human being who cannot answer this question. For I *am* truth."

Consequently, Christ is the truth in the sense that *to be* the truth is the only true explanation of what truth is. One, then, can ask an apostle or can ask a Christian what truth is, and then, in answer to the question, the apostle and this Christian point to Christ and say: "Look at him; learn from him; he was the truth." This means that the truth, in the sense in which Christ is the truth, is not a sum of propositions, not a conceptual definition, etc., but a life. The being of truth is not the direct redoubling of being in relation to thought, which only gives hypothetical being, only secures thinking against being a figment of the imagination that does not exist, reassuring it to think with validity, that what is thought exists—that is, has validity. No, the being of truth is the redoubling in yourself, in me, in him, that your life, that my life, that his life expresses the truth approximately in the striving after it; that your life, that my life, that his life is approximately the being of truth in the striving after it, just as the truth was a *life* in Christ. For he was the truth.

And, of course, that is why the truth, Christianly understood, is not to know the truth but to be the truth. Despite all the latest philosophy, there is an infinite difference in this, which is best seen in Christ's relation to Pilate. For Christ could not—could only falsely—answer the question "What is truth?" just because he was not the one who knew what truth is but was the truth. Not as if he did not know what truth is, but when one is the truth, and when the demand is to be truth, to know the truth is an untruth. For to know the truth is something that entirely of itself goes with being the truth, not the other way around. And just for that reason it becomes untruth when knowing the truth is separated from being the truth, or when knowing the truth and being the truth are made into a single thing, since they are related in reverse order: to be the truth is one with knowing the truth, and Christ would never have known the truth, if he had not been it. And no human being knows more of the truth than what he is of the truth.

Indeed, one cannot actually know the truth. For, after all, if one knows the truth one must know that the truth is to be the truth, and then one surely knows in his knowledge of the truth that to know the truth is an untruth. If one wants to say that one is the truth in knowing the truth, then one is indeed admitting that the truth is to be the truth, as one is saying that to know the truth is to be the truth, since one would have to say in the other case: the truth is to know the truth. Otherwise the question about the truth only returns, so that the question is not answered but the only decisive answer postponed, because, of course, one again must be able to know whether one is the truth or not. That is to say: my knowledge is related to the truth, but while I am falsely outside of myself. The truth is within me, in other words, when I am truly within myself (not falsely outside of myself). The truth, if it is there, is a being, a *life*. That is why it is said: "And this is life eternal, that they might know the only true God, and the one whom he sent," the truth. This means that I only know the truth in truth when it becomes a life in me. For that reason, Christ compares the truth with food and acquiring the truth with eating, because just as, bodily, food becomes that which sustains life by being acquired (assimilated), so also is the truth, spiritually, both that which gives and sustains life; it is life. And therefore one sees what a monstrous delusion it is—something close to the greatest possible—to didacticize Christianity. And hence one sees how changed Christianity has become through this continual didacticizing—that now all expressions are formed according to the view that truth is cognition, knowledge (now one talks constantly about comprehending, speculating, considering, etc.), whereas in original Christianity all expressions were formed according to the view that truth is a being.

There is a difference between truth and truths, and this difference is especially recognizable in the determination "to be," or it is recognizable in that a distinction is made between a *way* and a final decision, which is reached at the end, *the result*. In relation to the truth, where there is a difference between a way and what is reached by going or by having gone along the way, a change can set in for the successor in comparison with the predecessor. He can come to begin in a different place than this successor; he can be let off far more easily—in short, the change that takes place consists in the way being shortened, yes, shortened to the degree that, in certain cases, it seems to fall away entirely. Yet, when the truth is the way, to be the truth is a life—and, after all, Christ does say this about himself: "I am the way, the truth, and the life." In that case, no essential change is thinkable in the relation between predecessor and successor. Indeed, the change consisted in the fact that the way was shortened, which was possible because the way was not essentially synonymous with the truth. Yet, when the truth itself is the way, then the way cannot be shortened or fall away without the truth being distorted or falling away.

This is not difficult to understand; anyone who will just give himself a little time will be able to understand it easily. It can also become clearer by being illustrated in some examples, and it is important that it becomes clear—this difference between truth and truth. For what has utterly confused Christianity and what to a great extent has occasioned the fantasy of a triumphant church is this— that one has considered Christianity as truth in the sense of results, instead of its being truth in the sense of *the way*.

Here are some examples. A person invents something—for example, gunpowder. Perhaps he, the inventor, has spent many, many years of his life pondering and devising. Perhaps many before him have spent a long time in similar fashion but in vain. Now he is successful; now gunpowder is invented. In that same moment, the way almost entirely falls away; it is very shortened. That for which he has spent twenty years can be learned by another in half an hour with the help of his directions about how one sets about doing it. The twenty years stand in an altogether accidental relation to the invention. One actually cannot say that he has spent twenty years discovering gunpowder; no, he invented the gunpowder in half an hour really. One must rather say that he did not discover gunpowder in those twenty years; they have, in a certain sense, no worth, since they were not used to invent gunpowder but in a vain attempt to invent powder— consequently, not to invent gunpowder. If a person could prove with

306

evidence that he has worked to invent gunpowder day and night for thirty whole years but did not invent it, then "the way" as such has absolutely no meaning. If he who invented it invented it by stumbling over a gutter plank one evening as he walked home drunk from a party, then the way is absolutely a trivial matter. In such a case, the inventor will merely stand in a direct line with the dog who discovered purple, though his invention would have just as much worth for this generation—which, if the invention were of another kind, perhaps would call him a benefactor of the human race but not its teacher. For to be a teacher, especially of the human race, "the teacher of humanity," corresponds to the fact that the truth is *the way*.

A person laboriously works his way into an obscure period of history; no researcher has been capable of shedding light on it up till now. At last he is successful; he has spent twenty years bringing the historical truth to light and making it indisputable. This gain benefits the successor; the way is shorted quite significantly. The successor needs perhaps scarcely three months in order to have that obscure period's true context fully explained to him.

A person cultivates a language that no one has known up till now. He makes immense efforts his whole life through, but also leaves behind as the yield of his life and of his striving great means of help through which the successor perhaps comes just as far in the course of two years as he did in twenty years. Here the way is shortened significantly for the successor; the disciple (despite the fact that he perhaps is only a bungler in comparison with the master) is always above the master; through the master's preliminary work, he is able to begin at another point and to reach further than he. And this is pretty much the way it is wherever truth is knowledge.

But it is different where the truth is being, is "the way." Here, even if the world lasted for 18,000 years, it is impossible for any essential shortening in the relation between predecessor and successor to take place from generation to generation, since the truth is not different from the way but is exactly the way. Christ was the truth, was the way, or was the way in the sense that the truth is the way. That he has traveled over "the way" surely changes nothing at all in the relation for the successor, who, if he is of the truth and wants to be of the truth, can only be that by going along "the way." That up to a given time there have lived thirty generations who have traveled the way changes nothing at all in the relation for the next generation, or for each individual in this one, who must begin in absolutely the same place—from the beginning, at the beginning of the way—in order to travel it. For that reason, there is no cause or occasion to triumph, because only the who one has traveled the way could triumph. Yet, he is no longer in the world; he has entered into exaltation, as Christ was indeed also the way when he ascended into heaven. If, on the other hand, someone later wants to take occasion to triumph from the fact that someone earlier has traveled the way, then this is, after all, just as foolish as if a student were to triumph on the occasion of another student having finished his examination.

If one wants to hold fast to this—which is indeed Christ's own statement, that the truth is the way—one will perceive more and more clearly that a triumphant church is a fantasy in this world, that only a militant church can be truly talked about in this world. But the militant church relates itself and feels itself drawn to Christ in lowliness; the triumphant church has taken Christ's church in vain. To make this clear is the task of this exposition, and it simply must be remembered that what is constantly meant by a "triumphant church" is a church that wants to be triumphant here in this world. For a triumphant church in eternity is, of course, quite in order, corresponding to Christ's being taken up into exaltation.

What made one even come up with the fantasy of a triumphant church? And what is understood by a "triumphant church"?

It was already observed above that what has especially contributed to the delusion of a triumphant church is that people have understood Christianity as the truth in which there is a difference between result and way or Christianity's truth is understood as a result—what in Danish one perhaps could call the remainder, a profit. For in relation to the truth as the way, this is just what the emphasis lies on—that there is no remainder, no profit, no result left by the predecessor for the successor. That is, if Christianity were the truth in this sense, then it would be quite in order with triumph. Hence, with respect to the invention of gunpowder and the art of printing, etc., with respect to the many conquests that have been made in the fields of science, the arts, etc., this generation is deservedly triumphant. For here the truth is a result; here the emphasis is not laid on *the way* and on *each individual* who, responsible before God, has to decide himself whether or not he wants to go along the way, indifferent, absolutely indifferent, to whether no one or everyone is going along the same way, indifferent, absolutely indifferent, to whether no one or countless millions have gone along the same way. No, here the emphasis is placed upon the truth, *the profit*, and on the generation, human society, the company, "the community," which takes over the truth as a matter of course, and it is by accident that an individual has discovered it, invented it, fathomed it, etc.

Thus if Christ had been, for example, a teacher of the truth, a thinker, who had made a discovery or fathomed what perhaps had cost him indescribable intellectual trouble, but what also then (because *the way* only stood in an accidental relation to the truth) could become a result: then it would be quite in order that the succeeding generation would relate itself triumphantly to it as a matter of course. The successors, who were exempted from all these immense intellectual troubles—these many, many years of effort—could at most feel obliged to remember with gratitude him who had persevered. Yet, in other respects, there was nothing other to do than to triumph. That this is a delusion has already been shown. Here it only need be added that this is why Christ's teaching is infinitely exalted over all the inventions of this era and of all time, an eternity older and an eternity higher than all systems, even the very latest, also even the one that is the very latest in ten thousand years. For his teaching is the truth, but in the sense that the truth is the way, and he is and remains as the God-man the way himself—something that no human being, however zealously he professes that the truth is the way, would dare to say about himself without blasphemy.

Yet—besides the delusion that, as confused as is possible, has failed Christianity by understanding the truth as result—there is also another delusion that has contributed to producing the fantasy of a triumphant church. This delusion is the appearance, which has arisen over the course of time, that we as such are all Christians. For if this is a given, a militant church seems to be an impossibility. Wherever there seems to be—wherever people assume that there is—an established Christianity, there is an attempt to form a triumphant church, even if people do not use these words. For the militant church is in the making; an *established* Christianity *is*, is not becoming.

Finally, this fantasy lingers: a triumphant church, together with human impatience, wants to grasp in advance that which comes later. And just as one now almost universally sees the years of childhood or youth wanting to absorb the whole of life in advance, so that nothing remains for adulthood and old age: so has this generation—this generation or Christendom—wanted to absorb eternity with a similar impatience and (instead of that which is God's invention and thought with all existence—that temporality, this life, is the time of struggle, the time of testing, and eternity the time of victory) lodge triumph within temporality, which is to abolish Christianity. Because what Christ said, "My kingdom is not of this world," was not said in a special sense about the relation to those time periods; it is eternally valid, therefore a valid statement about the relation between Christ's kingdom and this world for every time period. As soon as Christ's kingdom makes a deal with this world and becomes a kingdom of this world, Christianity is abolished. When, on the other hand, Christianity is in truth, it is surely a kingdom in this world but not of this world. That is, it is militant.

What, then, is meant by a "triumphant church"? By this is meant a church that assumes that the time of struggling is over, that the church, although it is still in this world, has nothing more to struggle about or for. But then, of course, the church and this world have become synonymous, and this is the very situation not only with everything that has called itself the triumphant church, but with what is called an established Christendom. For truly Christ's church can only exist by struggling in this world, that is, by fighting to exist each moment. If it is the established church, then it is grounded in the fact that it has been victorious. The militant church exists by struggling, but, after all, the church that is called "established" must be the one that exists after having been victorious.

And this triumphant church or established Christendom resembles the militant church no more than the square resembles the circle. It would—if we imagined a Christian from those times when the church was truly militant—it would be absolutely impossible for him to recognize Christianity in this distortion. He would hear

Christianity declaimed and hear that what was said was entirely true, but, to his greatest surprise, he would see that the existential conditions for being a Christian had become the very opposite of what they were in his day, so that now to be a Christian did not resemble being a Christian in his day any more than walking on one's legs resembles walking on one's head.

In the militant church, to be a Christian means to express being a Christian within an environment that is the opposite of being a Christian. In a triumphant church, in an established Christendom, to be a Christian means to express being a Christian within an environment that is synonymous, homogeneous with being a Christian. If I am a true Christian in the first instance, then naturally this will (since, after all, the theater is the opposite) be *inversely* recognizable by what opposition I suffer, and to the degree that I am a Christian has more truth, to the same degree would this be recognizable by the fact that the opposition is greater. In the second instance, to be a Christian will of course (for, after all, the theater is homogeneity) be *directly* recognizable by the favor, honor, and prestige I win in this world. Why, however, am I saying "in this world"? After all, "this world" is Christendom; accordingly, it will be directly recognizable by the favor, honor, prestige I win in Christendom. To the degree that I am a Christian has more truth, to the same degree will this also be recognizable by the quite extraordinary prestige I enjoy in this world. But what am I saying? After all, "this world" is Christendom; accordingly, it will be recognizable by the extraordinary prestige I enjoy in Christendom.

This is an utterly unavoidable consequence when the assumption is: a triumphant church. There where, if I lived in a militant church, precisely suffering would come, now reward comes. There where, if I lived in a militant church, insult and derision would befall me, now honor and prestige beckon. There where death would be inevitable, now I celebrate the highest triumph. Since, according to the assumption, I am living among nothing but Christians, then surely they must recognize my genuinely Christian disposition at once and therefore hasten to meet me with honors and distinctions instead of offering me resistance. Yes, if one imagined a member of the Christian church from the time when it was militant—one who became a witness to this—I suppose he would almost have to laugh for a moment that what in his day was frightful earnestness has become a pleasant game.

There stands Christianity with its demands for self-denial: deny yourself—and then suffer because you deny yourself. This was Christianity. But how absolutely different it is now. If I imagine a youth who, with a lovely lack of sophistication, decided to adapt his life to Holy Scripture: how surprised would he be (yes, I wonder if he could help laughing at himself and at the whole of existence) because what happens in the very moment that, according to the instructions of Christianity, he had prepared himself to suffer—he comes into honor and prestige. He composes himself in order to endure the opposition; he dares to take the step—dash, and he is hailed with acclaim. He at least prepares for chilling derision and coldness, and he is received with the warm compress of an almost dainty admiration. That is, the youth had forgotten (what, after all, is not found in the Bible either) that he lived in Christendom, in Christendom where all are Christians, in the triumphant church where there is no more struggling, but where being the true Christian is rewarded with distinction.

This is the situation in the *triumphant* church, where it really pays to be a Christian, and the only thing that does not pay is not being a Christian. On the other hand, insofar as the so-called *established Christendom* does not call itself the triumphant church, perhaps it rejects this externality but produces the same confusion by way of *the hidden feeling*. For, again, the established Christendom, where all are Christians but in a hidden feeling, resembles the militant church just as little as the silence of death resembles the noisiness of passion.

Only the fantasy of a triumphant church was successful in really implementing the thought that those of a certain profession constituted the actual Christians. The task, the business, of this profession was to be Christian, and so here directness applied—that the more someone was a true Christian, the more he would increase in honor and prestige. The rest of the world indeed furnished the spectators, the chorus, but accordingly not any opposition to being a Christian;

on the contrary, it furnished an environment of admiration in relation to that profession, which represented being Christian.

Yet, when this difference in rank disappeared, the triumphant church disappeared as well. Since now everyone was supposed to join in the game, direct recognizability (the degree of being the true Christian in direct correspondence to the honor and prestige one enjoys) encountered a peculiar difficulty that made it impossible. The clergyman had essentially nothing other to do than to express being a Christian, and as long as the Christian masses were actually content with perceiving themselves in the rank representing them, it suited the triumphant church. But it was otherwise when this difference in rank no longer satisfied the Christian masses. The Christian masses also have—yes, viewed mainly in external fashion—something else to take care of in the world than to express being a Christian (in the sense of the triumphant church). Now how could the direct recognizability of being a Christian be expressed in what is heterogeneous with being a Christian but not really hostile to it, only indifferent? Yes, it was an impossibility. In the militant church, direct recognizability is impossible, because to be a Christian is expressed within the contrast of being a Christian. Now, on the other hand, direct recognizability became impossible, because to be a Christian was supposed to be expressed within what is indifferent in relation to being a Christian.

Please understand me properly. A citizen, for example, is a Christian. Let us assume that this citizen is, say, a shoemaker. It is his livelihood; naturally, he is occupied with the practice of his trade for the better part of the day. Now, should direct recognizability in relation to being a Christian be possible here, then the one who was the truest Christian among the shoemakers—or the fact that he was the truest Christian—would therefore have to be recognizable by his having the most to do, retaining the most assistants, so that perhaps the king, the queen, as well as the whole royal house (or, in any case, the clergy) let him make shoes for them. That this could not be carried out naturally became more and more obvious in the course of time. The direct recognizability in relation to being a Christian ran into another kind of opposition than the one known by the militant church. This opposition was not the contrast to being a Christian but

313

the indifference to being a Christian. This "opposition of indifference" does not turn the relation upside down to an inverted recognizability, as in the militant church, but it does make direct recognizability impossible.

So a complete change of scene in relation to being a Christian entered Christendom. People dropped the fantasy of a triumphant church; they let the whole externality stand and, in relation to it, the law of indifference toward being a Christian—that the best shoemaker was the one who sewed best, the best poet the one who wrote the best poems, etc., etc. In this way, people let go of the externality and now transferred being a Christian to a matter of feeling. A universal discharge is given and assumed for all of us; it is settled that we are all Christians, quite in the same sense as it is given that we are all human beings—the assumption, therefore, with which the game of life or of actuality first begins. For that reason, it would be foolishness, even madness, if someone were specifically to argue that he is a human being, since, after all, that would seek to bring a presupposition to consciousness that, assumed once and for all and by all, lies at the basis of everything.

Here we have the concept of established Christendom. In established Christendom, we are all Christians, albeit in a hidden feeling. The external world has nothing at all to do with the fact that I am a Christian; that is why my being a Christian is not detectable. If I own a pub, then I do not at all expect that my being a true Christian is supposed to be recognizable by the fact that I have the best patronage; no, whether I as a pub owner shall have the best patronage depends on the extent to which I know how to please an esteemed, cultured public, and the true Christian I am is something by itself, something for myself, something I am in a hidden feeling—quite like all the others, not only like all the other pub owners, but quite literally like every other person in Christendom. To the degree it is true that I am a Christian, it is absolutely just as true of me as of all the others. If I am a pastor, then I do not at all expect that my being a true Christian is going to be recognizable by the fact that I am the most heeded and most esteemed preacher. No, whether I will have the most support as a pastor depends on which gifts of eloquence I artistically possess, depends on whether I have a good voice, how the clerical gown becomes me, how much I have studied the latest philosophy, so that I can satisfy the demands of the times. The true Christian that I am, or that I am the true Christian, is something by itself, something for myself, something I am in a hidden feeling— quite like all the others. But that I am a true Christian—that is certain enough; it is just as certain as it is that all the others are.

And why this hiddenness then? Why this hiddenness, which I maintain by watching over it very carefully? Why, naturally, because I am afraid that, if one got to know to what degree I am a true Christian, then I would be rewarded with extraordinary honor and prestige. And I am too much of a true Christian for that, to want to be honored and esteemed *because* I am a true Christian. See, that is why I keep it stored in a hidden feeling. For if people got to know it, then it would not be possible to avoid being extraordinarily honored and esteemed, since it is, after all, established Christendom in which I am living—where we are all true Christians, albeit in a hidden feeling.

If a Christian from that time when the church was militant were to be thrown into established Christendom, he would fall into the most profound bewilderment. In the militant church, to be a Christian was recognizable by the opposition one suffered. In the triumphant church, it was recognizable by the honor and prestige one enjoyed. But "established Christendom" has invented something new: one hides that one is a Christian—out of fear that it would be rewarded with honor and prestige in an unchristian manner. In the militant church, it was indeed sometimes the case that one person or another would hide that he was a Christian out of fear of the opposition connected with being a Christian, but in "established Christendom" it is out of fear of receiving honor and prestige. So "established Christendom" really is something infinitely much higher than the militant church, which has hardly had an intimation of such exalted piety! In the militant church, it was piety to confess Christianity; in established Christendom, it is piety precisely to keep it secret! Oh, infinite depth of piety, since the whole thing could so very easily be a show! Oh, countless flock of pious people, when all the millions of every country are such pious people—and we are all that, after all! Take off your shoes, because the ground on which you stand is holy when you are standing in Christendom, where there are nothing but true Christians! Let God keep eternity, where, all in all, he will scarcely get as many true Christians as there are at any moment in established Christendom, where all are Christians.

Imagine a youth who grew up in established Christendom, but previously unacquainted with the conditions of actuality into which he is to enter, brought up by Holy Scripture in almost monastic remoteness from life: he will experience something extremely bizarre, something ridiculous in one sense. He is, then, well versed in Christianity—assuming that one can become this through Holy Scripture, and, indeed, one must allow this assumption for the poor little guy. It has been said to him that the requirement is to confess Christ before the world. He is well informed—that is to say, insofar as one can become that through Holy Scripture, and, indeed, one must allow this assumption for the youngster. He is informed about what the consequence of this will be. Having well considered all this, the youth is determined to adapt his life to the rule. But what takes place? He happens to live in established Christendom. While he makes as if to want to venture a step, a benevolent man, a kind of spiritual adviser, intervenes and "makes such a speech": "Young friend, you are delusional. You do not realize just where you are: this is established Christendom, and, in truth, there is nowhere to confess Christ. For between us—but it is between us and is already a weakness, an oversight, on my part to say so much—we are all Christians, and the true Christian is precisely the one who keeps it most hidden."

If a youth who was brought up on fairy tales in his childhood and is therefore familiar with the idea of monsters who dwell in the woods but are killed—if he, ready for battle with an immense broadsword at his side and equally immense courage in his heart, now went out into actuality, nothing stranger could happen to him than what happened to that youth in established Christendom. If, that is, a monster even stranger than anything he had heard or read about were to meet him, it would not be the strange thing, or still not be enough in comparison with the strange thing, that happened to him—that he could not at all catch a glimpse of anything that resembled a monster. Then a benevolent elderly man would come to him and say: "My young friend, you are delusional; you are not in the world of fairy tales but in the civilized and polished world, where no such monsters exist, where you are living among cultured and well-bred persons, and where, moreover, the police watch over your security, the clergy over your morality, and the gas lighting makes the night just as safe as the day. Consequently, since the time of monsters ended long ago, put your sword into its scabbard and learn what the task is now—to be an agreeable person, quite like the rest of us. Learn that you must recognize yourself in every other person, and every other person must recognize himself in you, up to the greatest possible disillusionment."

As has been said, the triumphant church resembles the militant church no more than the square resembles the circle, and "established Christendom" resembles it just as little. Nevertheless, the militant church alone is truth; the triumphant church and established Christendom are a fantasy.

"But," I hear someone say, "it is indeed an absurdity and an impossibility with a militant church nowadays. If we are all Christians, then what are we supposed to fight against?" Dear me! In order to find something to fight against, we could at the very least fight against this—that we are all Christians and, with that, how it all adds up. "How dare you presume to be a knower of hearts, who judges what lies deep within human beings! If a person himself says that he is a Christian, then surely you do not presume to deny it?" You see, we do have something to fight against. But does he really say that? I thought that, in established Christendom, it was the hidden feeling, that we were supposed to keep it hidden. "Yes, we certainly are to keep it hidden, precisely because it is a given that all are Christians." How, then, is it a given, when each person individually keeps it hidden? Are all Christians, because it is a given?

The situation is this. When, around the circle, everyone decides to be a Christian *just like* "the others," then no one, if you will, actually confesses Christ. On the other hand, it is well known that everyone, if you will, is a Christian of sorts. Everyone is baptized as a child and later confirmed—yes, also almost as a child (presumably so that everything in this respect can be in order and correct as early as possible regarding what really is necessary as a permit, if one is to go through the world without the indictment of the authorities). And it is certain that everyone who is baptized as a child and confirmed as

317

a boy or a girl is a Christian; after all, by opening the parish register, one can look it up. Yet, later in life, they presumably cannot come to confess Christ, because, of course, they are living in established Christendom, where it is known of all (see the parish register) that they are Christians. It applies even to the pastors in "established Christendom" that they do not so much "confess Christ" as "it is known of them" (as of everyone) that they are Christians. If one were to say that pastors obviously confess Christ through their sermons, then it must be replied that the fact that preaching is their livelihood, plus the fact that they do what they do as civil servants, has the result that the emphasis still does not fall upon *personally* confessing Christ.

All are Christians in a hidden feeling. Who would dare deny that? Indeed, the one who would take it upon himself to deny it quite rightly runs the risk of wanting to play the knower of hearts. Consequently, no one can deny it. That everyone is a Christian in a hidden feeling becomes a secretiveness that is, so to speak, jammed shut. It is impossible to get to know whether all these thousands and thousands actually are Christians, because, as it is said, they are all Christians in a hidden feeling. And it is valid, not only for the church but for everyone, that one does not judge of what is hidden, because one does not know how to judge.

But, really, should it not be possible to be able to break this secretiveness and to get a little disclosed without becoming guilty of being a knower of hearts? Well, yes! Then how? In this way—that someone simply and personally takes it upon himself to confess Christ in the midst of Christendom. He does not judge a single person, far from it. But many will be exposed by how they judge him. He does not claim to be a more perfect Christian than the others, no, far from it. On the contrary, he concedes to others that they certainly are more perfect Christians than he—they who keep it hidden out of a religious fear of winning honor and prestige, whereas he, being a poor simpleton, is so afraid for his own sake that it should become a pretense with such a decidedly steep Christianity, and that is why he holds to the old Christianity of confessing Christ. Therefore he does not indicate that any of the others are not Christians, oh, far from it. He only informs against himself—that he is such a poor simpleton. Still, the thoughts of many hearts would be disclosed by how they judge this poor simpleton, this imperfect Christian. He only expresses that, as he has been taught, he is a member of the militant church. Then it will be manifest whether or not this peaceful society, established Christendom, will come to help him—help him through persecution and the like, so that it will become entirely true that he is a member of a militant church.

But is the point, then, that as long as this world stands, or as long as the Christian church shall exist in this world, it is to be and must be a militant church? Answer: yes, this is quite certainly the point. It is quite certainly the point of Christianity, and, also quite certainly, there is meaning in this point. "What absurdity," I hear someone say, "what absurdity. After all, it is impossible that we all could become martyrs. If all of us are to become martyrs and be beaten to death, who, then, is going to kill us? If all of us are to become martyrs and be persecuted, mocked, reviled, who, then, is going to persecute and mock us?" This would be right on target—if only the presupposition that, as it were, tightens the bowstring for this shrewd objection were correct (the presupposition that we all are Christians), if this presupposition were correct (in other words, true at any given moment), or even if it were only at all true that it is Christianity's idea that the moment should come when literally all would truly be Christians in this world.

The situation is this. Through the continual observation of world history and the story of this generation, through continual talk about world-historical considerations, etc., it finally has gotten only all too easy to start making Christianity into revenue for world history; it has gotten to be entirely in order that Christianity becomes a development within the category, "the human race." People have utterly forgotten that Christ's life on earth (and this is Christianity, distinct from the history of Christians or the story about the lives, biographies, destinies of Christians, also of heretics, also of science) is the sacred history, which must not be confused with the history of the generation and of the world. People have utterly forgotten the essential heterogeneity of the God-man in relation to every other individual human being and to the entire human race. People have utterly forgotten that Christianity essentially relates itself to eternity, that life here on earth (to call to mind an earlier explanation) is a time of testing for every single individual of the innumerable millions who have lived and are going to live.

It is certainly Christianity's idea that it will be proclaimed to all persons. But does it ever follow from this that Christianity's idea has been that all persons should happen to adopt it and to become true Christians? If so, then I would have to say that one has not properly looked into God's counsel at the time it was decided from eternity that Christ should come into the world, Christ who proclaimed that life here on earth is a time of testing. One of two things: either it has been the thought of Providence (to be sure, in foreknowledge, Providence can be knowledgeable about the fact that something will happen, whereas human beings bear responsibility for the fact that something does happen) that it would never be the case that, at a given time, all persons or at least the greatest number of persons become true Christians, or even Providence has not seen far enough ahead. For if it is the case that all persons are actually Christians in truth, then this life is no longer the time of testing. The testing is, namely, self-denial, to deny oneself. To be a Christian is the test, and to be a Christian is to deny oneself. But if, at a given time, all persons are actually true Christians, then self-denial is not connected with being a Christian, at least not Christian self-denial.

Magister[2] Kierkegaard (at the conclusion of the first part of *Works of Love*) has shown what is understood by Christian self-denial—that it only exists where there is a double-danger, and that the decisive qualification is the second danger of suffering because one denies oneself. But, of necessity, this danger must fall away if all persons are true Christians during the time in which I live. For then, after all, everything around me will be sheer encouragement and incentive for me to become a true Christian as well. And if that is so, if I lived under such conditions, then it would not be true with regard to me and to my life to call this life in a Christian sense—and it is indeed Christianity that is the inventor of this expression—a time of

---

2. "Magister" refers to the highest academic degree attained by Kierkegaard, which, in his day, was equivalent to the doctorate. Note also that the pseudonymous author of this piece, Anti-Climacus, refers to Kierkegaard in the third person. (Tr.)

testing. No, then Providence has not actually known how to administer a test; it has overlooked one contingency, overlooked the possibility of its onset, a contingency that could turn upside down its whole purpose with Christianity.

But if one takes Christianity as it presents itself, instead of flippantly blurring Christianity with world history in a human way, if one believes that this life is a time of testing, if one believes that Providence sufficiently knows what it is doing, if one believes that it was and is Christianity's will to want to be proclaimed to all persons but that by no means is it Christianity's opinion that all will accept it: then everything is in order. Then this life becomes a time of testing for each individual, and the Christian church always becomes a militant church here in this world. A concept such as "congregation," with which people busy themselves so much in these times, is actually used in this life as an impatient anticipation of the eternal. "The individual" corresponds to struggling—that is to say, when struggling is in a spiritual and Christian sense, rather than in the fleshly sense of equipping a battlefield, where it does not so much depend on the individual as on how many thousands there are, how many cannons they have, etc. In Christian terms, struggling is always done by individuals, because the fact that each person is an individual before God is precisely spirit, that "community" is a lower category than "the individual," which everyone can and should be. And even if the individuals were in the thousands and thus struggling in union, each individual—Christianly understood—really is struggling within himself, as well as in union with the others, and shall give an individual account on judgment day, when his life will be judged as an individual. That is why the congregation actually belongs to eternity first; "the congregation" is in rest what "the individual" is in unrest. But, of course, this life is precisely the time of testing, the time of unrest, and therefore the "congregation" is not at home in time but only in eternity, where, in rest, it is the assembly of all the individuals who endured in the struggle and passed the test.

As long as this world stands and the Christian church in it, it is a militant church. However, it has the promise that the gates of hell shall not prevail against it. But woe, woe to the Christian church, when it wants to be victorious in this world. For then it is not the church that has been victorious; then the world has been victorious. Then the heterogeneity between Christianity and world has been cut out; the world has won, and Christianity has lost. Then Christ is no longer the God-man but a distinguished human being whose life is related homogeneously to the development of the human race. Then eternity is abolished, and the scene for the completion of everything is transferred within temporality. Then the way to life is no longer narrow and the gate strait, nor are there only a few who find it; no, then the way is broad and the gate wide open—the gates of hell have prevailed, and many, indeed all, are admitted.

Christ has never wanted to be victorious in this world. He came into the world in order to suffer; he called *that* being victorious. Yet, when human impatience and pert tactlessness ascribes its own thoughts and conceptions to Christianity, instead of letting its thoughts and conceptions be transformed by Christianity, when this has gotten the upper hand, then to be victorious takes on the old human meaning of being victorious in this world, and then Christianity is abolished. It was not a petty bickering that was between Christ and the world, so that, at bottom, he was in the wrong in not being able to get along better with the world; no, love of God is hate to the world. And the day when Christianity and the world become friends, yes, then Christianity is abolished. Then there is no more talk about the fact that Christ shall come again and judge; no, then the judgment has passed on him that, in the end, he was a dreamer, an imprudent human being. For, if he had not been so imprudent, then he would have gotten along well with the world; then he would not have been killed—something totally unnecessary. Then he would become something great in the world, just as his disciples in the triumphant church became something great in the world, which also abolished or rendered false the saying that the disciple is not greater than the master. For he was crucified, but they became powerful through honor and prestige, just as his disciples in established Christendom became great, not because of their Christianity, but because—they Christianly keep their Christianity in a hidden feeling and use their natural talents and gifts to be successful in the world.

In the meantime, however, the one we introduced before as an interlocutor, perhaps returns to his first remark and says: "In spite

322

of everything you say, I can do nothing other than repeat that it is and remains an impossibility that we all could become martyrs." Answer: "Is it, then, an impossibility for you to become a martyr?" "Yes, naturally, if everyone is supposed to be that." But what do you really have to do with everyone? Is your opinion actually this meaningless opinion—that you, as you will to arrange your life and to try yourself in the test of becoming and being a Christian, that you then must first ask about others or get to know something about everyone else before you can begin? I believed that the very beginning of the test to become and to be a Christian is to become so introspective that it is as if all the others did not exist in the least for a person, so introspective that one quite literally is alone in the whole world, alone before God, alone with Holy Scripture as guidance, alone with the archetype before one's eyes. And, in contrast, the language you are speaking is the language of extroversion according to the greatest possible degree; it quite resembles the way a newspaperman expresses himself.

This is easy to understand. The first condition for becoming a Christian is to become unconditionally introspective. Infinitely turned inward in this way, the introspective person has absolutely nothing to do with anyone else—this is earnestness, and it applies far more stringently than when the schoolteacher orders that each pupil keep his eyes to himself and not to look at the others at all. Turned inward in this way, the learner understands or comes to understand what the task is: to become and to be a Christian. Every moment he is turned outward is wasted, and if these moments become numerous, then everything is squandered. Perhaps, then, he is well informed about the task and has learned it by heart; perhaps he even recited it to others and actually became a pastor and was compensated by the state. But one thing has escaped him, the crucial point from a Christian perspective—that what he says concerns himself, and it concerns himself in infinite introspection, whereas perhaps he is of the opinion that what he says concerns the congregation and only the salary and the promotion concern him.

Accordingly, if he becomes introspective to the utmost, the infinitely introspective person comes to understand what the task is to the utmost—that to be a Christian is to believe in Christ and to suffer for the sake of this belief, or that to be a Christian is self-denial in a Christian sense. Yet, in order to properly show the foolishness of that objection ("it really is impossible that all could become martyrs"), let us now assume the absurd claim that literally all among whom this Christian is living are true Christians. Then, after all, it is impossible that he can become a martyr. Most certainly. But at what point will he come to know this? I wonder if it would be at the beginning, so that this becomes an evasion, an excuse, which hinders him in beginning the task? Impossible. For, after all, he is infinitely introspective; he knows nothing and wants to know nothing about the others. Therefore he will first come to know that he did not become a martyr at the end of his life. This "at the end of his life" must be taken quite precisely—that is, at the moment he dies, not before, because before he admittedly still cannot know whether or not it could happen to him. Yet, in the moment he dies, this indeed no longer concerns him in the least. So, in any case, he has experienced martyrdom in possibility. And this was, as said, under the assumption of what is most absurd—that literally all or merely the majority of the contemporaries were true Christians, and therefore the gate to life, in spite of Christ's statement, is not narrow but either unconditionally is wide open or nevertheless is considerably enlarged and expanded through renovation.

"But," I hear someone say, "do you who are speaking here have the strength to become a martyr in this way? Or do you have enough courage, to say nothing of impudence, to claim that no one was a true Christian who did not become a martyr? Or were you always so strong that you never felt the need for gentle and soothing words to be spoken to you? Or perhaps you are just in the situation that you yourself, anxious and afraid, need gentleness but take joy in scaring others, as is often the desire of one who is afraid?" I do not lack an answer to these questions, and I only wish that the questioner would not misunderstand the answer, since I by no means fail to appreciate the significance of the questions. That I feel the need for gentleness is granted. But I owe it to the truth to confess that I feel this need precisely because I have been brought up by and have lived under rigorousness for a long, long time—yes, I will be under it again at any moment. I have never taken joy in "making someone anxious." I myself am aware that I can talk gently and soothingly to the suffering, the sick, the sorrowful; I know that I have had my joy from that. I have never asserted that every Christian is a martyr or that no one was a true Christian who did not become a martyr, even if I think that, precisely in order to be a true Christian, every true Christian—and I include myself among them—is to make an admission of mortification that he really has gotten off easier than true Christians in the strictest sense. Moreover, he shall make this admission so that, if I dare put it this way, the Christian order of rank shall not be confused and the number one place altogether disappear while the number two place assumes its position.

And now, finally, this is my principal answer. Christianity has been quite literally dethroned in Christendom, but, if that is so, then it is abolished as well. For a king does not cease to exist because, for example, the place in which he lived made itself into a republic and him into a president. But Christianity is abolished as soon as it is kicked off the throne. Christianity is the unconditioned; it has only one way of being—the unconditioned being. If it is not unconditioned, it is abolished. In relation to Christianity, this is unconditionally valid—either/or. Now this brazen talk has been heard long enough and loudly enough—that one must go further, that one cannot stop at Christianity, with faith, with what is simple, with obedience, with this "you shall." And it has penetrated further and further down among the people, who naturally are influenced by the way the highest circles, if I dare say so, have passed judgment. It has penetrated, and only all too easily, since it is too bad that every human being has a natural, innate inclination to disobedience. That is why "reasons," believing for three reasons, were put in place of obedience: people were ashamed to obey. That is why lenience was put in place of rigorousness: people did not dare to command, and people shrank from letting themselves be commanded. The ones who should command became cowardly; the ones who should obey became defiant. Christianity was abolished in Christendom in this way—by lenience. Without authority, Christianity tiptoes around Christendom in worn-out, decrepit clothes, and we do not know whether we should doff our hats for it or whether it should bow before us, whether we need its compassion or whether it needs our compassion.

Yet, if Christianity is the only salvation for us, there truly is only one possible salvation for Christianity: rigorousness. It cannot be saved by the help of lenience—that is to say, it neither can nor shall be saved. This thought is a crime of high treason against Christianity, but by rigorousness it will be put in its rightful place again as ruler. And even if I myself should sink under the weight of the benchmark I am developing, and even if I should be the first who incurred judgment, and even if I should be the only one—I can do nothing else. I know well what I am doing; I also know what I—in fear and trembling, pursued by spiritual trials—have suffered by venturing out so far, solitary, occupied day and night with such thoughts, and solitarily occupied with them in escalating exertion for so long a time, and solitary even though I have lived in Christendom where, of course, all are Christians but where I have never really heard any talk or any conversation or sermon about which I (if this question were put to me before God) unconditionally would dare to say that it was Christian. For even the most Christian talk I have heard still always had an uneasy admixture of "reasons," a slight taste of human whining and pity, an ingratiating unpleasantness.

I had no monastery to which I could flee, seeking an environment that roughly corresponded to my intensive preoccupation. I chose the only way out that was left in Christendom: to seem to be the most irrational person of all, to "become a fool in the world," in order to guard (if possible in this earnest world) what I hid in my heart of hearts, a bit of earnestness, and in order that this intensity could get the peace of inner reserve to grow in stillness. By this life, I have further learned what perhaps in this way—through awareness of the thoughtless frivolity and self-satisfied bewilderment of human beings—one learns even better than in the desert and from the stillness of the night. By this life amid the human swarm—by this false life, if you will, because truly enough I hid something else in my heart of hearts, but I hid the best; I have never, never deceived in such a way that I have pretended to be better than I was—by this life amid the human swarm I learned with frightful certainty to understand that rigorousness is the only thing that can help.

I have used that. But I have no power, neither soldiers nor any other power. I have no powerful connections; I have zero, zero influence or power over the fates of others. In a worldly sense, I am the most solitary, the most powerless, of all persons. To use rigorousness can easily rile people up. That is why the one who wants to use rigorousness usually first secures power for himself. Thus I neither can nor want to use rigorousness, because I do not want to rule. I only want to serve the truth or, what is the same thing, to serve Christianity.

Rigorousness is the only thing that can help a human being. A child, then, is capable of so much and is much hardier than an adult, because there is still some rigorousness in being brought up. And what could a child not do, when rigorousness was greater! Therefore the Romans always prevailed in battle—why? Because rigorousness helped them, helped them to fear that which was worse than death, and therefore helped them be victorious. And so it is with Christianity too. There was a time when it, with divine authority, exercised dominion over human beings, when it directed the words "*You* shall" to each individual concisely, laconically, commandingly, when it terrified each individual with a rigorousness hitherto unknown: eternal punishment. This rigorousness helped. In fear and trembling, before the unavoidable life to come, the Christian was capable of scorning all the dangers and sufferings of this life as child's play and a half-hour's tomfoolery.

Yes, this rigorousness helped; it made it true that to be a Christian is to be in kinship with divinity. This was the militant church. Satan himself had no power against it, except to give the faith's heroes the desired occasion to shine with the incorruptible radiance of martyrdom, the necessary occasion for the hidden glory of a person to become transparent—for the Christian glory is an inner person, an intensity that must be held up to the light if it is to make itself truly manifest. Then Satan said to himself: "I am not winning like this," and he changed his method. Little by little he got the Christian church to imagine that it had now been victorious, that now it should have a good rest after the struggle and enjoy the win. And it looked seductive enough. For, during the time of the militant church, a man still hesitated to embrace Christianity. At that time, its growth was not even very great. But after it had been victorious—yes, then it won followers by the millions. What more does one want? For should there be any hesitancy connected with a victorious church, it would indeed have to be that it would gradually shrink, lose numbers. But just the opposite was the case. Yes, indeed, it did not shrink or decrease in number. No, it increased, truly like a person with edema grows larger; it swelled up in unhealthy fat, almost disgustingly thickened in fleshly chubbiness, scarcely recognizable.

Now all had become Christians. But power and authority were lost as well. People were pampered by hearing the never-ending litany of Christian truths recited—great things if anyone took the trouble to hear any more: good God, and the scene was in Christendom where all were Christians and where it nevertheless was doubtful whether anyone bothered to hear the Christian truths. But to speak in the now quite antiquated, almost laughable language that Christianity spoke when it exercised dominion over people with divine authority and brought them up by fear of eternal punishment with a previously unknown rigorousness—a punishment that only Christianity has attempted to apply: Christianity's preachers in Christendom dared not speak this language. "That will never do," such a person has said to himself. "Not only would I become laughable, not only would people perhaps even put me to death; but even if I would dare to do this, I would achieve nothing. I would only make persons so furious that they would totally throw off the yoke." Here was a difficult situation. Then a perhaps well-meaning human shrewdness began the saddest of all undertakings: to betray Christianity by defending it. And then the devil laughed to himself and said: "See, now I can keep calm; now the game is won."

Thus the ones who defend Christianity know not what they do. The secret is hidden deeply. They constantly want to seek the error in the defense's imperfection up till now and then rush ahead more and more zealously, become more and more absorbed in the defense— who would even guess that the one who defends is precisely the betrayer, even if he does not know it. So they defended Christianity— righteous God, and the scene was in Christendom. Accordingly, it was exactly to Christians that Christianity defended itself, as if a king had to defend himself directly before his subjects. They defended Christianity; there was never any talk about or use of authority. This "you shall" was never heard, lest it cause laughter. They defended

Christianity and said: "Do not reject Christianity; it is a gentle teaching, which contains all the gentle reasons for solace that every human being nevertheless can come to need so easily in life. Lord God, life is not always smiling; we all need a friend, and Christ is such a friend. Do not reject him. He means well by you." And it was successful. People actually listened attentively to this talk; people actually gave an audience to this beggar, the Lord Jesus Christ (for even if he himself was not the beggar, he was still the one on whose behalf the begging was done). There was something in it, they found. It tickled the ears of power-hungry Christendom, so that it indeed was almost as if there should be a vote by ballot: "Let it pass; we accept Christianity on these terms." Righteous God, and the scene was in Christendom, where all are Christians, and Christianity was accepted by Christians on these terms.

Christianity went backwards in this way. And now in established Christendom, where certainly there is never any talk about rigorousness, there lives a spoiled, proud, and yet cowardly, defiant, and in fact indulgent generation that occasionally hears these gentle reasons for solace recited but barely knows whether it will make use of them even when life smiles most beautifully and that is offended in the hour of need, when it is seen that they are not actually so gentle. Righteous God, and the scene is in Christendom! Righteous God—yes, whoever wants to see, he sees the righteous God precisely here. Terrible punishment, because the militant church became the triumphant church or established Christendom. Truly, when you see a person who is an addict, when you see him in all his wretchedness, disgrace, misery, if you can see the righteous God, then you must see the righteous God in "established Christendom," if you have been granted the grace that you were brought up with rigorousness in Christendom.

For only the militant church is truth, or the truth is that, as long as the church exists in this world, it is the militant church, which relates itself to Christ in his mortification even if drawn to him from on high. On the other hand, this talk whereby people flatter the human race and themselves—that the world is progressing—is untruth. For the world neither progresses nor regresses; it essentially remains the same, like the sea, like the air—in short, like an element.

That is to say, the world is and shall be the element that can administer the test of being a Christian, who is always a member of the militant church in this world. This is the truth. The triumphant church and established Christendom are untruth—an untruth that is the greatest adversity that can befall the church, is its downfall, and its punishment to boot, since, after all, it can only be self-inflicted.

WORKS CITED

WORKS BY SØREN KIERKEGAARD

Danish

Søren Kierkegaards Papirer. Edited by P.A. Heiberg, V. Kuhr, and E. Torsting. vols. I-XI-3. Copenhagen: Gyldendalske Boghandel, Nordisk Forlag, 1909–48.

Skrifter. Edited by Niels Jørgen Cappelørn, Joakim Garff, Johnny Kondrup, Karsten Kynde, Tonny Aagaard Olesen, and Steen Tullberg. Copenhagen: Gads Forlag, 1997–2013.

English

Søren Kierkegaard's Journals and Papers. Edited and translated by Howard and Edna Hong. 7 vols. Bloomington: Indiana University Press, 1967–78.

Kierkegaard's Writings. Edited and translated by Howard Hong and Edna Hong. 26 vols. Princeton, NJ: Princeton University Press, 1978–2002.

OTHER SOURCES

Arndt, Johann. *True Christianity*. Edited and translated by Peter C. Erb. New York: Paulist Press, 1979.

Baagø, Kaj. *Vækkelse og Kirkeliv in København og Omegn*. Copenhagen: Gads Forlag, 1960.

Barnett, Christopher B. "Erich Przywara: Catholicism's Great Expositor of the 'Mystery' of Kierkegaard." In *Kierkegaard's Influence on Theology: Tome III: Catholic and Jewish Theology*, edited by Jon Stewart, 131–54. Farnham, UK: Ashgate, 2009.

———. *From Despair to Faith: The Spirituality of Søren Kierkegaard*. Minneapolis: Fortress Press, 2014.

———. "Hans Adolph Brorson: Danish Pietism's Greatest Hymn Writer and His Relation to Kierkegaard." In *Kierkegaard and the Renaissance and Modern Traditions—Theology*, edited by Jon Stewart, 63–80. Farnham, UK: Ashgate, 2009.

———. *Kierkegaard, Pietism and Holiness*. Farnham, UK: Ashgate Publishing Company, 2011.

———. "Should One Suffer Death for the Truth?: Kierkegaard, *Erbauungsliteratur*, and the Imitation of Christ." *Journal for the History of Modern Theology* 15, no. 2 (2008): 232–47.

Barrett, Lee C. *Eros and Self-Emptying: The Intersections of Augustine and Kierkegaard*. Grand Rapids: Eerdmans, 2013.

———. "Jacob Böhme: The Ambiguous Legacy of Speculative Passion." In *Kierkegaard and the Renaissance and Modern Traditions—Theology*, edited by Jon Stewart, 43–62. Farnham, UK: Ashgate, 2009.

Barth, Karl. *The Epistle to the Romans*. Translated by Edwyn Hoskyns. London: Oxford University Press, 1933.

Barthes, Roland. "The Death of the Author." In *Image-Music-Text*, translated by Stephen Heath, 142–48. New York: Hill and Wang, 1977.

Blackburn, Simon. *Oxford Dictionary of Philosophy*. Oxford: Oxford University Press, 1996.

Brandes, Georg. *Søren Kierkegaard: En kritisk Fremstilling i Grundrids*. Copenhagen: Gyldendal, 1877.

Braw, Christian. *Bücher im Staube: Die Theologie Johann Arndts in ihrem Verhältnis zur Mystik*. Leiden: E.J. Brill, 1985.

Brorson, Hans Adolph. *Udvalgte salmer og digter*. Edited by Steffen Arndal. Borgen: Det Danske Sprog-og Litteraturselskab, 1994.

Bremer, Fredrika. *Lif I Norden: Skizz*. Stockholm: Bagge, 1849.

Brix, Hans. *Danmarks digtere: Fyvretyve kapitler af dansk digtekunsts historie*. Oslo: Aschehoug, 1944.

Buhl, H. O. "Søren Kierkegaard: Eksistensfilosof eller mystiker?" *Vestkysten* (Esbjerg), January 6, 1955.

Bukdahl, Jørgen. *Søren Kierkegaard and the Common Man*. Translated by Bruce H. Kirmmse. Grand Rapids: Eerdmans, 2001.

Burgess, Andrew. "Kierkegaard, Brorson, and Moravian Music." In *International Kierkegaard Commentary: Practice in Christianity*, edited by Robert L. Perkins, 211–43. Macon, GA: Mercer University Press, 2004.

Works Cited

——. "Kierkegaard, Moravian Missions, and Martyrdom." In *International Kierkegaard Commentary: Without Authority*, edited by Robert L. Perkins, 177–201. Macon, GA: Mercer University Press, 2007.

Cappelørn, Niels Jørgen. "Kierkegaard som bogkøber og bogsamler." In *Tekstpejle: Om Søren Kierkegaard som bogtilrettelæger, boggiver og bogsamler*, edited by Niels Jørgen Cappelørn, Gert Posselt, and Bent Rohde, 105–219. Copenhagen: Rosendahls Forlag, 2002.

Clapper, Gregory S. "Relations between Spirituality and Theology: Kierkegaard's Model." *Studies in Formative Spirituality* 9 (1988): 161–67.

Collins, James. *The Existentialists: A Critical Study*. Chicago: Henry Regnery Company, 1952.

Cruysberghs, Paul. "Transparency to Oneself and to God." In *At være sig selv nærværende: Festskrift til Niels Jørgen Cappelørn*, edited by Joakim Garff, Ettore Rocca, and Pia Søltoft, 127–41. Copenhagen: Kristeligt Dagblads Forlag, 2010.

Cunningham, Lawrence S., and Keith J. Egan. *Christian Spirituality: Themes from the Tradition*. New York: Paulist Press, 1996.

Dewey, Bradley R. *The New Obedience: Kierkegaard on Imitating Christ*. Washington, DC: Corpus Books, 1968.

Dooley, Mark. *The Politics of Exodus: Søren Kierkegaard's Ethics of Responsibility*. New York: Fordham University Press, 2001.

Drury, M. O'C. "Conversations with Wittgenstein." In *Recollections of Wittgenstein*, edited by Rush Rhees, 90–170. Oxford: Oxford University Press, 1984.

Eller, Vernard. *Kierkegaard and Radical Discipleship: A New Perspective*. Princeton, NJ: Princeton University Press, 1968.

Ellsberg, Robert. "Introduction: Little Brother of Jesus." In *Charles de Foucauld: Essential Writings*, 13–31. Maryknoll, NY: Orbis Books, 1999.

Erb, Peter C. "Introduction." In *True Christianity*, edited by Peter C. Erb, 1–27. New York: Paulist Press, 1979.

Evans, C. Stephen. *Kierkegaard: An Introduction*. Cambridge: Cambridge University Press, 2009.

Fabro, Cornelio. "Faith and Reason in Kierkegaard's Dialectic." In *A Kierkegaard Critique: An International Selection of Essays Interpreting Kierkegaard*, edited by Howard A. Johnson and Niels Thulstrup, 156–206. New York: Harper and Brothers, 1962.

——. "Influssi Cattolici Sulla Spiritualità Kierkegaardiana." *Humanitas* 17 (1962): 501–7.

SØREN KIERKEGAARD

Ferreira, M. Jamie. *Love's Grateful Striving: A Commentary on Kierkegaard's Works of Love*. Oxford: Oxford University Press, 2001.

Fiedler, Leslie A. "Introduction." In *Waiting for God*, translated by Emma Craufurd, vii–xxxiv. New York: Harper Perennial Modern Classics, 2009.

Foucauld, Charles de. *Charles de Foucauld: Essential Writings*. Maryknoll, NY: Orbis Books, 1999.

Furnal, Joshua. "Doing Theology with Cornelio Fabro: Kierkegaard, Mary, and the Church." *Heythrop Journal* 56 (2015): 931–47.

Garff, Joakim. *Søren Kierkegaard: A Biography*. Princeton, NJ: Princeton University Press, 2005.

Geismer, Eduard. *Lectures on the Religious Thought of Søren Kierkegaard*. Minneapolis: Augsburg, 1938.

———. "Søren Kierkegaard og Mystiken." *Dagens Nyheder* (Copenhagen), March 18, 1933.

Hannay, Alastair. *Kierkegaard: A Biography*. Cambridge: Cambridge University Press, 2001.

Hansen, Knud. *Søren Kierkegaard: Ideens digter*. Copenhagen: Gyldendal, 1954.

Hanson, Erik M. "Thomas Merton: Kierkegaard, Merton and Authenticity." In *Kierkegaard's Influence on Theology: Tome III: Catholic and Jewish Theology*, edited by Jon Stewart, 111–30. Farnham, UK: Ashgate, 2009.

Heidegger, Martin. *Being and Time*. Translated by John Macquarrie and Edward Robinson. San Francisco: Harper Collins, 1962.

Hong, Howard V., and Edna H. Hong. "Historical Introduction." In *Eighteen Upbuilding Discourses*, edited by Howard V. Hong and Edna H. Hong, ix–xxii. Princeton, NJ: Princeton University Press, 1990.

———. "Historical Introduction." In *The Moment and Late Writings*, edited by Howard V. Hong and Edna H. Hong, ix–xxxi. Princeton, NJ: Princeton University Press, 1998.

Kim, David Yoon-Jung, and Joel D. S. Rasmussen. "Martin Luther: Reform, Secularization, and the Question of His 'True Successor.'" In *Kierkegaard and the Renaissance and Modern Traditions: Tome II: Theology*, edited by Jon Stewart, 173–217. Farnham, UK: Ashgate, 2009.

Kingo, Anders. *Analogiens Teologi: En Dogmatisk Studie over Dialektikken i Søren Kierkegaards Opbyggelige og Pseudonyme Forfatterskab*. Copenhagen: Gad, 1995.

Works Cited

———. *Den Opbyggelige Tale: En Systematisk-Teologisk Studie over Søren Kierkegaards Opbyggelige Forfatterskab.* Copenhagen: Gad, 1987.

Kirmmse, Bruce, ed. *Encounters with Kierkegaard.* Princeton, NJ: Princeton University Press, 1996.

Koenker, Ernest B. "Søren Kierkegaard on Luther." In *Interpreters of Luther: Essays in Honor of Wilhelm Pauck*, edited by Jaroslav Pelikan, 231–52. Philadelphia: Fortress Press, 1968.

Lage, Dietmar. *Martin Luther's Christology and Ethics.* Lewiston, NY: Edwin Mellen Press, 1990.

Lindberg, Carter. "Luther's Struggle with Social-Ethical Issues." In *The Cambridge Companion to Martin Luther*, edited by Donald K. McKim, 165–78. Cambridge: Cambridge University Press, 2003.

Merton, Thomas. *Contemplative Prayer.* London: Darton, Longman & Todd, 1969.

Milbank, John. "Knowledge: The Theological Critique of Philosophy in Hamann and Jacobi." In *Radical Orthodoxy: A New Theology*, edited by John Milbank, Catherine Pickstock, and Graham Ward, 21–37. London: Routledge, 1999.

Mulder, Jack, Jr. "Bernard of Clairvaux: Kierkegaard's Reception of the Last of the Fathers." In *Kierkegaard and the Patristic and Medieval Traditions*, edited by Jon Stewart, 23–46. Farnham, UK: Ashgate, 2008.

Müller, Paul. "Begrebet 'det Opbyggelige' hos Søren Kierkegaard." *Fønix* 7 (1983): 1–16.

Mynster, J. P. [Kts., pseud.]. "Kirkelig Polemik." *Intelligensblade* 4 (1844): 97–114.

Pattison, George. *Kierkegaard and the Theology of the Nineteenth Century: The Paradox and the "Point of Contact."* Cambridge: Cambridge University Press, 2012.

———. *Kierkegaard's Upbuilding Discourses: Philosophy, Literature and Theology.* London: Routledge, 2002.

———. *The Philosophy of Kierkegaard.* Chesham, UK: Acumen, 2005.

Podmore, Simon D. *Kierkegaard and the Self before God: Anatomy of the Abyss.* Bloomington: Indiana University Press, 2011.

———. *Struggling with God: Kierkegaard and the Temptation of Spiritual Trial.* Cambridge: James Clarke & Co., 2013.

Polk, Timothy H. "Kierkegaard's Use of the New Testament: Intratextuality, Indirect Communication, and Appropriation." In *Kierkegaard and the Bible: Tome II: The New Testament*, edited by Lee C. Barrett and Jon Stewart, 237–48. Farnham, UK: Ashgate, 2010.

Poole, Roger. "The Unknown Kierkegaard: Twentieth-Century Receptions." In *The Cambridge Companion to Kierkegaard*, edited by Alastair Hannay and Gordon D. Marino, 48–75. Cambridge: Cambridge University Press, 1998.

Przywara, Erich. *Das Geheimnis Kierkegaaards*. Munich and Berlin: Verlag von R. Oldenbourg, 1929.

Ruhr, Mario von der. *Simone Weil: An Apprenticeship in Attention*. London: Continuum, 2006.

Šajda, Peter. "Kierkegaard's Encounter with Rhineland-Flemish Mystics: A Case Study." In *Kierkegaard Studies Yearbook 2009: Kierkegaard's Concept of Irony*, edited by Niels Jørgen Cappelørn, Hermann Deuser, and K. Brian Söderquist, 559–84. Berlin: de Gruyter, 2009.

Sampley, J. Paul. "The First Letter to the Corinthians." *The New Interpreter's Bible*, vol. 10, edited by Leander E. Keck et al., 771–1003. Nashville: Abingdon Press, 2002.

Scherz, G. "Alfonso di Liguori og S. Kierkegaard." *Kierkegaardiana* 3 (1959): 73–82.

Schneiders, Sandra M. "Christian Spirituality: Definition, Methods and Types." In *The New Westminster Dictionary of Christian Spirituality*, edited by Philip Sheldrake, 1–6. Louisville, KY: Westminster John Knox Press, 2005.

Sløk, Johannes. *Die Anthropologie Kierkegaards*. Copenhagen: Rosenkilde og Bagger, 1954.

———. "Kierkegaard and Luther." In *A Kierkegaard Critique*, edited by Howard A. Johnson and Niels Thulstrup, 85–101. Chicago: Henry Regnery, 1962.

Solomon, Robert. "Introduction." In *Existentialism*, edited by Robert C. Solomon, 81. Oxford: Oxford University Press, 2005.

Stewart, Jon, ed. *Kierkegaard and His Danish Contemporaries: Tome II: Theology*. Farnham, UK: Ashgate, 2009.

Strawser, Michael. *Both/And: Reading Kierkegaard from Irony to Edification*. New York: Fordham University Press, 1999.

Thulstrup, Marie Mikulová. "Efterfølgelsens dialektik hos Søren Kierkegaard." *Dansk teologisk Tidsskrift* 21 (1958): 193–209.

———. "Kierkegaard og kirkefædrene." *Nordisk teologisk Tidsskrift* 82 (1981): 129–40.

———. *Kierkegaard og pietismen*. Copenhagen: Munksgaard, 1967.

———. "Kierkegaard's Dialectic of Imitation." In *A Kierkegaard Critique: An International Selection of Essays Interpreting Kierkegaard*, edited by

Works Cited

Howard A. Johnson and Niels Thulstrup, 266–85. New York: Harper and Brothers, 1962.

———. "Lidelsens problematik hos Kierkegaard og mystikerne." *Kierkegaardiana* 3 (1959): 48–72.

———. "Præsentation af kristne mystikere i faglitteraturen, Kierkegaard kendte." *Kierkegaardiana* 11 (1980): 55–92.

Tullberg, Steen. "Denmark: The Permanent Reception—150 Years of Reading Kierkegaard." In *Kierkegaard's International Reception: Tome I: Northern and Western Europe*, edited by Jon Stewart, 3–120. Farnham, UK: Ashgate, 2009.

Wahl, Jean. "Kierkegaard et le Mysticisme." *Hermès* 1 (1930): 16–23.

Walsh, Sylvia. "Kierkegaard's Theology." In *The Oxford Handbook of Kierkegaard*, edited by John Lippitt and George Pattison, 292–308. Oxford: Oxford University Press, 2013.

Watkin, Julia. *Historical Dictionary of Kierkegaard's Philosophy*. Lanham, MD: Scarecrow Press, 2001.

Weil, Simone. *Gravity and Grace*. Translated by Emma Crawford and Mario von der Ruhr. London: Routledge Classics, 2002.

———. *The Notebooks of Simone Weil*. Vol. 2. Translated by Arthur Wills. London: Routledge, 1976.

———. *Waiting for God*. Translated by Emma Craufurd. New York: Harper Perennial Modern Classics, 2009.

Westphal, Merold. *Kierkegaard's Concept of Faith*. Grand Rapids: Eerdmans, 2014.

INDEX

Index

Index